Plans for Adding on and Remodeling

Plans for Adding on and Remodeling

Jerold L. Axelrod
Architect

McGRAW-HILL

New York   San Francisco   Washington, D.C.   Auckland   Bogotá
Caracas   Lisbon   London   Madrid   Mexico City   Milan
Montreal   New Delhi   San Juan   Singapore
Sydney   Tokyo   Toronto

McGraw-Hill

A Division of The **McGraw·Hill** Companies

Copyright © 2000 by McGraw-Hill, Inc. All rights reserved. Printed in the United States of America. Except as permitted under the United States Copyright Act of 1976, no part of this publication may be reproduced or distributed in any form or by any means, or stored in a data base or retrieval system, without the prior written permission of the publisher.

2 3 4 5 6 7 8 9 0   DOC/DOC   0 9 8 7 6 5 4

P/N 136160-X
Part of
ISBN 0-07-135236-8

The sponsoring editor for this book was Zoe G. Foundotos and the production supervisor was Sherri Souffrance. It was set in Century Schoolbook by Pro-Image Corporation.

Printed and bound by R. R. Donnelley & Sons Company.

 This book is printed on acid-free paper.

McGraw-Hill books are available at special quantity discounts to use as premiums and sales promotions, or for use in corporate training programs. For more information, please write to the Director of Special Sales, McGraw-Hill, Two Penn Plaza, New York, NY 10121. Or contact your local bookstore.

The first edition of this book was published as *Architectural Plans for Adding On or Remodeling*.

Contents

Dedicated to Florence, Sharron, Neil, Ahron, Gabrielle, and Julia

Acknowledgments

The inspiration for this book came from readers like you who purchased my earlier book on this subject, *Architectural Plans for Adding On or Remodeling*. I received hundreds of positive letters, praising the concept of a book on remodeling devoted exclusively to design. Many of you forwarded your own plans, and some of these have been incorporated into this volume. Whereas I initially had presumed there would be interest in reproducing my plans, what I found was that the uniqueness of each remodeling project made outright reproduction unlikely. However, what many of you asked for — CAD files — we were not yet ready to provide. We now are able to do just that. Back in 1991 our CAD files would have required 60 floppy disks. Today they fit on a single CD — and their accuracy can be assured.

This volume includes most of the drawings from the original book, an additional 200 or so new drawings, and some 50 new designs — all of which are also included on the accompanying CD. The new designs include a number of apartments, home offices, and some dramatic whole house renovations provided by my partner Glen Cherveny. These complement the original 240 plans that came from remodeling professionals around the country, and my personal travels and research.

The original book was a first ever attempt to graphically identify the most prevalent and common home improvement designs relevant today; this volume picks up on that theme, and provides the CAD files for these as well. The look of this book is all new. We have printed all the plans in a loose line, sketch format, which is more indicative of the purpose of this book — that it serve as a sketchbook of design ideas for hundreds of remodeling projects. Sincere appreciation is extended to my dedicated office staff, particularly Adam DeLumen whose CAD talents helped to produce the quality of drawings in the book and on the CD.

Introduction—What This Book Is— and Is Not

This book is primarily a sketchbook of architectural designs. The accompanying disk provides the user the unparalleled opportunity to prepare plans from these designs. Like its predecessor, *Architectural Plans for Adding On or Remodeling,* this book is unique in that it provides to the architect, designer, or professional remodeler a veritable potpourri of hundreds of practical plans for remodeling a home. With over 1,000 illustrations, and almost 300 different plans, it has something for every situation. There are beautiful room additions, exciting internal room remodelings, and even dramatic whole house renovations; they range from a charming three foot breakfast area bump-out, to a complete remake of a large two-story Victorian. There are porches, sunrooms, and vestibules, as well as kitchens, baths, bedrooms and family rooms. There are also garages, built-in or detached, and a whole range of apartments for parents or children.

There are plans that expand up or expand out, and some that rearrange and even reduce rooms. There are contemporary additions and traditional ones; but, most important, these are plans that are explicitly designed to remodel someone's home. That someone may be your client—or your customer—or maybe it's yourself. To avoid being unduly repetitive throughout the book, in defining the homeowner as your "client, customer, or yourself," the book is written in the personal "you" or "yours". The "your" may be the architect's or designer's client, the home improvement contractor's customer, or maybe it is really "yours".

The homes chosen are varied; there are one-stories, split-levels, one and one-half stories, old bungalows and cottages, and recent two-story traditionals too. The plans presented are a product of extensive research. It is likely that there is a plan for remodeling that both suits your specific needs and matches your subject home. The CAD files provided for each plan on the accompanying disk yield both 2 and 3D views, for your use in creating both presentation drawings and construction blueprints.

This book is also an encyclopedia of ideas—both graphic and written. It is notable for its profusion of artwork, but the written words are not meant to be glossed over. Much of my experience has been put down in the written material. Although this is a book about remodeling homes, it should not be confused with the majority of books that deal with the subject; most are how-to books, written to assist you, once you know what you want to build. This book is not that.

Many remodeling books attempt to teach the layman how to design his own project, and then how to draw the construction plans. For the majority of homeowners, I believe this proves to be an extremely frustrating task to learn. Most books, unfortunately, gloss over the subject of design, presuming the reader will gain that elsewhere. But where? The major source of such ideas are the home journals which do feature extensive examples of successful re-modelings. But most such examples have little practical value to the home-owner frantically trying to plan a remodeling project. The majority of photo-graphic features are, by nature, esoteric, one-of-a-kind essays on a custom renovation. In conversation with many clients, they tell me that they gain helpful ideas from the journals, but find it difficult to apply these to their own home.

Interestingly, the original inspiration for the predecessor book, *Architectural Plans for Adding On or Remodeling* was provided to me by the editor of one of these journals, more than seventeen years ago. He recognized the difficulty in the consumers' ability to find practical, readily usable, design ideas for their own homes. I resisted the concept at first, primarily out of fear of the magnitude of the undertaking. However, in the mid 1980s, I began to research and collect ideas for common themes. The almost infinite number of variations, however, that are possible for any one design, did speak against trying to standardize them.

The answer to that came (or so I hoped) when we purchased our first computer in 1985. After several years of frustration, and several aborted efforts, we returned to using pencils only finally to achieve success. All of the plans reproduced herein have been drawn on our CAD system; this makes it very easy to accommodate changes to affect individual nuances and variances in any home. This capability has enabled me to develop standardized, readily recognizable, existing home plans to work with as a base, with full knowledge that this base will grow over time, as will the remodeling projects themselves. That, in fact, has already occurred with the addition of some 25% new plans since the initial volume. Most important, however, is the technology that has now enabled us to duplicate all these CAD files on a CD for the user to use.

In 1991, this would have required 60 floppy disks or more—a very impractical proposal.

As to the organization of the book, resist the temptation to look at pictures first. There is a modest dose of helpful written material at the beginning to help you get started in the right direction.

The first three chapters of the book are designed to help you analyze needs, evaluate a home for change and develop a program. I do that with every custom client we have. It is a process you should not gloss over, as the satisfaction our clients ultimately receive from a finished remodeling project is directly related to the quality of the program we prepare.

A discussion ensues in chapter 4 on how to best use the prototype plans that make up the balance of the book. There is a discussion for the lay person about when you need an architect, and how to have these plans customized. I believe that architectural help is important, and that is why I prepared this book. My relationship with you may lack the personal contact, but the ideas—and plans—are the most important help that I can provide.

Part 2 of this book deals with the subject of creating appropriate additions, not in specific plans as of yet, but in shapes and concept only. My goal here is to help you create appropriate and attractive looking additions. In the first chapter of Part 2, chapter 5, I have identified some 25 different specific shapes that fit specific, recognizable home types. However, there are too many homes we come across that defy the norms. Therefore, in chapter 6, I deal with additions as simply forms. Thus, chapter 6 presents 60 prototype shapes for successful additions. I call them "blockforms" as that is all they are: simple block shapes that you may be able to easily recognize and relate to your home. If properly followed, any of them should lead to an addition that meshes well with the subject home.

The seventh chapter deals with what not to do. I debated frequently as to whether or not I should devote any valuable space to this subject. The problem was that to do it thoroughly could take a pictorial volume in itself. A brief discussion plus several pages of drawings was the compromise. If the project you are contemplating involves an addition, there could be some valuable information here.

The actual prototype plans are divided into four chapters in Part 3. Chapter 8 essentially presents room additions, that go up or out in every direction, on an extensive variety of existing homes; the additions comprise the full gamut of needs ranging from apartments to family rooms and kitchens to bedrooms and baths. If your plans include an addition, it is likely you will find one here.

Chapter 9 presents a voluminous collection of plans appropriately dubbed "bumps, bays, extensions and interior remodeling". Whereas the focus of the publishing world is usually directed at room additions, it is the identification and presentation of these smaller spatial undertakings that makes this book most unique. The majority of home remodeling projects usually include such smaller, bump-outs or interior space rearrangements, yet they have never been analyzed and presented in a usable format for your use. It is these that are readily prone to design error, more so than a self-contained addition; furthermore, even most additions incorporate such smaller spatial changes to the home and they can have a measurable affect on the ultimate success of the addition.

Chapter 10 presents a generous collection of stylish new front façade studies. Each portrays the old with the new, so you can relate these drawings to your home. Exterior remodeling has become increasingly popular, and I have provided ideas for your consideration. Whether the exterior is being remodeled alone, or as a by-product of a space addition or alteration, this chapter is on target with today's trends.

Finally, in chapter 11, there is a wonderful collection of whole house renovations. Included in this chapter are remakes of several old bungalows, cottages and "cape cods". The remodeling of these lovely old homes is presented very clearly so even if yours is not exactly the same, you can learn from them.

A second group of whole house undertakings is included, and these are derived from the prior chapters. This unique group of designs demonstrates how you can combine various plans, shown in the book, to create your own remodeling program. It is through the process demonstrated in this last group of homes, that I hope you will learn how to take my designs and ideas, and adapt them to your specific needs.

I have said that this is not a nuts and bolts, or how-to-build book; well, chapter 12 does do a little of that. My motivation in this chapter is to provide several construction details that are design driven, and which are not likely to appear in the how-to construction books.

Also, included here is a handy chart to aid you in sizing girders so that you can open up rooms to each other—an important design tool. The following chapter, chapter 13, presents a detailed discussion and graphic presentation on staging a project. This frequently neglected aspect of remodeling is an essential part of the design process itself. Whenever possible I try to plan any intricate, involved, project so that it can be developed in stages. The ability to do this can make the difference between a pleasurable and a miserable experience during construction.

Finally, chapter 14 takes a brief look at finishing the project, again not with sandpaper and paint, but within the broad concepts of interior and exterior design.

A detailed Addendum provides several graphic illustrations of what is provided on the included CD. It also discusses at length what kinds of files you can expect to find on it, and what you can do with these files. There is a discussion of how you can make your own CAD presentations and construction drawings from the files on the disk.

So, whether you're adding on, or remodeling, or contemplating a little—or a lot—of both, let's get going.

Developing a Program

Why Remodel?

The reasons to remodel are as individually different as are our fingerprints. Yet with all of our uniqueness, we tend to live in homes with a reasonable degree of sameness. These various homes eventually age the same, and although each of you may approach that problem differently, the decisions to remodel one's particular design, or style of home, tend to fall into certain likely patterns. This book latches on to those commonalties in the designs presented. But before one finalizes any design, or chooses a particular design, it is first necessary to identify why there is a need to remodel.

Identifying Needs

A successful remodeling project will likely satisfy some predetermined need; it was successful because it began with a need that clearly surfaced, was properly identified, and a correct path was chosen to satisfy that need. As an architect, I will become involved with my client in trying to help them identify needs, so that the design I propose will be relevant. When someone complains about a disappointment in their completed remodeling, I usually suspect an irrelevant design, which did not mesh with that person's needs.

Put these needs to paper; try to identify them — and don't skirt the process. Prospective remodelors have to be completely open and ask themselves what they expect to achieve in a contemplated remodeling. What changes have taken place, or will take place, that you should recognize? The answers to these questions are the beginning of a "program", something we will delve deeper into in chapter 3. This "program," that we will develop together, meshes needs with the inadequacies and opportunities presented in your current home; but for now let us concentrate on needs — and hopefully you recognize that "needs" are personal requirements. We are not yet talking about the needs of the home.

Changing Family Needs

As families grow—or decline—or change—their needs change; changing family needs are the most common reason to remodel. As children come into the family, there is a need for bedroom space. As they grow older, there is a need for adequate play or study space. When they marry and leave, there is usually a surplus of space poorly serving the remaining occupants. These are the most often cited reasons for adding or changing space; these needs frequently result in additions—they are physical space needs, as contrasted to lifestyle needs. The driving motivation is frequently simply more space, rather than the style or quality of the space.

A second marriage might demand some changes in lifestyle, but also may bring physical space needs due to the changed complexion of the new family. In any changing family, try to carefully define the new spatial needs by functions needed; i.e., more sleeping space, play space, study space, private space, eating space, formal dining space, and informal and formal entertaining space. Don't forget changed storage requirements, too.

Requirements for a different amount of space

Many of these family changes result in a new requirement for the size or number of rooms. Determining the number of bedrooms or baths required might be easy, as is evaluating that you now need a family room. Determining that you have to increase the *size* of the kitchen or living room may prove a little more difficult because you will get trapped in the "how much" syndrome. Don't worry about size now, the goal is to determine needs, the quantification process can come later.

Try to define where you feel that the home least fulfills the family's spatial needs. Does the kitchen feel cramped? Is there a desire for a formal dining room? Would you prefer a kitchen eating area? If so would you prefer a full breakfast table space, or is a snack counter with bar stools preferable?

What function will take place in the new family room and old living room? Do you need both? Would you prefer that they be interconnected for large scale entertaining—or should they be clearly separate? Remember to jot these needs down on paper.

Requirements for a different type of space

Many of these family changes also result in a need for new types of space that may not exist in the home. Some of these may also require that space be added, and as such, also affect the amount of space that may be needed—but many are also reconciled by "rearranging underutilized space" that we will later quantify.

Doing work at home may now demand the need for a home office. Is it simply a corner of your bedroom or living room, or is it a separate room? Is there enough space for the hobby enthusiast? A garden enthusiast might love a full-fledged greenhouse.

Does the lifestyle now demand more space for adult entertaining? Is there any place for the new media equipment? Do we no longer need distinct divisions between entertaining rooms? How do we feel about an open kitchen? What about a great room where all (or just some) of the cooking, dining and entertainment functions are combined, or opened to each other? Is a country kitchen to your liking? That's a great room of a less formal nature, where cooking, light meals and casual relaxation are combined into one flowing space?

Is there a need for more space for bathing or dressing? And what about the closets—do we have to benchpress to develop the strength to move clothes? Is there a preference for some extra space in the bedroom for reading?

The more your list of needs includes many of these contemporary living patterns, the more likely your current home will fall short, and the more likely you will need an extensive remodeling to satisfy them all. Therefore, unless you have no budget restrictions, which is unlikely, you should start to prioritize the list of needs; i.e., those we absolutely must have, and those that would be nice, but which we could live without. This is the time to dream, but let's try to make dreams come true.

Housing aging parents and newly married children

The nuclear family has stopped retreating. For many reasons, including emotional and economic ones, we are finding today that more and more extended families are living together again. Projects coming to my office often include the request for an apartment. If the apartment is for aging parents, it poses a major set of design restrictions as to where it can be located, particularly due to the potential need for handicapped accessibility. A first floor location is usually mandatory, but the need for a separate kitchen or entry might be unnecessary—but that is for you to define.

An apartment for a married child is a different need, with a very different set of requirements; a separate entrance and separate kitchen (codes allowing) is usually required; however, its location could be a second floor space. An apartment for income purposes could have the same requirements, but you are cautioned to check with your local municipality as to legal requirements.

Psychological or Emotional Needs

As important as it is to identify your physical, or spatial needs, it is equally necessary to clarify those very personal motivations, that may be driving the decision to remodel the home. It is here that I may fail to connect with a client, because of their inability to communicate a very private personal need. However, it is more important for the homeowner to be true to one's self. Now,

I am not talking about religion or mysticism. The issues that comprise this subject are real psychological or emotional needs that every remodeling project conjures within the client or homeowner, and being honest will help insure the successful remodeling I keep talking about.

The homeowner needs to ask, what are you looking to achieve beyond the addition or changes required? Is there an expectation to achieve a very personal gratification in the project? If there is, expect extensive involvement in every decision. Are there sensual or aesthetic demands that need to be satisfied? If so, be honest in requiring that the proposed remodeling will satisfy those yearnings. It's too late once it is finished. Or is it a perception to others that must be addressed? There is nothing wrong with that as a motive for remodeling. So many people thrive on satisfying that need, but for some reason we hesitate to acknowledge it. If that is the motivation, it is clear that just adding walls and a roof will not suffice. Many of the plans presented in this book, particularly the new faces, acknowledge this need.

Possibly one must satisfy a need to express a newfound stature in life. This might result in the same requirements as the previous need, but it could be different, if there is less concern with perception to others, as there is in achieving a personal gratification. Given this need, the chances are that the solution will be less conventional and more individual in your remodeling. So go ahead and be bold, because if we aren't, you could achieve less than satisfactory results.

The needs I am asking you to identify here are clearly very personal ones, and it is very possible that these could override purely spatial needs. In this vein, would be a decision to remodel a clearly inadequate home, despite all the arguments to move, because of an extremely personal attachment to the home or the community.

The identification of other personal requirements will likely help to clarify and define spatial needs. As an example, if you are a gourmet cook, you would probably prefer that the new kitchen be an expansive, beautiful space, because much time will be spent there. It might include a large center preparation island, commercial ranges and dual sinks. If, however, the most favorite meals are prepared in the neighborhood restaurant, your focus for a new kitchen would likely be more practical. A love for plants will require sunny places to put them, whereas a penchant for horticulture might demand a plant room.

There is a clear danger in identifying these needs—our inability to ultimately satisfy them all in a remodeling project. So at this point it would be helpful to start asking, are any of these needs compatible with others—or from a spatial demand—could they be combined? As an example, maybe a demand for a whirlpool spa could be merged into the same sunspace that houses the planting enthusiast. Or maybe that large screen TV, and its associated media equipment, doesn't need a separate room, but could find a happy place in a new country kitchen. Fortunately, many of the plans presented in the book have made some of these compromises for you.

Economic Needs

Alas, it would be such a beautiful world, if reality didn't present itself in the form of the checkbook. Although we may wish otherwise, in order to achieve that elusive, successful remodeling, I keep referring to, we must deal with the economic needs of a proposed remodeling.

Can we afford it?

Since the focus of this book is design, space does not allow me to delve into the myriad of issues concerning the financing of your project. I only touch upon these as they impact design decisions; there are numerous sources for us to consult for detailed information on this subject, including some of the how-to-books. What I am concerned with is how you approach the subject, as it affects the development of your design program. This is one of the most important things a professional can do to help the prospective client; providing advice on budgeting is so critical in these early stages of program development. The homeowner going along on their own is at a huge disadvantage in this regard. Once the scope of the proposed project is reasonably well defined, the do-it-yourselfer may be able to get a handle on how much you have to budget by inquiring of local contractors, or neighbors who have completed similar projects. Whereas you can't rely on these to provide you with your budget, it does establish a range so that you can determine whether or not you are reaching. Hopefully, the range is less than you expected because you will hear it here, and everywhere, that you have to allow at least ten percent more for those inevitable changes or unforeseen problems.

The most precise budgeting method is, of course, bidding from completed construction plans. However, at this stage we are far away from that process, yet we need to confirm that the project—even at this early stage—is within a workable budget. This process will be ongoing throughout the programming and design phases; we will likely modify our program, and the design, numerous times, so it remains aligned within our budget. This will be especially so in the larger, more complex projects. This is the most critical time to try to ballpark the range of cost, as the emotional ramifications will be less straining, should the project appear to be way over budget, than after you have spent months laboring over final plans. If this does occur, it will be necessary to redefine the program and bring it down in scope. But better at this point than when you are finished with final drawings, or worse yet, like when you are halfway through construction.

The project as an investment

I am sure that you have read that certain types of remodeling projects are very sound investments, in that they provide a return on the dollars spent. New kitchens, bathrooms and extra bedrooms usually provide very close to an immediate return on what one has spent; new family rooms return somewhat less. However, this is a very subjective matter, and it does vary by community.

Exterior remodeling projects, i.e., windows, siding, etc., also tend to fare well, especially if they achieve some energy-saving benefits. However, it is also my belief that any remodeling project that produces a significantly more attractive home will also bring a good return on the investment.

However, only the homeowner can evaluate how important this all is. I frown upon a decision that dictates what to do, that hangs solely on a return on your investment; it tends to negate all the subjectively beautiful things we can do that can make a house into a home. If one intends to remodel, and expects to be there for a number of years yet, investment return should play a lesser role. A more important goal should be to better one's living environment, so that they may enjoy a more rewarding lifestyle.

Remodeling versus moving

This entire subject is really directed at the homeowner. More than likely, once a client has come to an architect, designer or builder, they have likely weighed through this decision. However, very often that decision may be wavering, and what I, as a professional, can provide, is assistance in helping them make a learned decision that will inure to our joint benefit.

Although I tend to discuss the question of remodeling versus moving under an economic heading, since the pivotal issues are often cost concerns, this is not at all to underestimate the very emotional, as well as the many spatial issues, that must be reconciled in order to arrive at a learned decision. Let us start with the emotional issue.

Are your emotional attachments such that, regardless of your conclusions to the other questions, you will find it extremely difficult to move? If, after careful analysis, the answer is "yes" to this question, it is likely to take precedence over all other issues. Hopefully, the program you develop can be satisfied; but if it can not, you may have to make significant compromises on space needs, as well as other aesthetic or personal wants.

Remember to carefully weigh whether your current neighborhood is likely to retain those attributes that give rise to your decision to stay. It is also necessary to acknowledge that living within a home undergoing a significant renovation is not fun; be prepared to accept some emotionally upsetting times; although it might only last a few months, it could seem like an eternity.

Will remodeling satisfy your changing needs? The answer is usually "yes". How can I say that so unequivocally? Because of the inherent flexibility of most homes, and the infinite number of solutions that I can develop for almost any given home. Not finding a solution to your particular needs and your particular home in this book is not an indication that it can't be solved; on the contrary, it is likely that one or more solutions can be developed for you. A discussion on the subject of custom designs can be found in chapter 5.

There are, however, certain circumstances where your current home would not satisfy your needs. An example is a home on a very small lot, where there is no room to expand out or there is nothing available from existing internal spaces, but your requirements demand a new ground floor area, such as a new kitchen, a new garage, or a new handicap-accessible apartment. Another example could be a very old home, with historic relevance, that might demand that you move if your special needs can not be compromised with the special requirements of that home. But these are exceptions.

Now to the economic issues. Will the remodeling be an over-improvement? This is usually the only economic issue that may argue for moving. It is distinctly possible that your needs result in a remodeling project that could cost so much that when added to the home's current value, it outstrips the values in the neighborhood by an amount that is economically not sound. How will you know? You need to obtain a ballpark budget as discussed, add it to your home's current value and talk to real estate brokers and bankers. If the answer is affirmative, reduce the scale of your project—or move. Remember, you don't have to equal the average resale price of your neighborhood, you could exceed it by 20%, but talk to your local real estate professionals.

Can you afford to move? The answer to this question involves a myriad of issues such as financing options, the cost of new money, the true total cost of moving and the cost of new houses. The availability of equity financing and the additional costs associated with moving, such as landscaping, furniture, financing costs, brokers fees, etc., usually speak favorably toward remodeling. However, it is something that you should carefully evaluate before finalizing your decision.

Summing Up

We have looked at identifying physical needs, emotional needs and economic needs; together they form the basics for the need to remodel. Although it may prove difficult at first for a homeowner to think their way through these issues, it is an essential first step before embarking on the writing of a successful remodeling program.

An Overview of Remodeling Projects

Once you have identified your needs, you are ready to start developing a detailed program. However, before you plunge directly into another heady task, it might be helpful to take a broad look at the myriad of types of remodeling possibilities. Even if you think you know what you want to do, and you don't believe that writing a program will be meaningful, this could be a valuable exercise.

Specific versus General Projects

Specific needs are easier to find solutions for. For example, an identified need "for an extra bedroom" is fairly straightforward, whereas a need that concluded "that the house was too crowded" is too broad a general statement; it will require a more detailed analysis, before you get much further, to see what types of solutions best satisfy the existing house.

Exploring All Options

Whether your project is specific or general in nature, there are likely to be a number of solutions that will satisfy the requirements. It is important for you to look at all the solutions; you may find an alternative plan that runs contrary to a pre-conceived notion you had, but which, in actuality, works much better. Be open with yourself at this point, and avoid pre-conceived answers.

Let's try an example. Assume your goal is an enlarged dining room. The existing rear facing room is hemmed by the kitchen at one side, and the garage on the other. The likely solution, you say, is to expand into the rear yard; well maybe, but what if you also recognize that the kitchen is due for major remodeling, too. Maybe the dining room should expand into the old kitchen space and you build a brand new kitchen out the rear. The results of this might be far more exciting than expanding the dining room to the rear and remodeling the kitchen in place. Moreover, it is easier to stage this project, and it will avoid much of the mess.

The above remodeling happens to be pictured in the book, as plan number KD006 on page 183. One of my persistent themes is exploring alternatives; you will find a number of plans that provide different solutions to the same problem or need. I have done that with bedrooms, bathrooms, family rooms, kitchens and even whole house renovations.

Types of Projects

There are four types of remodeling projects. Let us look at each.

Projects that add a room or rooms

Whether the room is added up, out, or down, the following are possible room additions:

Bedroom	Bath
Kitchen	Breakfast Room
Country Kitchen	Laundry Room
Family Room	Porch
Dining Room	Sunroom
Living Room	Exercise Room
Great Room	Apartment
Office	Professional Suite
Master Suite	Barrier-Free Apartment
Bedroom Wing	Foyer
Media Room	Garage
Library/Study	Walk-in Closet
Playroom	Storage Room

Making the possibilities more intricate, any of these can be combined into a single project. For example:

Family Room, Bedroom, Bath
Kitchen, Breakfast Room, Family Room
Porch, Office, Garage
Kitchen, Family Room, Master Suite
etc, etc, etc.

When you consider that any of these can be combined, depending on the needs and your existing home, and that the solutions can be any mix of one or two-story plans, again depending on your home, you realize that there can be an infinite variety of types of remodeling projects. This book presents an extensive variety of such combined programs; however it goes beyond, by also showing you how to combine various ideas on your own to create your own personal program. An important aspect of a room addition is that it can open up the possibility of a significant relocation of other uses within a home, something you may not have considered.

Projects that add space to or remodel existing rooms

The same list of rooms applies, but the actual remodeling projects are very different. In this type of project, the existing room most often retains its original use; however, the space has been redesigned to better service needs. The potential variety of such projects is even more infinite than the prior list because we can alter virtually any space within the home.

Such a project can be as diverse as the following (all one project): remodeling the kitchen in place, bumping out a bay in the breakfast room, popping a clearstory for light in the living room, combining two bedrooms to create a new master suite, creating a garden bath, opening up a loft in the attic over the living room, creating an extra powder room from one bath, opening up walls to create a great room, popping a greenhouse on the dining room and bumping out a sitting alcove.

The list is potentially endless; whatever your program eventually tells you, if it concerns adding or remodeling space (as contrasted to rooms) it is likely you can accomplish it.

Projects that update the home

Included amongst these are:

1) Projects that simply update fixtures and equipment in bathrooms and kitchens.
2) Energy related projects such as new windows, heating systems, insulation, etc.
3) Projects that update the exterior of the home, by creating a new facade.

As a design book, I have only dealt with the last one. This can be a very important part of the design program you develop. A new facade can be readily combined into any of the other types of projects and become an integral part of your overall project.

Projects that remodel an entire home

Sometimes the scope of what we want to achieve is so all-encompassing that it involves virtually the entire house. Whereas this is more likely to occur in an older home, that is not necessarily a rule. The same could apply to a home only fifteen years old, if the program that you develop suggests wholesale changes, to bring all parts of the home up to contemporary standards.

Many homes that are fifty years old or more, may require a complete re-modeling, especially if very little has been done to them over the years. Some of these homes have unredeeming floor plans, that so inhibit modern living patterns, that you have no choice but to redo them stem to stern. Frequently, someone buys such an old home because it is charming to look at and is situated on a lovely parcel of land. Hopefully it was bought "right", leaving enough resources to completely remodel it.

This concludes my brief review of alternative types of remodeling projects. Keep in mind that many programs lead to a project that may simultaneously involve several of these types. It is less common to find a project that is tidy and neat and simple to define. Let us now begin to develop your program.

3

Creating the Program

I have mentioned this "program" before—what is it that I am talking about? A program is your guide to a successful remodeling project. It will lay out, in written form, the main objectives we are seeking to achieve: which rooms are to be remodeled; what is to be added; where it is to be added; what features we expect in each room; what exterior concerns we have; the stylistic preference and any other personal inclinations that are important, such as relationships between various rooms and where privacy is essential. It is still a wish list. We will prioritize these, for if the list is long, it is likely that certain compromises will have to be made, and we must know which items are not adjustable and which are. Don't worry about format. Whereas the bulk of this chapter is geared to helping the homeowner write a program, frequently the professional is called upon to finalize the program; it is something that we do in our office on almost every project.

The Steps to a Program

The program begins by writing down the personal needs we identified in chapter 1. Anything you write down from there on should be viewed against these needs. Do these now.

The second step will be an analysis of the home. The purpose of this step is to identify problem areas within the home; which areas fall short, which need updating, which are OK.

The third step will be an evaluation of the home for change. The purpose of this step is to identify where you can make changes or where you can add. There is a tendency to short circuit the process by combining steps two and three; do not fall to this temptation. You will achieve better results if you first identify problems, without simultaneously recording potential solutions.

The fourth and final step is to assimilate this information and develop the remodeling program as previously defined. Once the program is written, there is another step that can not be overlooked. It concerns retaining flexibility.

Remaining Flexible and Developing Alternates

It would be helpful after you finish the program—and prioritize its components—that you develop an alternate list that deals with issues such as, what if the program is way over budget, should you just strike something, or is there an alternate course to pursue?

A simple example: your program listed in priority order 1) a slightly expanded, remodeled kitchen, 2) a new breakfast room and 3) a new sunporch. You are over budget; you could just strike the sunporch, but maybe you could enlarge the breakfast room some, and add enough windows and skylights that it simulates a sunporch and leaves enough space for a small sitting area beside the table.

Also, remember that there are many potential solutions to the same problem; you can achieve that new larger kitchen by 1) either building out a new room, 2) reworking interior space, with or without a small addition, or 3) going up with something else and thereby freeing first floor area. So try to avoid pre-conceived solutions and give a fair review to all possibilities. The plans shown in this book should help you do that.

Analyzing A Home

I will now detail a systematic approach for you to follow in analyzing the home, but before we start, let's talk about obtaining a plan to work with. You will find it helpful to the overall process if you have a floor plan(s) of the current home. As a professional, it is often necessary that I measure and prepare an existing layout. However, there may be other solutions. The homeowner may have been given a set of plans when they purchased the home, or maybe they have a builder's brochure (actually that's the best because it is simple to read). Unless the home is very old, you should also be able to obtain a set of plans from your local building department. If all else fails, it will be necessary to measure your home and prepare a rough, sketchy layout. If you are unsure how to do this, talk to someone who has; it is really not that complicated. Once you have a plan in hand, you will analyze your home by visually walking through and examining the rooms, one at a time and identify possible problems.

Circulation problems

Circulation problems are most common in older homes and tract homes, but they can be prevalent in any home. The paths used in our daily travels through and around the home are the circulation paths you should observe. Do these paths cut through certain rooms? If they do, do they affect our ability to use or furnish these rooms? Such problems are common to living rooms, dining rooms, family rooms and kitchens. Sometimes just the simple relocation of an opening or a doorway can solve the problem; more often, though, it requires more serious remodeling, but that's the next step. Let's avoid looking at solutions now.

Circulation problems frequently result from the fact that the home was never designed with ample circulation routes to begin with. Rooms were expected to provide part of their area to serve as connection to the next room, and to the next, and so on. I am a fervent advocate of defined circulation routes; I believe they add to the functionality, furnishability, and livability of any home. I am not dogmatic about circulation routes necessarily being confined to designated halls, but if a room is to serve a circulation pattern, it must be studied as it concerns the ability to furnish it, and, if necessary, the room should be enlarged—or combined with another.

Congested places are another possible symptom of circulation problems. Although congested places are frequently a symptom of inadequate space (and we will deal with that shortly), it is also possible that a horrendous circulation problem is the cause. Study living habits; it is possible that the family has unknowingly adapted its living patterns to solve the problems of the home. A small example: if everyone must take off their shoes before entering, and if it is not by social custom, it is likely that your circulation patterns are not in order.

Wherever you identify a circulation problem write it down on your program notes, and make a note on the floor plan.

Underutilized areas

Every home has some underutilized space; the questions are how much and where it is, and whether it has some other potential use. The whole subject of space utilization has some disputable aspects; for example, the bathroom and kitchen probably get more use than the dining room or the living room. Should the bathroom be larger than either of these? Well, that is happening today, especially if the bathroom is going to be used by more than one person at a time. This discussion was improbable for the architect designing a bungalow in 1925.

The decision of where to allocate new space should include the possible redeployment of underutilized space; but the decision to declare space surplus is a personal one that each homeowner must decide for themselves. Can one truly live without that formal dining room? Could one do away with their living room? The answers to these questions help make each program unique.

Sometimes underutilization may be only a part of a room; the cause may be not that one doesn't need it, but that some other problem—like poor circulation—has rendered it underutilized. So look at each room carefully, and try to identify the actual problem.

Finally, don't confuse this phase with finding space; that is part of the next step. What you are seeking to clarify here is whether or not you have any excess existing space not serving you well. If so, write it down on your list and indicate it on the existing plan.

Congested spaces

I have spoken of crowded bathrooms; well, that's almost endemic to the species. If that's so, then write it down. What else is congested? Is the kitchen too crowded all the time? What about the family room (if there is one) or the living room? Is it crowded because there are too many activities that must take place there (i.e. eating, cooking, watching T.V., games, etc.), or is it that there is a poor circulation pattern that forces everyone through a tight space? These are questions that may take some careful analysis to resolve.

One of the best ways to answer the question, as it concerns activity rooms, is to list the family's activities, where they are currently being carried out, and where we would prefer they be centered. This will help you later decide how many different rooms are necessary, whether or not they should be connected, and how big they should be.

Some of the problem areas you identify as being congested may be very subjective. What may appear too cramped for one person may be more than adequate for the next. That is why each remodeling project develops its own program—and ultimately its own personality. So don't necessarily be guided by norms for room sizes. For this reason you will see in this book, for example, a new family room 11 ft. x 16 ft., another 20 ft. x 30 ft., and a third plan without a family room, but with a great room instead.

Inadequate places

The discussion of inadequate places may overlap with congested spaces, but there is a reason for me to discuss them separately. You might ultimately deal with these as one subject, but let us see the distinction. Whereas our master bedroom might appear congested because it is too small, that might be so because what is sought is a sitting room or alcove, furnished with a desk, plus two comfortable chairs, for reading. Is it not then, that you are short a place—or your home is inadequate in this regard—not congested?

This is a subtlety, but it is important to distinguish whether you need larger spaces to satisfy congestion, or whether you need new places to satisfy missing functions. An easy example is a shortage of the number of bedrooms or bathrooms; that is a problem that will be solved quantitatively by increasing the number of rooms, not by increasing the size of a room.

So, however you decide to review these potential shortcomings in the home, try to distinguish whether the space deficiency is one that is best resolved by increasing the size of rooms, or by adding new rooms—or spaces—or alcoves.

Rooms in need of repair or modernization

One of your tasks in going through each room is to try to list areas in obvious need of repair or modernization. If the repairs are purely cosmetic (something a paint job will take care of) and the room is otherwise a well-functioning part of the home, you would not likely look to focus any remodeling here. If, however, the room is in desperate need of remodeling or updating (an old kitchen, for example) then there is a greater likelihood that other efforts might be directed here simultaneously. Skylights, new windows or an extension, might be readily accomplished at the same time.

Whatever it is, put the item on your list. It could have some bearing on the overall scope of your project; and, anyway, the ability to "package" miscellaneous repairs into one project has cost-saving potential, as well as financing opportunities that might not otherwise exist.

Exterior repairs or modernization

Does the roof, siding, windows, gutters or trim need repair or replacement? If so, add the items to your program list. As discussed, there could be benefits in doing it all together with space additions or changes. In fact, it may well be that this is one of the motivations in undertaking a remodeling of the home. It is possible that this is a prime concern. If so, state it in your program. That is not at all unusual today. Chapter 10 deals with this subject in somewhat greater detail.

One of the major side benefits of any large remodeling project is the ability to purposefully redesign the exterior of the home to afford it some enhanced aesthetic appeal. I, in fact, encourage this approach; I believe that to undertake a costly project, and not to provide any consideration toward improving the appearance of the home, is an opportunity lost.

Landscaping, walks, patios, driveways

There are several areas you should consider here. First, do any of the exterior site improvements to the home need any repair? If so, add them to your program list; the same logic prevails about doing them simultaneously with other improvements.

But there is a second area of concern. If your program will lead to room additions or space enlargements it is very likely that some disturbance will take place in landscaping, walks or patios, and possibly even the driveway.

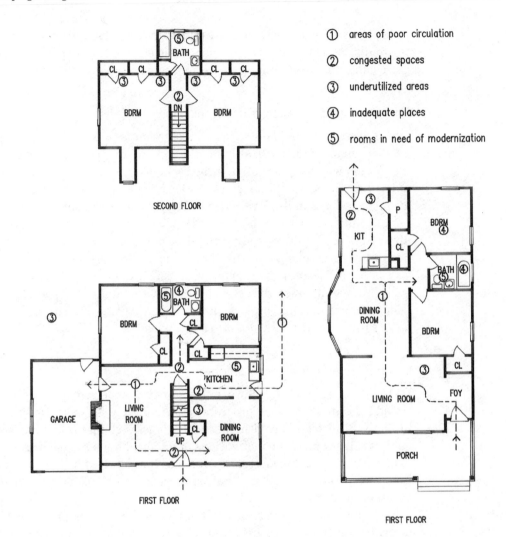

ANALYZING A HOME

You should consider these disturbances very carefully within your overall program. You might have to move some extremely ornate shrubs, and, if so, that could affect the project's timing. More often than not, however, this is an opportunity that should be seized upon. As with the opportunity to redesign the exterior of your home, look upon this as a chance to improve the landscaping and the patios. Climate and personal tastes will figure importantly.

Before you think that I am callous with your money, there is a distinction between planning the design of new landscaping and patios and actually doing the work. You should certainly seize the opportunity to replan your yard, but the work could be deferred. We'll talk more about finishing the project in chapter 14.

Determining current market value

As a knowledgeable local I am often asked to help a client with this subject. However, most homeowners are usually pretty savvy on this subject; if you are not, one of the unrelated items you might consider doing, as you are analyzing your home, is to try to determine its current value. This could be an opportune time to work on this, since you will be focusing intently on your home, its room sizes and its pluses and minuses.

The only reason to do it, though, is if there is any serious concern about the potential for over-improving. I tend to minimize this issue, as stated before, but if you are worried, then this is an opportune time to deal with the subject.

As an aid to help visualize the potential deficiencies we have discussed so far, several floor plans are presented on page 20, with their problem areas identified.

Evaluating the Home for Change

You have identified the problem places you see in the home; you will now move on to the task of identifying how, or where, the home can be modified to satisfy these problems.

Where can you make interior changes?

The first area we will look at is the existing home itself. Before you consider any exterior additions, let us try to identify where you can effect changes within the shape of the current foundation. Such changes are usually (but not always) cheaper than additions, but it may also be that you do not have any room to expand out.

Finding space

In the prior step we analyzed the home for underutilized space. If you have identified some, let us take a look at it. Maybe the space was an unused bedroom opposite your master bedroom. If your goal is a new master bath and dressing room — the answer is pretty clear. This remodeling, as any we discuss in this part, is a reallocation of space; unless you go up — or out — and add new space, any of the changes we talk about here are a redistribution of existing space.

Combining rooms and removing walls

Sometimes the answer to finding space can be found by removing partitions and combining rooms. Although no new floor area is added, the combining of several spaces provides a visual enhancement that may equate to an expansion. One of the increasingly popular applications of this technique today is in the great room, which removes walls between your kitchen, dining room and living room. Several such plans are shown in this book, including KDL03 on page 293.

Maybe it's only a partial removal of a wall, which preserves some separation, which you may prefer. A low wall with a counter above can do the same for a small kitchen, while allowing it to visually be part of a larger space.

Sometimes you can achieve most of the same affect by creating larger openings in existing walls; this may be necessary if the walls are structurally bearing, which we will discuss later. It also could be beneficial where you feel the need to maintain some greater definition of a room because of wallpaper or some other decorating concern. An excellent example of this is the opening up of a small dining room to the adjacent space, whether it be a foyer, a family room or living room. Similar spatial enhancement occurs, but short walls at each side and a header maintain the definition of the room. You will also see plans in this book that use interior columns in lieu of walls; this is another, very stylish technique that is in use today.

Moving partitions

On occasion, it might be advantageous to move an interior partition a few feet. This could prove beneficial, say in a kitchen, where 2 feet more might allow a return counter, and thereby make an inadequate kitchen workable. Of course the 2 feet would have to be such that the room it is taken from can still function.

Another common example might be several feet taken from a secondary bedroom to create a new modern bathroom. If an up-to-date modish bathroom is high on the program, and there is no other place to gain the area to achieve it, someone in the family will learn to adjust to a smaller bedroom. Plan number B0006 on page 240 is an example. Maybe that bedroom can be enhanced by larger windows, or raising its ceiling to provide volume or a loft. This latter comment is important; compromises are going to be necessary every step of the way, and there may always be some way to compensate the losing part of the compromise.

Creating halls and foyers

In certain circumstances it may be necessary to reduce the size of a room to create a hall or a foyer. When? Only when you have such a serious circulation problem that nothing else will work. We can sometimes satisfy circulation problems by a change in flooring, or using columns, or low walls, or moving an opening, or even using furnishings to define the traffic flow. But there may be occasions where the best solution is a new wall. Plan CAP04 on page 341 is such an example.

Using volume

One of the best methods available to visually enhance a cramped space is the utilization of volume. Volume is that space above our head, usually covered up in an attic. All it usually takes to uncover it is the removal of ceiling beams. If your house has a trussed roof you would be limited to a smaller area, but it can still be achieved. Skylights are a common addition to a vaulted or cathedral ceiling; with the addition of extra light, an otherwise small room is further enhanced.

Another place to find living space is from unused volume in the attic. Space under the eaves is potentially available for storage needs, or to expand second floor rooms or create new rooms. It will take a little investigation on your part, but if you find attic area that you can stand in for a width of at least four or five feet, it is space worth pursuing. There could be space for a bath lurking there (see plan B0010 on page 245). If it is 8 or 10 feet in width you might have a whole playroom (see plan F0013 on page 268). Another potential use for unused attic space is the development of finished loft space that overlooks, or serves as an adjunct to first floor rooms.

Going up

Finding space in an attic is great, but if your needs can only be met by a large infusion of new square footage, you should look up. Unless there are zoning restrictions that prohibit your use of the air and sky overhead, adding up is a very potent solution for cramped spaces. It becomes the only solution if you are prevented from expanding out. There are a number of different styles of such expansions, depending on what type of home we have, and how much space is needed. The book is full of such expansions, too numerous to list here; perusing through the plans is required. Let's talk about five types of additions that go up.

If the current home is a one and one-half story design with a partial second floor, the balance of the area over the first floor could be added; this would create a full two story home and could enable you to free much first floor space for living or entertainment needs. You also may be able to create a luxurious first floor master bedroom. Such an addition requires care in developing a new facade; since the home is now a two story design, new relationships are created between first and second floor forms, windows and rooflines. Many disasters have been created by an unthinking remodeler adding a full second floor. Follow the examples shown in this book and you won't go wrong.

If the current home is a split level, the area over the living room wing has ready potential for adding space. Likely uses include a spacious new master suite or an apartment. Stairs are easily located. Extreme care must be exercised in the forms added here; a setback from the front wall is important and rooflines must echo the existing house.

If the subject is a one-story home, there's a great deal of possible space obtainable on a second floor. You could add more bedrooms, even a whole bedroom wing, or a private master suite, possibly even a whole apartment. As with the one and one-half story home, the relocation of some bedrooms here offers the potential freeing of first floor area to enhance other uses.

There are, however, two areas of significant concern, when adding up on a one-story home. The first involves finding a location for a stair. If there is a basement, the likely place to look is over the basement stair, but that could be poorly located. If you have to create a new stair, the 3 ft. x 10 ft. space required might be an unpalatable loss that forces you to abandon the idea. This very much depends on your exact floor plan, and what you hope to achieve on the second floor.

The second concern with adding up on a one-story home, involves the aesthetic balance of the home. A small dormer or clearstory will always look fine on a one-story roof, but once the space reaches the outer walls, it must be studied very carefully. If the element on the second floor is too small, it could be out of proportion with the home. The size of the addition, plus the styling of its roofline are best left to a professional or patterned on the ideas shown in this book.

The fourth type of plan, that utilizes space overhead, is one that adds above a garage. The space over a garage is ideal for a playroom, an apartment or a bedroom. On a two-story design, it can also be used to expand the second floor. Caution is the word again concerning exterior forms.

The fifth is actually the simplest. It involves the addition of bumps for small second floor additions to a one and one-half story design. These are commonly called dormers.

New windows and the use of glass

What does this have to do with making interior changes? A whole lot! Much of our efforts are aimed at trying to find space to enhance rooms. The addition of large windows, maybe even some very stylish shapes, or the use of large unbroken areas of fixed glass, or glass block can help to visually expand interior space. By doing so, the outdoor spaces that rooms face out to can help enhance tight indoor spaces. With the addition of garden lighting, privacy walls and landscaping, this enhancement is available day and night. It is a tool one should seriously consider using.

① finding space

② moving partitions

③ combining rooms

④ creating halls and foyers

⑤ creating volume

⑥ going up

⑦ adding out

⑧ bearing partitions

⑨ remodeling baths or kitchens in place

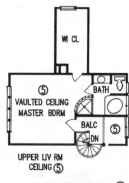

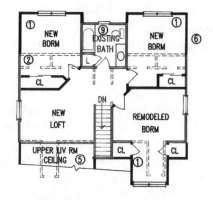

REMODELED SECOND FLOOR ⑥

ALL NEW SECOND FLOOR ⑥

- - - → new circulation

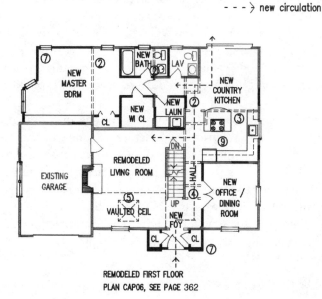

REMODELED FIRST FLOOR
PLAN CAP06, SEE PAGE 362

REMODELED FIRST FLOOR
PLAN CTG02, SEE PAGE 353

IDENTIFYING WHERE YOU CAN MAKE CHANGES

Remodeling kitchens and baths in place

Just a few words to those who choose to remodel kitchens and baths by merely replacing fixtures and finishes. If your decision is purely economic I will not dissuade you; there is absolutely no question that the cheapest solution is to remodel in place. If, however, you choose this route, because you truly believe that no space exists to enhance them, look again. I assure you there is some way to achieve those few feet of space so essential to solving the problems of many older kitchens and baths. Chapter 9 presents a number of such plans.

All of the subjects we have just discussed are graphically shown in the drawing on page 25. In that drawing, you will see how I have proposed to resolve the problems that we had identified in the plans shown on page 20.

Potential problems of interior remodeling

There are several problems common to all of these remodeling projects that stay inside the exterior walls. The first is identifying bearing partitions that may limit your freedom in removing or relocating walls. If you have obtained a set of construction plans on the home these will be labeled; if you are not sure, some probing, and even some educated guess work, may be required. If you are a do-it-yourselfer, you may have to ask a contractor with experience. All of the plans shown in this book have addressed that concern. If you discover an unexpected bearing wall during construction, the chart in chapter 11 should help you get a quick answer on necessary girders.

Homes with masonry exterior bearing walls may inhibit your ability to create large new openings, not necessarily because of the loads on girders, but because of the extensive labor required to make the openings. If the subject is a masonry home, we might have to reduce expectations—or increase the budget.

Interior renovations may obviously cause disruptions in the heating, electrical and plumbing systems. Whereas cost factors are one concern, the larger unanticipated one is the disruption factor that is impossible to prepare for. No matter how well I plan for these and prepare the homeowner for being without them, it will seem like an endless eternity. The same holds true for the mess in general, but it is an unavoidable factor that we must try to plan for. One avenue of help is to plan for staging the construction. A detailed discussion, plus some examples, are presented in chapter 13.

Where can you add to your home?

In the prior pages we have reviewed where we can effect changes within the home, including going up, but not going out. Additions bring a different set of issues and concerns that we will now review.

Finding space

Finding space for additions presents entirely different search criteria; the space we are looking for, to create an addition, is exterior space—part of the front, rear or side yards. The space could also be in the form of a recess or a courtyard. Other places to look at are underutilized parts of the lot, like the area behind a garage, or the area in front of a garage on an L-shaped home. Wherever you find this space, there are a number of significant considerations and constraints you will have to identify before you can consider using the space.

Zoning considerations

Foremost amongst the possible constraints are zoning considerations. Most communities have established criteria for minimum front, rear and side yards. There are also restrictions on the percentage of the lot that can be covered by structures. Sometimes there are even total floor area restrictions and height restrictions. All of these could inhibit your use of what you thought was found space.

The first step necessary to evaluate these is a review of the survey of the home; most homeowners likely received one at closing, when they purchased the home. If one can't be found, a call to the attorney or bank should produce one. The survey is to solving exterior space needs as the floor plan was to solving interior problems. From a survey you can sketch a site plan which sets out all the constraints—and benefits—that will control your ability to build out. From the survey you will find out what the current yards are. Don't rely on what you think they are—it must be verified by the survey. You can then contact the local municipality and inquire about the zoning restrictions. You will usually find that there is plenty of room to expand to the rear, and very little, maybe even no room at all, to expand to the front and sides. However, if you believe that the home would be best served by adding within one of these required yards, there is usually an appeal process called a variance.

Variances

Depending upon the municipality, the process of filing for a variance could be a routine matter, that you could handle yourself, or a legal proceding that demands you bring along an attorney. It is usually necessary to show a hardship to convince the board that the request should be granted, as well as some proof (or a statement) that granting the variance will not result in reduced property values.

An example for discussion: say the kitchen is in the front; it is dark, dingy and awfully cramped, but the front of the home is right on the setback line.

Well, you might be able to argue a hardship; that you should not be prevented from enlarging the kitchen, and to relocate it elsewhere is a total impracticality. The way to sell it though is to bring a professionally drawn sketch of the new front and demonstrate that you will be upgrading the streetscape. The same two-part approach should be used for any variance. Sometimes certain types of structures like porches, vestibules and terraces, are permitted to encroach into a required yard, so check the ordinance carefully.

Natural site constraints and easements

Sometimes it's not zoning that controls where we can place an addition, but a natural condition of the site. A steep drop-off or a steep up-slope are one type of severe restraint; rock out croppings are another—unless we are prepared to remove the rock. A modest drop-off in grade or a modest up-slope, however, can actually be advantageous in creating an attractive setting for an addition. If it drops away, a walk-out basement could be a bonus; on an up-slope a small retaining wall could add interest to the view; such a wall is also technically a necessity, so that when the addition is finished the lot will still maintain a positive flow of drainage away from the home.

A drainage ditch or swale could be an impediment; a buried sewer main could be another. Both of these are probably located within easements, which are areas of the lot that restrict building. These would be shown on the survey.

Other buried items to look for are water mains, utility lines, septic systems and oil tanks. None of these would prevent us from building, however you would have to plan to relocate them elsewhere, which are additional items of cost.

Finally there are the planted shrubs and patios and walks that might be in the way of a potential addition. It isn't likely we would change our mind because of these, but just keep them in mind, in terms of developing a thorough program that lists everything to be done.

Orientation

Where the sun rises, and falls, and how it affects the lot are design issues you should look at. All too often, the orientation of the existing home doesn't allow you to take full advantage of—or protect against—the affects of the sun. However, when planning an addition there may be some opportunities for you to exploit. If your goal is to take advantage of the sun, you could try to locate the addition where it would receive more hours of sun. If that were not practical you could place windows in the appropriate walls, and skylites in the appropriately facing roof plane. If your goal was to avoid sun, you could readily make sure that windows facing south would be protected by overhangs, and make certain not to locate windows on a westerly wall.

Choosing the size and shape of the addition

As mentioned before, the determination of size (assuming there are no zoning or physical constraints) is a very subjective matter to be decided. The size of the current home should not be a factor; the purpose of the addition is to provide the space needed so don't limit it for some abstract reason like that. Size could be an aesthetic concern, but I discuss that under "problems," coming up next.

As concerns shape, an addition is a wonderful opportunity to break with the rigid shapes of the current home. This requires a little daring and good design. You will see good examples of some exciting shapes in the chapters on plans.

All of these factors that affect the design of an addition are shown in the sample site plan pictured on page 30.

Potential problems of additions

As with the remodeling of interior space there are potential problems associated with all additions that you should be aware of. The first is the potential loss of light to the room(s) that adjoin the addition. It is usually necessary to compensate for this loss with the use of skylights, if possible, and the use of recessed lighting. However, another method is to design the new addition, particularly if it is a family room, kitchen, dining room, etc., to be fully open to the old room it adjoins; this, of course requires careful placement of the addition.

A second possible problem is a significant design concern; it is the problem of roof design, and the attachment of the addition, so it appears as an integral part of the home. It is easy to make a mistake and end up with one of those additions that clearly looks like an addition, and which is at odds with the original home. The only certain way to avoid this is to hire a professional, or follow the pre-designed plans shown in the book. This is an area so prone to error, that I have even pursued it further by developing a special chapter, known as "blockforms", which are 60 schematic forms showing attachments that work. There is also another group, located in another chapter, that show you what not to do.

Additions also have a tendency to expand the scope of exterior work. When you add something new it is likely the sidings won't match; chances are you will also use lots of windows in the addition — and that you might prefer windows of a different style and design than the original house. What do you do?

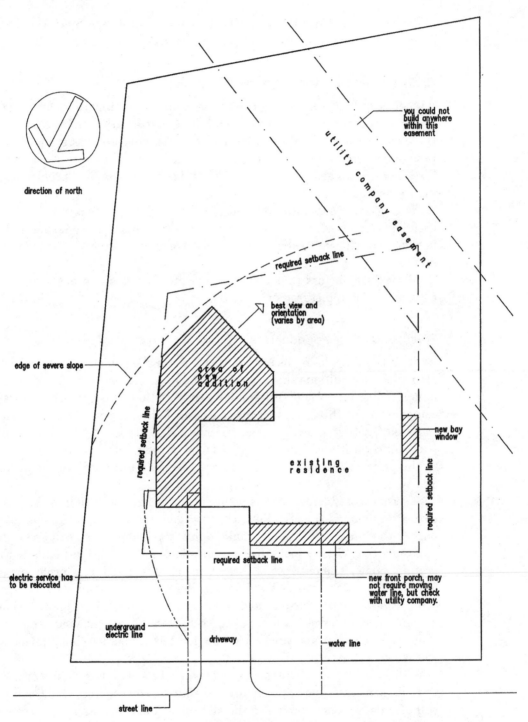

direction of north

you could not build anywhere within this easement

utility company easement

required setback line

best view and orientation (varies by area)

edge of severe slope

area of new addition

required setback line

new bay window

existing residence

required setback line

required setback line

new front porch, may not require moving water line, but check with utility company.

electric service has to be relocated

underground electric line

driveway

water line

street line

SAMPLE SITE PLAN

Do you replace all the windows in the house and redo the siding? Very often the answer is yes, not just for the sake of exterior harmony, but also because these items were due for replacement anyway. If the house does not warrant this wholesale change—or the budget prescribes against it—you will have to carefully choose new sidings and windows that blend with the existing, and locate the addition so that there is no flush match line; the best match line that avoids this problem is a 90 degree intersection.

Finalizing the Program

Unless the scope of the project was narrow, and well-defined to start, the likelihood is that a final program will involve a mix of some interior remodeling of space and some exterior addition. The addition might only be a bay or a few feet, but it is also very common to see large new additions combined with significant renovations to interior space; many of the plans shown in chapter 8 do just that.

The fact is that your program may not be very tidy; it is probably several pages of some scribbled notes you have made in trying to evaluate needs and the home. You may have many uncertainties, and be unsure, for example, whether to build out, or add up, or do both. But do not fret—that dilemma is not uncommon. To try to gain a firmer picture of what may ultimately work, now is the time to rewrite your notes and spend a reasonable amount of time helping to prioritize this wish list. It will then be necessary to prepare the list of alternates as discussed in the introduction to this chapter. Once that has been completed, you have a program that can be used as a guide in preparing a design.

Remember, compromises will be necessary. In looking through this book, you will not likely find a plan that meshes 100% with your program, but do not back off on features that are strongly desired. The ability to make changes to any plan is a given fact, and you can customize and rework any of the plans shown in this book. We will talk more about that in chapter 5.

How to Utilize the Plans

Your use of the plans that follow will largely depend on how well you have defined the remodeling project. If you know, for certain, that you will only be adding a front porch, you will likely turn to that part of chapter 9 that shows new front porches. If you are clearly not considering any additions, up or out, you could readily bypass chapter 8. If, however, like most, you are not certain and are in search of ideas, you may well want to review all the plans.

Reviewing the Plans

I will briefly summarize the organization of the plans again: the next two chapters present sketch diagrams designed primarily for additions. The first chapter presents 24 recognizable home types; the following chapter presents 60 generalized shapes. These are merely blockforms to help orient you on shapes that may suit your home. Chapter 8 presents 128 detailed designs for additions of every sort. They are generally organized by room types. Following that is a collection of 91 detailed designs for interior remodels and small space additions; these are also generally organized by room type. Following these are 26 designs for new exterior facades. Finally, in chapter 11, are 27 whole house renovations. If you are seeking specific types of plans, consulting the index might prove helpful.

If you purchased this book with the accompanying computer disk, all of the plans may be viewed, copied, or changed, depending on the software you own. You will also find lots of other helpful drawings on the disk, including various sketch drawings as well as sample construction drawings. See the Addendum for a detailed discussion on how to use the disk. The following notes are common to all the plans.

Text

It is important to read the accompanying text with each plan. The text not only highlights the salient components of each plan, but also provides helpful tips and hints for better design. The text may also provide the overall dimensions of an addition as it is drawn, which would indicate whether the size might require adjustment to suit your lot. The text could also direct you to other plans for consideration, especially if there are alternates for your review. Finally the text might provide tips on staging, cost considerations, or other facts for review.

Combining, reversing or modifying plans

Keep in mind that all plans can be reversed. If the current home is a mirror image—or you would prefer a mirror image of an addition—any of the plans could be constructed in reverse. Also keep the door open for changes. Remember these are, generally, very flexible plans that can be readily modified to suit your specific requirements, so don't look for a precise fit—custom tailoring is expected. Also remember that plans can be combined. Many of the plans shown remodel two or more rooms, and all of those in chapter 11 remodel the whole house; the potential for other combinations is almost infinite.

Rules for viewing plans

Some further facts about each plan: the general orientation of each floor plan presumes that the street is at the bottom of the page. Although that may not always be the case for your particular home, it is the general rule. As such, a front addition is generally indicated below the existing house in the floor plan and a rear addition is indicated above the existing rooms. Even on additions to a side, or on internal renovations, the plan has been drawn the way it is most frequently found. Where the perspective view shows an exterior addition, the view could be from the side, rear or front. The direction is indicated by the view-wizard on the floor plan, plus the addition is shaded, so you should be able to tell from which direction the view is taken. When rooms are dimensioned, the first number is always the horizontal dimension, the second number is the vertical dimension. This holds true regardless of the shape of the room—and remember every room can be stretched or reduced as you deem necessary. See the first drawing in chapter 8, which is an explanatory sample drawing.

Study all the options

One of my persistent themes is exploring alternatives. You will find throughout these chapters on plans various solutions to the same problem. In certain instances, where I invite direct comparison, you will be told so, and which plans to compare; however, the majority of options are dependent on your requirements, so unless the program is extremely well-defined, and you have very few alternatives listed, it is probably worthwhile to review all the plans that deal with your needs.

As an example, assuming the home was a typical three-bedroom split-level and the goal (or one of them) was a new master suite, you could consider the addition of only a new private master bath, or the rear or side addition of an entire new master suite, or going up internally over the living room. These are three distinctly different solutions to the same problem. All are pictured in the book, but it will be for you to perceive them as viable options for your consideration.

The extras or bonuses of each plan

You will find, occasionally, in the text a reference to an "extra" or a "bonus"; these are not intended in the same way a builder of new homes uses these terms. Very often there is a secondary benefit of a plan, which was not the main focus of the plan, but which results as a by-product. It is not that this is an accident, but in the design process, as I see this occurring, these other elements are studied and are perfected in the final design along with the main subject. If they are not studied, these secondary affects of most remodeling projects could prove to be an unwelcome afterthought. I have seen these all too often as a result of an unprofessionally planned design. By being aware, in advance, of all the potential impacts of a particular improvement, they can be studied and made a beneficial aspect of the project.

As an example, take the split-level previously referred to; say you opted for a side addition. Do you build it on posts? Never, unless you absolutely had to. An extra garage becomes a likely bonus to the new master suite, but it could be more. If you didn't need an extra garage, you could increase the potential living area by expanding into the old garage—you might even be able to develop an apartment. These then are all studied, pre-planned bonuses to the plan. Many are more subtle and significantly smaller than this example.

Creating construction blueprints

Once you have singled out one or more designs in this book as a starting point, you can, of course, have new revised preliminary design drawings prepared that will permit a better study of your modified design. These drawings could be created directly from the drawings in this book, particularly if utilizing the files on the accompanying disk.

Construction drawings can similarly be created by utilizing the files on the disk. Imported into your CAD program they can be modified, stretched, etc. For further details on utilizing the files on disk see the Addendum. If you are creating drawings by hand, the designs in the book can be used as a guide.

The creation of a sound set of construction drawings is best undertaken by an experienced professional—one who has prepared such drawings many times. Such drawings must spell out all the technical information necessary to build the project. When accompanied by a set of specifications, which I shall discuss shortly, these drawings will permit accurate estimating to establish a firm price.

There are no firm rules as to what must be shown on a set of construction drawings; the variables include the nature of the project itself, whether the drawings are going to be bid, or be part of a contract for construction, and finally the requirements of the local municipality. If the drawing is for a small bump-out that will be utilized only by a contractor, without the need to bid a price, in a municipality with little regulation, then the drawing could be rudimentary; one might even simply add notes, annotations and structure to the floor plan shown in this book. However, if it is a complicated addition/renovation for a homeowner who wants to obtain bids, and it is located in an overly regulated community, these drawings would likely comprise foundation plans, floor plans, cross-sections, elevations, site plan and numerous details that elaborate on special situations of the project. Samples of several construction drawings are provided on the computer disk. As a design book, it is not my intent here to go into a detailed discussion on how to create construction drawings; again there are many books on that subject, if you need further information. For the do-it-yourselfer, caution is necessary here; despite your desire and willing effort, an architect may still be necessary. I will review the role of the architect shortly.

Specifications

Specifications have the same relationship to construction drawings as the accessory/option list has to the manufacturers list price for automobiles. Specifications define the quality of all the materials to be utilized in the construction, ranging from concrete to fixtures to switch plates. It can be very detailed, but does not have to be so detailed to be effective. Specifications may not even be needed at all, if the contractor has his own. If the project is to be bid by several contractors, specifications serve to establish an even playing field for all bidders, eliminating any guesswork.

Creating a detailed set of specifications for a project, if desired by the homeowner, can be a very time consuming endeavor. One has to pick all the plumbing fixtures, including all the colors and fittings, all the flooring, including actual samples, etc. Since the time required to pick these can be so extensive, and the homeowner is often not yet prepared to choose everything before bidding, dollar allowances can be used on a set of specifications to establish the range of quality and a bid price. For example, the specification can state that the allowance for floor tile material will be $5.00 per square foot. This has every contractor bidding the same, but allows the homeowner time to actually pick the tile. A sample specification has been included on the accompanying disk. However, regional techniques, practices and preferences will play a significant role in developing your own specifications.

Building codes, building permits, approvals

Alas, there are rules—sometimes very few—but more often, very many rules. Someone in the building team has to check these out beforehand to assume that the project will pass all approvals. This person could be the architect, designer, contractor or even the homeowner himself. If you are planning an addition, the *zoning* code must be first consulted to establish required yards, easements, coverage rules, etc. Then, the *building* code used in the municipality needs to be consulted to establish construction code rules, which could affect everything from foundation wall rebars to interior door sizes. Sometimes there are various other agencies that need to be contacted to obtain their rules. These include the local health department, environmental agencies, and architectural review committees, amongst others. If yours is a very regulated community you might need permits and approvals from all these agencies.

The role of the architect

The architect could be the master in charge of it all; preliminary design, design development, construction drawings, specifications, bidding, permits, approvals and even construction administration could all be provided by the architect, if so desired, in one given project. There may not be an architect involved at all in another project. The scope of the project, the homeowner's goals and the regulatory nature of the community will influence that decision. In many situations, the contractor will provide many of these services. A do-it-yourselfer could try to do it alone—but that may not be wise, considering all the possible pitfalls the home remodeling process has to skirt.

The above has been a brief discussion of what one needs to do once they have finalized on a particular design scheme. The next few chapters provide an enormous range of conceptual design ideas, as well as many detailed, specific, design programs for you to review and consider. Remember, it is likely that nothing will be a perfect fit to your particular home; adjustments will be required.

A Review of Exterior Forms

Common Home Types—
Patterns for Adding On

As I stated in the introduction, one of the goals of this book was to identify those common house types that proliferate across North America, and find and document sound, common solutions. This chapter starts that process. It shows 24 different sketches of various house types and some 50 different types of additions that will be suited to these homes. It is also the first of three chapters that deals with the process of finding attractive, workable forms that can be successfully added to different types of homes. This first chapter identifies very specific, recognizable, home types; the next chapter deals with generalized abstract forms; and the third chapter provides a collection of unacceptable solutions. The first 12 sketches in this chapter represent more recent housing types built after World War II; the last 12 are sketches of older homes, many of which are distinct historical styles.

You may ask why have I devoted so much effort to this subject? Simply, I am horrified at the preponderance of ugliness emanating from so much of our existing housing stock. Sometimes this ugliness can be attributable to the original design, as in the case of many of the post-war tract homes, but it also is a function of inappropriate additions. These stand out like a sore thumb and they dot our landscape; they cut across all styles, from older historic homes, that have been poorly added to, to more recent tract homes with additions that only added to their lack of appeal.

Unfortunately, so many of our homes have been added to inappropriately; all too often space has been added purely for function with no concern for aesthetics. As I have stated elsewhere, that was an opportunity lost because every time we tinker with the exterior of a home we need to consider what we can simultaneously do to improve its overall appearance. The way we approach this, however, is greatly determined by the type of home we are working on.

If we are adding to a home built prior to 1940, more than likely, it has a distinct historical style. In general, our options are restricted by the nature of the home, its shape, its roofline and its exterior materials and trim. Most such older homes are not short in looks, but in livability, as contrasted to postwar suburban homes. Many such older homes have rich oak woodwork and hand-carved detailing and trim which would be prohibitive to duplicate today. When adding to such a home, the addition should be true to the original style; it must complement and add to the original design. Rooflines, materials and windows should be as seamless as possible; this is often costly, but the alternative could serve to devalue the home.

In that regard, one of the steps necessary to consider when adding to an older historical home is to see if there were any inappropriate earlier additions that could be corrected in a new project. Look carefully at rear one story additions, that include kitchens and baths, or second floor dormered bathrooms. These could be the products of a do-it-yourselfer at some time in the past history of the home. Very often these older additions were not built to the same quality as the original home, and they could be in serious need of repair, thus creating an opportune time to improve their aesthetics. We often find porches that have been poorly enclosed; yet today we are adding porches to new and existing homes. Maybe this is the opportunity to return the porch to its original use. If you do, research it first; try to find old pictures or look at old plan books.

One thing that becomes abundantly clear when we review techniques for adding on to older, historical, home styles, is that the fronts are inviolate, allowing only minor tinkering; we usually can add to the rear of these homes, and sometimes to the side. We can see this in the last 12 or so of the sketches that follow. For this reason, when we are engaged to remodel an older, historical home, we are often forced to focus more heavily on interior remodeling solutions, particularly bathrooms and kitchens, which are usually their most serious deficiencies.

On the other hand, when remodeling a post-1940 home, the opposite often becomes the focus of our direction. Since so many of these homes lack any true discernable style other than "contractor modern", we may choose to utilize additions to produce a "style". Although purists frown upon such restyling, the reality is that most homeowners today, who own such a banal home, are desirous of modifying the appearance of their home so it reflects their lifestyle. Common themes for restyling prevalent today include neo-Victorian and "Country", an eclectic, non-descriptive style that attempts to emulate the Folk Victorian styles of the mid-1800's.

When remodeling an older, historical home, the size, shape, roofline, materials, trim and even the color of an addition must be carefully chosen to match the existing home. When remodeling a post-1940 home, where restyling is part of the program, we only need to choose the correct size, shape and roofline of an addition so that the form complements the existing home, but the details of the façade could be a second step. For that reason the first 12 sketches, which deal with post-1940 homes, show additions in mass only; the following chapter does the same. Ideas for restyling the façades can then be found in chapter 10.

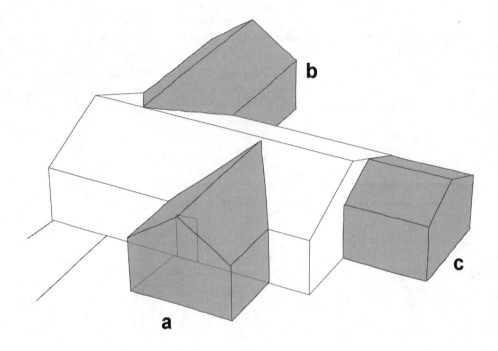

Wide-line ranch

This is the first of four sketches showing possible forms for additions to wide-line ranch homes. The front addition, "a", is one of the most attractive forms we can add to such a home. It is a reverse gable form that can add significantly to the appearance of the home; if you style it with dramatic windows it can be exceptionally attractive. This type of addition can be used to enlarge a front living room or dining room and entrance foyer. We strive to make the pitches as steep as the existing ridge allows us to.

Similarly, addition "b", is a rear reverse gable, often used for a new family room or bedroom. It too can be a very attractive form added to the existing ranch home. Its ridge line cannot exceed the height of the existing roof.

Addition "c" is a wing to the side. It is best being smaller in depth than the original home, so there is no need to align ridges or perfectly match siding; the roof pitch also must match the existing roof. This form is ideal for adding a bedroom, expanding a dining room or adding a garage.

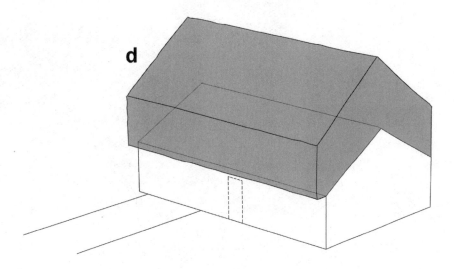

Wide-line ranch

Probably the most common home type being remodeled today is the one-story or "ranch" or "rambler"; millions of these were built over the past 50 years. Many were small, modest starter homes, devoid of any frills and as such, are ripe for remodeling. Fortunately, for the owner, it is probably the most flexible home to remodel. There are no second floor problems, no complicated roof patterns, and plumbing and mechanical issues are usually readily resolved.

The sheer variety of ranch homes offers endless possibilities for adding on or remodeling; internal use changes are easily accommodated, either alone or with an infinite variety of exterior add-ons, such as the forms pictured in the sketches on these four pages.

The form pictured here in "d" is a full two-story addition. When done, it is usually a whole house renovation such as those shown in chapter II. Façade issues are the biggest concern here, as windows may be difficult to align on both floors. If that is a problem, cantilevering the second floor, as shown, is a good solution. Many plans in chapters 8 and II deal with this subject further.

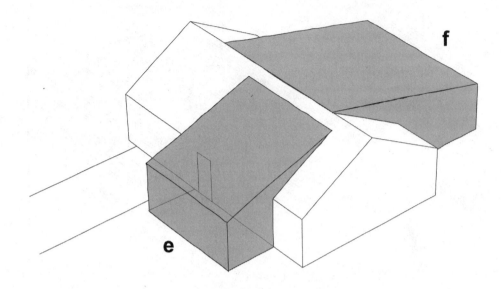

Wide-line ranch

The choices that designers have to make when preparing plans for a major remodeling, are sometimes compromises that we are forced to accept. Because many tract ranch homes were built with very low roof pitches, it often poses a serious concern when proposing a large addition. Although reverse gable forms are infinitely more appealing, if either "e" or "f", as pictured, would have been sketched as reverse gables, they would not work. Why? Because an attractive reverse gable would place the ridge of the additions higher than the existing roof, unless we raised the entire existing roof. Very often we can exceed the existing ridge, but this requires careful study of the massing; in the two pictured above, it would not work, as the additions would overwhelm the existing form.

Therefore, when designing a large addition, we often must accept the less appealing shed roof forms pictured in "e" and "f". If, however, the home were to be "restyled" as a prairie or craftsman style, for example, a low pitch reverse gable could be considered, so there is much to be considered before finalizing a decision.

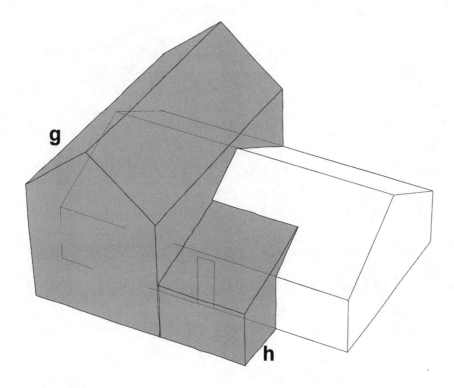

Wide-line ranch

This, the last sketch showing alternative types of additions to the typical ranch home, is probably the most appealing. It mixes one and two-story forms in attractive proportions, which produces a more varied and interesting home. The two-story element, which runs perpendicular to the existing home is an ideal form to redo the bedroom wing in a typical ranch. Additional bedrooms can be added on the second floor, while the first floor rooms are enlarged and modernized.

This form is also well suited to create a great new first floor master suite out of the existing bedroom wing, while adding two or three children's bedrooms on the second floor. This type of home is becoming increasingly popular in new homes built today in many regions.

The front shed addition can be either a covered porch or space that creates a new entrance foyer—or some combination of both.

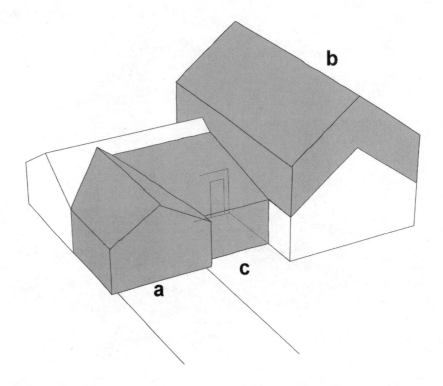

L-Shaped Ranch

The L-shaped ranch may utilize many of the forms presented in the prior four drawings; however, it does also offer several new possibilities that are unique to this shape. The L ranch permits front additions without the need for variances. The recessed areas can be infilled, as represented in "a" and "c". These additions can also add a great deal of exterior appeal to the home. The "a" addition is likely a new garage, which would free the existing garage to be converted to living area.

The "c" addition is either a covered porch or an enhancement to the entrance foyer. The two-story addition is self-evident; it is likely new bedrooms built over the existing bedroom wing. This would free the first floor area, allowing the creation of a lavish master suite. Not all such volume need be additional rooms; for example the rear of this form could enable the creation of a two-story volume for a rear living space.

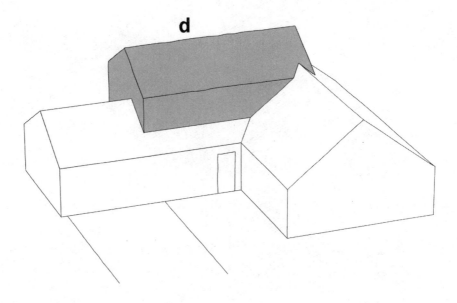

L-Shaped Ranch

The addition pictured here is a very different approach to going up in a ranch home. Whereas most of the other forms pictured affected the front façade, this addition adds an interesting second floor mass, but to the rear. This type of addition can also be used for a conventional wide-line ranch; it poses less problems in locating and aligning second floor windows, and it requires less concern about matching materials and roofing. As in all the additions that run parallel to an existing roofline, the new roof pitches, however, should match the existing.

In the typical L ranch pictured, this type of addition can create new second floor children's bedrooms. This would allow you to redesign the first floor bedroom wing and create a luxurious new master suite, by combining the existing master bedroom with the adjacent bedroom. There are numerous plans in chapter 9 that show such rearrangements of existing bedrooms to create a new master suite.

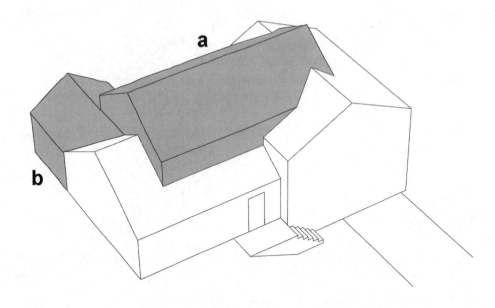

Split Level

There are generally two types of common additions to an existing side-to-side split-level home. Pictured in "b" is a rear one-story reverse gable addition; depending on the layout of your home, this can add a family room or enlarge a kitchen or dining room—or both. Shed room forms are also possible for large additions (see sketch "f" for the wide-line ranch).

The most intriguing addition to a split-level, however, is the form pictured in "a". What this enables us to do is add a room—or rooms—over the living room wing. This is an ideal location for a new master suite, or a guest suite; it usually ties in directly and easily to the existing stair hall, and is a half flight up from the existing bedroom floor. There are many different ways to do this form attractively, and several plans are presented in chapter 8 and another in chapter 10. Any of these can turn an ordinary drab split-level into an exciting home. One rule to remember, don't bring the addition out to the front wall. It doesn't look good at all, unless you extend the front with a porch.

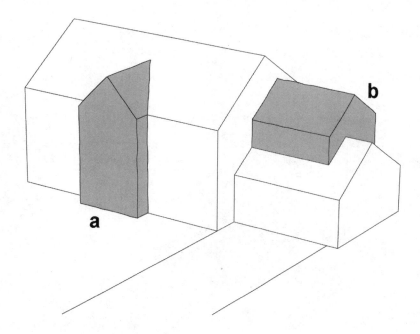

Two-Story

The next two pages deal with the typical suburban "two-story colonial"; some sketches also apply to older, historical, two-story homes, such as Georgian, Federal or Greek Revival homes, but they are intended primarily for suburban tract two-story homes. The form pictured in "a" is usually an enlargement of the front entry. It is often accompanied by a plan revision that moves a room from above the existing foyer to create a two-story high entry, a feature very popular today in new homes. Several of these are shown in chapter 9.

The form pictured in "b" is a second floor addition above the existing garage. This is a great location for an extra bedroom, or a playroom, or guest suite or apartment. Many of today's newer two-story homes utilize the space above the garage, which enables the creation of high ceiling, large volume, rooms elsewhere on the first floor. That also becomes a possibility with this type of addition in an existing home.

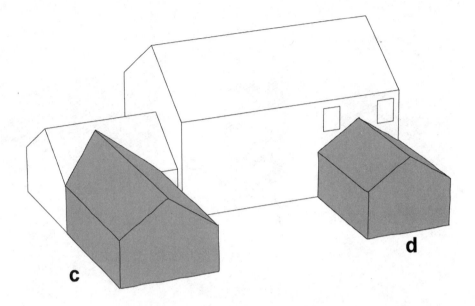

Two-Story

The prior page pictured front additions. This shows potential rear additions. These would tend to be applicable to almost all two-story homes, including most older, historical styled homes. The one-story addition pictured in "c" is a very common addition behind an existing garage that adds either an extra bedroom, or an apartment. Many plans for these are provided in chapter 8. If your existing garage is a side-entry garage, this could also be an addition to the garage.

The one-story addition pictured in "d" is a common room size addition for a new study, den or family room. Smaller versions could also be bump-outs that enlarge existing kitchens and family rooms. Shed roof forms are also possible, but they run more into the problem pictured here—that of keeping the roof of the addition below existing second floor windows.

A third type of addition, not pictured, but self-evident, is a full two-story addition to the rear, which enables enlargement of second floor bedrooms as well. Plans for all the above are profusely provided in chapters 8 and 9.

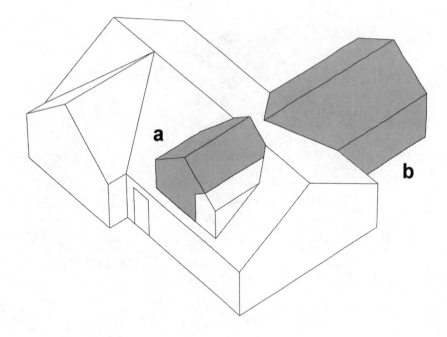

I¹/₂ Story

The next three pages show possible additions to typical I¹/₂-story development homes. As contrasted to ranches, these homes usually have some finished room or rooms in a second floor attic. Some of the forms we use for wide-line ranches are also applicable here, but there are others that are particular to this style of home.

For example, the addition pictured in "b" is a rear one-story reverse gable addition, very much like that shown for the ranch. It can be a new bedroom or family room and in a smaller revision it can be a room expander for a kitchen, dining room, family room, bedroom or bath. As in a ranch, a shed roof is also possible.

Pictured in "a", however, is a new reverse gable front addition on the second floor. Very often the second floor bedrooms in these homes have small dormers and low ceilings. An addition such as the one pictured can improve the size and height in such a room, while also enhancing the appearance of the home.

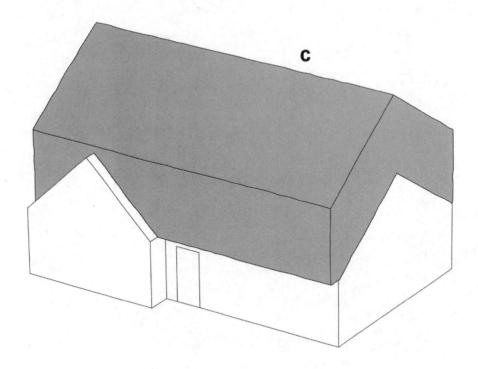

1¹⁄₂ Story

Many of these existing homes are so small that there is a frequent call to "raise the roof" and add a full second floor, effectively doubling the size of the home. These become whole house renovations, and a number are shown in chapter II. The possibilities are such that it could become a two-story home, with all the bedrooms upstairs, or the master could stay down. In either event, the internal changes are usually very extensive.

The exterior form presents some very real challenges. If the second floor wall is built flush with the first, some serious window relocations become necessary to allow us to align windows on both floors. As such, a better solution is to overhang the second floor a foot or so, eliminating that problem. In such a façade, we create balance within each floor, but the relationships between floors are less dictating. Another approach to this problem is to add a one-story porch—if the setbacks allow us to.

This form, incidentally, and all of its problems and concerns, is equally available as a solution to also enlarging a wide-line ranch.

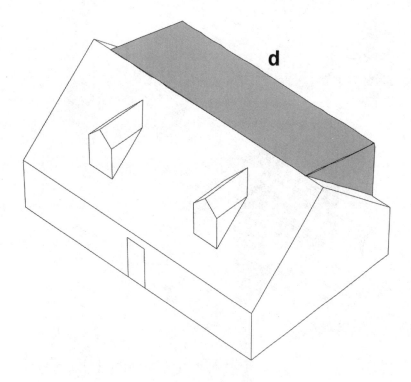

1½ Story

This is probably the most common addition to the 1½-story home. Whether it's called a Cape, Cape Cod, Williamsburg, or Farm Ranch, this style of home has filled thousands of subdivisions coast-to-coast. Most do-it-yourselfers are afraid to tinker with the front, so "raising the rear roof" is an often utilized solution to gaining more space. It is easily accomplished and very economical to boot. Unfortunately it doesn't add a thing to the exterior appeal of the home; in fact very often it hurts. Because the ridge line of the existing home is often low, the pitch of this rear shed roof is frequently very flat—and very unappealing—something you should consider if you undertake this.

This addition is not necessarily "wrong"; if it was, I would have located it in chapter 7. However, we need to see it for what it is; an affordable solution to adding more space— usually two bedrooms—in an otherwise very small home. For several whole house renovations of 1½-story homes, see CAP01-06 in chapter 11.

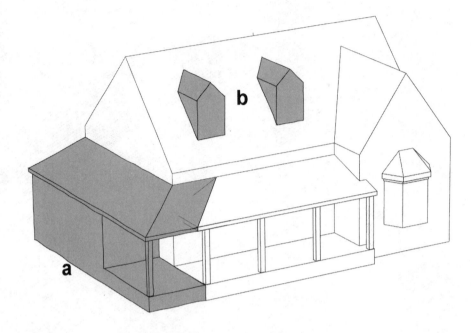

Folk Victorian 1½ Story

All of the prior sketches dealt with post-war suburban home styles. The remainder of this chapter sketches solutions to older, historical, home styles. Typically, there is less tinkering in the front and more within the roofline, to the side, or to the rear. That's exactly the solutions pictured here when confronting a Folk Victorian 1½ story.

Pictured in "a" is a side one-story addition. It has to tie into the existing porch line, so the solution is to "wrap" the front porch around to the addition. Whatever the trim details, they have to match perfectly, and the front porch roof may have to be redone as well.

Shown in "b" are two front dormers; for whatever reason, most of these homes underutilized their second floor areas. There is often large unused volume in the attic, which is readily convertible to living space with the addition of windows, such as the dormers shown.

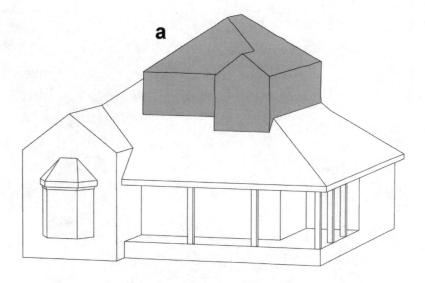

Folk Victorian 1½ Story

This further example of a pyramidal roofed Folk Victorian 1½-story home shows that often the most logical way to expand is up. Houses such as this can be found coast-to-coast. Depending on when they were built, and their original budget, they might proliferate with significantly beautiful wood work and trim on their façades, something we can't duplicate today. For that reason, we wouldn't want to tinker with the front. If, however, this were an older (pre-1870 home), that was built more for shelter than beauty, we might consider more extensive revisions—that is a call you have to make. The program, the budget, and the condition of the existing home will determine how extensive a modification is called for.

Presuming the decision was not to tinker much, the addition shown is a logical one. It takes advantage of the unused volume in the high attic of the home by "popping up" walls through the roofline where we can place windows to create new rooms. Try to mimic existing window and trim details as much as possible.

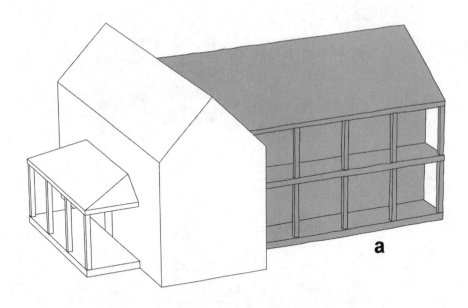

a

Folk Two-Story

   This is one of the common shelter home styles built in the mid-1800's. It is usually a one room deep house that was often added to. Part of the program will likely be to determine what is authentic, which additions are salvageable, and which should be removed either because of shoddy workmanship or stylistic irreverence. Although the existing front may be non-specific as to any classical or Victorian style, it still might be so nice that we really do not want to mess with it. As such, since these homes are often so small that a proposed new wing could overwhelm the existing house, the most logical addition is one that is placed at ninety degrees to it at the rear. This way we can make the additions as grand as we want, while not deploring the original character of the home.

   This philosophy can hold for other small historically preserved homes. Do not let the addition overwhelm the existing façade.

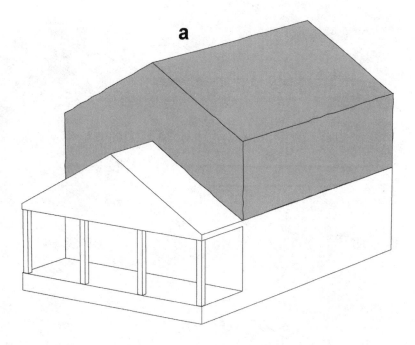

Bungalow

The next four pages deal with the bungalow—another uniquely American home. The bungalow, which began in California about 100 years ago, rapidly spread across the country; it was the "tract" home a century ago. Many, like post-war tract homes, were plain vanilla boxes without any particular stylistic treatment; others, like the last two in this group, were developed in a distinct style known as Craftsman. The common denominator to most bungalows is that they are small; if they are on a nice lot, in a nice area, they may be worth adding to (rather than tearing them down).

Because lot sizes usually preclude adding out, the only way to expand a bungalow is usually to go up. The sketch shown in "a" is the simplest solution to doubling the size of a bungalow; it adds a full second floor with a reverse gable to match the existing front porch. It is a utilitarian solution.

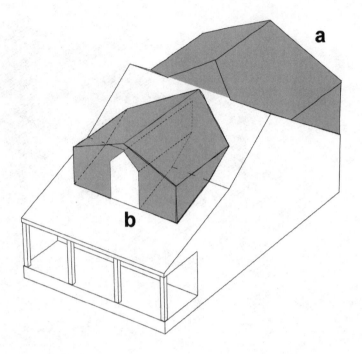

Bungalow

The prior sketch showed a simple reverse gable bungalow, which makes adding up easy. Most bungalows, however, turned their gable side-to-side so as to "look bigger" to the street. This type of bungalow also frequently has a small attic which may have one or two very small rooms. Many bungalows also have front porches which are the only stylistic element potentially worth saving. Therefore, if we add up, we usually begin behind the porch at the line of the house itself.

The two elements shown above include a full width raising of the roof at the rear to create a full two-story rear. This will usually raise the ridge higher than the existing. The front addition shown in "b" significantly increases the size of the front dormer without towering over the existing ridge. A number of whole house remakes of bungalows appear in chapter 11 as CTG01-03 and TWS02. A number of the bump outs in chapter 9 also deal with bungalow forms.

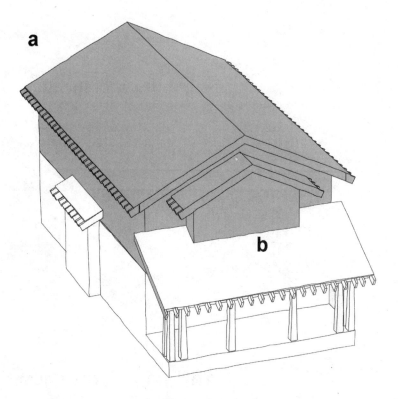

Craftsman Bungalow

The craftsman style also originated in California and moved east across the country around 1900. It was hugely popular for 30 years and has become a favorite of many buyers today. Although there are two-story Craftsman-style homes, and other Craftsman homes of much larger proportions, I have chosen to sketch two Craftsman bungalows to illustrate how style affects the decisions we make on additions.

Although this sketch shows a similar full two-story reverse gable addition, it is heavily influenced by style. The very flat roof pitch is characteristic of Craftsman as contrasted to the reverse gable two pages prior. The small reverse gable bump out shown in "b" adds some detail and interest, often associated with Craftsman style.

Whatever we did, we would want to preserve and protect the front porch which, although it might need lots of care, is likely so intricate and charming.

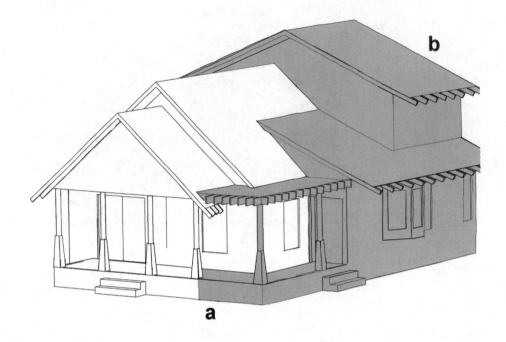

Craftsman Bungalow

This addition to a Craftsman bungalow is significantly more complex than the one sketched in the prior page, but it is also a good deal more interesting. Although the existing home is likely on a small lot, there is a good likelihood that we can add a few feet in width on one side. Those few feet can make a huge difference to the interior layout—which usually needs a lot of help—as well as the exterior appearance. By adding a little width we can improve circulation within the first floor, and also reduce the need to add a full second floor.

This latter benefit enables us to produce additions that add to the richness and character of a Craftsman home. The addition represented by "b" is essentially a raising of the entire rear to create a full two-story addition, but it breaks down into one-story elements, which embellish its appeal.

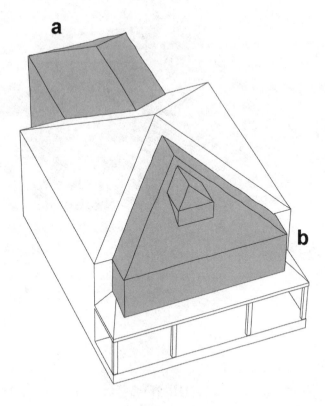

Four-Square Two-Story

One of the most popular housing forms that came into mainstream housing in the early 1900's is the four-square, a kind of urban folk vernacular to the prairie style. Virtually any town in the midwest has hundreds of these. Like the bungalow, the four-square usually has little lot area to expand into. Where there may be some room is fortunately in the rear, where most of these homes desperately need additional square footage to improve their kitchen and related plumbing. This addition could be either one or two stories. There are a number of plans in chapter 9 that do just that.

Another place to expand is indicated in "b"; this shows a small bump-out at the second floor over the front porch; very often the front porch has already been enclosed, and as long as the structure is adequate, a second floor addition is possible— but do not extend to the front of the porch. Also shown in this sketch is a third floor dormer, a distinct possibility in this house type due to its large hip roof; however check your local code as to its legality.

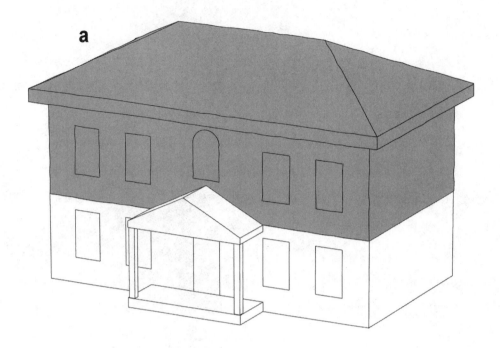

Italianette I to 2 Story

The subject of this sketch is one of those historical styles rarely seen in urban America, but numerous examples still exist in rural places. What I am referring to is not the highly intricate large masonry Italianette-styled homes we find in older cities, but the simple one-story frame homes that were cousins to the Folk Victorians that had distinct Italianette detailing. Most are very formal and balanced homes. They may or may not have front porches, and are usually small homes.

The classic addition to such a home is to go up and repeat the Italianette hip roof above. The detailing can be kept quite simple, as the original façade is also likely simple. This is one instance where we can add flush to the front wall and create a very appealing two-story home. The reason is that the existing façade is symmetrical and balanced, unlike the majority of one-story homes. Do not disturb the existing front porch.

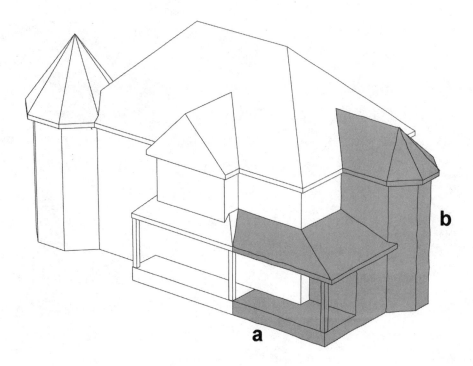

Queen Anne Victorian

Because of the infinite variety of Queen Anne Victorians around, I hesitated whether to include an example. Many of these charming homes still exist and more often than not they require a great deal of work. Usually the remodeling is on the interior with exterior remodeling confined to replacement of windows, trim and siding. But what if you have to add to one? It is not easy. Adding to such a distinct style requires excruciatingly careful attention to design, especially if you are going to tackle the front or side. The resulting finished home can not show a seam where old meets new.

So if you want to add to a porch, as shown in "a" or add a bump-out as shown in "b", the forms must be studied to perfectly match the subject existing house. Since there is no one Queen Anne form, each home will require an independent appraisal as to whether any addition is practical. I have shown one such whole house renovation in Chapter II.

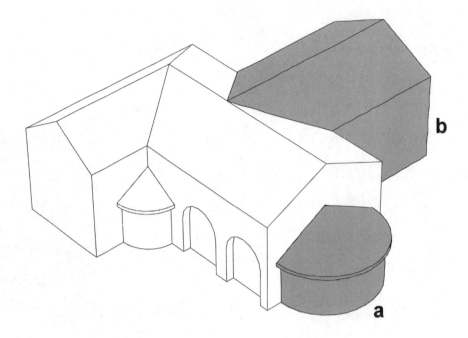

Spanish Eclectic

Spanish Eclectic styled homes enjoyed much of the same variety as Queen Anne Victorians and, as such, also defy creating any norm. However, as a very popular house style of the early 20th century, there are still thousands around; therefore, there is a need to discuss them. As with most of these distinct historical styles, if the front was well done, it is not likely you can do much there—nor do you really want to.

A two-story reverse gable is an appropriate rear addition; it can provide the missing family room and a brand new master suite above. A side addition, such as that pictured in "a", is also possible, but the form, windows, siding and detailing must match with the front. This can be particularly difficult if the façade is done in brick, with the beautiful brick detailing common to these older homes.

If the subject were a one-story home, the same type of one-story additions could be considered.

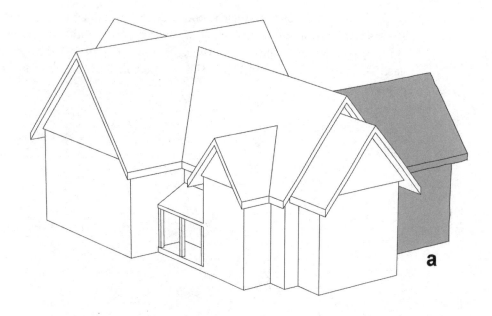

Tudor or Elizabethan Two-Story

There were several periods when Tudor styling was popular; one goes back to the 1800's, and some examples still exist. But the Tudor style has come (and gone) at least twice since; many were exceptionally well-done homes that enjoyed many luxuries and amenities. They are rarely replicated today, but we are occasionally called upon to remodel one.

Most of the time there is ample space internally to modernize one of these with interior renovations only. However, if you must add on to an old Tudor or Elizabethan home, you most likely will not touch the front—or even the side. The rear might lend itself to a one or two-story addition for a new family room or expanded kitchen, and bedroom over it. The roof must be a reverse gable that matches the existing rooflines in both pitch and finish detailing.

This concludes our historical tour. There are dozens of other historical homes I haven't sketched for either of two reasons; 1) they defy creating logical "prototypes" for additions, or 2) there are not enough left that we ever really see. The next chapter continues the discussion of additions, but as abstract shapes and forms.

Blockforms—Generalized Patterns for Adding On

The prior chapter dealt with suggested additions to common recognizable home types. But what if the home in question does not fit one of these? Maybe it is a hybrid, a do-it-yourselfer's creation, or for whatever reason we really can not find a match. That is the subject of this chapter. It deals with additions as simple shapes—or blockforms. The current chapter provides 60 examples of building shapes that will lead to successful additions. You may say, "Why waste time, they are only simple blocks; I don't see windows and doors or other details"? It is because, by perusing through these, you may be able to recognize and then match the shape of the existing home to a potential addition. The addition is always pictured shaded.

The process of designing an addition does involve this somewhat abstract concept of creating a "shape" or "form" that will complement the home. If done properly, this new shape could do more than just match the home; it could also make it exciting to look at, and thereby enhance its market appeal too.

Therefore, I would recommend that if you are a do-it-yourselfer planning an addition, and are uncertain about shapes, the process for you to follow would involve first finding those blockforms that fit, and then reviewing the chapter on additions to find floor plans that would match these shapes. Professionals should find these helpful in discussions with clients.

The text under each form may also list other similar new roof shapes other than the one pictured. One of the important decision factors that this section deals with is the shape of the roof on the addition. The decision as to which roof shape to use is a complex factor that involves the relationships created between the existing and the new. To make matters more complicated, there are frequently several combinations that are suited to any one situation. As a simple example, usually a rectangular addition, to the front or rear of a simple rectangular home, can be roofed as a shed, a reverse gable, a hip, or even a flat roof; since all could be correct, the decision then is a personal preference as to the style of the exterior or the quality of the interior space (sloped ceilings, high ceiling, skylights, etc.). In many circumstances, however, there may be only one roofline that is preferable. That usually occurs when the existing home is a distinct roof shape in itself; but it is also possible that the shape of certain additions may also dictate a particular roof design.

Adding one-story forms to one-story homes

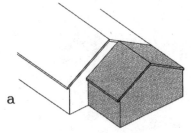

a

The setback form is attractive and may save you from matching siding. On a hip roof, use a hip roof addition.

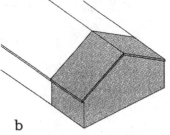

b

The flush match is OK, as long as it is not a garage. This will require the perfect match of roofing and siding.

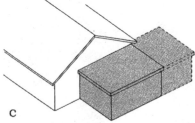

c

A flat roof is acceptable on the side, even though it won't help to broaden the front façade.

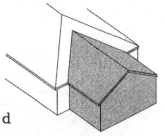

d

A gable intersecting a hip is a very stylish treatment. Make sure the gable is smaller than the hip.

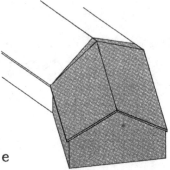

e

Attaching at an angle can be attractive, but it gets a little tricky at the intersection. Be sure to match pitches.

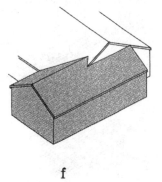

f

Attaching at a corner with a reverse gable that becomes a shed is a very appealing form.

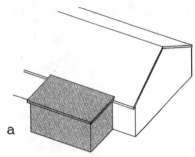

a

A flat-roof addition at the eave of a gable roof addition is fine for a porch or vestibule.

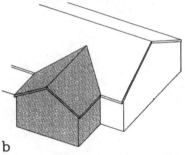

b

A reverse gable intersecting another gable is probably the best form. A hip would be acceptable too.

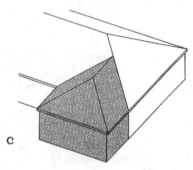

c

Attaching flush to the corner requires care. The hip roof matches the existing hip perfectly as long as it is lower.

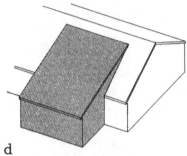

d

The one-story shed is acceptable as long as the width of its front wall is twice its height.

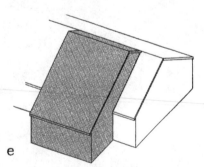

e

This is a better way to use a shed—by matching the existing pitch of the roof. It requires matching the roof shingles at the top.

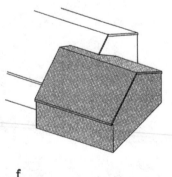

f

This is another acceptable corner attachment. Match the pitch of the existing roof. A cricket might be required.

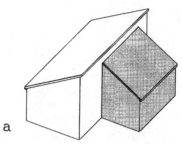

a

Use an opposing pitch to attach a narrow shed roof addition to the tall side of an existing shed form.

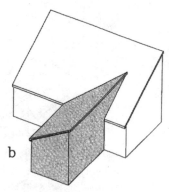

b

An intersecting shed works, but be careful. Keep the addition smaller than the existing form.

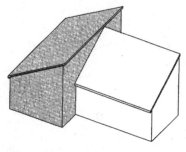

c

The attractive opposing shed is turned 90 degrees to the existing. Keep the heights different, even if it's inches.

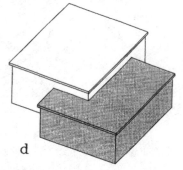

d

A flat-roof addition that is lower than the existing looks just fine, and is better if it wraps as shown.

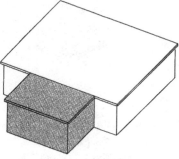

e

When adding to a large flat roof, you can also keep the addition flush with the existing.

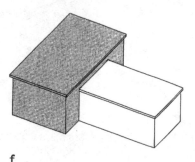

f

A flat-roof addition can also be higher than the existing. The two contrasting forms look good.

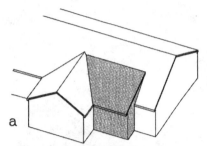

a

Attaching between two intersecting gables is tricky. The shed is an excellent solution as long as it's not too big.

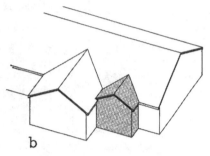

b

A matching reverse gable can be a stylish solution to the same addition. A cricket might be required.

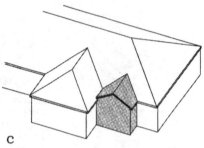

c

Between two hip roofs, you could install another hip roof for certain, but the reverse gable might be more exciting.

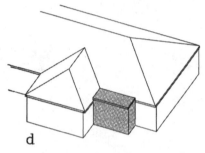

d

The flat roof connection between the two hips—or two gables—is OK for a porch or vestibule.

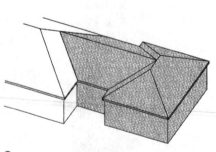

e

Multiple roof forms are very common in better looking additions. Roofs blend or intersect at similar pitches.

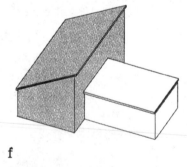

f

A shed and a flat roof can be successfully combined. Keep the forms contrasting or opposing each other.

Adding one-story forms to two-story homes

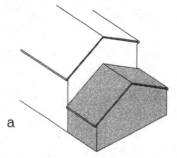

a

Flush ends mean matching siding. If the gable is a side wall, the scale must be proportional to the existing front.

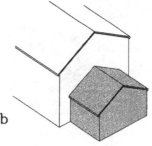

b

Setback form is fine, especially if gable is a front or rear wall. As a side wall, the size is critical.

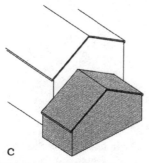

c

This looks excellent if the attachment is a side wall. The width of front wall should be a minimum of $1/3$ of the existing front.

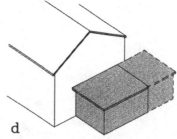

d

This is acceptable for a porch or carport, whether the gable end is a front or side wall.

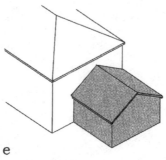

e

A hip on the new addition would be best if it is large. If it is small, use a gable as shown.

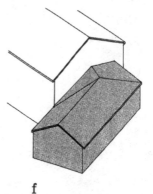

f

The angle addition could be an excellent solution. The pitches do not have to match. Be careful along the common wall.

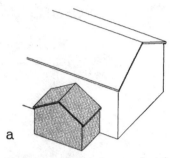

a

The reverse gable is a perfect form for almost any size addition. The pitch determined by the aesthetics of the new element.

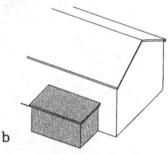

b

The flat roof is just fine for many additions and is perfect for a vestibule, porch or carport.

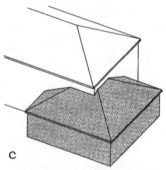

c

Wrapping the corner with a hip produces attractive forms. The pitch of new roof must match and be lower than the eave.

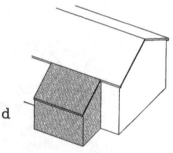

d

A continuation of the two-story gable roof creates a unified addition. New end wall may be higher than standard.

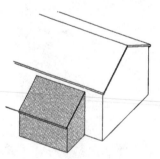

e

This is almost the same, but clearly an addition. The separtate shed roof does not have to match the existing roof pitch, but could.

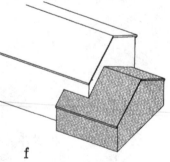

f

Wrapping the corner with a gable is an excellent marriage of new to old. Be sure to maintain the same roof pitches.

Adding two-story forms to one-story homes

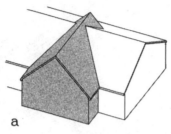

a

The steep one and one-half story reverse gable provides a small second floor room. It is an excellent attachment.

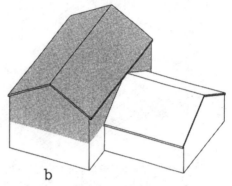

b

A second floor over one wing of an L-shaped one story is a good looking solution to adding lots of space.

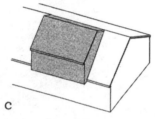

c

Extending the ridge to create second floor space at one side is an excellent tool. Keep overhangs to a minimum.

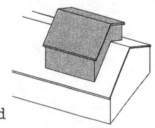

d

Popping up through the roof is fine —but dangerous. Proportions must be carefully analyzed to the existing bulk.

e

Adding a full second floor is also fine —and dangerous. First floor windows must relate to new second floor openings.

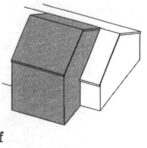

f

Extending the ridge to create a full two-story addition produces a thoroughly integrated solution. Be sure to match pitches.

Adding two-story forms to two-story homes

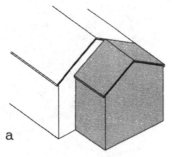

a

The offset is attractive, especially if the gable is a front or rear wall. If a side wall, watch the scale.

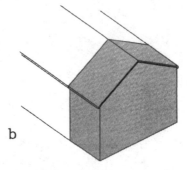

b

The flush form achieves a seamless end result and is best for a small addition, but requires perfect matching.

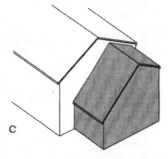

c

The asymmetrical form is best if the gable is an end wall, the addition appears as one-story from front.

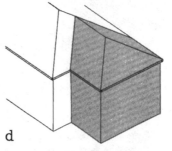

d

Match a two-story hip with a two-story hip addition. The same rules apply for flush or setback walls, as above.

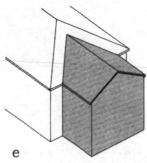

e

Attaching a two-story gable to a hip can produce a good look, if the gable end is made a feature wall.

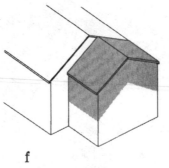

f

Adding a second floor over a one-story element is fine, but it requires coordination of first and second floor openings.

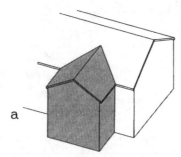

a

The ever-successful reverse gable produces the best results on vertical additions. The depth of the addition is unlimited.

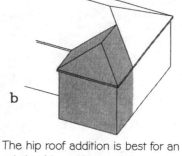

b

The hip roof addition is best for an existing hip, and especially so at a corner.

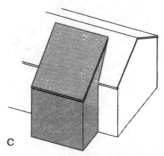

c

The shed roof form is best for wide but shallow additions, where a reverse gable would be too high.

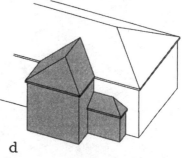

d

A complex roof of one and two-story additions requires following rules for both. Keep roof types similar.

e

Building up over a driveway requires following the rules for two-story forms, but the proportions may be different.

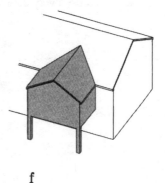

f

A second floor reverse gable on posts requires understanding that the mass of the addition is less than a full two-story home.

Forms for 1½ story homes

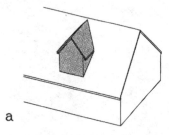

a

The perennial favorite, the reverse gable dormer, is one of the most acceptable and widely used forms.

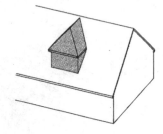

b

A hip roof dormer keeps a lower profile on the roof, and might permit a somewhat wider addition.

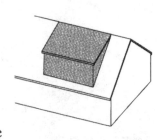

c

The shed roof dormer is the choice for larger additions, where a reverse gable would require a very flat pitch.

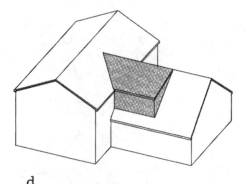

d

Adding at a complex intersection requires roofs to marry to both forms, as this shed on the lower roof demonstrates.

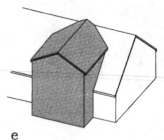

e

A full two-story reverse gable can be added for a tall vertical addition. Use a shed for a wider addition.

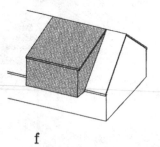

f

The overhanging shed roof addition is no longer a dormer, since it breaks the roofline. It adds more space.

What Not to Do

In all likelihood, I could probably prepare a complete volume, including hundreds of plans, of what one should not do. Twenty-five years of private practice, and thousands of miles of travel, have offered me the perspective to do that, but I do not believe it is a productive avenue to follow. Rather than perusing the endless possibilities for failure, this book is devoted to providing positive ideas and sound examples for you to follow.

One of the most obvious traps I tell homeowners to avoid is not being true to themselves — and their needs. Somehow when it comes to our homes, every friend or relative has their own helpful idea. I tell my clients to listen to them all, but try to analyze these thoughts against their own needs — and our heretofore prepared program. Their contemplated remodeling is one that should bring years of enjoyment, but only they can evaluate what will achieve that goal. As professionals we can only help steer them in the right direction, but I won't live in their home — they will.

This is not to suggest being smug; homeowners are advised to acknowledge where they are uncertain and where they need assistance. Foremost, unless they possess the talent to be their own designer, and they can visualize three dimensionally, I strongly recommend that they hire the skills of a professional. It is possible that they or someone in their family possess the talent to build an addition, or undertake the remodeling, but learning to design is not the same as learning to use a circular saw.

Although I encourage the pursuit of highly individualized home improvements, I caution against producing a remodeled home that is so out of place, that it loses marketability. Inputting one's personality into a project is usually a positive; the only exception is when the remodeling becomes so unique that it is bizarre. An earth covered underground addition to a tract split level might preserve the lawn, and be an energy efficient improvement, but not only will it excite few others — it would likely detract from the home, and reduce its marketability. As I indicated earlier, not every improvement has to be measured in terms of its return on investment (a return for personal gratification is perfectly acceptable); however, an improvement should not decrease the value of the home.

The potential for planning errors exist whether the remodeling is an interior renovation or an exterior addition. An interior renovation, however, is not likely to be fatal — an exterior addition can be. For that reason I have prepared a few pages of sketches to show some examples of what not to do; these deal primarily with the issue of attachment. Although certainly not all-inclusive, they are suggestive of potential error. The subsequent chapter of drawings presents a whole series of sketches that show what is correct.

Presented on the next two pages are common examples of additions that attach very poorly to their homes, or are awkward shapes that relate poorly to the existing home. The addition is indicated shaded. All should be avoided.

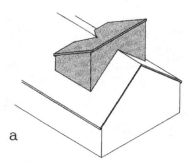

a

The roof structure of the new addition is not harmonious with the simple gable roof below.

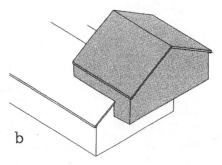

b

The second floor addition looks like it was just stuck on—and it may fall off. Don't cantilever a gable wall.

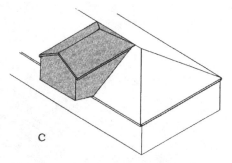

c

The new dormer element looks like it wants to fly away. Keep small second floor elements inside the roofline.

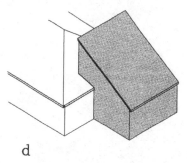

d

The shed roof side addition is fighting the hip roof structure it is attached to. Use another hip.

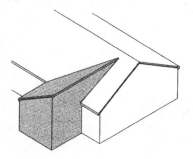

e

A side-to-side shed roof on the gable doesn't work without lots of study. Stay away from it. Use a reverse gable.

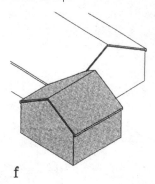

f

Attaching at a corner is dangerous. It would be better if the addition also extended along the side wall.

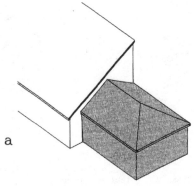

a

The hip roof addition is discordant with
the existing shed. Use another shed
roof or a flat roof.

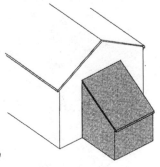

b

A shed roof addition on a side gable
wall is an unappealing form, and it
looks like an addition.

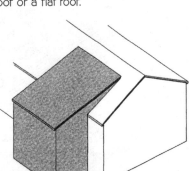

c

The two-story shed roof form is simple
to build—but unattractive. A reverse
gable is much nicer.

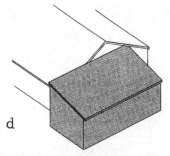

d

The side addition makes no effort to
harmonize with the existing form. It
needs a reverse gable at the front.

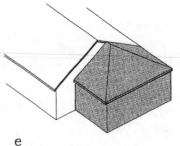

e

The shape is fine, but the new roofline
doesn't belong. It should be a
matching gable.

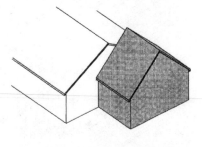

f

The pitch of the new addition does
not match the existing roofline, and
should be flush or lower than it.

Remodel Plans

Remodel Plans—Room Size Additions

Whereas the prior two chapters dealt with additions in general forms only, this chapter presents an extensive collection of architectural designs for specific room additions of every nature. There are one room bath or kitchen additions, and five room additions involving a kitchen, family room, master bedroom, dining room and laundry room. There are room additions that go up— and out. The plans are generally grouped by room type, but that is not universally possible; in a complex plan, like the five room addition mentioned, the plan may be placed near other kitchens, so the bedroom or laundry room would not be with other similar rooms. Therefore, depending on your precise needs you may have to peruse all the designs.

The plan viewing rules discussed in chapter 4 prevail as to front orientation and dimensions. There are, however, other viewing instructions. All darker colored (black) walls are new walls; all lighter colored (gray) walls are existing walls; dotted gray lines represent walls to be removed, or fixtures being removed. When clarity is required, I have prepared a separate existing plan, representing the way it is assumed that the home currently exists. A sample page follows this introduction explaining all the viewing conventions.

With each plan, there is also a perspective view. For the majority of these additions, the view is an exterior of the addition, showing its likely attachment to the home. The area of the addition is shaded so you should be able to tell the direction from which the view is taken; views could be from the front, rear or side, depending on which seemed more appropriate. Materials and window details are intentionally removed to create views that are simple sketches. Materials should obviously complement (or on occasion, contrast) with the existing home. Further discussion on materials is presented in chapter 14.

On occasion, rather than an exterior view, I have chosen to show an interior view where it provided more information on the addition. Shading has not been used on these interiors, as it would make the drawings very difficult to read, but these are only utilized for very simply additions, and you should be able to discern the area of addition from the floor plan itself.

A few words about the specificity of the existing home pictured. The majority of additions are shown attached to a home of some fairly defined shape or character. This is not to say that the same addition could not be attached to a very different house. This is where the blockforms in chapter 6 should help provide you the confidence that the two (addition plus existing home) will match well. Also keep in mind that one-story additions can usually attach to most one, one and one-half, and two-story homes. Furthermore, where a two-story addition has been pictured, it is possible to take either floor and build it as a one-story addition. You could readily accommodate that change from the accompanying CAD files.

There are also a number of generic types of additions shown where, the existing home is only vaguely outlined. These additions are planned to permit the greatest flexibility of attachment to any home—only the rooflines have to be considered, and these are usually pictured.

Finally, many designs also show some renovation to interior space as well. As I have indicated, this is a very common practice; the addition leads to some reason to alter the interior space as an integral part of the remodeling project. You may decide to forgo this part of the renovation, or to modify it to suit the specific home. I fully expect that any remodeling project undertaken from these designs will produce many changes necessary to suit specific needs, lifestyle or the existing home, so don't feel inhibited by change.

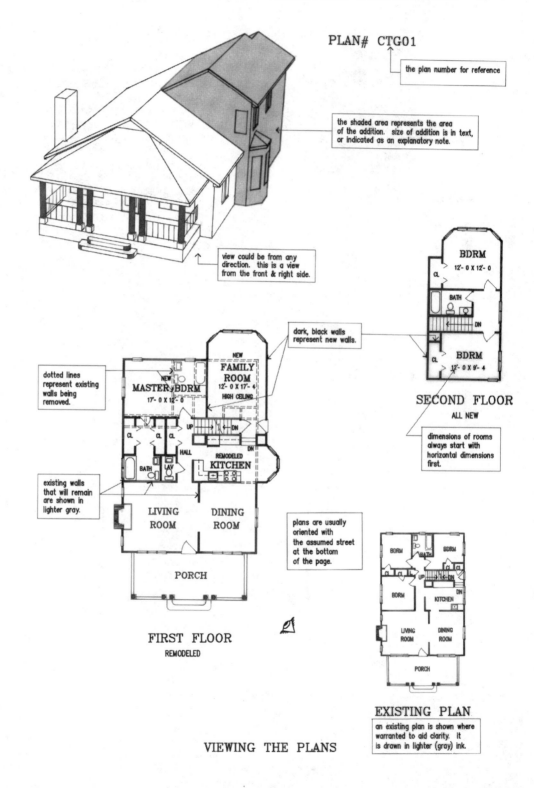

PLAN# CTG01

the plan number for reference

the shaded area represents the area of the addition. size of addition is in text, or indicated as an explanatory note.

view could be from any direction. this is a view from the front & right side.

BDRM
12'- 0 X 12'- 0

CL

BATH

DN

CL

BDRM
12'- 0 X 9'- 4

dark, black walls represent new walls.

dotted lines represent existing walls being removed.

NEW
FAMILY ROOM
12'- 0 X 17'- 4
HIGH CEILING

NEW
MASTER BDRM
17'- 0 X 12'- 0

CL CL CL

UP

DN

HALL

DN

BATH   LAV

REMODELED
KITCHEN

existing walls that will remain are shown in lighter gray.

LIVING ROOM

DINING ROOM

PORCH

SECOND FLOOR

ALL NEW

dimensions of rooms always start with horizontal dimensions first.

plans are usually oriented with the assumed street at the bottom of the page.

BDRM

BATH

BDRM

CL   CL

UP

DN

BDRM

KITCHEN

LIVING ROOM

DINING ROOM

PORCH

FIRST FLOOR

REMODELED

EXISTING PLAN

an existing plan is shown where warranted to aid clarity. it is drawn in lighter (gray) ink.

VIEWING THE PLANS

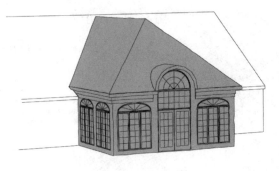

P0024

THIS BEAUTIFUL LOOKING 22'x15' SUN PORCH WOULD MAKE A STUNNING ADDITION TO THE REAR OF ANY HOUSE. ITS THREE SIDES BOAST AN ABUNDANCE OF WINDOWS, INCLUDING A HANDSOME USE OF ELLIPTICAL AND HALF-ROUND SHAPES. WHETHER IT IS USED AS A PORCH, FAMILY ROOM, DINING ROOM— OR WHATEVER—IT WILL BE A WONDERFUL SPACE TO ENTERTAIN IN. A ROOM OF THIS SHAPE USES UP LESS OF THE REAR YARD, BUT IT DOES INVOLVE MORE OF THE REAR WALL AND COULD BE MORE OF A CONNECTION PROBLEM THAN PLAN P0025 WHICH FOLLOWS. WHEREAS IT ALSO MIGHT LOOK BETTER THAN A NARROW, LONG ADDITION LIKE P0025, ITS ROOF COULD CAUSE MORE OF A PROBLEM IN CONNECTING TO THE EXISTING ROOF.

EXISTING

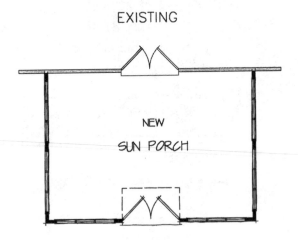

NEW

SUN PORCH

REMODELED FLOOR PLAN

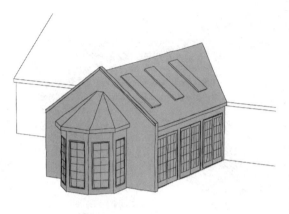

P0025

THIS STRIKING ROOM IS A 16'×27' NEW SUNROOM
THAT CAN BE ADDED TO THE REAR OF MOST ANY
HOUSE. IT IS NOT A PREFAB GREENHOUSE TYPE
STRUCTURE, BUT A CONVENTIONALLY FRAMED ROOM
ADDITION THAT SPORTS AN ABUNDANCE OF
WINDOWS, DOORS AND SKYLIGHTS. THE ROOM
COULD FUNCTION AS A SUN PORCH, FAMILY ROOM,
DINING ROOM—OR WHATEVER YOU WANT IT TO BE.
BOTH SIDE WALLS ARE WALL-TO-WALL FRENCH
SLIDING DOORS, AND THE REAR WALL INCLUDES A
BEAUTIFUL, DEEP BAY WINDOW. THE END GABLE
WALL COULD BE A BRICK WALL WHICH WOULD IMPART
A EUROPEAN FLAIR. IF IT IS BUILT AS A SOLID
MASONRY WALL, REMEMBER TO USE STEP FLASHING
ON THE SHINGLED ROOF.

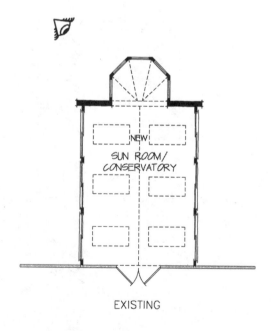

NEW

SUN ROOM/
CONSERVATORY

EXISTING

REMODELED FLOOR PLAN

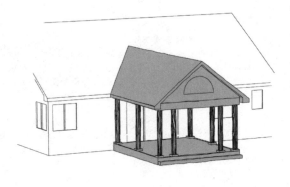

P0018

THE SIMPLE, REVERSE GABLED PORCH ADDITION IS
SECOND ONLY TO THE SHED ROOF PORCH IN
POPULARITY, BUT IT COULD BE FIRST IN LOOKS. WITH
ATTENTION TO DETAIL, AND THE USE OF ROUND
COLUMNS, A SIMPLE ROOFED PORCH COULD BECOME
A CLASSICAL STATELY ADDITION TO YOUR HOME.
THE FORM, AS PICTURED, IS SUITED TO END WALLS
OR FRONT WALLS AND TO TWO-STORY HOMES, AND
IT COULD BE BUILT WITH EITHER A CONCRETE SLAB
FOR A FLOOR OR WITH A RAISED WOOD FLOOR. A
SCREEN ENCLOSURE COULD BE ADAPTED TO THIS
DESIGN, BUT YOU MAY WANT TO CONSIDER OTHER
POSTS OR RESPACING THE ROUND COLUMNS TO
ACCOMMODATE STANDARD SCREEN SECTIONS.

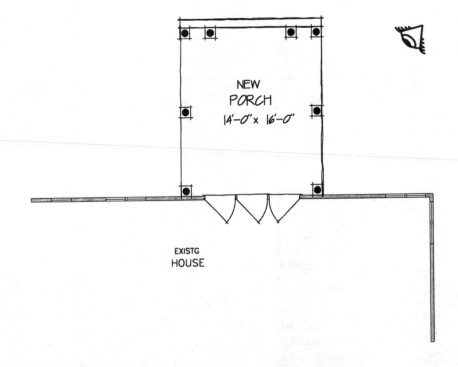

NEW
PORCH
14'-0" x 16'-0"

EXISTG
HOUSE

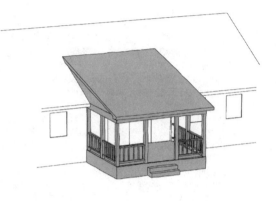

P0017

THE SHED ROOFED PORCH IS PROBABLY THE MOST
COMMON TYPE OF PORCH ADDED TO THE REAR OF
THE TYPICAL HOME; IT IS ALSO THE MOST COMMON
ADDITION OF ALL. BUT WITH A LITTLE FLAIR, IT
COULD HAVE SOME CHARACTER, TOO. A FAIRLY
REGULAR SPACING OF POSTS, EVEN ON THE NON-
BEARING SIDE WALLS, AND A RAILING HELP PROVIDE
THE PORCH PICTURED WITH A WARM, INVITING
CHARACTER. THE PORCH COULD BE BUILT ON A
CONCRETE SLAB, OR WITH A RAISED WOOD FLOOR,
DEPENDING ON YOUR WISHES AND THE STYLE OF
HOUSE. THE SAME DESIGN IS ALSO SUITED TO THE
REAR OF A TWO-STORY HOME, BUT IT WOULD NOT
LOOK WELL ON THE SIDE. A REVERSE GABLE IS MORE
APPROPRIATE TO A SIDE GABLE WALL.

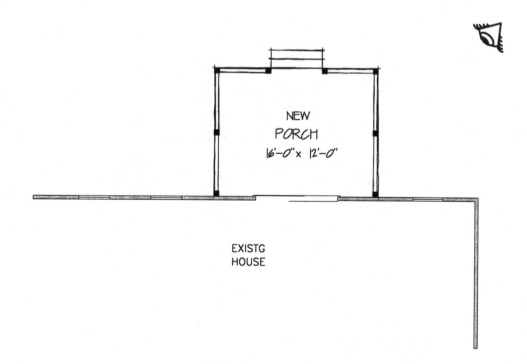

NEW
PORCH
16'-0" x 12'-0"

EXISTG
HOUSE

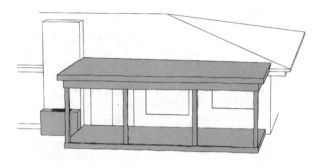

P0004

PORCHES COME IN ALL SIZES AND SHAPES AND, MORE IMPORTANTLY, IN ALL TYPES OF ROOFS. THE FLAT-ROOF PORCH, AS SHOWN HERE, IS CERTAINLY THE MOST ECONOMICAL STRUCTURE TO BUILD; BUT IT IS ALSO THE MOST PRACTICAL FOR MANY HOMES AND MANY LOCATIONS. THE CORNER OF THIS LOW PITCHED, HIP-ROOFED ONE-STORY IS A GREAT SPOT FOR A PORCH; IT IS WELL SUITED FOR A MATCHING HIP-ROOFED SHAPE, BUT THAT'S POTENTIALLY MORE EXPENSIVE. A GABLE ROOF WON'T GO HERE, SO THE FLAT IS IDEAL. THE EXTRA THICKNESS I'VE DESIGNED INTO THE ROOF STRUCTURE TAKES AWAY THE SKIMPY, FLIMSY APPEARANCE COMMON TO MANY SUCH PORCHES.

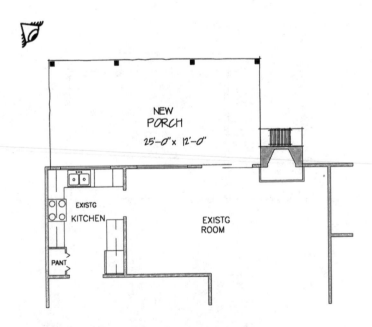

NEW
PORCH
25'-0" x 12'-0"

EXISTG
KITCHEN

EXISTG
ROOM

PANT

REMODELED FIRST FLOOR PLAN

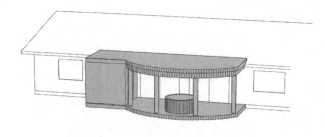

P0005

THERE'S A REAR PORCH IN YOUR PROGRAM—
AND A POOL CABANA AND BATH. WELL WHY
NOT COMBINE THEM. THIS CLASSY LOOKING
ADDITION ARTFULLY COMBINES A DRESSING
ROOM AND SHOWER BATH WITH A SEMI-
CIRCULAR SHAPED FLAT-ROOFED PORCH.
ROUND COLUMNS PROVIDE A NICE DETAIL AS
DOES A DROPPED HEADER FRIEZE FOLLOWING
THE CIRCULAR SHAPE. THE BATH IS LOCATED
ON THE REAR WALL AND MAY WELL BE IN THE
VICINITY OF EXISTING PLUMBING AS INDICATED.
THIS PORCH COULD BE A GREAT PLACE TO
LOCATE A SPA AS SHOWN.

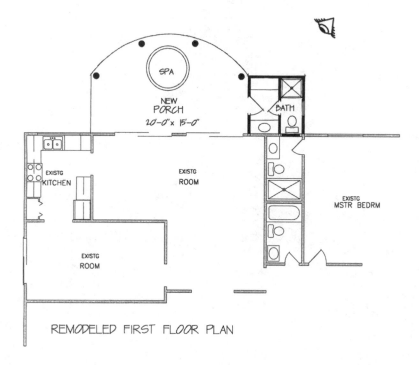

REMODELED FIRST FLOOR PLAN

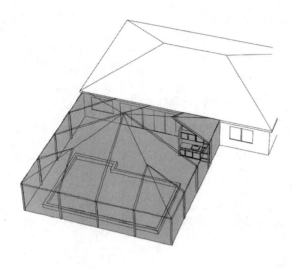

P0006

THIS 37'6" SQUARE ADDITION IS NOT QUITE A ROOM. ALTHOUGH NICKNAMED A "FLORIDA ROOM" BY ITS ORIGINATORS, IT IS ACTUALLY A GIANT SCREENED ENCLOSURE THAT PERMITS EVENING ENJOYMENT OF YOUR BACKYARD SWIMMING POOL, FREE FROM INSECT ATTACK.   THE ONLY ACTUAL ROOFED STRUCTURE IS THAT HOUSING A NEW POOL BATH AND A MINI-KITCHEN, WHICH ARE TUCKED AGAINST THE HOUSE WALL, CLOSE TO EXISTING PLUMBING.   THE SIZE OF THE STRUCTURE IS SITE DEPENDENT, VARYING BY VIRTUE OF THE SIZE OF THE POOL AND POOL DECK. A GLASS ROOF IS AN OPTION TO CONSIDER FOR COLDER CLIMATES.   HOWEVER, BEFORE DOING ANYTHING, YOU ARE CAUTIONED TO CHECK ON LOCAL CODES, ZONING REQUIREMENTS AND TAXING RULES, AS WELL AS TRYING TO LOCATE A LOCAL MANUFACTURER OR DISTRIBUTOR OF SUCH ROOF SYSTEMS.

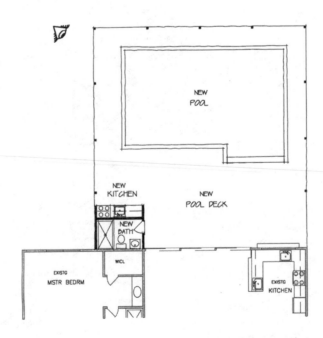

REMODELED FIRST FLOOR PLAN

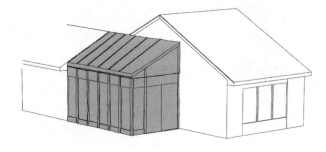

P0002

MOST NEW ROOMS ARE FOR PEOPLE.
SOMETIMES WE ADD FOR CARS. THIS ROOM IS
FOR PLANTS. IT IS A SOLAR GREENHOUSE
STRUCTURE AVAILABLE FROM A NUMBER OF
MANUFACTURERS. THERE ARE OTHER
GREENHOUSES IN THIS BOOK DESIGNED AS
LIVING SPACES; THIS ONE IS TRULY A PLANT
ROOM FOR THE GARDEN ENTHUSIAST. IT IS
SHOWN TUCKED INTO A CORNER. IT WOULD
OBVIOUSLY BE A SUNNY CORNER OF YOUR
HOME, WHERE THE PLANTS WOULD RECEIVE
AMPLE SUNLIGHT. THE ROOM IS SHOWN
ACCESSED FROM THE GARAGE AND VIEWED
FROM THE KITCHEN; THE KITCHEN WINDOWS
SHOULD BE LEFT TO OPEN TO THE NEW
GREENHOUSE. THE GREENHOUSE STRUCTURE
REQUIRES THAT IT NOT BE FLUSH WITH
ADJACENT WALLS OR ROOFS, BUT BE
SOMEWHAT LOWER FOR PROPER FLASHING.

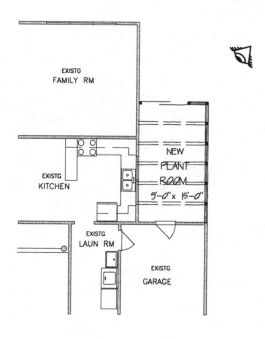

REMODELED FIRST FLOOR PLAN

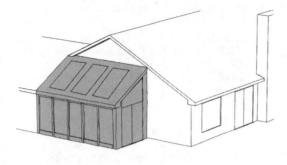

P0003

THERE'S A SUNNY CORNER OFF THE SUBJECT HOUSE—THE GOAL IS TO CAPTURE IT INDOORS IN A GLASSED-IN SUNROOM. THAT'S THE SUBJECT OF THIS PLAN. THE CORNER SHOWN IS A KITCHEN, GARAGE AND FAMILY OR DINING ROOM, BUT IT COULD BE ANY SET OF ROOMS. THE SUN PORCH IS DISTINGUISHED FROM A GREENHOUSE IN THAT IT INCORPORATES WINDOWS AND SKYLIGHTS INTO A CONVENTIONAL WOOD FRAME STRUCTURE; THE WINDOWS COULD BE WALL-TO-WALL AS SHOWN HERE. THE ROOFLINE OF THE SUN PORCH HAS TO BLEND WITH EXISTING ROOFLINES, WHEREAS THE GREENHOUSE IS FREQUENTLY (BUT NOT NECESSARILY) A SEPARATE ROOF STRUCTURE. MATERIAL COSTS TEND TO BE LESS IN A SUN PORCH.

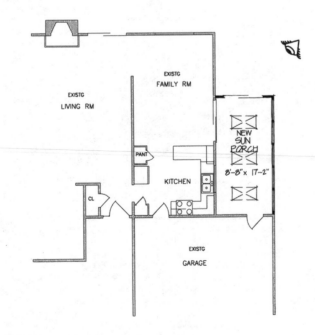

REMODELED FIRST FLOOR PLAN

P0001

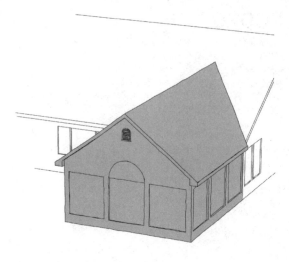

THIS CLASSY LOOKING SQUARE-SHAPED ADDITION
ADDS A SPARKLING, BRIGHT NEW SUN PORCH TO
ANY HOME. IT FEATURES WINDOWS WRAPPING ITS
THREE EXPOSED SIDES, AN EXPANSIVE VAULTED
CEILING AND FOUR LARGE SKYLIGHTS, THEREBY
CREATING AN OPEN FEELING SIMILAR TO THAT OF A
PREFABRICATED METAL AND GLASS STRUCTURE.
YOU MAY FIND THAT A CONVENTIONALLY BUILT
STRUCTURE SUCH AS THIS IS MORE APPROPRIATE TO
YOUR HOME THAN A GREENHOUSE STRUCTURE—AND
IT COULD BE LESS EXPENSIVE. FOR EVEN MORE
GLASS THAN SHOWN, ALL THE WINDOWS COULD
EXTEND TO THE FLOOR AND BECOME SLIDING GLASS
DOORS. TO PREVENT BOWING WALLS, DO NOT
ATTEMPT TO BUILD A ROOM SUCH AS THIS (OR ANY
OTHER FOR THAT MATTER) WITHOUT PROPER
CONSTRUCTION PLANS.

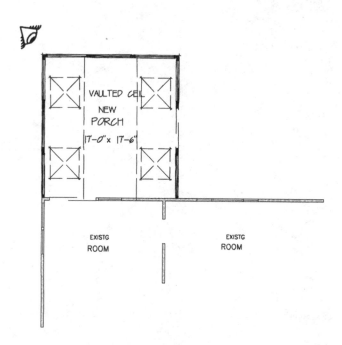

VAULTED CEIL

NEW
PORCH

17'-0" x 17'-6"

EXISTG
ROOM

EXISTG
ROOM

REMODELED FIRST FLOOR PLAN

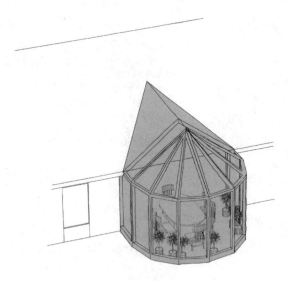

P0020

ADDITIONS DON'T HAVE TO BE ENCLOSED BY STEREOTYPICAL WALLS AND ROOFS. IF ONE HAS A PENCHANT FOR A GLASS ENCLOSED SPACE, WHETHER TO USE FOR DINING UNDER THE STARS OR TO USE AS A SUNNY FAMILY ROOM ADDITION, THIS COULD BE THE PLAN TO CONSIDER. THERE ARE A NUMBER OF OTHER GLASS ROOFED PORCH ADDITIONS FOR YOU TO LOOK AT WHICH COULD ALSO SERVE YOUR NEEDS, BUT THIS ONE IS UNUSUAL FOR ITS SHAPE. ITS EIGHT SIDES ARE GLAZED, AS ARE ITS EIGHT SECTIONS OF ROOF, AND IT WILL LIKELY REQUIRE CUSTOM FABRICATION. NOTE THE NEW REVERSE GABLED SECTION OF CONVENTIONAL ROOF BEYOND, WHICH IS NECESSARY TO ENABLE YOU TO ATTACH SUCH A STRUCTURE TO A ONE-STORY HOME.

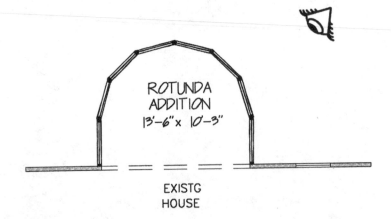

ROTUNDA
ADDITION
13'-6" x 10'-3"

EXISTG
HOUSE

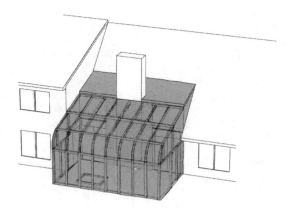

P0022

THIS BEAUTIFUL ENCLOSED SUNSPACE IS A
GENEROUS SIZE ROOM, LARGE ENOUGH FOR A
DELIGHTFUL, BUILT-IN, WHIRLPOOL SPA AND A WOOD
STOVE TO HEAT THE ROOM.   THE REAR WALL IS
DESIGNED AS A MASONRY HEAT STORAGE (OR
TROMBE) WALL, TO CAPTURE AND STORE THE HEAT
FROM THE SUN AND THE WOOD STOVE.   IF YOU DO
INSTALL A WHIRLPOOL, MAKE SURE TO PROVIDE AN
OVERSIZED VENTILATION SYSTEM.   THIS TYPE OF
STRUCTURE IS AVAILABLE FROM MANY
MANUFACTURERS, AND CAN BE PURCHASED AS A KIT
OR FULLY INSTALLED.   NOTE THE PIECE OF NEW
CONVENTIONAL ROOF FRAMING REQUIRED.

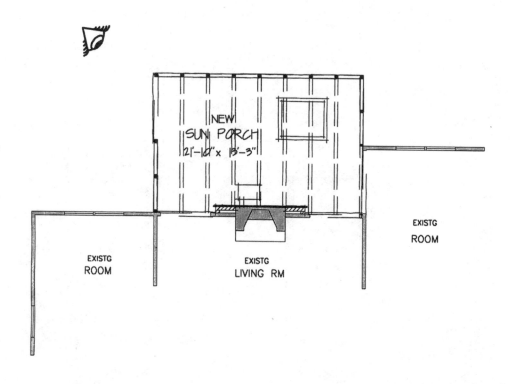

NEW
SUN PORCH
21'-10" x 13'-3"

EXISTG
ROOM

EXISTG
ROOM

EXISTG
LIVING RM

EXISTG
ROOM

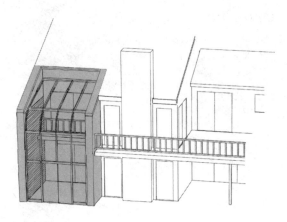

P0023

OF THE MANY SUN PORCHES PRESENTED, THIS IS THE ONLY TWO-STORY DESIGN. THE PLAN TUCKS A NEW PORCH INTO AN EXISTING CORNER ON TWO FLOORS. IT IS ALSO DESIGNED AS A PASSIVE SOLAR COLLECTOR SPACE WITH A MASONRY FLOOR AND A SIDE WALL OF BRICK FOR HEAT STORAGE, COMMONLY REFERRED TO AS A TROMBE WALL. THE TWO-STORY GLAZED FORM IS AN EXTREMELY ATTRACTIVE SPACE, BOTH FROM THE EXTERIOR AND FROM WITHIN. THE PLAN CALLS FOR A NARROW BALCONY AT THE SECOND FLOOR WITHIN THE SUNSPACE, THEREBY PROVIDING A CHARMING RETREAT FROM THE ROOMS IT PROVIDES ACCESS TO.

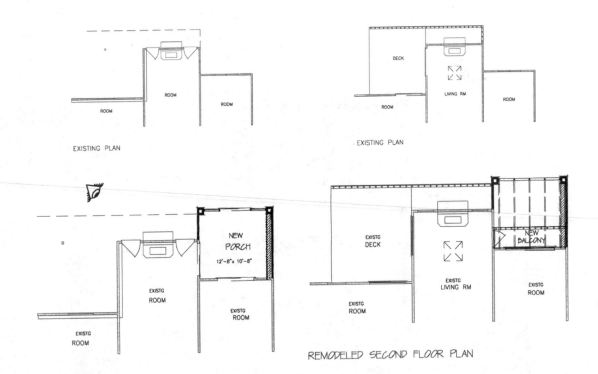

EXISTING PLAN

EXISTING PLAN

REMODELED FIRST FLOOR PLAN

REMODELED SECOND FLOOR PLAN

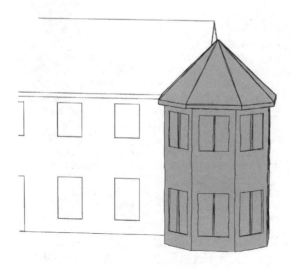

PBR04

THIS TWO-STORY TOWER, WITH ITS CONICAL SHAPED ROOF, MAY BE JUST THE ADDITION, IF YOU ARE SEARCHING FOR THE UNUSUAL. THE PLAN IS A PICTURESQUE OCTAGON, 12 FEET SQUARE, ENVELOPED WITH WINDOWS ON ALL ITS SIDES, EXCEPT FOR ONE, THAT BEING THE SIDE THAT PROVIDES CONNECTION TO THE HOUSE. THE SAME PLAN IS DUPLICATED ON EACH FLOOR; JUST THE USE MAY VARY. IN THE DESIGN SHOWN, WHERE IT IS ATTACHED TO THE CORNER OF A TWO-STORY HOME, THE FIRST FLOOR IS A LIKELY SUNROOM OR PORCH, AND THE SECOND FLOOR COULD BE AN ENGAGING NEW SITTING ROOM CONNECTED TO YOUR MASTER BEDROOM. WHATEVER ITS USE, IT COULD BECOME A STRIKING ADDITION TO YOUR HOME.

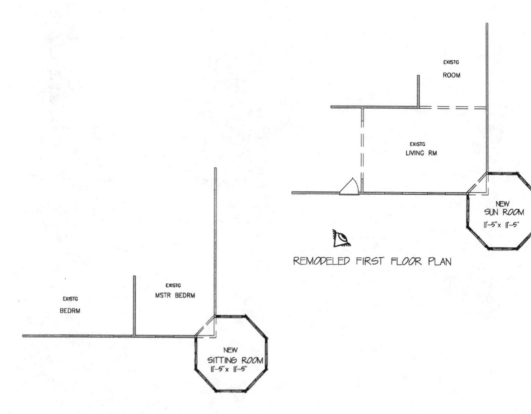

REMODELED FIRST FLOOR PLAN

REMODELED SECOND FLOOR PLAN

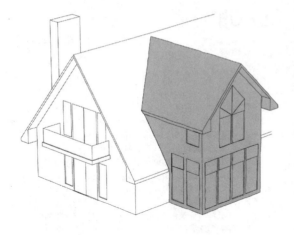

PBROI

WHEN A HOME ENJOYS A STRONG DISTINCTIVE EXTERIOR CHARACTER IT IS VERY IMPORTANT TO PLAN ANY NEW ADDITION SO THAT IT IS IN HARMONY WITH THE EXISTING FORMS.   AN A-FRAME STYLE IS SUCH A HOME.   THE ADDITION PICTURED HERE IS DESIGNED TO SATISFY THE DEMAND FOR ANOTHER SECOND FLOOR BEDROOM, AND TO CREATE A NEW FIRST FLOOR SUN PORCH IN THE SPACE GENERATED BELOW THE BEDROOM.   THE ROOFLINE OF THE NEW ADDITION COMPLEMENTS, AND EVEN ENHANCES, THE EXISTING ROOFLINE.   THE SUN PORCH FEATURES WRAP-AROUND WINDOWS ON THREE SIDES, AND THE NEW BEDROOM INCLUDES A DRAMATIC VAULTED CEILING. IT IS WORTHWHILE TO NOTE THAT THE BEDROOM IS LARGER THAN THE PORCH BECAUSE THE NEW TWO-STORY FORM PICKS UP SOME AREA HERETOFORE LOST UNDER THE EXISTING ONE AND ONE-HALF STORY ROOFLINE.

REMODELED FIRST FLOOR PLAN

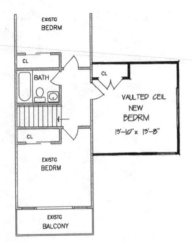

REMODELED SECOND FLOOR PLAN

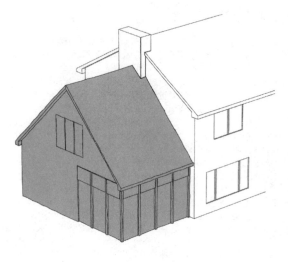

PBR02

HERE'S AN EXAMPLE WHERE THE BONUS OR EXTRA (SEE CHAPTER 3 FOR DISCUSSION) COULD BE AS IMPORTANT AS THE MAIN PURPOSE OF THE REMODELING. WHEREAS THE GOAL OF THIS PLAN IS TO ADD A FIRST FLOOR HOME OFFICE AND ENCLOSED PORCH (OR SUNROOM), THE SECOND FLOOR DRESSING ROOM OR SITTING ROOM IS NOT AN AFTERTHOUGHT. IN PLAN LD001 ON PAGE 191, WE SEE A ONE-STORY ADDITION TO THE SIDE OF A TWO-STORY HOME—ITS AESTHETIC PROPORTIONS COULD BE A PROBLEM, ESPECIALLY ON A WIDER HOME. THEREFORE I RECOMMEND THE STEEPER, ONE AND ONE-HALF STORY ROOFLINE TO ACHIEVE BETTER BALANCE, AND, AS SUCH, WE GAIN THE SECOND FLOOR SPACE. IF YOU WANT TO CONSIDER GOING ALL-OUT, THERE ARE A NUMBER OF PLANS IN CHAPTER 8 THAT SHOW YOU HOW TO REMODEL THE MASTER BATHROOM TOO.

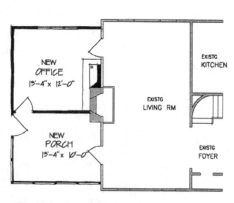

REMODELED FIRST FLOOR PLAN

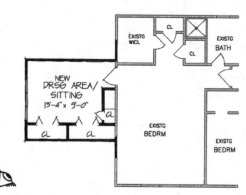

REMODELED SECOND FLOOR PLAN

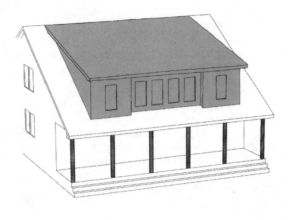

BRBI7

YOUR SUBJECT IS AN OLD CAPE, BUNGALOW, OR
SHINGLE STYLE I½ STORY HOME AND THE BEDROOMS
ARE TIGHT. LOOK UP TO THE ROOF. THE DORMERS
ARE LIKELY VERY SMALL, AND THERE IS PROBABLY
MUCH SPACE TO BE FOUND BY PUSHING OUT ONE OR
MORE DORMERS. YOUR MAJOR CONCERN IS
EXTENDING THE ROOFLINES SO THEY ARE IN
CHARACTER WITH THE EXISTING HOME. THIS MODISH
27'0"×7'0" ADDITION SHOWS YOU HOW TO DO IT
WITH CLASS. IT REMOVES AN EXISTING SMALL
FRONT BEDROOM, AND PROVIDES A SENSATIONAL
NEW MASTER SUITE WITH A FABULOUS BATH AND
SPACIOUS WALK-IN CLOSET. MOST IMPORTANTLY,
THE NEW ROOFLINES ECHO THE EXISTING LINES OF
THE HOUSE, AND THE ADDITION LOOKS SMASHING.

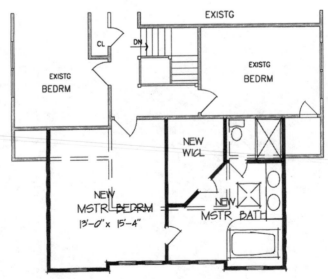

REMODELED SECOND FLOOR PLAN

BRB15

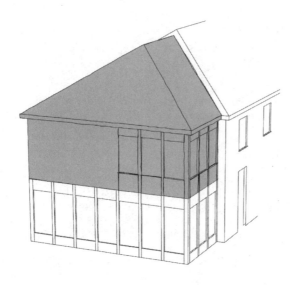

A SPLENDID MASTER BEDROOM SUITE IS CREATED BY THIS 9'6"×21'8" SECOND FLOOR ADDITION OVER AN EXISTING FIRST FLOOR SUN PORCH. BY COMBINING AN EXISTING BEDROOM WITH THE NEW FOUND AREA OVER THE PORCH, MORE THAN AMPLE FOOTAGE IS AVAILABLE TO CREATE A DELICIOUS, UP-TO-DATE MASTER SUITE. TWO SMALL CLOSETS ARE COMBINED—AND ENLARGED INTO A SPACIOUS WALK-IN CLOSET. THE NEW MASTER BATH INCLUDES A COMPARTMENTED WATER CLOSET, A PLATFORM WHIRLPOOL TUB, A SEPARATE CORNER STYLE STALL SHOWER AND A DOUBLE VANITY. BEDROOM WINDOWS COMPLEMENT THE PORCH BELOW, CREATING A BRIGHT, CHEERFUL BEDROOM. AN ALTERNATE PLAN FOR THIS SPACE MIGHT CALL FOR THE EXTENSION OF THE HALL AND THE CREATION OF A SMALLER EXTRA BEDROOM LOCATED ONLY WITHIN THE ADDITION, SIMILAR TO PLAN BRB08 ON PAGE 115.

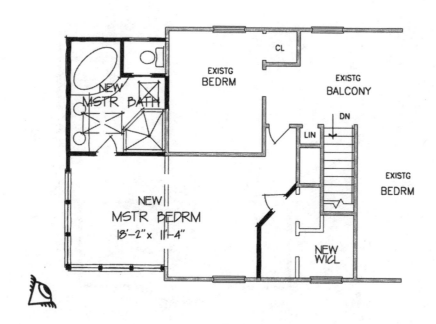

REMODELED SECOND FLOOR PLAN

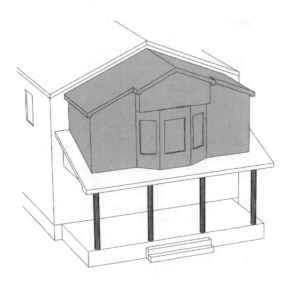

BRB16

THIS IS ANOTHER SECOND FLOOR BEDROOM EXPANSION PLAN OVER AN EXISTING FIRST FLOOR PORCH. THIS PLAN ADDS 21'0"×8'0" TO ENLARGE ONE BEDROOM INTO A MASTER-SIZED SUITE. A PRIVATE BATH AND WALK-IN CLOSET ARE ADDED, AS WELL AS ADDITIONAL FLOOR AREA, TO CREATE A VERY INVITING BEDROOM SUITE. CLOSET DOORS ARE RELOCATED TO PROVIDE AMPLE WALL SPACE FOR FURNISHING—A FACTOR OFTEN IGNORED IN MANY OLDER HOMES. MOST ADDITIONS OVER A PORCH WILL LIKELY REQUIRE REPLACING THE CEILING OF THE PORCH, AS THE STRUCTURE IS USUALLY INADEQUATE FOR A FLOOR; HOWEVER, THE SPACE OVER A PORCH IS TRULY FOUND SPACE, AND THE RESULTING RENOVATION CAN ENHANCE THE APPEARANCE OF THE HOME.

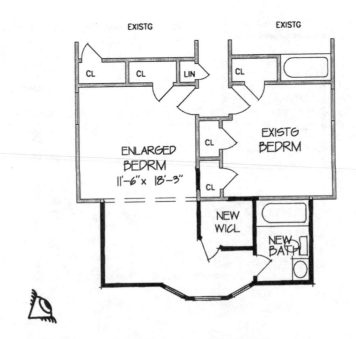

REMODELED SECOND FLOOR PLAN

BRB05

THE HOME HAS A SPACIOUS FOUR-BEDROOM LAYOUT, BUT THE MASTER BEDROOM IS JUST NOT UP TO TODAY'S STANDARDS; THE GOAL IS A SENSATIONAL NEW SUITE WITH A SPARKLING NEW BATH, PLENTY OF CLOSETS AND SOME OFFICE SPACE TO BOOT. THE ROOF OVER THE GARAGE AND LAUNDRY ROOM IS WAITING. PICTURED HERE, IS AN ARCHITECTURALLY DELIGHTFUL ADDITION, THAT SATISFIES THOSE WISHES; IT PROVIDES ALL THE SPACE ASKED FOR AND DOES IT WITH FLAIR. IT EVEN REDESIGNS THE FRONT OF THE HOME TO GIVE IT A STYLISH NEW CHARACTER. VAULTED CEILINGS, SKYLIGHTS AND BUILT-IN SPACE ARE SOME EXTRA BONUSES OF THE PLAN.

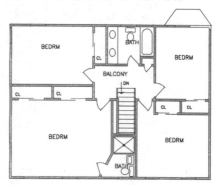

EXISTING PLAN

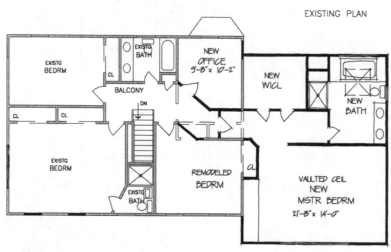

REMODELED SECOND FLOOR PLAN

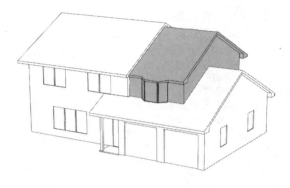

BRB20

THE SUBJECT IS A 3-BEDROOM SIDE-HALL TWO-
STORY WITH AN ATTACHED 2 CAR GARAGE, AND
NOTHING BUT SKY ABOVE. WELL, IF YOU WOULD LIKE
TO ADD A FOURTH BEDROOM OVER THE GARAGE,
THIS PLAN SHOWS HOW TO DO IT. THE PLAN, AS
DRAWN, CALLS FOR AN ENTIRE NEW MASTER SUITE
COMPLETE WITH ITS OWN SHOWER BATH, DRESSING
ALCOVE AND WALK-IN CLOSET. IT IS PREDICATED ON
A ONE-STORY WING BELOW THAT IS 29' or 30' DEEP,
WHICH IS FAIRLY COMMON IF THERE IS A LAUNDRY,
UTILITY ROOM OR KITCHEN BEHIND THE GARAGE. THE
ROOM COULD BE MADE WIDER OR SHALLOWER, AS
NECESSARY, TO ACCOMMODATE THE EXISTING
DIMENSIONS OF YOUR HOUSE.

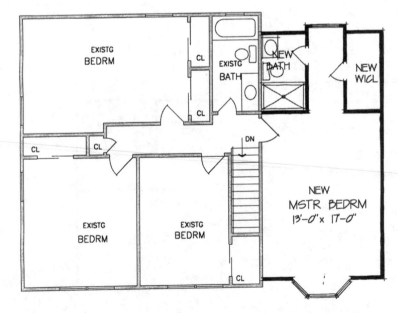

REMODELED SECOND FLOOR PLAN

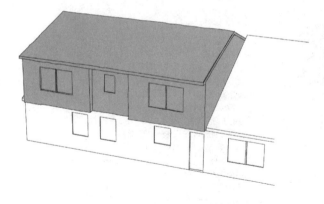

BRBOI

GIVEN: THE REAR CORNER OF A ONE-STORY HOME; YOU NEED AT LEAST ONE NEW BEDROOM (TWO WOULD FREE UP ANOTHER EXISTING BEDROOM FOR USE AS AN OFFICE), AND YOU NEED TO EXPLORE THE OPTIONS OF GOING OUT OR GOING UP. THIS PLAN SHOWS HOW TO ACCOMPLISH THE LATTER VERY ECONOMICALLY. IT RAISES THE ROOF, PLACES A NEW STAIR TO THE SECOND FLOOR OVER THE BASEMENT STAIR, A NEW BATH OVER THE EXISTING HALL BATH, AND TWO BEDROOMS FLANKING ON EITHER SIDE. THE BEDROOMS ARE CANTILEVERED, WHICH ADDS SOME NEEDED SQUARE FOOTAGE, WHILE IMPROVING THE AESTHETIC OF THE PARTIAL SECOND FLOOR. THE ROOF FORM UTILIZED HERE IS MORE SPECIFIC TO A FLATTER PITCHED ONE-STORY HOME, RATHER THAN A STEEPER ONE AND ONE-HALF STORY ROOFLINE.

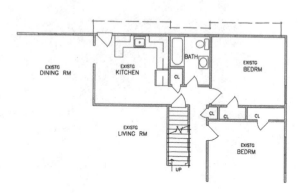

FIRST FLOOR PLAN

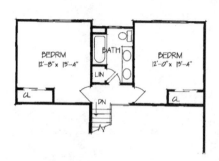

SECOND FLOOR PLAN
ALL NEW

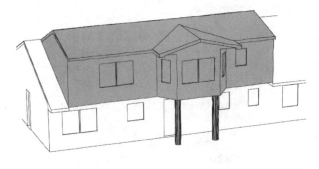

BRB03

AN ENGAGINGLY PRIVATE BEDROOM SUITE IS THE RESULT OF THIS SECOND FLOOR ADDITION THAT REQUIRES VIRTUALLY NO CHANGE TO THE EXISTING FIRST FLOOR. THE STAIR IS LOCATED ABOVE YOUR EXISTING BASEMENT STAIR, AS SHOWN. SINCE SOME MODEST CEILING DAMAGE MAY OCCUR, YOU MIGHT CONSIDER REMODELING THE KITCHEN AND FIRST FLOOR BATHROOMS, BUT THAT IS NOT REQUIRED AT ALL. THE CHANGE CAN BE ACCOMPLISHED WITH MINIMAL INTERRUPTION TO YOUR DAILY PATTERNS. THE ADDITION PROVIDES A LUXURIOUS BEDROOM, A SPACIOUS BATH, A FABULOUS WALK-IN CLOSET, AND A LOVELY SITTING AREA IN FRONT OF THE BAY WINDOW. THE BATH INCLUDES A WHIRLPOOL TUB, SEPARATE STALL SHOWER, DOUBLE VANITY AND A SKYLIGHT.

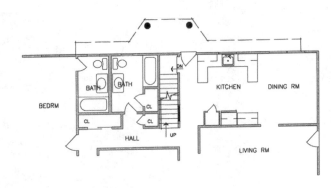

FIRST FLOOR PLAN

SECOND FLOOR PLAN
ALL NEW

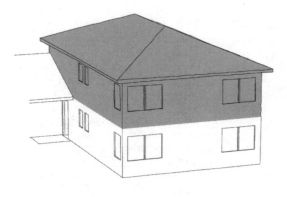

BRB02

CRAMPED SMALL BEDROOMS ARE ELIMINATED WHEN THIS MODEST L-SHAPED RANCH BECOMES A STUNNING TWO-STORY IN THIS REMODEL. THE ROOF IS RAISED OVER THE BEDROOM WING AND THREE BEDROOMS AND A BATH ARE ADDED ON THE SECOND FLOOR. THERE'S NOW LOADS OF CLOSET SPACE AND EVEN A DRAMATIC BALCONY OVERLOOKING A NEWLY RAISED CEILING AREA OF THE LIVING ROOM. THE FIRST FLOOR BEDROOM WING IS REMODELED AND A FABULOUS, PRIVATE, MASTER SUITE IS CARVED OUT. IT INCLUDES TWO WALK-IN CLOSETS AND A GREAT BATH WITH A WHIRLPOOL TUB, SEPARATE SHOWER AND CURVED VANITY. SUCH AN EXTENSIVE PROJECT WILL LIKELY REQUIRE MAJOR DECISIONS ON NEW WINDOWS, SIDING, ROOFING & EVEN THE HEATING & AIR CONDITIONING SYSTEM. SEE CHAPTERS 2 AND 12 FOR FURTHER DISCUSSION.

EXISTING PLAN

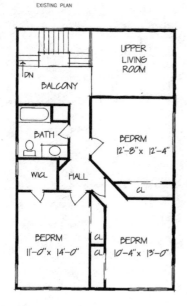

REMODELED SECOND FLOOR PLAN

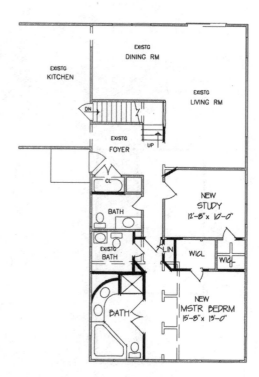

REMODELED FIRST FLOOR PLAN

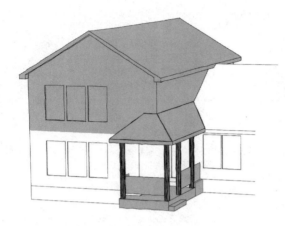

BRB04

PROBLEM: THREE BEDROOMS SHARE ONE BATH, THE MASTER IS TOO SMALL, AND YOU REALLY DON'T HAVE ENOUGH ROOM TO EXPAND OUT.   SOLUTION: MOVE THE ENTIRE BEDROOM WING UP, AND CREATE A DELICIOUS NEW FIRST FLOOR MASTER SUITE FROM THE EXISTING SPACE.   THIS PLAN SHOWS HOW TO DO IT WITH STYLE.   THE NEW MASTER SUITE ENJOYS THE PRIVACY OF THE REAR PART OF THE OLD BEDROOM WING; A LOVELY BAY WINDOW IS ADDED TO THE REAR WALL AND A LUXURIOUS COMPARTMENTED BATH AND SPACIOUS WALK-IN CLOSET ARE CARVED FROM THE OLD MIDDLE BEDROOM.   THE FRONT BEDROOM REMAINS INTACT AND SERVES AS AN IDEAL GUEST OR PARENTS' BEDROOM, OR AS AN OFFICE. THE COVERED FIRST FLOOR PORCH IS A SMART BY-PRODUCT OF THE DESIGN.

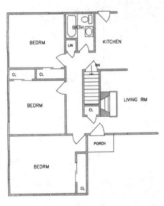

EXISTING FIRST FLOOR PLAN

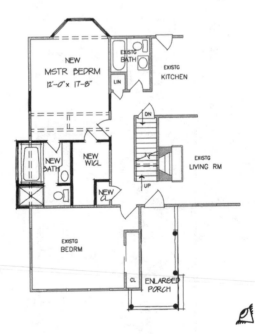

REMODELED FIRST FLOOR PLAN

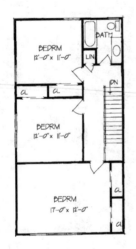

SECOND FLOOR PLAN

ALL NEW

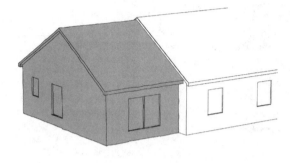

BRB08

THIS 13'10"×25'4" ONE-STORY ADDITION PROVIDES A COMFORTABLE NEW MASTER SUITE, COMPRISING A LOVELY BEDROOM, A PRIVATE TUB BATH AND A SPACIOUS WALK-IN CLOSET. THE ATTACHMENT SHOWN IS TO THE SIDE OR REAR OF A VERY COMMONLY FOUND BEDROOM WING. THE PLAN SHOWS YOU HOW TO EXTEND THE BEDROOM HALL BY REMOVING AND RELOCATING THREE EXISTING CLOSETS; A REMODELING OF THE EXISTING HALL BATH IS ALSO INDICATED. DON'T BE TEMPTED TO GAIN EVERY INCH OF SPACE BY ALIGNING THE ADDITION FLUSH ON BOTH THE FRONT AND REAR (OR BOTH SIDES); DOING SO WOULD LIKELY REQUIRE RE-ROOFING, RE-SIDING AND A HARD LOOK AT MATCHING WINDOWS TOO; THE BREAK, AS SHOWN, AVOIDS THOSE CONCERNS.

REMODELED FIRST FLOOR PLAN

BRB09

THIS PLAN, WHEN COMPARED TO THE ONE ON THE
PRIOR PAGE, SHOWS THE IMPORTANCE OF
EVALUATING OPTIONS WHEN DECIDING HOW TO
APPROACH A REMODELING PROJECT.   THIS REMODEL
ALSO ADDS A NEW MASTER SUITE TO THE SAME
BEDROOM WING; HOWEVER, IT DOES SO IN A
13'4"×37'8" ADDITION, THAT PLACES THE NEW
MASTER BEDROOM IN A REAR-FACING REVERSE GABLE
WING.   OTHER DIFFERENCES INCLUDE LOCATING THE
NEW MASTER BATH AND A BRAND NEW HALL BATH IN
THE SPACE FORMERLY OCCUPIED BY THE SMALL REAR
BEDROOM.   THE NEW ADDITION REPLACES THIS
BEDROOM—IN A LARGER FORM—IN THE FRONT OF
THE NEW WING.   OTHER NUANCES: A TRAY CEILING IN
THE MASTER BEDROOM, CORNER WINDOWS, AND THE
OLD HALL BATH CONVERTED TO A SPACIOUS
LAUNDRY ROOM.

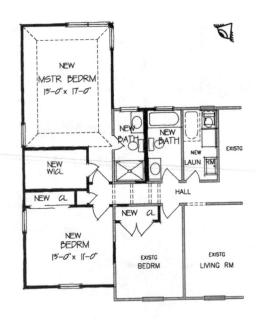

REMODELED FIRST FLOOR PLAN

BRB10

GIVEN: AN EXISTING CONGESTED FIRST FLOOR
BEDROOM WING AND A PROGRAM CALLING FOR A
NEW MASTER BEDROOM AND BATH.   THE ENTIRE
EXTENSION (18'6"×21'2") IS TO THE REAR.   TWO NEW
TUB BATHS ARE CONSTRUCTED IN THE NEW WING,
WHICH ALLOWS A VERY EASY STAGING PROCESS.
THE OLD BATH WOULD BE THE LAST TO BE DONE,
SINCE REMOVING IT IS NECESSARY TO PROVIDE THE
HALL ACCESS, TO THE NEW WING WHILE ALSO
PROVIDING LAUNDRY SPACE.   THE NEW SIDE DOOR IS
AN INTERESTING ASPECT OF THIS DESIGN.

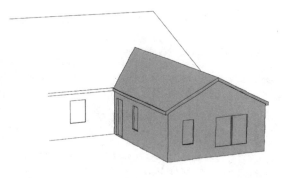

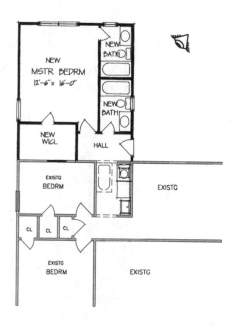

REMODELED FIRST FLOOR PLAN

BRBII

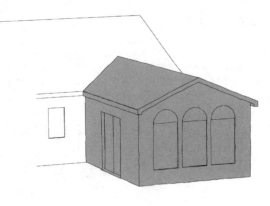

A COMMON EXISTING CONDITION: A SMALL REAR CORNER BEDROOM AND AN ANCIENT HALL BATH. A COMMON PROGRAM NEED: A LARGER MASTER BEDROOM WITH PLENTY OF CLOSETS AND A PRIVATE BATH. THIS PLAN MESHES BOTH; A 13'8"×19'8" REAR ADDITION, COMBINED WITH THE SPACE FROM THE SMALL BEDROOM, CREATES A STYLISH CONTEMPORARY MASTER SUITE. THE NEW BEDROOM FEATURES A BEAUTIFUL REAR WINDOW WALL, A VAULTED CEILING AND OPTIONAL FRENCH DOORS TO THE SIDE. THE BATH PROVIDES A COMPARTMENTED STALL SHOWER AND WATER CLOSET ALCOVE, AND A LOVELY BAY WINDOW AT THE TUB AREA. THE OLD HALL BATH CAN BE SIMPLY REMODELED, OR DIVIDED INTO A POWDER ROOM AND A SEPARATE LAUNDRY ALCOVE, DEPENDING ON YOUR NEEDS.

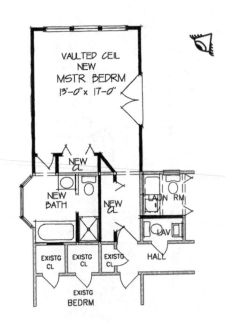

REMODELED FIRST FLOOR PLAN

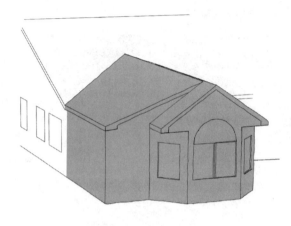

BRB06

PROBLEM: THE THREE BEDROOMS SHARE A HALL BATH, THERE IS NO NEED FOR AN EXTRA BEDROOM, BUT A GOAL FOR A GRAND NEW MASTER SUITE; FURTHERMORE, THE ONLY PLACE TO EXPAND OUT IS IN THE REAR, WHICH REQUIRES REMOVING THE OLD BATH. ACTUALLY THE REMOVAL OF THE OLD HALL BATH BECOMES A BENEFIT, AS THE SOLUTION SHOWN CREATES A NEW BATH, WHICH CAN BE FINISHED OFF EARLY IN THE RENOVATION PROCESS, ALLOWING YOU TO COMFORTABLY STAGE THE ALTERATION. THE NEW MASTER SUITE IS LUXURIOUS AND EXQUISITE. IT BOASTS A STYLISH WRAP-AROUND BAY WINDOW, A BEAUTIFUL VAULTED CEILING, AND A FABULOUS PRIVATE BATH; THE BATH INCLUDES AN OVERSIZED PLATFORM WHIRLPOOL TUB, A LARGE SEPARATE STALL SHOWER AND AN IMPRESSIVE WALK-IN CLOSET. THE DIMENSIONS OF THIS ADDITION ARE 18'8" WIDE BY 17'4" DEEP.

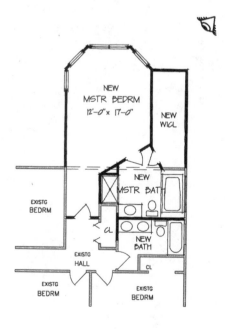

REMODELED FIRST FLOOR PLAN

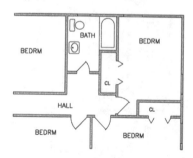

EXISTING PLAN

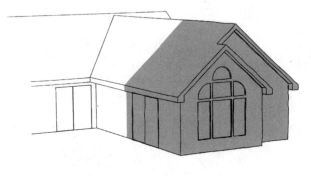

BRB32

THE EXISTING REAR-FACING MASTER BEDROOM
IS DATED; IT IS SMALL, INCLUDES ONLY A HALF
BATH AND A SINGLE CLOSET. THE GOAL IS AN
UPDATED MASTER SUITE THAT WILL INCLUDE A
NEW FIVE-FIXTURE BATH, DUAL WALK-IN
CLOSETS AND A BEDROOM WITH SOME
INTERIOR DRAMA. THE PLAN PICTURED
ACCOMPLISHES THAT, AND CREATES A
SENSATIONAL NEW MASTER SUITE. THE NEW
BATH IS EASILY CONNECTED TO THE EXISTING
PLUMBING AND INCLUDES A LARGE WHIRLPOOL
TUB IN A PLATFORM UNDER A WINDOW. THE
DRAMATIC REAR WINDOW WALL, WITH ITS HIGH
CEILING, BATHES THE NEW ROOM IN AN
ABUNDANCE OF LIGHT. A BONUS OF THE PLAN
IS THE OFFICE ALCOVE CREATED UPON
ENTERING THE BEDROOM.

REMODELED FLOOR PLAN

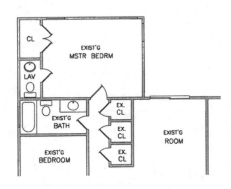

EXISTING FLOOR PLAN

BRB29

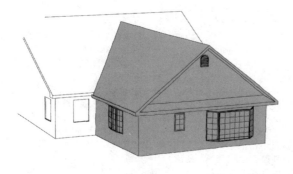

THIS 25'×18' GABLE ROOFED ADDITION IS A FULL NEW MASTER SUITE THAT CAN BE ATTACHED TO THE REAR OF MOST ONE AND TWO-STORY HOMES. IT PROVIDES A 14'×18' NEW BEDROOM WITH A TRAY CEILING AND CHARMING REAR BAY WINDOW WITH A SEAT. THE NEW MASTER BATH INCLUDES A SEPARATE TOILET COMPARTMENT, DUAL WALK-IN CLOSETS, AND DUAL SINKS, A SEPARATE STALL SHOWER AND A WHIRLPOOL TUB IN A CENTRAL PLATFORM. THE KEY TO THIS ADDITION IS FINDING AMPLE REAR OR SIDE WALL, WHERE THERE ARE NO REQUIRED WINDOWS FOR EITHER ROOMS.

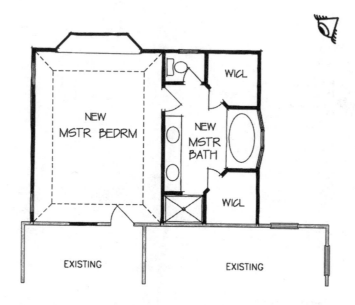

REMODELED FLOOR PLAN

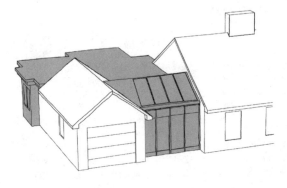

PBR03

THE OUTRAGEOUS NEW FIRST FLOOR MASTER SUITE, PICTURED HERE, IS A STUNNING EXAMPLE OF THE USE OF FOUND SPACE. THE OLD BREEZEWAY, BLANK SIDE OF THE DINING ROOM AND REAR OF THE GARAGE ARE LIKELY TO BE UNDERUTILIZED AREAS OF YOUR LOT; WHAT A PERFECT SPOT FOR A PRIVATE MASTER RETREAT. ALTHOUGH PICTURED AS A ONE-STORY HOME, THE SAME PLAN WORKS FOR AN EXISTING SPLIT-LEVEL OR TWO-STORY HOME. THE OLD BREEZEWAY IS NOW TRANSFORMED INTO A BEAUTIFUL SUN PORCH, WHICH NOT ONLY ENHANCES THE EXISTING LIVING ROOM, BUT ALSO SERVES AS A LOVELY ENTRANCE AND ADJUNCT TO THE NEW MASTER BEDROOM. IT'S DELICIOUS.

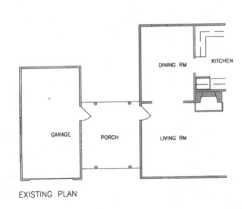

EXISTING PLAN

REMODELED FIRST FLOOR PLAN

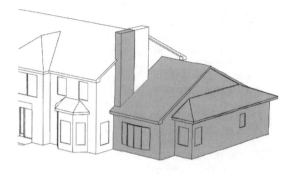

BRB24

A WINNING NEW MASTER SUITE IS THE SUBJECT OF THIS LARGE ONE-STORY ADDITION. ALTHOUGH SPECIFICALLY PLANNED TO ATTACH TO THE LIVING ROOM SIDE OF A TWO-STORY HOME, THIS SPLASHY DESIGN COULD BE CONNECTED TO MANY DIFFERENT HOMES, AND MAYBE YOURS. THE PLAN PROVIDES FOR A LARGE, TRAY-CEILINGED BEDROOM WITH AN ADJOINING SITTING AREA, AND A LUXURIOUS BATHROOM, DRESSING AND CLOSET SUITE. A LARGE BOW WINDOW PROVIDES AN ABUNDANCE OF LIGHT TO THE SITTING AREA, WHERE THERE IS ALSO A FIREPLACE. THE SPACIOUS DRESSING AREA INCLUDES A DRAMATIC DOUBLE VANITY THAT WRAPS AROUND A CORNER, A LARGE WHIRLPOOL TUB AND TWO GRAND WALK-IN CLOSETS, ALL DESIGNED INTO A STYLISH PLAN THAT IS DOMINATED BY STRIKING ANGLES.

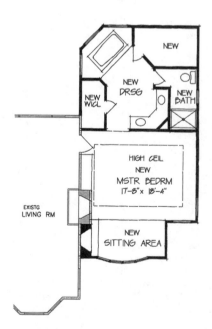

NEW

NEW
DRSG

NEW
WICL

NEW
BATH

HIGH CEIL
NEW
MSTR BEDRM
17-8" x 18'-4"

EXISTG
LIVING RM

NEW
SITTING AREA

REMODELED FIRST FLOOR PLAN

BR008

LET'S SAY YOU'RE GIVEN AN ORDINARY PITCHED-ROOF SPLIT-LEVEL AND THERE'S A PROGRAM TO ADD A ROOM OVER THE KITCHEN AND DINING ROOM, BUT THE LOCAL ORDINANCE HAS A 26 FT HEIGHT RESTRICTION TO THE HIGHEST POINT OF THE ROOF. WHAT DO YOU DO? SINCE AN ORDINARY PITCHED ROOF WOULD EXCEED THAT HEIGHT, WE HAVE NO CHOICE BUT TO USE A FLAT ROOF OVER THE ADDITION. WE KNOW, HOWEVER, THAT THIS WILL LOOK VERY UGLY, SO WHAT CAN WE DO TO MITIGATE THAT LOOK? CONSIDER CREATING A FALSE "MANSARD" ROOF AT THE UPPER LEVEL; THIS AT LEAST PUTS ROOFING SHINGLES ON THE ELEMENT TO MIRROR THE OTHER PART OF THE HOME. WITH THE RIGHT CHOICE OF MATERIALS WE CAN MAKE THIS ADDITION LOOK "RIGHT."

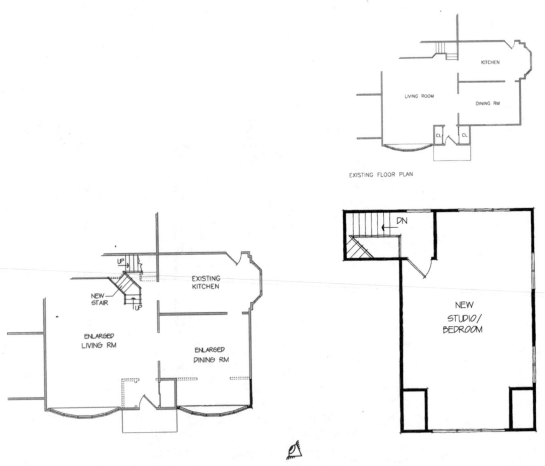

EXISTING FLOOR PLAN

KITCHEN

LIVING ROOM

DINING RM

CL   CL

EXISTING KITCHEN

NEW STAIR

UP

UP

ENLARGED LIVING RM

ENLARGED DINING RM

REMODELED FLOOR PLAN

DN

NEW STUDIO/ BEDROOM

REMODELED FLOOR PLAN

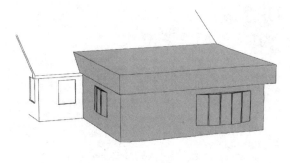

BRB14

A STUNNING AND CHIC MASTER BEDROOM SUITE IS THE SUBJECT OF THIS 25'2"×18'4" ONE-STORY ADDITION. IT CAN BE ADDED ANYWHERE TO AN EXISTING REAR, SIDE, OR EVEN FRONT WALL; YOUR MAIN CONCERN IS CLOSING OF EXISTING WINDOWS AND WHERE TO PLACE THE DOOR TO THE SUITE. THE BEDROOM BOASTS AN ELEGANT TRAY CEILING AND A BEAUTIFUL BAY WINDOW. THE EXTRAORDINARY BATH INCLUDES A BEAUTIFUL ANGLED INTERIOR FORM, WITH HIS AND HER WALK-IN CLOSETS FLANKING A LARGE SOAKING TUB. THERE IS A SEPARATE COMPARTMENT FOR THE WATER CLOSET, PLUS A LARGE STALL SHOWER AND AN 8' DOUBLE VANITY. THE FLAT ROOF, AS SHOWN, IS READILY CONVERTED TO A GABLE, HIP OR SHED AS MAY BE REQUIRED OR PREFERRED. SEE CHAPTER 6 ON AVAILABLE BLOCKFORMS.

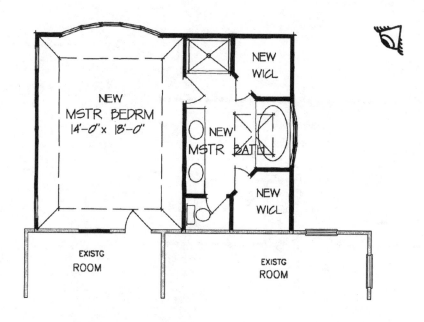

REMODELED FLOOR PLAN

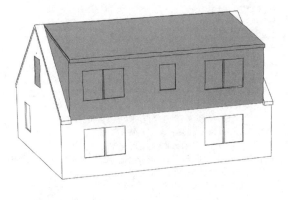

BRB12

THIS PLAN PROVIDES TWO NEW LARGE BEDROOMS AND A BATH IN A NEW DORMERED REAR. THE DORMER SHOWN IS 29'4" WIDE AND THE EXISTING HOME IS 32'0" WIDE; BOTH COULD BE WIDER OR SMALLER. THIS TYPE OF SHED ROOF DORMER IS ADAPTABLE TO ALMOST ANY EXISTING ONE OR ONE AND ONE-HALF STORY HOME; HOWEVER, IT IS MOST SUITED TO A HOME THAT ALREADY HAS A STAND UP ATTIC UNDER A STEEPLY PITCHED ROOF. A DESIGN ISSUE YOU SHOULD BE CONCERNED WITH IS KEEPING AT LEAST A SMALL SLIVER OF THE OLD ROOF ON EACH SIDE; THIS AVOIDS THE AWKWARD BULK LOOKING SIDE FORM SO OFTEN SEEN ON SUCH HOMES. ALSO, CONSIDER RAISING THE CEILING ALONGSIDE THE STAIR ON THE FIRST FLOOR TO ACHIEVE A MORE INVITING ENTRY TO BOTH FLOORS.

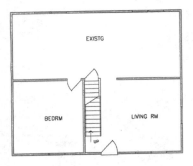

EXISTING FIRST FLOOR PLAN

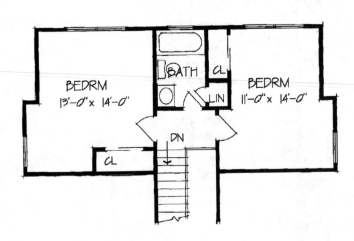

SECOND FLOOR PLAN
ALL NEW

BRB23

ADDING UP ON A ONE-STORY HOME MUST BE DONE WITH CARE, PARTICULARLY WHEN THE SPACE ADDED IS SMALL IN RELATION TO THE EXISTING HOME. THE DESIGN PRESENTED HERE ADDS JUST A SMALL BEDROOM AND BATH (OR A MINI-APARTMENT), BUT IT DOES SO WITH A FLAIR THAT PROVIDES THE PLAIN FLUSH ONE-STORY WITH A NEW FOUND EXTERIOR APPEAL. THE NEW, STEEPLY PITCHED ONE AND ONE-HALF STORY REVERSE GABLE ADDITION ADDS A 4'0" DEEP ONE-STORY PORCH IN THE PROCESS, WHICH SHELTERS THE FRONT DOOR. THE SECOND FLOOR COULD BE READILY EXPANDED BY WIDENING THE ADDITION, OR BY DORMERING THE REAR. IF USED AS A MINI-APARTMENT, THE FRONT AREA COULD SUPPORT A SMALL KITCHENETTE.

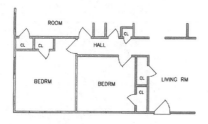

EXISTING PLAN

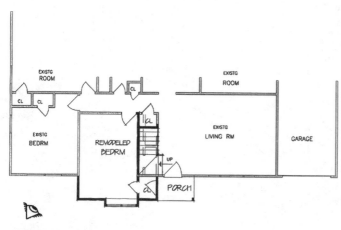

REMODELED FIRST FLOOR PLAN

SECOND FLOOR PLAN
ALL NEW

BRB19

ONE OF THE MOST POPULAR HOMES FOR DECADES—
THE SPLIT-LEVEL—IS NOW ONE OF THE MOST
POPULAR REMODELING SUBJECTS.   THE VARIETY OF
TYPES THAT WERE BUILT OFFERS A MYRIAD OF
POTENTIAL SOLUTIONS, BUT COMMON TO VIRTUALLY
ALL SPLIT-LEVELS IS THE ABILITY TO PLACE A LARGE
BEDROOM SUITE OVER THE LIVING ROOM WING.
HOWEVER, IT IS ALSO ONE OF THE MOST COMMONLY
FLAWED ADDITIONS UNDERTAKEN.   UNLESS CAREFUL
ATTENTION IS GIVEN TO EXISTING ROOFLINES THE
ADDITION COULD LOOK AWFUL.   THIS PLAN SHOWS
YOU HOW TO CREATE A SPECTACULAR NEW MASTER
BEDROOM SUITE, WHILE ENHANCING THE HOME'S
APPEARANCE.   THE SUITE INCLUDES A SENSATIONAL
BATH AND A LOVELY SITTING AREA, ALL UNDER A
STYLISH VAULTED CEILING.   THE PERFECT RETREAT.

NEW
WICL

NEW
MSTR BATH

DN

NEW
MSTR BEDRM
20'-2" x 15'-0"

SECOND FLOOR PLAN
ALL NEW

DINING RM

KITCHEN

BATH

BEDRM

LIVING RM

BEDRM

BEDRM

EXISTING PLAN

BRB18

THIS DAPPER NEW BEDROOM SUITE MAKES AN IDEAL NEW MASTER RETREAT; TUCKED OUT OF SIGHT ON ITS OWN LEVEL, WITH ITS OWN PRIVATE BATH AND PRIVATE BALCONY, IT WILL BE A JOY TO COME HOME TO. IT IS ESPECIALLY DESIGNED TO BE ADDED ABOVE THE LIVING ROOM WING OF A TYPICAL SPLIT-LEVEL, A PLACE WHERE THE UNTRAINED DESIGNER IS PRONE TO MAKE AN AESTHETIC MISTAKE. THIS ADDITION ACTUALLY ENHANCES THE LINES OF THE HOME. THE SUITE INCLUDES A GENEROUS BEDROOM, A COMPARTMENTED BATH WITH A WHIRLPOOL TUB AND DOUBLE VANITY, PLUS A LARGE WALK-IN CLOSET. THIS SPACE IS AVAILABLE IN MOST SPLIT-LEVELS, AND IF IT'S NOT A BEDROOM YOU DESIRE, IT COULD BE UTILIZED AS AN APARTMENT OR EVEN A PLAYROOM.

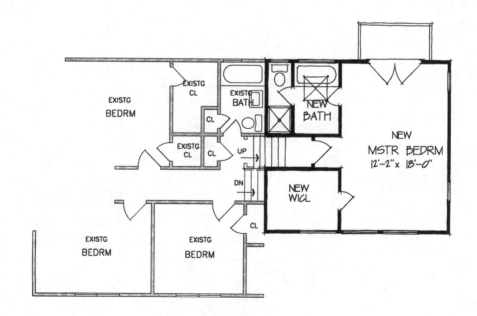

SECOND FLOOR PLAN

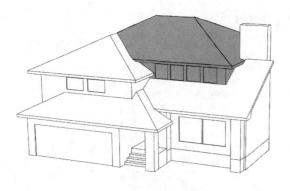

BROO7

THE NARROW STYLE, SIDE-TO-SIDE, SPLIT-LEVEL OR TWO-STORY PICTURED USUALLY HAS LOTS OF HIGH VOLUME OVER THE LIVING ROOM, DINING ROOM AND KITCHEN; BUT IT IS USUALLY SHORT A BEDROOM, AND ITS MINIMAL BASEMENT (IF ONE EXISTS AT ALL) DOESN'T PROVIDE SPACE FOR A RECREATION ROOM. THIS ARCHITECTURALLY WELL-COMPOSED ADDITION PROVIDES THE SPACE FOR BOTH; THE TRADE OFF IS THE LOSS OF THAT HIGH VOLUME, BUT YOU COULD GO UP A FEW EXTRA STEPS IN THE ADDITION AND CREATE A 9', OR EVEN A 10', HIGH CEILING BELOW. A SUGGESTION: USE SOUND DEADENING BOARD AS AN UNDERLAYMENT ON THE RECREATION ROOM FLOOR AND AN EXTRA THICK CARPET AND PAD.

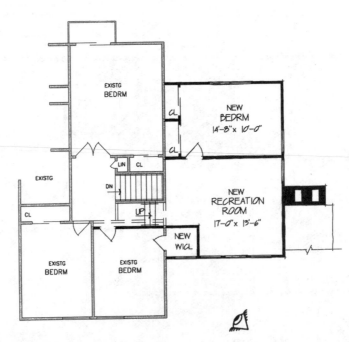

REMODELED SECOND FLOOR PLAN

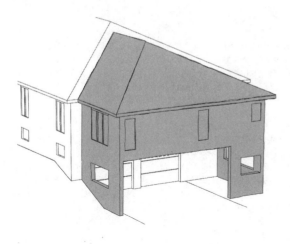

BRB25

ARE WE LOOKING TO ADD A SPACIOUS NEW MASTER BEDROOM SUITE, BUT THE LIKELY PLACE TO BUILD HAS A DRIVEWAY BELOW, WHICH LEADS TO THE GARAGE? IF SO, THIS PLAN SHOWS HOW. THE DESIGN CONCERN HERE IS TO MAKE THE ADDITION AN INTEGRAL PART OF THE HOME AND NOT APPEAR AS A FRAGILE ATTACHMENT ON A FEW POSTS. THIS IS ACCOMPLISHED BY BUILDING SEVERAL WALLS BELOW THE BEDROOM, WITH OPENINGS TO ECHO THE WINDOWS ABOVE. THE WALLS OBVIOUSLY SUPPORT THE NEW ROOM, BUT ALSO SERVE TO PROVIDE A SENSE OF PERMANENCE TO THE ADDITION. THE BEDROOM IS HIGHLIGHTED BY A TRAY CEILING, AND AN ADJOINING DRAMATIC BATHROOM, WITH AN ANGLED TUB PLATFORM. THIS SUITE COULD BE BUILT, OF COURSE, WITHOUT THE BASEMENT.

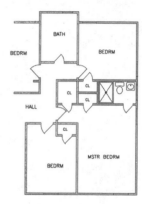

EXISTING UPPER LEVEL PLAN

REMODELED UPPER LEVEL PLAN

REMODELED LOWER LEVEL PLAN

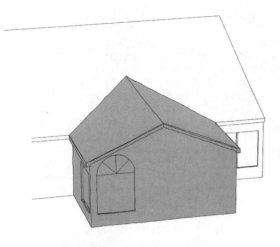

BRB07

A FABULOUS NEW MASTER BATH AND ROOM-SIZE
WALK-IN CLOSET ARE THE SUBJECTS OF THIS
19'4"×11'8" ADDITION.   A SPLENDOROUS MASTER
SUITE IS THE ULTIMATE RESULT.   THE BEDROOM
ITSELF BENEFITS FROM THE REMOVAL OF THE
EXISTING BATHROOM AND CLOSET; THE AREA FROM
THE OLD CLOSET IS IDEAL FOR BUILT-INS, AND THE
AREA FROM THE OLD BATH GRACIOUSLY ENLARGES
THE BEDROOM, CREATING AN ATTRACTIVE SITTING OR
DRESSING AREA.   THE MASTER BATH FEATURES A
DRAMATIC ANGLED ENTRY AND A CORNER PLATFORM
TUB AT A COMPLEMENTARY ANGLE.   MODISH CORNER
WINDOWS ABOVE THE TUB AND A VAULTED CEILING
ADD TO THE HIGH FASHION OF THIS BATHROOM.

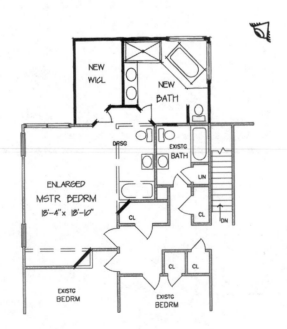

REMODELED FIRST FLOOR PLAN

B0008

THIS 17'0"×14'6" ADDITION CREATES A DAZZLING GARDEN BATH THAT IS DESIGNED TO BE ADDED OFF A CORNER OF YOUR MASTER BEDROOM, INCORPORATING THE OLD BATH AS A TOILET AND SHOWER COMPARTMENT. GARDEN WALLS ENCLOSE SOME ADDITIONAL OUTDOOR SPACE TO PROVIDE PRIVACY FOR THE NEW BATHROOM, WHICH BOASTS A SPACIOUS DRESSING AREA, A FABULOUS WHIRLPOOL TUB, AND A BUILT-IN SAUNA. AN EXCITING PLAY ON ANGLES CREATES SPATIAL DRAMA, WHICH WOULD BE FURTHER ENHANCED BY THE USE OF MIRRORED WALLS BEHIND THE TUB AND VANITY. THE LARGE WINDOW OVER THE TUB AND SLIDING DOORS BOTH FACE THE PRIVATE GARDEN, AND A SKYLIGHT ADDS FURTHER NATURAL LIGHT.

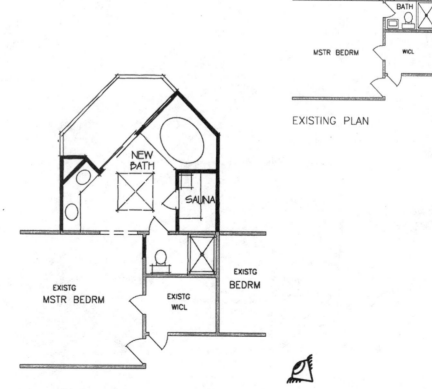

EXISTING PLAN

REMODELED FIRST FLOOR PLAN

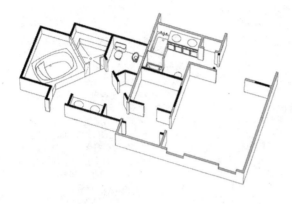

B0013

THE EXISTING MASTER BATH IN THIS RANCH IS
TYPICAL OF THOSE BUILT 25–35 YEARS AGO; IT'S
ABOUT 30 SQ. FT. IN TOTAL AREA, WHEREAS TODAY
WE INSTALL WHIRLPOOL TUBS THAT ARE 30 SQ. FT.
IT'S SIMPLY A REFLECTION OF THE INDULGENCES
THAT MANY NOW EXPECT IN A NEW HOME.   TO
CREATE THAT SAME EFFECT IN THIS OLD RANCH
REQUIRES US TO ADD A NEW BATHROOM THAT IS
ALMOST AS BIG AS THE BEDROOM ITSELF.   ASIDE
FROM THE TUB, THERE IS A HUGE SHOWER, DOUBLE
VANITY AND A PRIVATE COMPARTMENT FOR THE
TOILET AND BIDET.   THIS PLAN ALSO ENLARGES THE
EXISTING HALL BATH BY ADDING A SEPARATE STALL
SHOWER.

EXISTING FLOOR PLAN

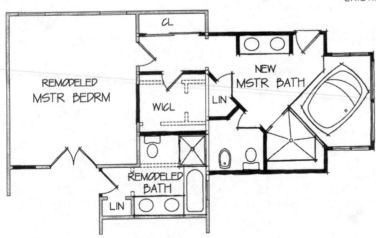

REMODELED FLOOR PLAN

LBRBI

FEW MAJOR ADDITIONS EXPAND TO THE FRONT DUE TO LACK OF AVAILABLE FRONT YARD, BUT IF THERE IS ROOM, AND THE CURRENT HOME IS A DATED IN-LINE RANCH, YOU COULD CREATE THE STYLISH U-SHAPED DESIGN PICTURED. THE 18'-DEEP ADDITION PLACES AN INVITING NEW GREAT ROOM AT THE FRONT OF THE EXISTING LIVING ROOM, AND A SMART NEW MASTER SUITE IN FRONT OF THE EXISTING BEDROOMS. IT IS AN EASY ADDITION TO STAGE AND WHEN IT IS COMPLETE, AND THE OLD FRONT WALL IS REMOVED, THE NEW ENTERTAINMENT WING WILL BECOME A SPACIOUS, OPEN, FLOWING SPACE THAT CAN BE DECORATED AND FURNISHED TO SUIT ONE'S LIFESTYLE. THE NEW MASTER BEDROOM INCLUDES A PRIVATE, COMPARTMENTED, BATH AND A LARGE WALK-IN CLOSET. BOTH NEW ROOMS FEATURE LARGE BOW WINDOWS AND HIGH-TRAYED CEILINGS.

EXISTING PLAN

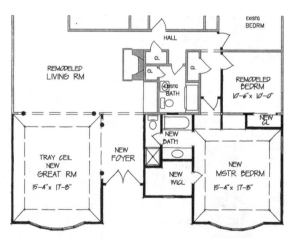

REMODELED FIRST FLOOR PLAN

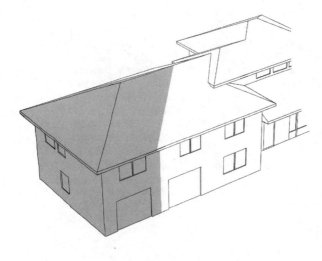

BRG01

A FOURTH BEDROOM AND A SECOND GARAGE ARE THE SUBJECTS OF THIS ADDITION; THE HOME PICTURED IS A THREE-BEDROOM SPLIT-LEVEL WITH A ONE-CAR GARAGE BELOW, BUT THE PLAN IS ALSO PERFECTLY SUITED TO ANY MULTI-STORY HOME. THIS IS THE TYPE OF ADDITION THAT SHOULD MARRY PERFECTLY TO THE EXISTING HOME, SO THAT IT APPEARS AS AN ORIGINAL PART OF THE DESIGN; MATCHING SIDING, WINDOWS AND ROOFING ARE THEREFORE ESSENTIAL. THE FOURTH BEDROOM IS SHOWN AS A NEW MASTER BEDROOM SUITE, COMPLETE WITH ITS OWN PRIVATE, COMPARTMENTED BATH AND A LARGE WALK-IN CLOSET; ACCESS TO THE BEDROOM IS PROVIDED BY SIMPLY EXTENDING THE EXISTING HALL.

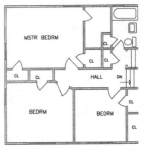

EXISTING SECOND FLOOR PLAN

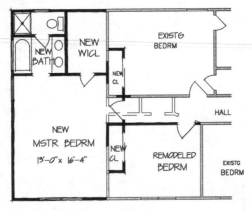

REMODELED SECOND FLOOR PLAN

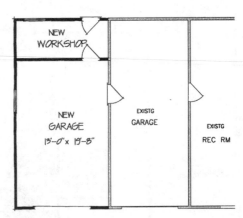

REMODELED FIRST FLOOR PLAN

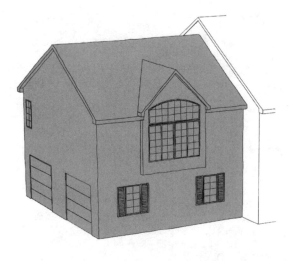

BRG02

THIS IS ONE OF THOSE SELF-CONTAINED ADDITIONS THAT REQUIRES LITTLE, IF ANY, CONNECTION TO THE EXISTING HOUSE. IT IS A 26'×23' ADDITION THAT INCLUDES A TWO-CAR GARAGE ON THE FIRST FLOOR AND A "MASTER BEDROOM" SUITE ON THE SECOND FLOOR. THERE IS A STAIRCASE INCLUDED THAT PROVIDES ACCESS TO THE SECOND FLOOR BEDROOM; THIS STAIRCASE COULD BE ACCESSED FROM THE EXISTING HOUSE, OR FROM THE GARAGE. THE SECOND FLOOR SUITE INCLUDES A SPACIOUS BEDROOM, A LARGE COMPARTMENTED FIVE-FIXTURE BATH AND A VERY LARGE WALK-IN CLOSET. THE SECOND FLOOR COULD ALSO BE UTILIZED AS AN APARTMENT OR "GRANNY FLAT." AS WITH ALL THE PLANS IN THE BOOK, THE CAD FILE ON THE INCLUDED DISK ALLOWS YOU TO ENLARGE, SHRINK OR OTHERWISE MODIFY THIS PLAN TO SUIT YOUR SPECIFIC NEEDS.

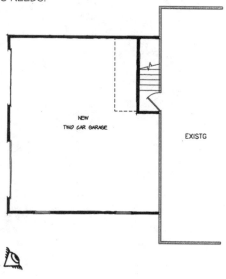

REMODELED FIRST FLOOR PLAN

REMODELED SECOND FLOOR PLAN

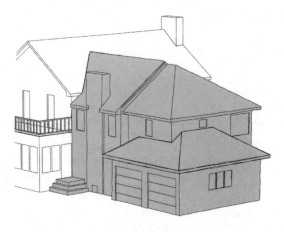

FBRGI

THE SUBJECT IS A LOVELY OLD TWO-STORY HOME, BUT IT IS MISSING A FAMILY ROOM AND GARAGE. THIS CLEVER ARCHITECTURAL DESIGN SHOWS YOU HOW TO ADD BOTH, PLUS A FABULOUS NEW MASTER SUITE ABOVE, TO BOOT. WHETHER THE ADDITION IS TO THE REAR OR SIDE OF YOUR HOME, IT WILL BE AN ATTRACTION. THE FAMILY ROOM IS SHOWN ATTACHING TO THE REAR OF THE STAIR HALL AND KITCHEN, BUT THAT MIGHT VARY IN YOUR HOME. A FIREPLACE WITH SPACE FOR BUILT-INS AT EITHER SIDE IS FEATURED IN THE FAMILY ROOM, AS IS A WALL OF WINDOWS AND DOORS AT THE OPPOSITE SIDE. THE NEW MASTER SUITE IS AN EXQUISITELY DELICIOUS AREA; IT INCLUDES A FIREPLACE AND BAY WINDOW IN THE BEDROOM PLUS A FABULOUS MASTER BATH, DRESSING AREA, AND SPACIOUS WALK-IN CLOSETS.

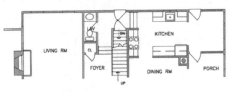

EXISTING FIRST FLOOR PLAN

REMODELED FIRST FLOOR PLAN

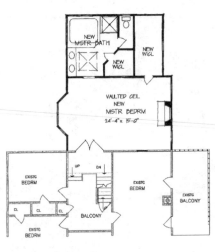

REMODELED SECOND FLOOR PLAN

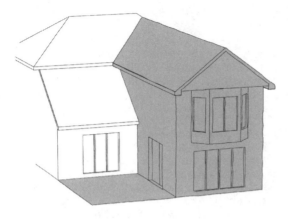

FBROI

NARROW TWO-STORY ADDITIONS REQUIRE ATTENTION TO DETAIL, PARTICULARLY IN THE MANNER OF ATTACHMENT TO THE ROOFLINES OF THE EXISTING HOME. THIS 13'4"×16'8" ADDITION DOES JUST THAT, IN THE SHAPE OF A CRISPLY DESIGNED REVERSE GABLE BLOCKFORM. IT PROVIDES A LOVELY FIRST-FLOOR FAMILY ROOM, PLUS A NEW SECOND-FLOOR MASTER BEDROOM. THE BATHROOM AND CLOSETS FOR THE NEW BEDROOM ARE CARVED FROM AN EXISTING SMALL BEDROOM (OF COURSE, NOW THE OLD MASTER BEDROOM IS AVAILABLE TO REPLACE THE LOST SMALL BEDROOM). THE NEW WALK-IN CLOSET IN THE MASTER BEDROOM IS TOO WIDE TO WASTE ON 2 RODS, TOO NARROW TO MAKE TWO FULL WALK-INS, THUS THE 3-ROD CLOSET WHERE THE CENTER ROD IS REACHED FROM EITHER SIDE.

REMODELED FIRST FLOOR PLAN

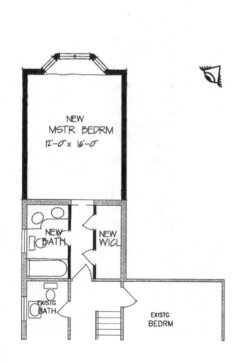

REMODELED SECOND FLOOR PLAN

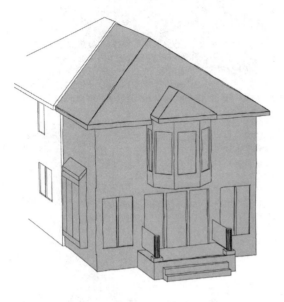

FBR03

A BRIGHT NEW SUNROOM AND A CLASSY NEW MASTER SUITE ARE THE SUBJECTS OF THIS 21'6"×13'10" TWO-STORY ADDITION. BOX BAY WINDOWS ON EITHER SIDE AND TRIPLE FRENCH DOORS FLANKED BY ADDITIONAL WINDOWS FLOOD THE SUNROOM WITH LIGHT, BUT DO SO WITH STYLE. THE MASTER SUITE INCLUDES A LOVELY WALK-IN ANGLED BAY, A LARGE WALK-IN CLOSET AND A NEW FASHIONED, COMPARTMENTED BATH WITH A PLATFORM TUB AND CURVED VANITY. ATTACHMENT OF SUCH AN ADDITION IS A MAJOR CONCERN, ESPECIALLY AS IT IMPACTS ON THE EXISTING ROOF. ALTHOUGH NOT MANDATORY, THIS PLAN SHOWS ATTACHMENT TO A WALL AT LEAST 4" LONGER ON EITHER SIDE. SUCH A 4"-OFFSET ALLOWS THE ADDITION TO BE INDEPENDENT OF THE EXISTING ROOF AND SIDEWALLS, MAKING THE MATCHING OF MATERIALS LESS OF A CONCERN.

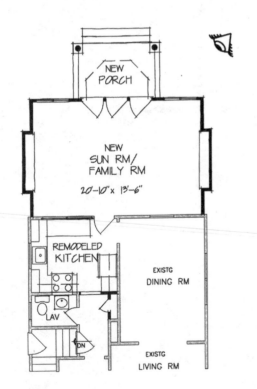

FIRST FLOOR PLAN

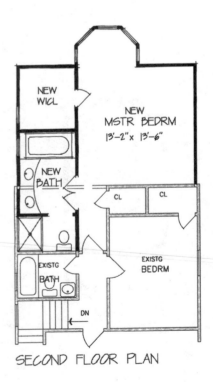

SECOND FLOOR PLAN

FBR04

A SENSATIONAL GREAT ROOM AND COMPACT MASTER SUITE ARE PROVIDED IN THIS 22′0″×13′10″ TWO-STORY ADDITION.   THE GREAT ROOM INCLUDES A FIREPLACE AND AN ADJACENT ALCOVE FOR A BUILT-IN MEDIA UNIT.   A GREENHOUSE ROOF IS INCLUDED AT ONE END, AND A FLOOR-TO-CEILING BAY AT THE OTHER END IS IDEALLY DESIGNED FOR TABLE SPACE—ESPECIALLY IF IT'S ADJACENT TO THE KITCHEN AS INDICATED IN THE SPECIFIC PLAN SHOWN.   THE ACCESS TO THE NEW MASTER SUITE FROM THE TOP OF THE STAIRS (COMMON IN MANY OLDER TWO-STORY HOMES) PROBABLY REQUIRES ONLY THE REMOVAL OF A WINDOW AT MOST. ATTACHMENT COULD BE TO MANY OTHER TWO-STORY HOMES AS WELL.

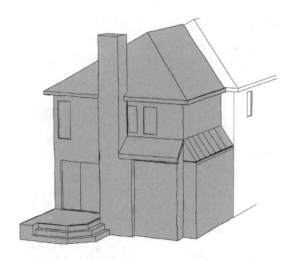

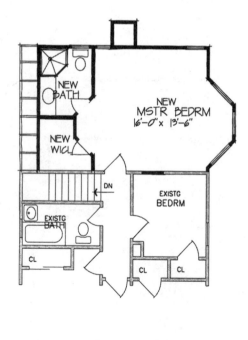

SECOND FLOOR PLAN

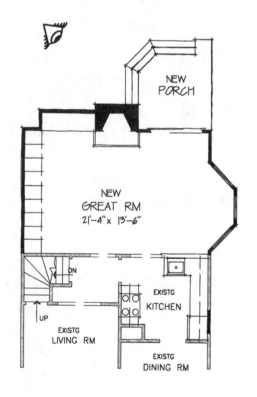

FIRST FLOOR PLAN

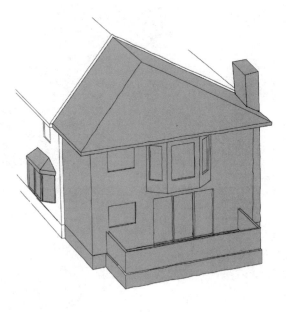

KFBRI

AN OLDER ONE-STORY KITCHEN WING IS REMOVED IN THIS DESIGN, AND IS REPLACED BY A 25'0"×12'0" STYLISH TWO-STORY ADDITION THAT CREATES A NEW KITCHEN AND FAMILY ROOM, PLUS A LOVELY NEW MASTER SUITE. THE NEW U-SHAPED KITCHEN IS A WORKING DELIGHT; A PENINSULA RETURN IS GREAT FOR SNACKS AND, WHILE SEPARATING THE KITCHEN, IT DOES NOT DISTURB THE VISUAL CONNECTION TO THE FAMILY ROOM. THIS PLAN COULD BE VIEWED AS TWO SEPARATE PLANS. IF WE LOVE THE NEW MASTER SUITE, BUT DON'T NEED A NEW FAMILY ROOM, THE BEDROOM CAN BE BUILT ALONE, EITHER AS A ONE-STORY ADDITION ON A FIRST FLOOR OR AS A SECOND FLOOR ADDITION OVER A PORCH (OR WHATEVER). SIMILARLY, THE NEW KITCHEN AND FAMILY ROOM COULD BE CONSTRUCTED AS A ONE-STORY ADDITION WITHOUT THE SECOND FLOOR.

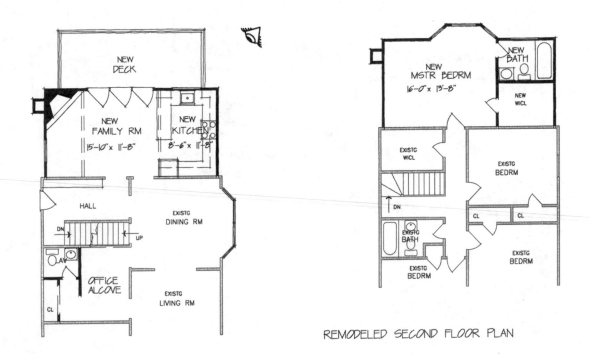

REMODELED FIRST FLOOR PLAN

REMODELED SECOND FLOOR PLAN

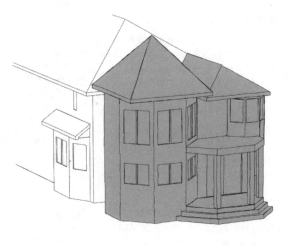

KFBR2

IF ANGLES TURN YOU ON, TAKE A HARD LOOK HERE. THIS PLAN CREATES A STUNNING OCTAGONALLY-SHAPED NEW MASTER BEDROOM ABOVE A FABULOUS OCTAGONAL KITCHEN. A COMPLEMENTARY OCTAGONALLY-SHAPED PLATFORM TUB IS THE FOCAL POINT OF THE MASTER BATH, AND THE OVERALL EFFECT IS CERTAINLY DISTINCTIVE. THIS TWO-STORY ADDITION COULD BE ATTACHED TO MANY TWO-STORY HOMES, BUT IS ESPECIALLY SUITED TO A CLASSIC OLDER HOME, WHERE SUCH FORMS ALREADY EXIST. IN THE PLAN SHOWN, THE ADDITION IS MARRIED TO THE REAR OF A NARROW, HIP-ROOFED, TWO-STORY. THE OLD KITCHEN IS REMOVED AND THE SPACE COMBINED WITH THE BREAKFAST AREA OF THE NEW ADDITION TO CREATE A LONG FAMILY ROOM. THE ADDITION ALSO INCLUDES AN ATTRACTIVE COVERED PORCH.

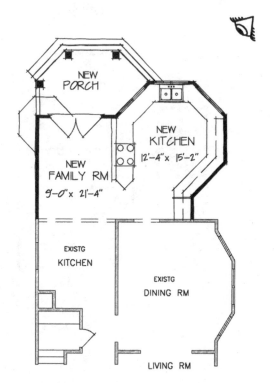

REMODELED FIRST FLOOR PLAN

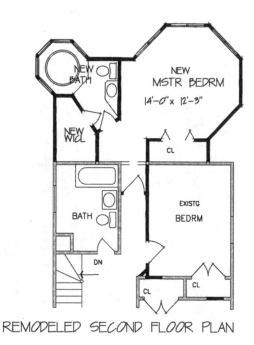

REMODELED SECOND FLOOR PLAN

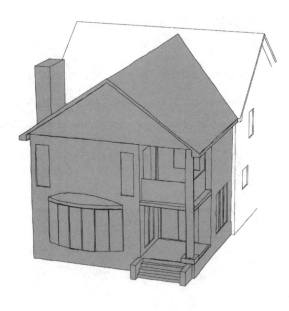

KFBR3

A LUXURIOUS NEW FAMILY ROOM AND NEW BREAKFAST ROOM ARE CROWNED BY A FABULOUS MASTER SUITE IN THIS 25'0"×18'4" TWO-STORY ADDITION. FIREPLACES AND COVERED DECKS ARE INCLUDED ON BOTH FLOORS, AS ARE AN ABUNDANCE OF WINDOWS AND GLASS; FRENCH DOORS CONNECT TO BOTH DECKS. THE COMPARTMENTED MASTER BATH WITH ITS WHIRLPOOL TUB AND SEPARATE SHOWER, PLUS TWO WALK-IN CLOSETS, ADD TO THE LUXURIOUS QUALITY OF THIS ADDITION. ALTHOUGH SUITED TO ATTACHMENT TO VIRTUALLY ANY TWO-STORY, THE REVISIONS SHOWN TO THE SPECIFIC 30'0" WIDE TWO-STORY PLAN INCLUDE A REMODELED KITCHEN, A POSSIBLE NEW POWDER ROOM AND A SMALLER REMODELED SECOND FLOOR HALL BATH. ACCESS TO THE NEW MASTER SUITE IS FLEXIBLE DEPENDING UPON YOUR HOME.

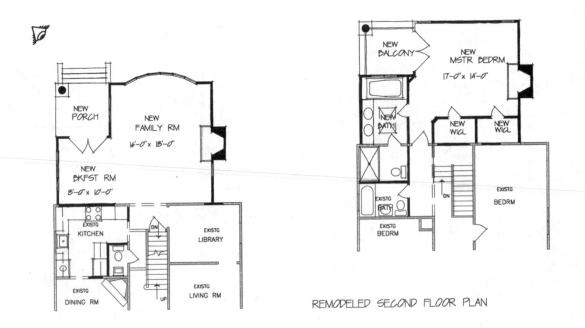

REMODELED FIRST FLOOR PLAN

REMODELED SECOND FLOOR PLAN

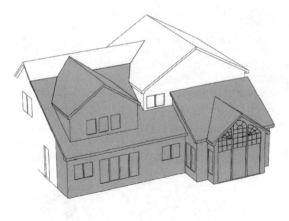

KFBR5

DESIGNING EXPANSIONS TO TWO-STORY HOMES CAN BE INFINITELY COMPLEX, AND PARTICULARLY SO WHEN THE ADDITION IS PRIMARILY A ONE-STORY EXPANSION. THE DESIGNER MUST BE CONCERNED WITH HOW ROOFLINES INTERSECT THE TWO-STORY, HOW THEY AFFECT SECOND FLOOR WINDOWS, HOW THE VOLUME CAN BE USED ADVANTAGEOUSLY ON THE SECOND FLOOR, AND EVEN MORE IMPORTANT, FROM MY POINT OF VIEW, HOW IT ALL LOOKS AND FEELS. THE PLAN ON THIS PAGE EXPANDS A VERY DATED REAR KITCHEN AND BREAKFAST ROOM, ADDS A MISSING FAMILY ROOM AND A FIRST FLOOR LAUNDRY ROOM, AND TURNS AN ORDINARY SECOND FLOOR BEDROOM INTO A MARVELOUS NEW MASTER SUITE. WHAT'S MORE, IT DOES IT CREATIVELY AND WITH STYLE. THE NEW ADDITION FUNCTIONS WELL, LOOKS EVEN BETTER, AND WILL LIKELY BE A SOLID INVESTMENT WITH EXCELLENT RETURN POTENTIAL.

EXISTING FIRST FLOOR PLAN   PLAN# KFBR5

EXISTING SECOND FLOOR PLAN

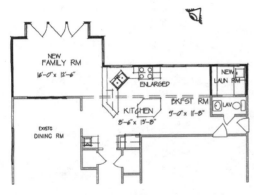

REMODELED FIRST FLOOR PLAN

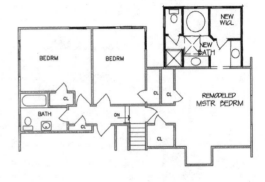

REMODELED SECOND FLOOR PLAN

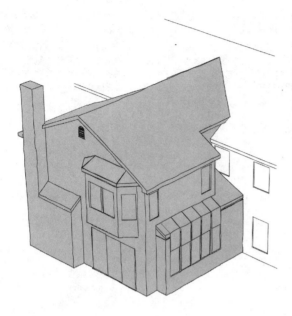

FBR06

THIS FABULOUS TWO-STORY ADDITION PROVIDES YOU WITH A WONDERFUL NEW FAMILY ROOM ON ITS FIRST FLOOR AND A DRAMATIC NEW MASTER BEDROOM SUITE ABOVE. THE PLAN IS DIFFERENT, NOT ONLY IN ITS DISTINCTIVE ARCHITECTURAL STYLING, BUT ALSO WITH THE INCLUSION OF ITS OWN STAIR TO THE SECOND FLOOR. THIS STAIR ENABLES EASE OF CONNECTION, SINCE NO SECOND FLOOR ACCESS IS NEEDED (UNLESS YOU DESIRE IT). THE PLAN IS ALSO VERY FLEXIBLE REGARDING THE LOCATION AND STYLE OF HOME IT ATTACHES TO. FURTHERMORE, THE DESIGN OF THE NEW SECOND FLOOR HAS BEEN CAREFULLY PLANNED TO REDUCE ITS IMPACT ON EXISTING WINDOWS. THE NUANCES OF THE DESIGN ARE JUST LOVELY—STUDY THEM ALL.

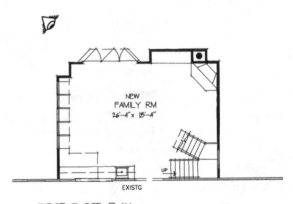

NEW
FAMILY RM
26'-4" x 18'-4"

UP

EXISTG

FIRST FLOOR PLAN

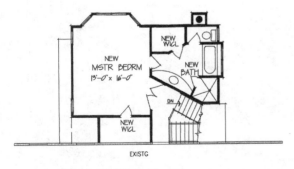

NEW
MSTR BEDRM
13'-0" x 16'-0"

NEW
WICL

NEW
BATH

DN

NEW
WICL

EXISTG

SECOND FLOOR PLAN

FBRIO

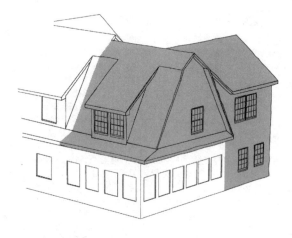

THIS EXPANSIVE TWO-STORY ADDITION SHOWS A VERY SPECIFIC ROOF TYPE—A GAMBREL ROOF. THE GAMBREL IS A VERY SPECIAL ROOF SHAPE AND YOU WOULD CONSIDER USING IT IF THE EXISTING HOUSE HAD A GAMBREL ROOF BEYOND. IN THE EXISTING HOUSE, THE DEN WING AT THE RIGHT IS A CONVERTED PORCH—A COMMON OCCURRENCE IN OLDER HOMES, WHERE YOU OFTEN FIND A PORCH CONVERTED TO LIVING SPACE. ADDING OVER IT REQUIRES CAREFUL ANALYSIS TO MAKE CERTAIN THE FOUNDATION AND SUPERSTRUCTURE CAN PROPERLY SUPPORT A SECOND FLOOR. SOMETIMES IT MAY BE NECESSARY TO REBUILD SOME OF THE FOUNDATION AND FLOOR STRUCTURE BEFORE ADDING A SECOND FLOOR.

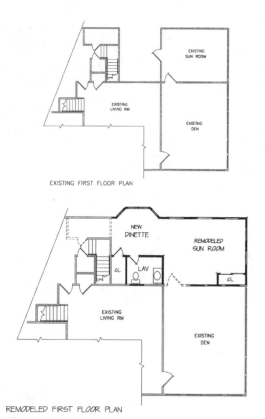

EXISTING FIRST FLOOR PLAN

EXISTING SECOND FLOOR PLAN

REMODELED FIRST FLOOR PLAN

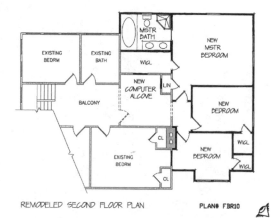

REMODELED SECOND FLOOR PLAN   PLAN# FBR10

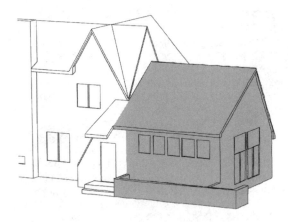

FBR09

CERTAIN STYLES OF HOMES PRESENT MORE OF A PROBLEM—AND A CHALLENGE—IN DESIGNING AN ADDITION. THE TUDOR TWO-STORY, WITH ITS STEEP ROOFLINES AND PROTRUDING CORNER VESTIBULE, POSES A SERIOUS ARCHITECTURAL CONCERN, IF YOU ARE CONSIDERING AN ATTACHMENT ALONGSIDE. THE ADDITION SHOWN HERE PROVIDES A WONDERFUL NEW FAMILY ROOM—OR BEDROOM—PLUS A FULL BATH, BUT WHAT IS EVEN MORE APPEALING IS ITS BEAUTIFUL INTEGRATION INTO THE EXISTING FRONT FAÇADE. THE NEW ROOM IS AN EXCITING SPACE WITH WINDOWS ON THREE SIDES, INCLUDING HIGH FRONT WINDOWS, UNDER WHICH YOU CAN INSTALL A WALL OF BUILT-INS. THERE IS ALSO A VAULTED CEILING AND A SKYLIGHT. THE NEW ROOFLINE MERGES WITH THE EXISTING AND EVEN ADDS A 3' OVERHANG AT THE FRONT DOOR.

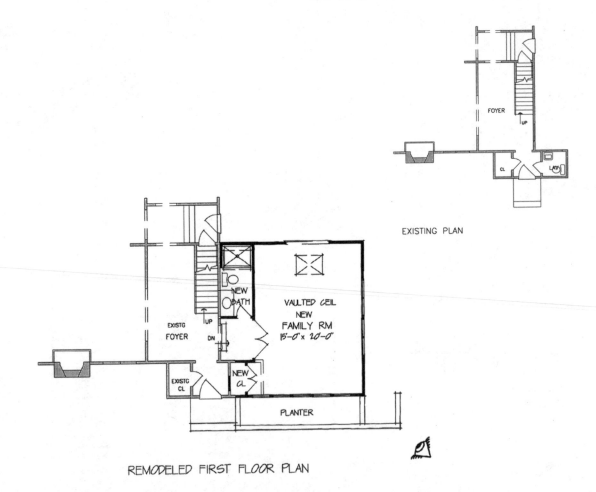

EXISTING PLAN

REMODELED FIRST FLOOR PLAN

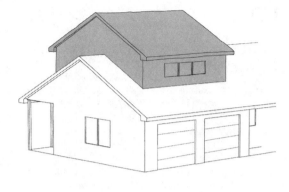

FBR07

THIS IS ONE OF SEVERAL DESIGNS THAT MAKES USE OF THE FOUND SPACE OVER A GARAGE. ADDITIONAL BEDROOMS OR APARTMENTS ARE THE SUBJECT OF THE OTHER PLANS; THIS ONE PROVIDES FOR A LARGE PLAYROOM, BUT IT TOO COULD BE TURNED INTO A BEDROOM. THIS PARTICULAR PLAN IS ESPECIALLY DESIGNED FOR THE ROOFLINE OF A ONE-STORY HOME. IN ADDING OVER A GARAGE IN A ONE-STORY HOME, ONE HAS TO BE CAREFUL NOT TO LET THE TWO-STORY ELEMENT APPEAR TOO BULKY OR TOO HIGH. THE SOLUTION IS TO SET IT BACK FROM ALL SIDES AND TO WRAP IT IN ROOF, IN ORDER TO GIVE IT THE APPEARANCE OF A DORMER. THE NEW STAIR TO THE PLAYROOM IS SHOWN ENTERING FROM A FAMILY ROOM OR BREAKFAST ROOM, BUT THE CONNECTION COULD ALSO BE FROM OTHER ROOMS, DEPENDING ON YOUR HOME.

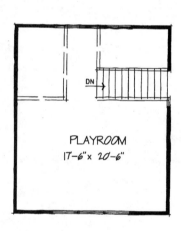

PLAYROOM
17-6" x 20-6"

SECOND FLOOR PLAN
ALL NEW

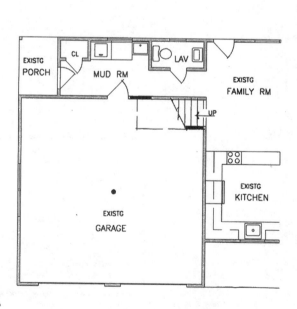

REMODELED FIRST FLOOR PLAN

F0010

A 35' TO 40'-DEEP ONE-STORY HOME USUALLY PROVIDES THE NECESSARY HEIGHT IN ITS EXISTING ROOFLINE TO ENABLE YOU TO ADD A PARTIAL SECOND FLOOR ADDITION THAT WILL APPEAR ATTRACTIVE. IN THE HIP-ROOFED VERSION PICTURED, A LARGE SECOND FLOOR PLAYROOM IS ADDED AT THE MIDDLE PART OF THE REAR OF THE HOME. IT HAS MINIMAL IMPACT ON THE FRONT FAÇADE AND LOOKS QUITE NICE IN THE REAR. NOTE THAT IT IS SET BACK FROM THE FIRST FLOOR WALL—AN IMPORTANT DESIGN ELEMENT IN SUCH AN ADDITION— TO PERMIT THE ROOFLINE TO REMAIN UNBROKEN. A NEW STAIRCASE IS PROVIDED AT THE FRONT OF THE FAMILY ROOM, AND IT REMAINS OPEN AT BOTH FLOORS TO ALLOW FOR A SPATIAL CONNECTION.

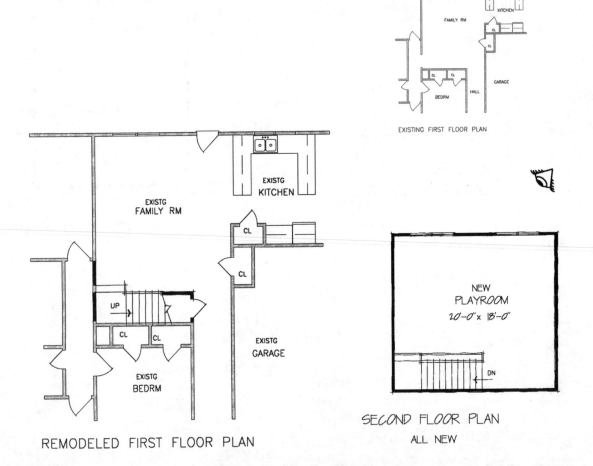

EXISTING FIRST FLOOR PLAN

REMODELED FIRST FLOOR PLAN

SECOND FLOOR PLAN
ALL NEW

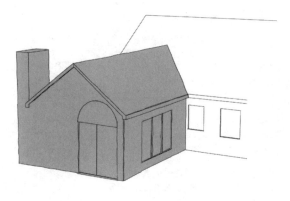

F0004

NEED A FAMILY ROOM? IS THE ONLY PLACE TO ATTACH IT AT THE REAR OF YOUR KITCHEN? THIS PLAN SHOWS YOU HOW TO DO JUST THAT. ATTACHMENT TO THE KITCHEN MEANS A POTENTIAL LOSS OF LIGHT TO THE KITCHEN, THEREFORE THE NEED TO VISUALLY OPEN IT TO THE FAMILY ROOM. A WIDE COUNTER, WHICH SERVES BOTH AS A PASS-THROUGH AND AS A SNACK COUNTER IS AN EXCELLENT IDEA. IT'S ALSO A GOOD PLACE FOR THE SINK, AS THIS PART OF THE KITCHEN WILL BENEFIT MOST FROM BORROWED LIGHT FROM THE NEW FAMILY ROOM. THE FAMILY ROOM SHOWN INCLUDES A VAULTED CEILING, SKYLIGHTS, AND A CORNER FIREPLACE. IF YOU PREFER A CENTERED FIREPLACE, SEE PLAN F0001 ON PAGE 156. ALSO, ALTERNATE ROOFLINES ARE READILY AVAILABLE BY REFERRING TO THE BLOCKFORMS NOTED IN CHAPTER 6.

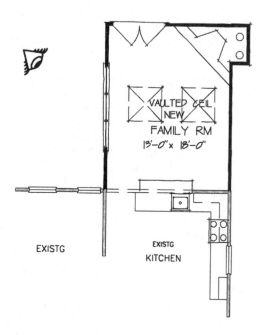

VAULTED CEIL
NEW
FAMILY RM
13'-0" x 18'-0"

EXISTG

EXISTG
KITCHEN

REMODELED FIRST FLOOR PLAN

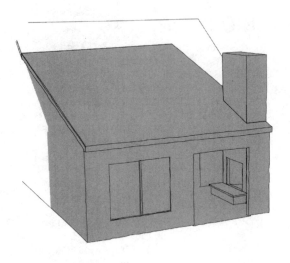

F0003

FAMILY ROOMS ARE AVAILABLE IN ALL SHAPES AND FORMS TO ACCOMMODATE VARYING DESIRES, OR LOT CONSTRAINTS OR EXISTING HOMES.   THIS 17'8"×12'4" ADDITION TURNS A NEW FAMILY ROOM ADDITION LENGTHWISE AND IS SUGGESTIVE OF A SHED ROOF AS SHOWN.   THIS LENGTHWISE ADDITION MAY ELIMINATE WINDOWS IN MORE THAN ONE ROOM; IN THE PLAN INDICATED, THE ATTACHMENT IS TO THE REAR OF A KITCHEN AND BATH.   SINCE THE DESIGN GOAL IS TO VISUALLY INTEGRATE THE NEW FAMILY ROOM WITH THE KITCHEN, A WIDE PASS-THROUGH, WHICH CAN DOUBLE AS A SERVING OR SNACK COUNTER, IS SUGGESTED.   THIS, THEN, FURTHER SUGGESTS THAT THE SINK BE LOCATED HERE, AS THE RANGE OR REFRIGERATOR ARE NOT SUITED TO A PASS-THROUGH LOCATION.

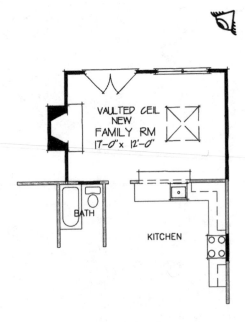

VAULTED CEIL
NEW
FAMILY RM
17'-0" x 12'-0"

BATH

KITCHEN

REMODELED FIRST FLOOR PLAN

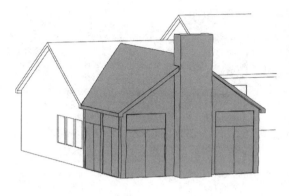

F0006

A FABULOUS NEW GREAT ROOM, 21'6"×14'4", IS THE SUBJECT OF THIS ROOM ADDITION. IT IS SHOWN ATTACHED TO THE REAR KITCHEN AND ADJOINING DINING ROOM OF A MODEST SPLIT-LEVEL; HOWEVER, IT COULD ATTACH TO ALMOST ANY STYLE OR TYPE OF HOME. WHETHER IT'S A ONE OR TWO-STORY, OR A SPLIT-LEVEL, AS SHOWN, THE NEW ROOM IS A STUNNING SPACE. IT BOASTS SIX SETS OF SLIDING GLASS DOORS THAT WRAP AROUND ALL THREE SIDES, A CENTERED FIREPLACE AND A DRAMATIC VAULTED CEILING. WHEN ADDED AS SHOWN, IT IS SUGGESTED THAT THE EXISTING REAR WALL OF THE DINING ROOM BE REMOVED; THE NEW SPACE WILL NOW VISUALLY MERGE WITH THE EXISTING ROOMS, ENHANCING THEIR CAPABILITY TO FUNCTION AS ONE CONTINUOUS SPACE.

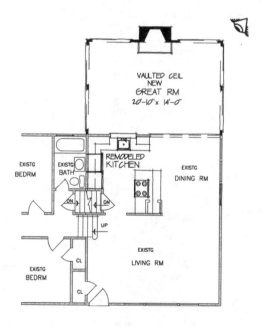

REMODELED FIRST FLOOR PLAN

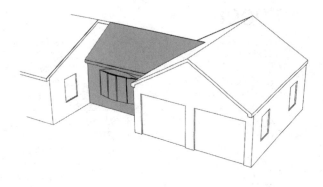

F0002

THE BREEZEWAY WAS A VERY COMMON
FEATURE OF HOMES BUILT 30 TO 40 YEARS
AGO. OVER THIS PERIOD, MANY HAVE BEEN
CONVERTED TO LIVING SPACE, THE MOST
COMMON USE BEING THAT OF A FAMILY ROOM.
IF IT EXISTS IN THE SUBJECT HOUSE, IT IS
SPACE WAITING TO BE CLAIMED FOR BETTER
USE. OTHER IDEAS TO CONSIDER INCLUDE A
SUN PORCH, GUEST BEDROOM OR EVEN A NEW
MASTER SUITE, WHICH WOULD REQUIRE ADDING
SPACE AS WELL (SEE PLAN NO. PBR03 ON
PAGE 122). THE BREEZEWAY OFTEN DISJOINED
THE GARAGE BY USING A DIFFERENT TYPE OF
ROOF THEN ON THE HOME; WHEN CONVERTING
IT TO LIVING AREA I RECOMMEND INSTALLING A
NEW ROOF, SUCH AS THE GABLE ROOF SHOWN,
TO TIE THE ELEMENTS TOGETHER.

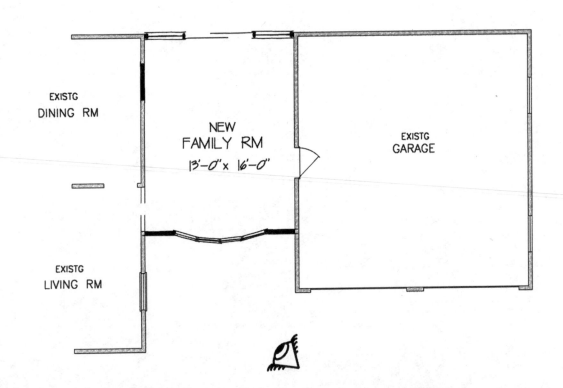

EXISTG
DINING RM

NEW
FAMILY RM
13'-0" x 16'-0"

EXISTG
GARAGE

EXISTG
LIVING RM

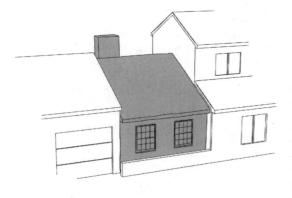

FOO16

THIS PLAN PROVIDES AN ENCLOSURE TO AN EXISTING UNROOFED BREEZEWAY THAT IS LOCATED BETWEEN THE HOUSE AND THE GARAGE. THE ROOM IS SHOWN AS A PROPOSED FAMILY ROOM, ALTHOUGH IT COULD BE WHATEVER YOU WANT. AS A FAMILY ROOM, IT IS DESIGNED TO FURNISH AROUND A REAR WALL THAT INCLUDES A FIREPLACE FLANKED BY FRENCH DOORS. THE EXISTING DOOR TO THE GARAGE DOESN'T DISTURB THE FURNISHABILITY OF THE ROOM BECAUSE IT IS LOCATED AT THE VERY FRONT. THE SIZE OF THE OPENING TO BE MADE TO CONNECT TO THE EXISTING HOUSE IS A FUNCTION OF THE ROOM WE ARE CONNECTING TO AND ITS FURNISHABILITY. NOTE THAT THE NEW ROOF OVER THE BREEZEWAY IS INTENTIONALLY DESIGNED SO AS NOT TO BE FLUSH WITH EITHER ROOF ON EACH SIDE; IF THE ROOF SHINGLES ARE A GOOD MATCH, THIS COULD SAVE HAVING TO REROOF THE ENTIRE HOUSE.

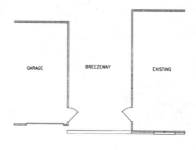

EXISTING FLOOR PLAN

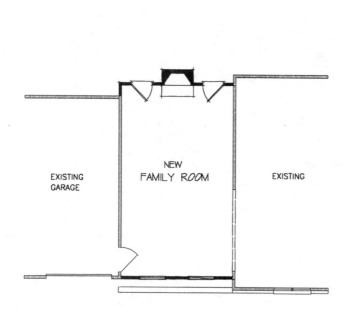

EXISTING GARAGE   NEW FAMILY ROOM   EXISTING

REMODELED FLOOR PLAN

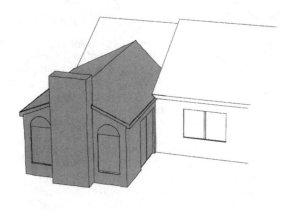

FOOOI

A COMMON EXISTING CONDITION: A LITTLE USED PATIO SLAB BEHIND A GARAGE THAT ADJOINS AN L-SHAPED LIVING AND DINING ROOM. A COMMON NEED: A FAMILY ROOM. THE SOLUTION: REMOVE THE PATIO (OR PORCH, IF ONE EXISTS) AND CONSTRUCT AN INVITING, REVERSE GABLE, FAMILY ROOM ADDITION. THE ROOFLINE MAY NEED A CRICKET, BUT THAT'S O.K. THE CENTERED FIREPLACE, FLANKED BY TALL, CIRCULAR-CAPPED WINDOWS, ALL UNDER A VAULTED CEILING WILL CREATE A VERY MODISH, YET TASTEFUL INTERIOR SPACE. SUGGESTION: OPEN THE CONNECTION TO THE EXISTING HOUSE AS WIDE AS POSSIBLE TO VISUALLY CONNECT THE NEW FAMILY ROOM.

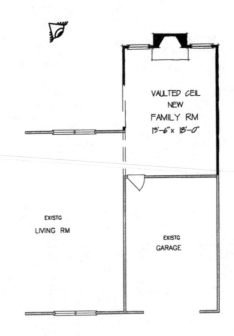

REMODELED FIRST FLOOR PLAN

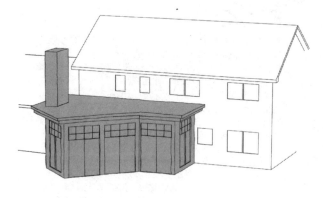

F0008

THERE ARE TIMES WHEN CONDITIONS DICTATE AN ATYPICAL SOLUTION. FOR THE STRIKING NEW FAMILY ROOM PICTURED HERE, IT MIGHT HAVE BEEN A LIMITING REAR YARD (SWIMMING POOL OR HILL AT ONE SIDE) OR A DESIRABLE ORIENTATION. HOWEVER, BEYOND THESE THERE MUST ALSO BE A WILLINGNESS TO BE DIFFERENT AND UNIQUE. THIS MODERN FAMILY ROOM WORKS EXCEEDINGLY WELL WITH THE KITCHEN—AND THE ENTIRE HOUSE IT IS ATTACHED TO—BUT IT CLEARLY DOES NOT TRY TO MIMIC THE FORMS OF THE EXISTING HOME. THE ROOM FEATURES A HIGH CEILING, A FIREPLACE AND A WALL FOR BUILT-INS; THE KITCHEN IS COMPLETELY REMODELED AND OPENED TO THE NEW FAMILY ROOM WITH A HIGH SNACK COUNTER SEPARATING THE TWO.

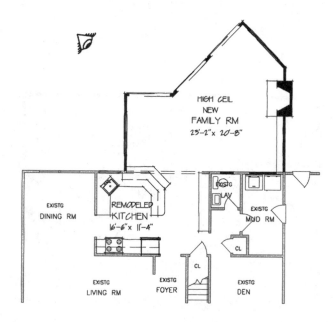

REMODELED FIRST FLOOR PLAN

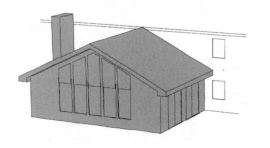

F0012

IF YOUR DEMANDS INCLUDE A LARGE CONTEMPORARY
FAMILY ROOM, YOU SHOULD STUDY THIS DESIGN.
ENCLOSED WITHIN ITS WALLS IS A 30'×20' SPACE
DOMINATED BY A HIGH, VAULTED CEILING, FOUR
LARGE SKYLIGHTS, A FIREPLACE WALL FLANKED BY
BUILT-INS AND A STUNNING PANORAMA OF GLASS.
TWO SETS OF SLIDING DOORS AT ONE SIDE AND A
DRAMATIC WINDOW WALL ON THE GABLE END BATHE
THE ROOM IN NATURAL LIGHT. THIS IS ONE OF
THOSE DESIGNS THAT IS NOT SPECIFIC TO ANY
GIVEN EXISTING HOUSE, BUT WHICH YOU CAN READILY
ATTACH TO ALMOST ANY ONE OR TWO-STORY HOME.
THE PLANS CAN BE READILY ADJUSTED IN SIZE, AS
REQUIRED, AND CAN BE ADAPTED TO THE
REQUIREMENTS OF ANY SPECIFIC ATTACHMENT.

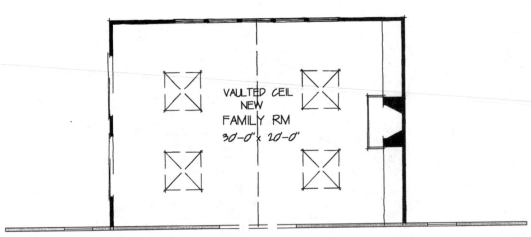

VAULTED CEIL
NEW
FAMILY RM
30'-0" x 20'-0"

EXISTG
HOUSE

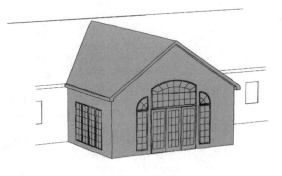

F0015

SOME PLANS IN THIS BOOK ARE VERY SPECIFIC TO CERTAIN EXISTING HOMES. OTHERS, LIKE THE ADDITION PICTURED, ARE GENERIC, AND ARE READILY ADAPTABLE TO MANY HOMES. ONE OF THE MOST COMMON ROOMS ADDED TODAY IS A NEW FAMILY ROOM—OR GREAT ROOM. THE PLAN SHOWN IS A 22'×14' ADDITION THAT CREATES A SPECTACULAR NEW SPACE. THE ROOM INCLUDES A VAULTED CEILING AND A FABULOUS REAR WINDOW WALL THAT MAKES THE ROOM. THIS PLAN, LIKE ALL OF THE PLANS, IS LOCATED ON THE CAD DISK AND IS READILY STRETCHED OR MODIFIED IN YOUR CAD PROGRAM. WINDOWS COULD ALSO BE CHANGED TO SUIT YOUR PREFERENCE, IF DESIRED, AND THE CONNECTION TO THE HOME ADJUSTED TO SATISFY YOUR SPECIFIC CONDITION.

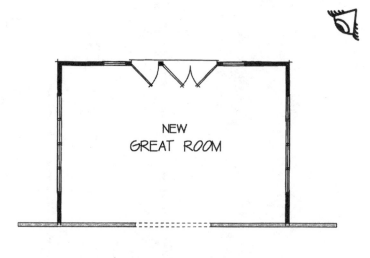

NEW
GREAT ROOM

EXISTING

REMODELED FLOOR PLAN

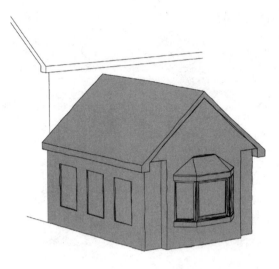

FOOI7

THIS IS ANOTHER IN THE SERIES OF GENERIC ROOM
ADDITIONS THAT CAN BE ADDED TO ALMOST ANY
HOME. THE SUBJECT IS A 14'×21' FAMILY ROOM
WITH A SINGLE CONNECTION TO THE EXISTING HOME.
THE FAR END OF THE ROOM FEATURES AN
ATTRACTIVE BAY WINDOW WITH A BUILT-IN SEAT.
FRENCH DOORS FROM ONE SIDE PROVIDE ACCESS TO
A REAR PATIO OR DECK. THE ROOF OVER THIS
ADDITION IS BEST AS THE REVERSE GABLE PICTURED,
WHICH ALLOWS IT TO BE EASILY CONNECTED TO
MOST ONE AND TWO-STORY HOMES. IF YOU ARE
CONNECTING TO THE REAR OF A TWO-STORY HOME,
EXISTING WINDOW LOCATIONS ON THE SECOND
FLOOR WALL COULD BECOME AN OBSTACLE TO
BUILDING THIS SHAPE.

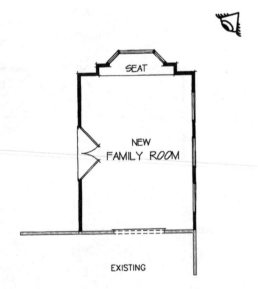

REMODELED FLOOR PLAN

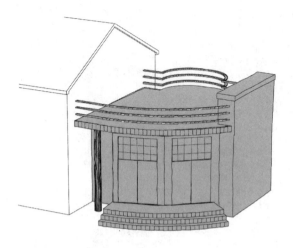

F0014

THIS IS A DESIGN FOR THOSE WHO DARE TO BE DIFFERENT. IT IS A VERY MODERN FAMILY ROOM OF GRAND PROPORTIONS THAT IS NOT INTENDED TO MIRROR THE EXISTING ARCHITECTURE OF YOUR HOME. IT IS DESIGNED WITH A FLAT ROOF WHICH REQUIRES THAT THE CONNECTION BE AN EXISTING WALL HIGHER THAN THE NEW ROOF; THIS COULD BE THE SIDE OR REAR OF ANY TWO-STORY. ALTHOUGH THE FORM OF THIS ADDITION MAY DEPART FROM EXISTING STYLE, IT IS IMPORTANT THAT MATERIALS BLEND AND UNITE WITH THE EXISTING HOME. THE ROOM FEATURES A BEAUTIFUL SEMI-CIRCULAR SEATING ALCOVE, A WALL FOR A FIREPLACE AND BUILT-INS, PLUS AN EXHILARATING 11'-HIGH CEILING THROUGHOUT.

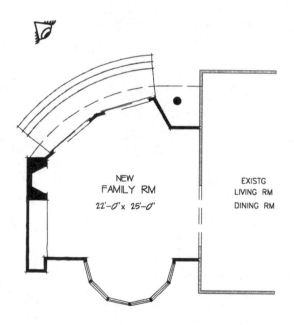

REMODELED FIRST FLOOR PLAN

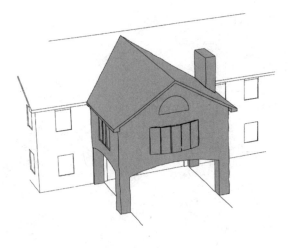

F0011

IS THE PLACE YOU ARE CONSIDERING ADDING A NEW FAMILY ROOM SITUATED ABOVE AN EXISTING LOWER LEVEL DRIVEWAY? IF SO, LOOK HERE. WHETHER IT IS THE SIDE OR REAR—OR EVEN THE FRONT—OF YOUR HOME, THIS BEAUTIFUL DESIGN SHOWS YOU HOW TO ADD A NICE SIZED ROOM, COMPLETE WITH ALL THE DESIRED FEATURES OF A FAMILY ROOM, WITHOUT DISTURBING THE REQUIRED ACCESS TO YOUR GARAGE. THE NEW ROOM POSSESSES BOTH A LOVELY EXTERIOR AND INTERIOR CHARACTER, INCLUDING A BOW WINDOW, A VAULTED CEILING, AND A BUILT-IN FIREPLACE WITH RECESSED LOCATIONS FOR MEDIA EQUIPMENT ON EACH SIDE. THE FIREPLACE, OF COURSE, WOULD BE A PREFAB VARIETY. SKYLIGHTS ADD NATURAL LIGHT.

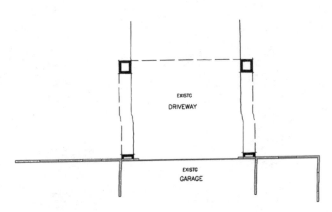

EXISTG
DRIVEWAY

EXISTG
GARAGE

LOWER LEVEL PLAN

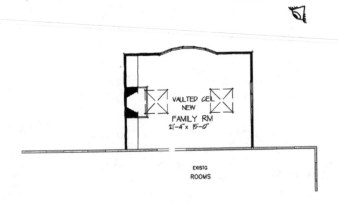

VAULTED CEIL
NEW
FAMILY RM
21'-4" x 15'-0"

EXISTG
ROOMS

UPPER LEVEL PLAN

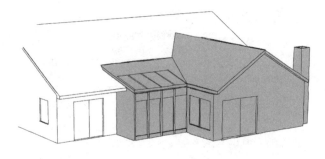

FD001

THIS HANDSOME LOOKING 21'0"×13'4" FAMILY ROOM ADDITION ALSO SHOWS A 5'6" DEEP GREENHOUSE ADDITION TO AN ADJACENT DINING ROOM.   HOWEVER, BOTH ADDITIONS ARE SEPARATE AND COULD BE ACCOMPLISHED INDEPENDENTLY.   THE STUNNING FAMILY ROOM EMPHASIZES NATURAL LIGHT WITH WRAP-AROUND CORNER WINDOWS AND SLIDING DOORS, PLUS TWO SKYLIGHTS.   THE ROOM IS DESIGNED WITH A VAULTED CEILING AND A DRAMATIC CORNER FIREPLACE, AND IS SHOWN A STEP DOWN FROM THE ADJACENT KITCHEN. IT IS SUGGESTED THAT THE EXISTING REAR WALL OF THE KITCHEN BE REMOVED AND REPLACED WITH A LOW WALL.   THE DINING ROOM IS SHOWN ENLARGED BY THE FOUR-BAY GREENHOUSE, WHICH MAKES FOR A VERY CHIC ADDITION.

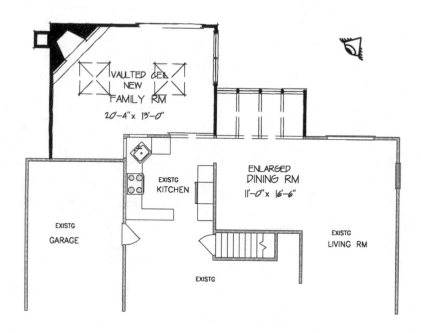

REMODELED FIRST FLOOR PLAN

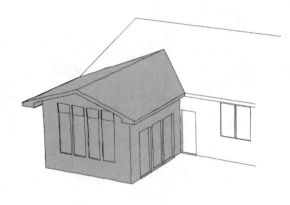

KF003

THIS FASHIONABLE 14'8"×14'4" FAMILY ROOM ADDITION CAN STAND BY ITSELF AS A SMART ADDITION—OR IF COMBINED WITH AN ADJACENT REMODELED KITCHEN, AS SHOWN, IT WILL BECOME A SPLASH.   THE FAMILY ROOM BOASTS A 10'-HIGH CEILING AND LOTS OF GLASS, INCLUDING HIGH, TRANSOMED WINDOWS AND FRENCH DOORS TO THE PATIO AREA.   THE FAMILY ROOM TIES TO AN EXISTING KITCHEN BY WAY OF A SPLIT STAIRWAY THAT LEADS TO THE OUTSIDE, AS WELL AS THE BASEMENT—A COMMON CONDITION IN MANY HOMES.   THIS ALLOWS THE HIGH CEILING, WHILE MAINTAINING THE SAME ROOFLINE.   THE REMODELED KITCHEN, OPEN TO THE FAMILY ROOM, WITH ITS ANGLED SERVING/SNACK TOP AND THE BALCONIED BREAKFAST AREA, MAKES THE ENTIRE SPACE A GORGEOUS RENOVATION.

EXISTING PLAN

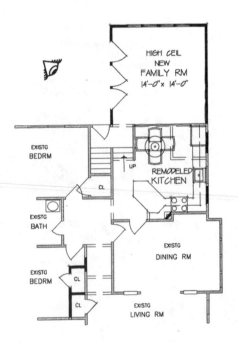

REMODELED FIRST FLOOR PLAN

KFOI4

THE EXISTING BREEZEWAY BETWEEN THE KITCHEN AND GARAGE IN THIS TWO-STORY HOME MAKES FOR AN IDEAL LOCATION FOR A NEW FAMILY ROOM; HOWEVER, IF WE DID NOT ALSO REDO THE KITCHEN, THERE WOULD BE VERY LITTLE VISUAL CONNECTION BETWEEN THE TWO ROOMS. BY REVERSING THE KITCHEN AND BREAKFAST ROOM WE ARE ABLE TO OPEN THE NEW FAMILY ROOM SIGNIFICANTLY MORE TO THE KITCHEN. THE NEW BAY ROOF BUMP-OUT FOR THE BREAKFAST ROOM IS BOTH FUNCTIONAL AND AN ATTRACTIVE CONNECTING ELEMENT BETWEEN THE NEW FAMILY ROOM AND THE REMODELED KITCHEN. THIS BAY PROVIDES THAT EXTRA LITTLE BIT OF SPACE NEEDED TO MAKE THE ENTIRE PLAN WORK.

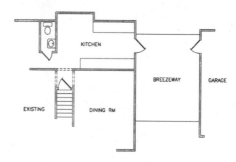

EXISTING FLOOR PLAN

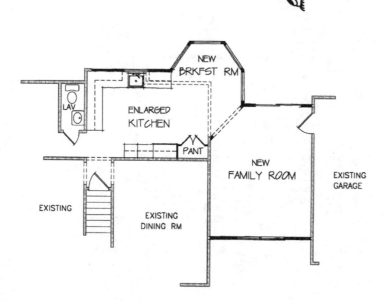

REMODELED FLOOR PLAN

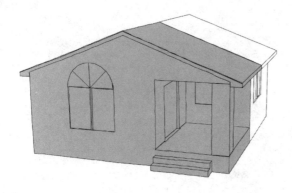

KF002

A GREAT ROOM (OR FAMILY ROOM) WITH A VAULTED
CEILING AND A LOVELY COVERED PORCH RESULT
FROM THIS 25'6"×12'4" ONE-STORY ADDITION. IF
MARRIED TO THE REAR OF A GABLED COTTAGE, AS
SHOWN, THE ROOFS WOULD ALIGN, RESULTING IN THE
LIKELY NEED FOR AN ENTIRE NEW ROOF. BUT THIS
SAME ADDITION IS EASILY ATTACHED TO A REVERSE
GABLE ROOF OR TWO-STORY WALL, AS WELL. THE
ADDITION IS MAINTAINED AT THE SAME LEVEL AS THE
HOME, NOT DOWN THE 3 OR 4 STEPS, AS IN SOME
OTHER PLANS IN THE BOOK. IF IT ADJOINS A
KITCHEN, AS SHOWN, THE KITCHEN WALL SHOULD BE
OPENED TO VISUALLY ENHANCE BOTH ROOMS. THE
SIDE BAY CREATES A DELIGHTFUL TABLE SPACE, IF
THAT'S IN YOUR PROGRAM.

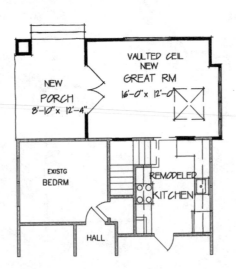

REMODELED FIRST FLOOR PLAN

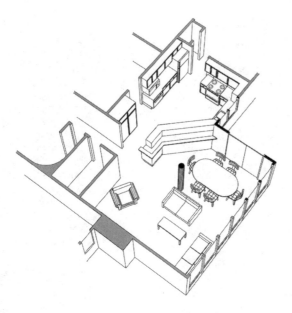

KF008

TWENTY YEARS AGO THIS WAS A TOP-SELLING FAMILY ROOM AND KITCHEN, AND TO MANY, ESPECIALLY IF ONE IS COMING FROM A SMALL HOME, THAT STILL MAY BE SO. BUT, IF THE OWNERS HAVE LIVED WITH IT FOR TWENTY YEARS, THEY MAY BE DREAMING OF A FASHIONABLE NEW FAMILY-LIVING CENTER THAT INTEGRATES THE KITCHEN AND FAMILY ROOM. THIS PLAN ACCOMPLISHES THAT WITH STYLE. AN 8'4"×10'0" ADDITION TO THE SIDE OF THE FAMILY ROOM PROVIDES A NEW BRIGHT, SUNNY SPACE FOR A TABLE. WALLS ARE REMOVED AND THE ENTIRE AREA IS VISUALLY CONNECTED. THE NEW EXPANDED KITCHEN IS OPENED TO THE FAMILY ROOM, WHERE A DRAMATIC ANGLED SERVING AND SNACK COUNTER IS LOCATED.

EXISTING PLAN

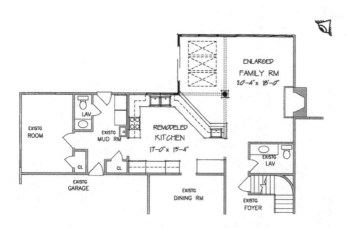

REMODELED FIRST FLOOR PLAN

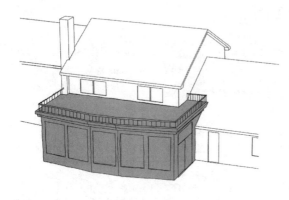

KF009

THIS IMPRESSIVE, FLAT-ROOFED, FAMILY ROOM ADDITION IS BOTH STUNNING TO LOOK AT AND DRAMATIC TO LIVE IN. IT HELPS CREATE AN EXTRAORDINARY FAMILY LIVING CENTER FROM A NICE, BUT ORDINARY, FAMILY ROOM AND KITCHEN FOUND IN A TYPICAL TWO-STORY. THE BOW-SHAPED ADDITION ENCOMPASSES THE WIDTH OF BOTH ROOMS; THE INTERNAL DIVIDING WALLS AND OLD EXTERIOR WALLS ARE REMOVED, CREATING AN OVERALL SPACE THAT MEASURES 29'4"×27'4", WHICH IS A STATEMENT IN ITSELF. THE LUXURIOUS NEW KITCHEN FEATURES A LARGE CENTER ISLAND AND AN ABUNDANCE OF STORAGE. IT IS VISUALLY PART OF THE FAMILY ROOM, WHICH INCLUDES A HIGH CEILING, FIVE SKYLIGHTS AND A HANDSOME WINDOW WALL.

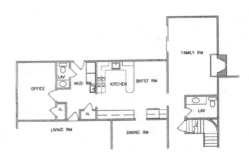

EXISTING PLAN

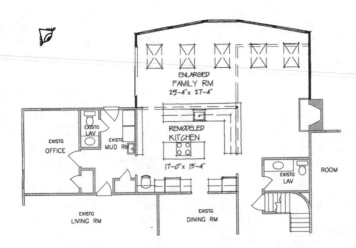

REMODELED FIRST FLOOR PLAN

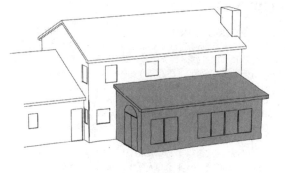

KF012

YOU KNOW THAT THE FAMILY ROOM, KITCHEN AND BREAKFAST ROOM OF THIS CENTER HALL TWO-STORY ARE OK, BUT WE NOW ARE SEEKING SOMETHING MUCH LARGER AND MORE IN FASHION. THIS ARCHITECTURAL DESIGN ACCOMPLISHES THAT. IT PROVIDES AN ADDITION TO THE FAMILY ROOM THAT VIRTUALLY DOUBLES IT IN SIZE, AND ALSO ADDS ENOUGH SPACE FOR A BRIGHT NEW BREAKFAST ROOM, WHICH, IN TURN, FREES UP ENOUGH AREA TO CREATE A FABULOUS NEW KITCHEN. THE KITCHEN NOW BOASTS CORNER WINDOWS OVER A CORNER SINK, A LARGE CENTER ISLAND AND A PANTRY WALL COMBINED WITH STYLISH ANGULAR SHAPES. THE AREA OF THE ADDITION VISUALLY FLOWS TO THE NEWLY OPENED INTERIOR SPACE, CREATING A WONDERFUL SPACIOUS FEELING THROUGHOUT.

EXISTING PLAN

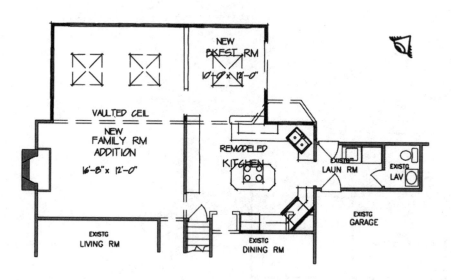

REMODELED FIRST FLOOR PLAN

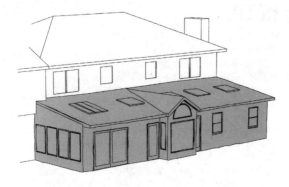

KFOI3

THE EXISTING PLAN PICTURED IS DIFFERENT FROM THE NORM; WE ARE LOOKING AT THE REAR WALL OF A LARGE TWO-STORY HOME. THERE IS A SPACIOUS KITCHEN AND DEN—BUT A VERY UNAPPEALING BREAKFAST AREA; THE PROGRAM ALSO CALLS FOR A NEW STUDY TO BE ADDED SOMEWHERE, AND THE OWNER IS ALSO DESIROUS OF ADDING A SUNROOM SPACE. THE ADDITION PICTURED ACCOMPLISHES THAT VERY HANDSOMELY. THE PITFALL IS THE VERY SHALLOW ROOF PITCH OVER THE ADDITION BECAUSE WE HAVE TO STAY BELOW THE SILL OF THE SECOND FLOOR WINDOWS. THIS IS A VERY COMMON PROBLEM WHEN ADDING A ONE-STORY WING TO THE REAR OF A TWO-STORY HOME. DEPENDING ON THE ACTUAL PITCH OF THE ROOF, SPECIAL ROOFING MATERIALS MAY BE REQUIRED, SUCH AS DOUBLE FELT UNDERLAY OR EVEN A BUILT-UP HOT ROOF.

EXISTING FLOOR PLAN

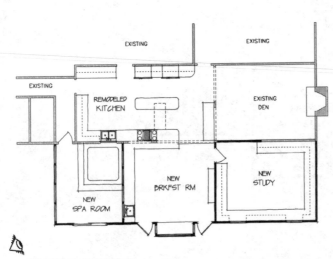

REMODELED FLOOR PLAN

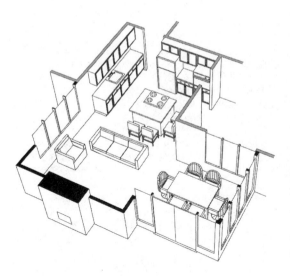

KFOII

EXPANDING A DATED KITCHEN INTO SOMETHING OTHER THAN JUST A LARGER ONE WAS THE GOAL OF THIS DESIGN. THE PLAN CREATES THREE DISTINCT SPACES THAT MESH INTO ONE MARVELOUS NEW COUNTRY KITCHEN: AN UPDATED NEW WORKING KITCHEN, WITH A LARGE CENTER ISLAND, A ROOMY BREAKFAST AREA, SITUATED WITHIN A GLAZED GREENHOUSE STRUCTURE, AND A COZY SITTING AREA, FOCUSING ABOUT A FIREPLACE AND BUILT-IN MEDIA. THE THREE SPACES EACH ENJOY THEIR DISTINCT AND SPECIAL CHARACTER, YET THEY MERGE TOGETHER TO CREATE A SPACIOUS, YET EXTREMELY CHARMING AND FUNCTIONAL FAMILY LIVING CENTER. IT IS A PLACE THAT CAN SUPPORT MULTIPLE, SIMULTANEOUS ACTIVITIES, AND IN WHICH THE KITCHEN IS THE HUB.

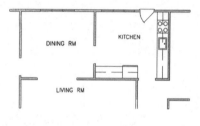

EXISTING PLAN

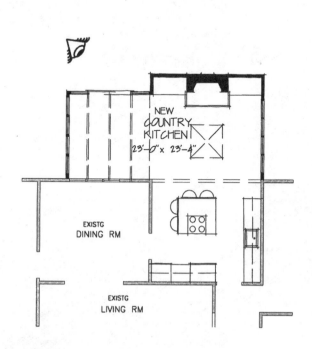

REMODELED FIRST FLOOR PLAN

KFO15

THE EXISTING KITCHEN AND BREAKFAST ROOM IN
THIS OLDER TWO-STORY HOME ARE INADEQUATE.
NEITHER ENJOYS A GOOD VIEW OF THE REAR YARD,
AND THERE IS NO FAMILY ROOM IN THE HOME. THE
MULTI-ROOM REMODELING DEPICTED IN THIS DESIGN
IS AN EXCEPTIONALLY HANDSOME ADDITION, BOTH
INSIDE AND OUT. THE NEW KITCHEN IS AN
EXPANSIVE LAYOUT THAT INCLUDES A CENTER
ISLAND; IT IS WIDE OPEN TO THE NEW FAMILY ROOM
AND A REMODELED BREAKFAST ROOM. THE EXISTING
LAVATORY AND BREAKFAST ROOM SWAP LOCATION,
SO THE BREAKFAST ROOM CAN ENJOY A REAR YARD
VIEW. THE KITCHEN INCLUDES A DOUBLE WINDOW,
AND THE FAMILY ROOM BOASTS AN ATTRACTIVE
WINDOW WALL.

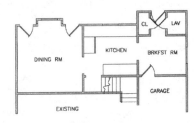

EXISTING FLOOR PLAN

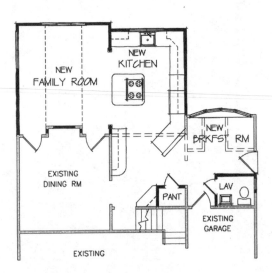

REMODELED FLOOR PLAN

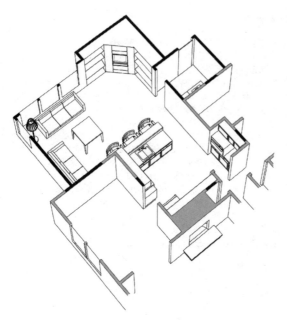

KFO1O

A STYLISH NEW FAMILY ROOM, A NEW LAUNDRY ROOM AND A REMODELED KITCHEN ARE THE SUBJECTS OF THIS DESIGN. THE LOCATION IS TO THE REAR OF THE KITCHEN AND DINING ROOM OF A CONVENTIONAL L-SHAPED LIVING-DINING ROOM. THIS IS THE TYPE OF PLAN FOUND VERY FREQUENTLY IN SPLIT-LEVEL AND ONE-STORY HOMES, AND EVEN MANY TWO-STORY HOMES. THE NEW FAMILY ROOM IS DESIGNED TO FOCUS ITS SEATING ABOUT A BUILT-IN MEDIA CENTER THAT WRAPS AROUND A CORNER. THE DINING ROOM WINDOW IS RELOCATED TO THE SIDE TO GAIN WALL SPACE FOR THE FAMILY ROOM. FINALLY, THE KITCHEN IS OPENED UP AND VISUALLY CONNECTED TO THE NEW FAMILY ROOM, AND THE NEW LAUNDRY ALSO SERVES AS A MUD ROOM, PROVIDING ACCESS TO THE REAR YARD.

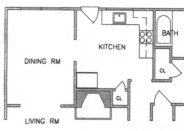

EXISTING PLAN

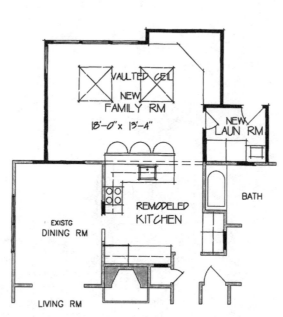

REMODELED FIRST FLOOR PLAN

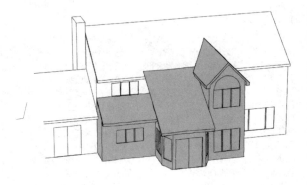

KEBOI

A LARGE NEW KITCHEN AND BREAKFAST ROOM ARE THE PRIME REASONS TO REMODEL THIS TWO-STORY HOME. AN EXPANDED MASTER BATH IS ANOTHER INTEREST, BUT HOW WILL YOU ENLARGE THE BATH IF THE MASTER BEDROOM IS NOT CLOSE TO THE KITCHEN SO WE MAY TAKE ADVANTAGE OF SPACE OVER THAT CONTEMPLATED EXPANSION? WELL, WE WILL CREATE A NEW FIRST FLOOR SPACE BEHIND THE EXISTING LAUNDRY, AND ADJACENT TO THE NEW BREAKFAST ROOM, SO THAT WE MAY EXPAND THE MASTER BATH. THIS AREA CAN SERVE AS A SEWING ROOM, OFFICE, OR EVEN A MODERN EXERCISE ROOM. THE NEW KITCHEN IS A SENSATIONAL, DRAMATIC SPACE, WITH SKYLIGHTS IN THE NEW EXTENSION AND A FABULOUS CENTER ISLAND. THE EXPANDED MASTER BATH IS EQUALLY DELIGHTFUL.

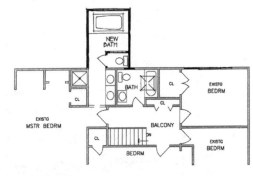

REMODELED SECOND FLOOR PLAN

EXISTING PLAN

EXISTING PLAN

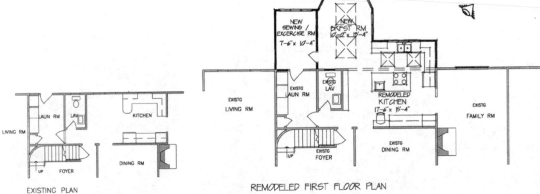

REMODELED FIRST FLOOR PLAN

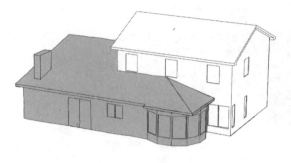

KFD03

A BEAUTIFUL ROTUNDA-SHAPED BREAKFAST ROOM WITH WRAP-AROUND WINDOWS, A BRIGHT NEW KITCHEN, AND A SPACIOUS NEW FAMILY ROOM ARE THE SUBJECTS OF THIS DESIGN. IT IS PLANNED AS A ONE-STORY ADDITION TO THE REAR OF A SIDE-HALL TWO-STORY HOME. LOW WALLS SEPARATE THE NEW FAMILY ROOM AND KITCHEN, WHICH AUGMENTS A VISUAL INTEGRATION ACROSS THE ENTIRE NEW ADDITION. SKYLIGHTS, A VAULTED CEILING AND A FIREPLACE, WITH SPACE FOR BUILT-INS AT EITHER SIDE, ARE FURTHER HIGHLIGHTS OF THE FAMILY ROOM. SOME SECONDARY BENEFITS, OR BONUSES, INCLUDE AN ENLARGEMENT OF THE DINING ROOM INTO THE SPACE FORMERLY OCCUPIED BY THE KITCHEN, NEW LARGE DINING ROOM WINDOWS, A NEW LAVATORY AND TWO EXTRA CLOSETS.

EXISTING PLAN

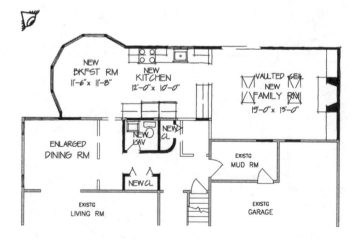

REMODELED FIRST FLOOR PLAN

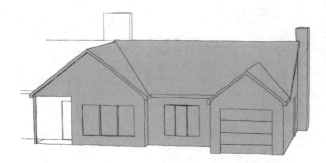

KFLD1

THIS 23'8" WIDE SIDE ADDITION ADDS A
FABULOUS NEW FAMILY ROOM, A DINING ROOM
AND A GARAGE TO A ONE OR 1½-STORY HOME.
IT IS ONE OF THE MORE SPECIFIC PLANS,
DESIGNED TO ATTACH TO THE SIDE OF A
KITCHEN AND LIVING ROOM, WITH THE PLAN
SHOWING HOW TO REMODEL THESE ROOMS
AND THE BATH AS WELL. IF YOUR EXISTING
BASEMENT STAIR IS INFRINGING INTO THE
KITCHEN AREA, CONSIDER MOVING IT AS
INDICATED. THE RESULTING PLAN GIVES YOU
A COVERED PORCH, A DEFINED ENTRANCE
FOYER, A NON-TRAFFIC LIVING ROOM AND A
GREAT KITCHEN WITH A CENTER ISLAND, PLUS
THE NEW FAMILY ROOM, DINING ROOM AND
GARAGE. THE ADDITION ALSO EXTENDS
APPROXIMATELY 9' FORWARD OF THE FRONT
LINE OF THE HOME, BUT THE CONSTRUCTION
DRAWINGS COULD BE MODIFIED TO MOVE THE
NEW ADDITION BACK, IF NECESSARY.

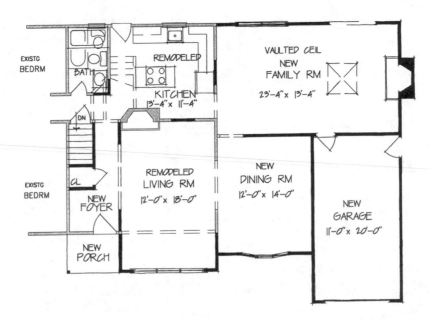

REMODELED FIRST FLOOR PLAN

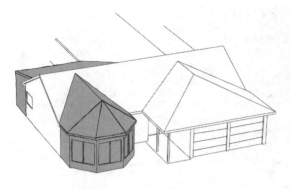

KFLD2

SIMILAR TO THE L-SHAPED PLAN, THE T-SHAPED ONE-STORY HOME OFFERS READILY FOUND SITE AREA TO EXPAND INTO. IN THE DESIGN SHOWN, THE FRONT-FACING LIVING AND DINING ROOM, PLUS THE REAR-FACING FAMILY ROOM AND KITCHEN, ARE EXPANDED IN TWO SEPARATE RENOVATIONS. A SENSATIONAL GREAT ROOM IS THE RESULT OF THE EXPANSION INTO THE FRONT YARD; A LARGE, ELEGANT BAYED SHAPE, ACTUALLY $5/8$ OF AN OCTAGON, IS ATTACHED, BEAUTIFULLY ENHANCING THE FORMAL ROOMS. THE ADDITION TO THE REAR YARD IS ONLY A MODEST 6'8", BUT IT SQUARES OFF THE FAMILY ROOM AND KITCHEN, ENABLING IT TO NOW FUNCTION AS ONE LARGE COUNTRY KITCHEN. THE KITCHEN ITSELF BENEFITS FROM A STYLISH NEW REMODELING.

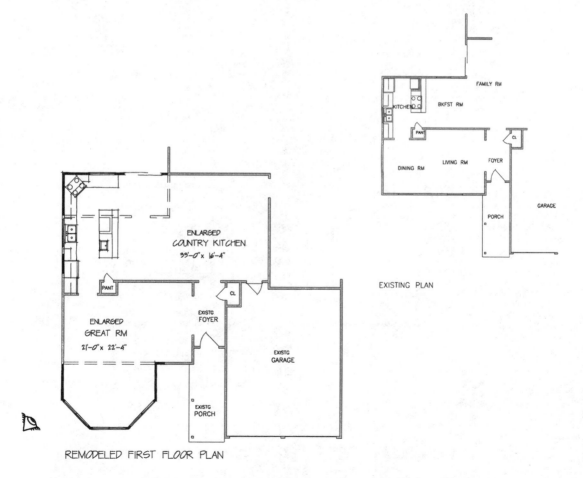

EXISTING PLAN

REMODELED FIRST FLOOR PLAN

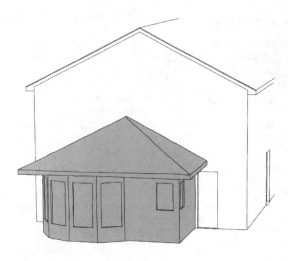

K0004

EXISTING SIDE-FACING KITCHENS POSE EXPANSION PROBLEMS; GOING OUT TO THE REAR USUALLY MEANS REARRANGING THE ENTIRE HOUSE, WHICH, DEPENDING ON THE QUALITY OF THE HOME—AND YOUR BUDGET, IS A SERIOUS CONSIDERATION. GOING OUT THE SIDE IS AN EXCELLENT IDEA—AS LONG AS YOU HAVE THE ROOM; THIS PICTURESQUE, HIP-ROOFED, 10'6"-WIDE BY 17'6"-DEEP ADDITION ASSUMES YOU HAVE THE ROOM. IT RESULTS IN A SPLENDROUS KITCHEN AND AN EQUALLY BEAUTIFUL AND SPACIOUS ROTUNDA STYLE BREAKFAST ROOM. ALTHOUGH THE OLDER PART OF THE KITCHEN IS STILL BROKEN BY THE CONSTRAINTS OF EXISTING DOORWAYS, THAT PART SERVES MAINLY FOR PANTRY, STORAGE AND A DESK. THE NEW WORKING PART OF THE KITCHEN IS A CHEERFUL, BRIGHT, DELIGHTFUL SPACE.

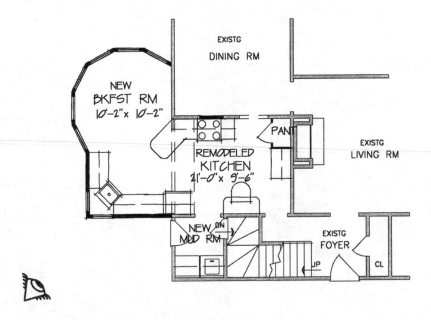

REMODELED FIRST FLOOR PLAN

DOOO4

THIS CHARMING SHED ROOF BUMP-OUT PROVIDES
THREE WALLS OF WINDOWS TO SHED LIGHT ON A
BRAND NEW BREAKFAST ROOM INSIDE. IT IS AN IDEAL
ADDITION TO A DATED KITCHEN, WHICH ALLOWS YOU
TO EXPAND AND UPDATE THE KITCHEN ITSELF, BY
UTILIZING ALL THE EXISTING SPACE FOR THE KITCHEN
WORK AREA. WITH THE KITCHEN REMAINING INSIDE, A
SNACK COUNTER BECOMES A NICE SEPARATOR FROM
THE BREAKFAST ROOM. AS WITH ALL THE PLANS IN
THE BOOK, THIS PLAN CAN BE FOUND ON THE
ACCOMPANYING CAD DISK AND IT CAN BE MODIFIED
AS NEEDED. THE SHED ROOF IS AN IDEAL ADDITION
TO A TWO-STORY WALL, PROVIDED NO WINDOWS
INTERFERE AT THE SECOND FLOOR.

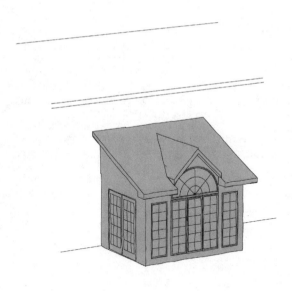

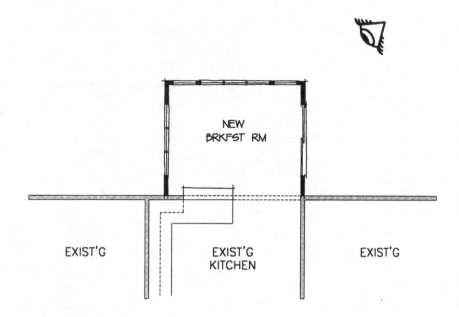

NEW
BRKFST RM

EXIST'G

EXIST'G
KITCHEN

EXIST'G

REMODELED FLOOR PLAN

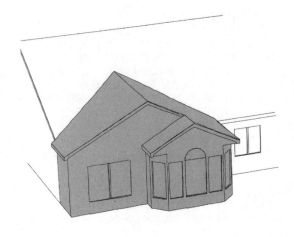

KDOOI

THIS PLAN ADDS 9'0" TO A TIGHT KITCHEN AND 5'0" TO THE ADJOINING DINING ROOM; TOGETHER THEY FORM A SMART LOOKING ADDITION THAT RESULTS IN A BEAUTIFUL NEW EAT-IN KITCHEN, AND A DINING ROOM THAT CAN HANDLE THAT HOLIDAY CROWD. BY RELOCATING THE KITCHEN/DINING ROOM CONNECTION, THE REAR WALL OF THE KITCHEN IS NOW USABLE. THE NEW U-SHAPED KITCHEN IS ATTRACTIVE AND HIGHLY FUNCTIONAL. A PENINSULA COUNTER SEPARATES IT FROM A CHARMING NEW BREAKFAST ROOM. A BAYED END, VAULTED CEILING AND CONTEMPORARY WINDOW WALL GIVE THIS SMALL SPACE AN INVITING CHARACTER. THE NEW DINING ROOM IS LONG ENOUGH, BUT STILL MAY BE A LITTLE NARROW. THEREFORE, ADD A 5'. WALL AT THE OPEN END. THIS WILL ACCOMMODATE THE BREAKFRONT OR HUTCH.

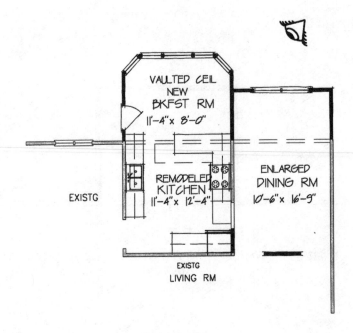

REMODELED FIRST FLOOR PLAN

KD002

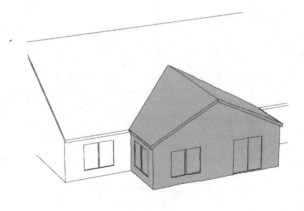

PROBLEM: AN AMPLE KITCHEN, BUT NO TABLE SPACE, AND A DINING ROOM THAT WOULD BE OK, IF IT DIDN'T HAVE TO DOUBLE AS A CIRCULATION ROUTE TO THE DEN AND GARAGE. SOLUTION: A 10'0" ADDITION OUT THE REAR THAT SOLVES BOTH PROBLEMS. THE RESULT ALSO SIGNIFICANTLY HELPS IMPROVE THE KITCHEN ITSELF. THE NEW U-SHAPED LAYOUT IS PERFECTION IN FUNCTION AND ATTRACTION. THE ANGLED CORNER SINK IS LOCATED CLOSE TO NEW WINDOWS, AND THE WIDE PENINSULA COUNTER ALLOWS COMMUNICATION WITH THE FOLKS AT THE BREAKFAST TABLE. SLIDING DOORS, A SKYLIGHT AND A VAULTED CEILING ENHANCE THE NEW BREAKFAST ROOM. THE NEW DINING ROOM IS FORMAL AND SEPARATE FROM THE NEW GALLERY THAT HAS BEEN CREATED TO SATISFY THE CIRCULATION FUNCTION.

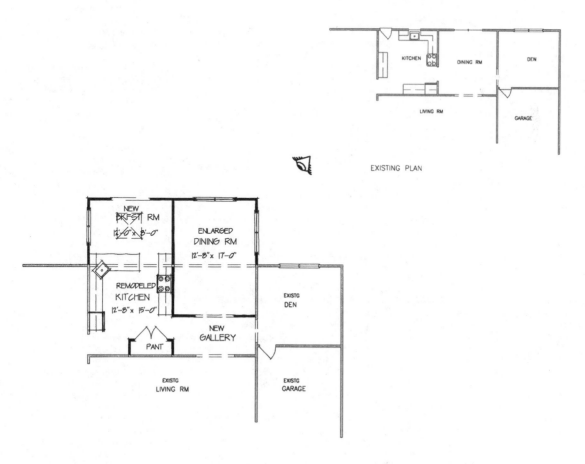

EXISTING PLAN

REMODELED FIRST FLOOR PLAN

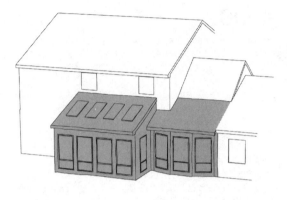

KD009

THE PROGRAM: TO REMODEL THE KITCHEN INTO A SPACIOUS GOURMET KITCHEN, PROVIDE A LARGE BREAKFAST AREA AND EXPAND THE ADJACENT DINING ROOM AS WELL. THE SOLUTION: BUMP THE DINING ROOM OUT A FEW FEET, BUT ADD A WHOLE NEW ROOM OUTSIDE THE EXISTING KITCHEN. THE NEW KITCHEN WILL OCCUPY THE ENTIRE SPACE OF THE OLD ROOM, AND THE NEW ADDITION WILL HOUSE A SUN-FILLED BREAKFAST ROOM. THE KITCHEN INCLUDES A HUGE CENTER ISLAND THAT INCLUDES THE SINK AND A PANTRY STYLE WALL ADJOINING THE DINING ROOM. THE BREAKFAST ROOM IS DESIGNED WITH WRAP-AROUND WINDOWS AND DOORS, AND INCLUDES A SLOPED CEILING BELOW FOUR LARGE SKYLIGHTS.

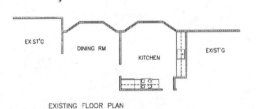

EXISTING FLOOR PLAN

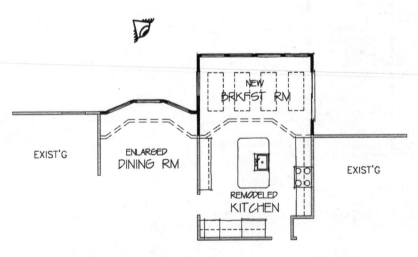

REMODELED FLOOR PLAN

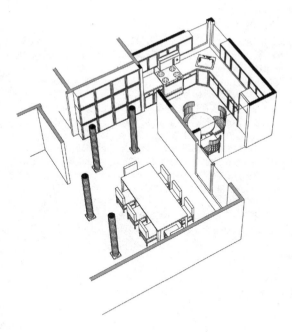

KD006

GIVEN: A CONVENTIONAL L-SHAPED LIVING / DINING ROOM WITH AN ADJOINING OLD KITCHEN. GOALS: A BRIGHT NEW CHEERFUL KITCHEN AND A LARGER DINING ROOM. THIS PLAN IS FOR THE PERSON WHO WOULD LIKE SOME TABLE SPACE IN THE KITCHEN, BUT WHOSE REAL PREFERENCE IS AN EXPANSIVE FORMAL DINING ROOM. THE INTERESTING SOLUTION DEVELOPED HERE EXPANDS THE DINING ROOM INTO THE FORMER KITCHEN SPACE, AND IN DOING SO IT CREATES AN IMPRESSIVE, OPEN PLANNED, LIVING / DINING ROOM; THE NEW KITCHEN IS CREATED IN A 12'8"×10'4" REAR ADDITION. CABINETS ARE IN THE FORM OF AN "L" WITH A CORNER SINK UNDER CORNER WINDOWS, AND SLIDING DOORS LEAD TO A NEW TERRACE BEHIND THE DINING ROOM. THIS IS AN EASY ADDITION TO STAGE, BECAUSE THE KITCHEN IS COMPLETELY NEW.

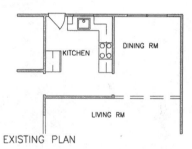

EXISTING PLAN

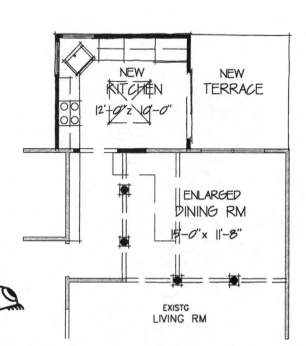

REMODELED FIRST FLOOR PLAN

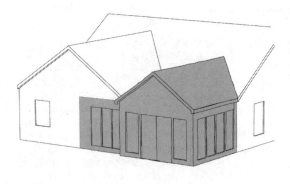

KF004

A REALLY TIGHT KITCHEN THAT IS DIFFICULT TO WORK WITH IS ENLARGED AND REMODELED IN THIS PLAN, AND A DELIGHTFUL SUNROOM IS TUCKED INTO THE CORNER. DOORWAYS TO THE HALL, DINING ROOM, BASEMENT STAIR AND A PANTRY MAKE THE REAR WALL OF THIS KITCHEN ALMOST USELESS. THE NEW KITCHEN IS CREATED IN AN L-SHAPE AND A SERVING/ SNACK COUNTER IS DESIGNED ALONG THE CIRCULATION CORRIDOR, THEREBY MAKING USE OF THIS AREA. COZY TABLE SPACE IS PROVIDED UNDER THE NEW LARGE WINDOW. A BEAUTIFUL NEW SUNROOM OR PORCH IS PROPOSED FOR THE CORNER BEHIND THE DINING ROOM. THE OLD WINDOWS IN THE DINING ROOM SHOULD REMAIN AND NEW WINDOWS ADDED FROM THE KITCHEN FACING INTO THE PORCH, BRINGING BORROWED LIGHT TO BOTH ROOMS.

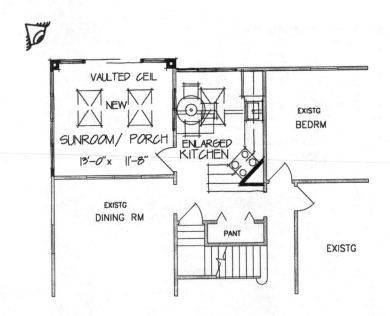

REMODELED FIRST FLOOR PLAN

KD004

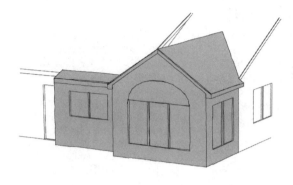

THIS CHARMING LITTLE 11'10"×8'6" ADDITION PROVIDES FOR A SUNNY BREAKFAST ROOM—OR A SUN PORCH OR SUNROOM IF YOU PREFER—OFF AN ADJACENT EXISTING KITCHEN. IF YOU HAVE A SMALL CORNER RECESS ADJACENT TO THE KITCHEN, THE PLAN WOULD NEATLY ATTACH AS SHOWN; OTHERWISE IT WOULD ATTACH FLUSH TO THE REAR. WINDOWS ABOUND ON TWO SIDES, INCLUDING A DECORATIVE CURVED TOP WINDOW ON THE LONG SIDE. THE ROOM ALSO INCLUDES A VAULTED CEILING. THE KITCHEN ITSELF IS SHOWN AS BEING REMODELED. THE REAR WALL IS BUMPED OUT 2'0" TO ALLOW FOR A COUNTER TOP WITH THE SINK UNDER A NEW LARGE WINDOW. THE LAYOUT ALSO SHOWS AN INTERESTING ANGLED RANGE AT AN INSIDE CORNER; CONTEMPLATE THIS IN ANY KITCHEN YOU ARE CONSIDERING REMODELING.

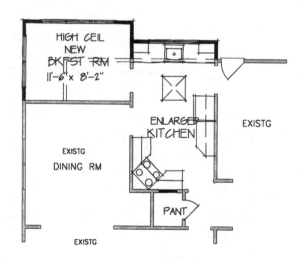

REMODELED FIRST FLOOR PLAN

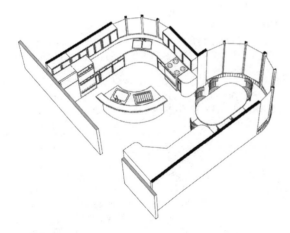

K0011

THIS MIGHT BE DUBBED A DREAM KITCHEN—AND RIGHTFULLY SO; IT IS A VERY EXPANSIVE (ALMOST 22'×22') ADDITION THAT DOES CREATE A DAZZLING NEW KITCHEN AND BREAKFAST ROOM. THE DESIGN THEME IS CURVES. THE KITCHEN ROUNDS A CORNER IN A QUARTER CIRCLE, INCLUDES A CURVED ISLAND AND SNACK COUNTER, AND CULMINATES IN A SEMI-CIRCULAR WRAP-AROUND WINDOW WALL IN THE BREAKFAST AREA. AN AREA FOR BUILT-INS, INCLUDING SPACE FOR A PANTRY AND TV IS INCLUDED IN THE DESIGN. THIS IS ONE OF THE PLANS THAT IS LESS SPECIFIC AS TO WHERE YOU ATTACH IT TO THE HOME; THAT IS FOR YOU TO RESOLVE, INCLUDING THE QUESTION OF WHICH ROOFLINES TO PLAN. PLAN F0014 ON PAGE 161 IS A FAMILY ROOM ADDITION OF SIMILAR ARCHITECTURAL DESIGN.

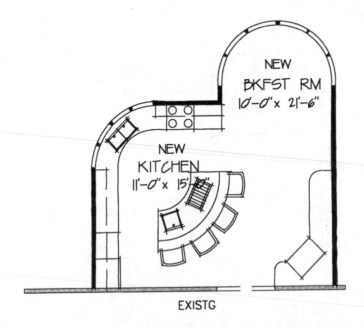

NEW
BKFST RM
10'-0" x 21'-6"

NEW
KITCHEN
11'-0" x 15'-?"

EXISTG

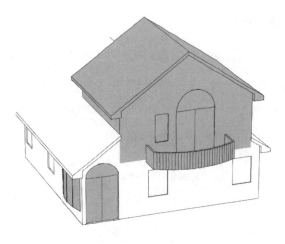

KBR0I

PROBLEM: THE PROGRAM CALLS FOR A NEW MASTER SUITE, BUT THE HOME IS A SMALL ONE-STORY HOME WITH NO ROOM TO EXPAND OUT—AND IF YOU COULD MODERNIZE THE KITCHEN AT THE SAME TIME, THAT WOULD BE A BONUS. THIS PLAN SHOWS YOU HOW TO DO BOTH. THE SOLUTION, WORKING WITHIN THE EXISTING GABLE ROOFLINES, ADDS A FABULOUS NEW MASTER SUITE UPSTAIRS, AND REMODELS THE EXISTING KITCHEN TO CREATE A STYLISH NEW ROOM WITH A SMALL BREAKFAST NOOK TO BOOT. ACCESS TO THE NEW PARTIAL SECOND FLOOR IS OVER THE EXISTING BASEMENT STAIR. THE NEW MASTER SUITE INCLUDES A LAVISH, COMPARTMENTED, SKYLIT BATH, A SPACIOUS WALK-IN CLOSET, AND A LOVELY BALCONY OFF THE VAULTED CEILING BEDROOM.

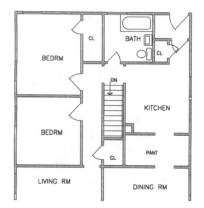

EXISTING PLAN

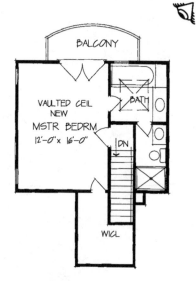

SECOND FLOOR PLAN
ALL NEW

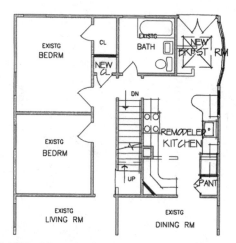

REMODELED FIRST FLOOR PLAN

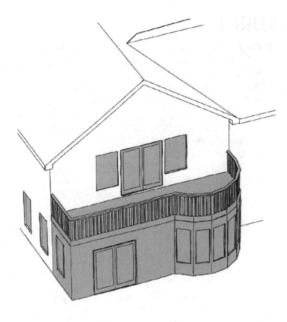

KDOIO

MOST OLDER HOMES SUFFER FROM INADEQUATE EATING SPACE, BOTH IN THEIR KITCHENS AND DINING ROOMS. WHAT'S THE POINT OF HAVING A DINING ROOM AT ALL IF ON THOSE FEW OCCASIONS EACH YEAR IT IS NEEDED, IT IS TOO SMALL FOR THE CROWD WE WANT TO INVITE. THIS CHIC LITTLE BUMP OUT SOLVES BOTH EATING SPACES; IT CREATES A CHARMING BOW-WINDOWED BREAKFAST ROOM TO THE REAR OF THE EXISTING KITCHEN WHILE ENLARGING THE DINING ROOM AS WELL. CLOSING THE EXISTING OPENING BETWEEN THE KITCHEN AND DINING ROOM CREATES A SIGNIFICANTLY MORE ATTRACTIVE KITCHEN, AND IT'S NOT A BIG PROBLEM TO SERVE THE DINING ROOM BY GOING AROUND. THE SECOND FLOOR DECK IS A LOVELY BONUS TO THE PLAN.

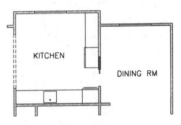

EXISTING FLOOR PLAN

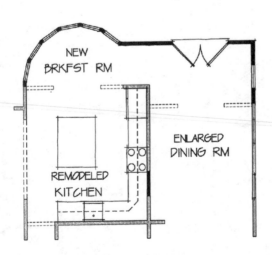

REMODELED FLOOR PLAN

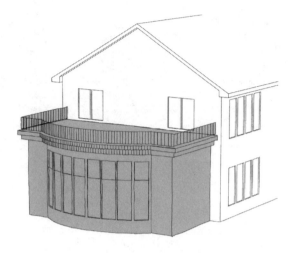

L000I

LOOKING TO ENLARGE A LIVING ROOM AND CREATE
AN EXQUISITE GREAT ROOM FOR ENTERTAINING?
THIS 10' ADDITION TO THE SIDE OF A TWO-STORY
DOES JUST THAT. IT TAKES THE CURRENT LIVING
ROOM AND VIRTUALLY DOUBLES IT IN SIZE. THE OLD
END WALL IS REMOVED IN ITS ENTIRETY, CREATING
ONE LARGE, FLOWING SPACE. THE ADDITION SPORTS
A 12'-HIGH CEILING—AN IMPORTANT NEED FOR A
ROOM OF THIS SIZE. THE NEW END WALL IS
SUGGESTED AS A GREAT BIG BOW WINDOW WHICH
WILL ADD FOCUS AND DRAMA TO THE SPACE.
WINDOWS, AS WELL AS THE SIZE OF THE ROOM,
COULD BE MODIFIED TO FIT THE REQUIREMENTS OF
YOUR HOME AND LOT.

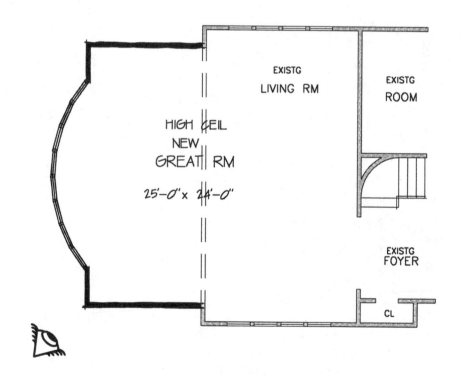

EXISTG
LIVING RM

EXISTG
ROOM

HIGH CEIL
NEW
GREAT RM

25'-0" x 24'-0"

EXISTG
FOYER

CL

REMODELED FIRST FLOOR PLAN

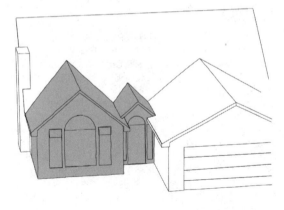

L0002

THE EXISTING L-SHAPED PLAN, AS PICTURED,
USUALLY ALLOWS EXPANSION INTO THE FRONT YARD.
WHAT A WONDERFUL WAY TO EXPAND THE
ENTERTAINMENT WING AND GIVE YOUR HOME A NEW
STRIKING APPEARANCE TOO! A BEAUTIFUL REVERSE
GABLE ADDITION ADDS A GENEROUS AMOUNT OF
FOOTAGE TO THE EXISTING LIVING ROOM. WHEN THE
OLD WALL IS REMOVED, THE AREA OF THE NEW
SPACE IS SUCH THAT IT COULD NOW FUNCTION AS A
MULTI-USE GREAT ROOM. THE MAIN ENTRANCE TO
THE HOME IS ALSO SIGNIFICANTLY ENHANCED, IN THIS
DESIGN, WITH THE ADDITION OF ANOTHER REVERSE
GABLED SPACE. BOTH ELEMENTS INCLUDE ARTY
HALF ROUND WINDOWS AND VAULTED CEILINGS, AND
TOGETHER THEY FORM A HIGHLY ATTRACTIVE NEW
FRONT FAÇADE OF ARCHITECTURAL MERIT.

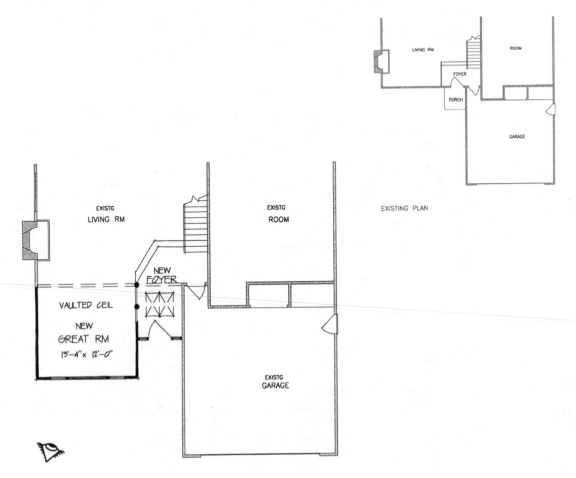

EXISTING PLAN

REMODELED FIRST FLOOR PLAN

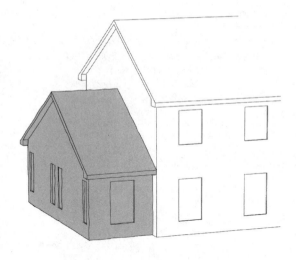

LD001

GIVEN: THE SIDE OF A TWO-STORY CONTAINING AN
L-SHAPED LIVING AND DINING ROOM.   PROGRAM
REQUIREMENTS: EXPAND THE DINING ROOM AND ADD
AN OFFICE OR LIBRARY.   THIS 8'0"×24'4" ADDITION
HELPS ACHIEVE BOTH.   THE NEW OFFICE BORROWS
2' FROM THE SELDOM USED LIVING ROOM, CREATING
A 10'-0" OFFICE/LIBRARY.   IF DESIRED, AN OUTSIDE
DOOR COULD BE INSTALLED TO THIS OFFICE, AND
THE DOUBLE DOORS TO THE LIVING ROOM COULD BE
CLOSED.   THE NEWLY EXPANDED DINING ROOM IS AN
IMPRESSIVE SIZE, CERTAINLY CAPABLE OF HANDLING
THE HOLIDAY DINNER.   A WORD OF CAUTION: THE 8'0"
ADDITION IS OK IF THE TWO-STORY SECTION IS NO
MORE THAN 27 TO 28' IN LENGTH.   IF IT IS LONGER,
THE 8'0" IS TOO SMALL.

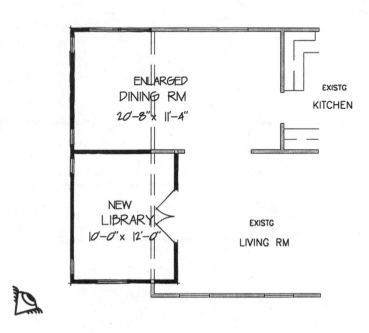

REMODELED FIRST FLOOR PLAN

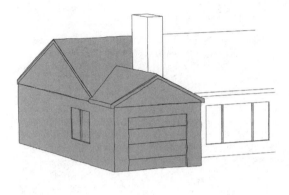

DMG01

AN ATTACHED GARAGE, LAUNDRY/MUD ROOM, AND
EXPANDED DINING ROOM ARE THE SUBJECT OF THIS
TRIM 12'4"×32'4" ADDITION.   IF YOUR LOT PERMITS,
THE GARAGE COULD BE FURTHER EXPANDED TO
ACCOMMODATE TWO CARS.   THE APPROXIMATELY
6'-ADDITION TO THE DINING ROOM IS A WELCOME BY-
PRODUCT, SINCE ALL TOO OFTEN THIS L-SHAPED
DINING ROOM IS TOO TIGHT FOR THE FEW
OCCASIONS WHEN IT IS REALLY NEEDED.   THE EXTRA
SPACE ALSO MAKES IT A LITTLE MORE COMFORTABLE
FOR TRAFFIC FLOW TO THE MUD ROOM AND GARAGE.
THE LAUNDRY/MUD ROOM PROVIDES SPACE FOR A
CLOSET PLUS COUNTER SPACE FOR EITHER A SINK
OR FOR FOLDING AND IRONING.

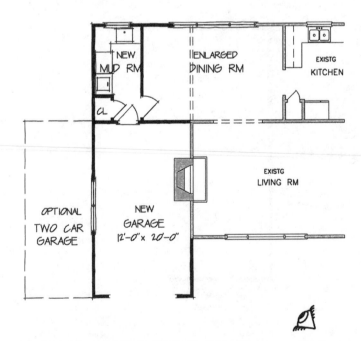

REMODELED FIRST FLOOR PLAN

DMG02

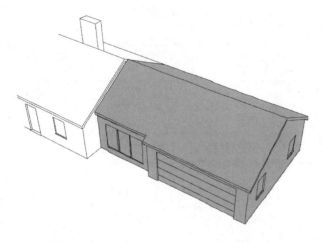

A NEW TWO-CAR GARAGE, A CONVENIENT LAUNDRY/MUD ROOM, A NEW DINING ROOM OR FAMILY ROOM (YOUR CHOICE AS TO USE) AND A REMODELED KITCHEN ARE THE SUBJECTS OF THIS 33'8"×22'8" ONE-STORY ADDITION. THE ATTACHMENT, AS SHOWN, IS TO THE LIVING ROOM/KITCHEN SIDE OF A ONE-STORY HOME; HOWEVER, IT IS EQUALLY SUITED TO ANY MULTI-STORY HOME. WHEREAS YOU MIGHT PREFER AS MUCH SPACE AS POSSIBLE, THE ALL IMPORTANT DESIGN CONSIDERATION SUGGESTS VARYING THE SETBACKS FOR THE DINING (OR FAMILY) ROOM AND GARAGE FROM THE ORIGINAL LINE OF THE HOUSE. OPENINGS IN THE OLD END WALL ALLOW VISUAL INTEGRATION BETWEEN THE LIVING ROOM AND THE NEW DINING OR FAMILY ROOM AND DIRECT CIRCULATION FROM THE KITCHEN TO THE NEW LAUNDRY ROOM AND GARAGE.

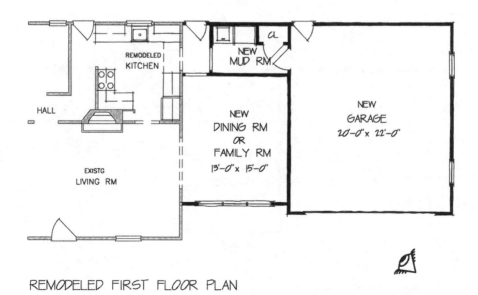

REMODELED FIRST FLOOR PLAN

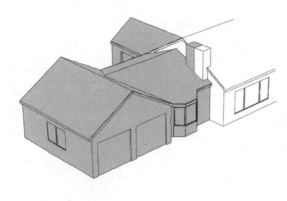

FDG01

A LARGE FRONT-TO-REAR FAMILY ROOM, ATTACHED
TWO-CAR GARAGE AND ENLARGED DINING ROOM ARE
ATTRACTIVELY COMBINED IN THIS EXPANSIVE
ADDITION TO THE SIDE OF AN L-SHAPED LIVING AND
DINING ROOM.   THE ADDITION IS VERY FLEXIBLE AND
IS SUITED FOR ANY STYLE OR TYPE OF HOME,
INCLUDING A ONE- OR TWO-STORY OR A SPLIT-LEVEL.
THIS ADDITION SHOWS THE IMPORTANCE OF
PROGRAMMING.   IF ALL YOU INTENDED TO ADD WAS
THE FAMILY ROOM AND GARAGE, YOU MIGHT NOT
HAVE CONSIDERED THAT IN ORDER TO PROVIDE AN
UNCRAMPED CONNECTION BETWEEN THE KITCHEN
AND FAMILY ROOM, THE DINING ROOM WOULD SUFFER
BADLY.   THUS THE REAR EXTENSION FOR THE DINING
ROOM.   THE PLAN ALSO SHOWS A NEW FIREPLACE
ATTACHING TO THE REAR OF THE EXISTING LIVING
ROOM FIREPLACE.

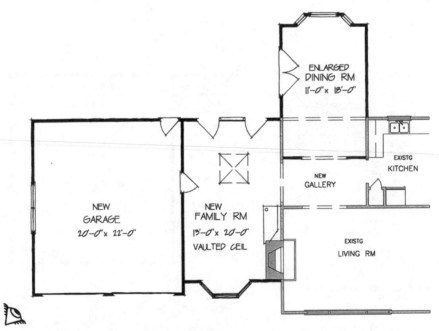

REMODELED FIRST FLOOR PLAN

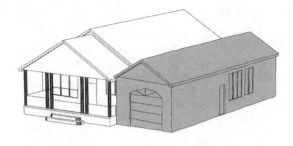

FDG02

PROBLEM: THE PROGRAM CALLS FOR A FAMILY ROOM AND GARAGE, BUT THE HOME IS AN OLD COTTAGE WITH A LOVELY FRONT PORCH. ALTHOUGH THE SPACE EXISTS ALONGSIDE, CAN YOU DO THIS GRACEFULLY? IT'S A TOUGH CALL. THE BETTER SOLUTION MIGHT BE A DETACHED GARAGE AND A REAR FAMILY ROOM, BUT PRACTICAL CONSIDERATIONS MAY DICTATE THAT YOU ATTACH THEM. IF SO, FOLLOW THIS PLAN CAREFULLY. A REVERSE GABLE IS THE BEST SOLUTION, EVEN THOUGH IT REQUIRES SPECIAL ROOF FLASHING IN THE FORM OF A CRICKET (SEE PAGE 378). THE FAMILY ROOM IS LOCATED AT GRADE SINCE IT IS CONNECTED AT THE LANDING OF THE SIDE STAIR. A DRAMATIC NEW BALCONIED BREAKFAST ROOM IS CREATED, WHICH VISUALLY CONNECTS THE NEW FAMILY ROOM TO THE REMODELED KITCHEN.

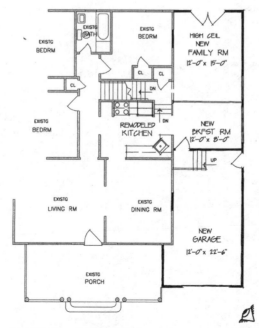

REMODELED FIRST FLOOR PLAN

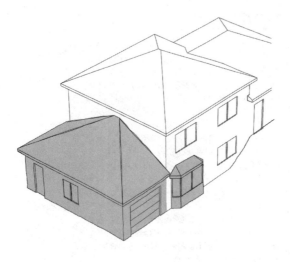

FG00I

ONE OF THE MORE OBVIOUS WAYS TO ENLARGE A
FAMILY ROOM IN A SPLIT-LEVEL IS TO BREAK
THROUGH INTO THE ADJOINING GARAGE.   HOWEVER,
IF YOUR LOT PERMITS, A NEW GARAGE (I- OR 2-CAR)
CAN ALSO BE ADDED ALONGSIDE.   SUCH AN
ADDITION USUALLY ENHANCES THE LINES OF THE
TYPICAL SPLIT-LEVEL, BY PROVIDING AN AESTHETIC
BALANCE TO THE ONE-STORY LIVING ROOM WING AT
THE OPPOSITE SIDE.   THIS PLAN SHOWS YOU HOW TO
ADD THE GARAGE AND EXPAND THE FAMILY ROOM.
THE ENTIRE WALL CAN EASILY BE REMOVED BETWEEN
THE FAMILY ROOM AND THE CURRENT GARAGE, AS
THIS IS USUALLY A NON-BEARING WALL.   NEW DOORS
TO THE REAR YARD ARE PLACED IN THE REAR WALL,
AND A LARGE BAY WINDOW IS DESIGNED IN PLACE OF
THE OLD GARAGE DOOR.

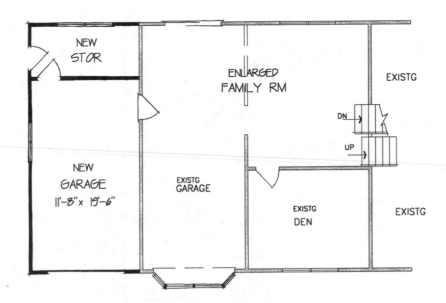

LOWER LEVEL PLAN

FG002

PROBLEM: THIS CENTER HALL TWO-STORY LACKS A GARAGE AND A FAMILY ROOM; FURTHERMORE THERE IS NO ROOM TO ADD ON EITHER SIDE, AND THE REAR YARD IS TOO SMALL TO ACCOMMODATE BOTH. SOLUTION: BUILD AN ADDITION THAT INCLUDES A LARGE SECOND FLOOR FAMILY ROOM (OR PLAYROOM) WHICH IS NEVERTHELESS STILL ACCESSIBLE TO THE KITCHEN.   BY CAREFUL DESIGN, THIS SENSATIONAL ROOM IS ONLY A SHORT FLIGHT AWAY FROM THE FIRST FLOOR.   IT IS ALSO EASILY REACHED FROM THE BEDROOMS, IN EFFECT BECOMING A REAR CONNECTOR BETWEEN THE TWO FLOORS.   THE ROOM FEATURES A DRAMATIC VAULTED CEILING AND WINDOWS ON THREE SIDES, INCLUDING A STUNNING WINDOW WALL AT THE REAR, COMPRISED OF ARCHED HEAD WINDOWS OF VARYING HEIGHTS.   THE DESIGN ALSO ADDS A LOVELY NEW BREAKFAST ROOM ADJACENT TO THE KITCHEN.

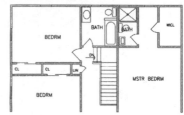

EXISTING FIRST FLOOR PLAN

EXISTING SECOND FLOOR PLAN

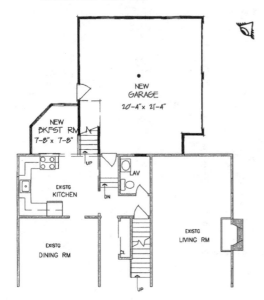

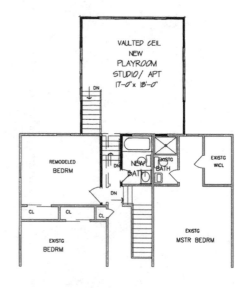

REMODELED FIRST FLOOR PLAN

REMODELED SECOND FLOOR PLAN

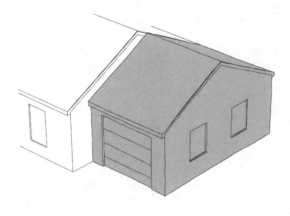

GAR02

A SIMPLE ONE- OR TWO-CAR ATTACHED GARAGE IS
THE ONLY SUBJECT OF THIS PLAN. THE GARAGE
SHOWN CAN BE ATTACHED TO THE SIDE OF ANY
HOUSE TYPE (ONE-STORY, TWO-STORY, SPLIT-LEVEL,
ETC.); A MIRROR IMAGE PUTS IT ON THE OPPOSITE
SIDE. AS SIMPLE AS IT SEEMS, IT IS EASY TO BOTCH
THIS ONE UP. THE SETBACK FROM THE FRONT WALL
IS AN IMPORTANT DESIGN CONSIDERATION. THE
ELEMENTS OF A GARAGE DOOR DO NOT MIRROR ANY
OTHER PART OF THE FRONT ELEVATION AND, AS
SUCH, DESERVE A SEPARATE DEFINITION. ALSO,
CONSTRUCTION BENEFITS OF THE SETBACK INCLUDE
THE ELIMINATION OF THE NEED TO PERFECTLY
MATCH ROOFING AND SIDING, AND A GREATER
FLEXIBILITY IN ESTABLISHING THE LEVEL OF THE
GARAGE FLOOR. ON A ONE-STORY DESIGN, AS
SHOWN, IF THE REAR IS SET FLUSH TO THE EXISTING
HOME, THE ROOFS DO HAVE TO PERFECTLY MATCH,
UNLESS YOU MAKE THE REAR WALL LOWER.

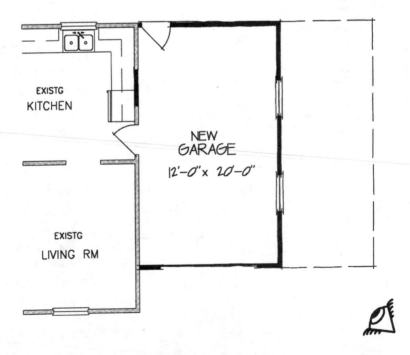

EXISTG
KITCHEN

NEW
GARAGE
12'-0" x 20'-0"

EXISTG
LIVING RM

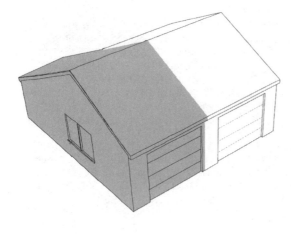

GAR0I

NEED A SECOND GARAGE? THIS PLAN NEATLY ACCOMPLISHES THAT AND ADDS SOME STORAGE TOO. THE DEPTH OF STORAGE IS A FUNCTION OF THE ROOF PITCH AND THE LEVEL OF THE FLOOR IN THE GARAGE. THE BETTER APPEARANCE OF THIS ADDITION CALLS FOR MAINTAINING THE SAME ROOF PITCH AND RIDGE LINE OF THE EXISTING ROOF, ALTHOUGH THIS WOULD LIKELY REQUIRE THAT YOU RE-ROOF COMPLETELY. IF YOU MAKE A BREAK AT THE FRONT, THIS REQUIREMENT WOULD BE ELIMINATED AS THE ROOFS WOULD NOT ALIGN. IF YOU CAN ONLY ADD LESS THAN 10', IT STILL MIGHT BE POSSIBLE TO CREATE A TWO-CAR GARAGE BY ELIMINATING THE OLD END WALL. HOWEVER, KEEP IN MIND, A TWO-CAR GARAGE OF LESS THAN 18' IN TOTAL WIDTH IS TOO TIGHT FOR COMFORT. IF THAT IS YOUR SITUATION, CONSIDER JUST ADDING STORAGE, SUCH AS SHOWN IN PLAN STR0I ON PAGE 305.

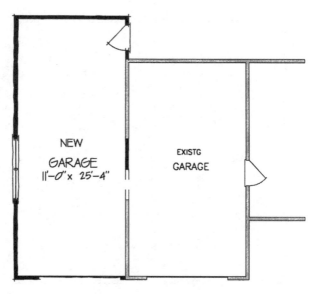

NEW
GARAGE
11'-0" x 25'-4"

EXISTG
GARAGE

REMODELED FIRST FLOOR PLAN

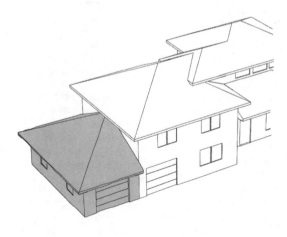

GAR05

THIS PLAN ACCOMPLISHES ONE THING—IT ADDS A 13'
WIDE ONE-CAR GARAGE TO A SPLIT-LEVEL OR TWO-
STORY HOME. IT RETAINS THE EXISTING GARAGE,
THEREBY CREATING A TWO-CAR GARAGE, AS
CONTRASTED TO PLAN FG001, ON PAGE 196, WHICH
ADDS A SOMEWHAT NARROWER GARAGE AND ALSO
CONVERTS THE OLD GARAGE TO ENLARGE THE
FAMILY ROOM. AS WITH THE OTHER PLAN, THIS
ADDITION DOES SIGNIFICANTLY ENHANCE THE LINES
OF THE HOME. MAKE SURE TO ALIGN THE GARAGE
DOOR HEAD WITH THE EXISTING OPENING, AND RE-
SIDE THE ENTIRE FRONT TO MATCH. THERE IS NO
NEED TO REMOVE THE OLD GARAGE WALL.

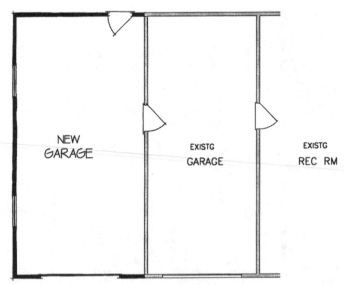

NEW
GARAGE

EXISTG
GARAGE

EXISTG
REC RM

LOWER LEVEL PLAN

GAR04

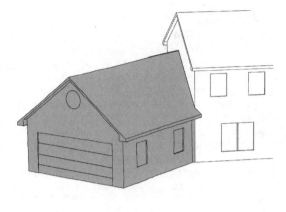

LOOKING TO ATTACH A TWO-CAR GARAGE? GIVE SOME CONSIDERATION TO SOMETHING OTHER THAN A 90 DEGREE ANGLE. MAYBE THE SHAPE OF YOUR LOT REQUIRES IT, OR THERE IS A GRADE DROP-OFF, OR SOME OTHER PHYSICAL CONSTRAINT THAT WOULD SUGGEST TURNING THE GARAGE. ONE OF THE OTHER MORE COMMON REASONS IS A DESIRE FOR THE LOOK OF A SIDE ENTRY GARAGE, WHERE THERE IS A SHORTAGE OF SPACE. ALTHOUGH THE ANGLED GARAGE ACTUALLY REQUIRES MORE YARD FOR THE STRUCTURE (ABOUT 10'0" MORE), THE TOTAL SPACE FOR STRUCTURE PLUS DRIVEWAY CAN BE ACHIEVED IN ABOUT 40 TO 42', WHICH IS 10' LESS THAN REQUIRED FOR A TRUE SIDE ENTRY GARAGE. THE ANGLED GARAGE PLAN ALSO PRESENTS SEVERAL BONUSES, INCLUDING THE FOUND SPACE FOR LAUNDRY, LAVATORY, PANTRY, STORAGE, ETC., AS SHOWN, AS WELL AS A DIFFERENT AESTHETIC APPEAL.

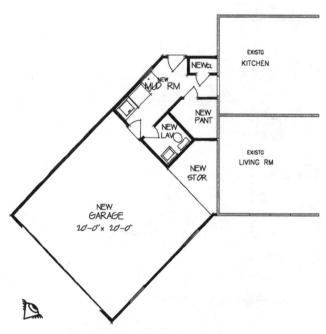

REMODELED FIRST FLOOR PLAN

GAR03

A PLAIN, CHARACTERLESS, L-RANCH IS TURNED INTO A SPARKLING SPANISH-STYLE COURT HOME IN THIS PLAN. THE OPEN SITE AREA OF THE L IS SPACE WAITING TO BE BETTER UTILIZED. IN THIS DESIGN, A NEW GARAGE IS BUILT FLUSH WITH THE FRONT WALL AND A LARGE NEW ROOM IS BUILT ALONGSIDE. THIS ROOM IS IDEAL FOR USE AS AN OFFICE, ALTHOUGH IT IS ALSO PERFECT AS A STUDIO, PLAYROOM, OR SPACIOUS BEDROOM SUITE. THE FORMER GARAGE IS SPACE THAT CAN BE CONVERTED TO MANY USES, SUCH AS AN APARTMENT, A NEW MASTER SUITE OR A FABULOUS NEW FAMILY ROOM. A STYLISH WALL IS CONSTRUCTED AT THE FRONT TO ENCLOSE THE NEW COURTYARD AND HELP CREATE THE SOUTHWESTERN FAÇADE.

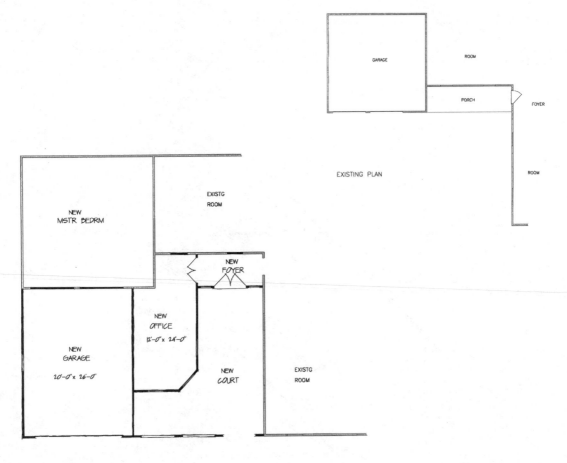

REMODELED FIRST FLOOR PLAN

GAR06

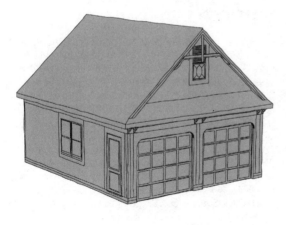

ALTHOUGH NOT A TRADITIONAL REMODELING
PROJECT, THE ADDITION OF A DETACHED GARAGE IS
A VERY COMMON UNDERTAKING. BECAUSE IT IS A
PLAN FOR "ADDING ON," IT HAS ITS PLACE IN THIS
BOOK, AND IN ACTUALITY A GARAGE OF THIS NATURE
COULD BE ATTACHED TO MANY HOMES. THIS
GARAGE IS A SIMPLE 20'×24' RECTANGLE WITH A
MODESTLY STEEP ROOF PITCH THAT PROVIDES
STAND UP ATTIC STORAGE. A PULL-DOWN STAIR—
OR EVEN A REGULAR STAIR—COULD BE LOCATED AT
THE REAR. IT COULD BE BUILT AS PLAIN VANILLA—
WITHOUT ALL THE TRIM AND DETAILING SHOWN, IF
YOU CHOOSE. THIS PLAN, OR THE NEXT GARAGE
PLAN, AS WELL AS PLAN NUMBER APT08 ON PAGE
216, COULD ALSO BE MODIFIED TO BE ATTACHED TO
AN EXISTING STRUCTURE.

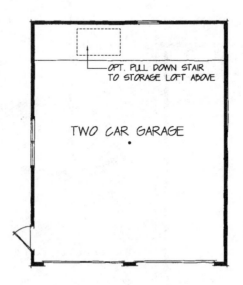

OPT. PULL DOWN STAIR
TO STORAGE LOFT ABOVE

TWO CAR GARAGE

FLOOR PLAN

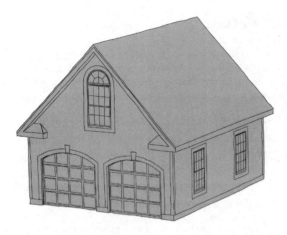

GAR07

SOMETIMES A NEW GARAGE IS NEEDED BECAUSE
THE EXISTING GARAGE WAS CONVERTED TO LIVING
SPACE. IN SUCH AN INSTANCE, IT IS VERY POSSIBLE
THAT WE WOULD BE ADDING A DETACHED GARAGE
SOMEWHERE ON THE LOT. CHECK YOUR ZONING
REQUIREMENTS FOR YARD REQUIREMENTS FOR AN
"ACCESSORY STRUCTURE," THE TERMINOLOGY
USUALLY USED FOR A DETACHED GARAGE. THIS
PARTICULAR PLAN IS A LITTLE WIDER THAN GAR06
AND INCLUDES A STEEPER ROOFLINE THAT ENABLES
YOU TO CREATE A HABITABLE ROOM ABOVE THE
GARAGE—A PERFECT PLACE FOR A HIDEAWAY,
STUDIO OR EVEN A GUEST BEDROOM.

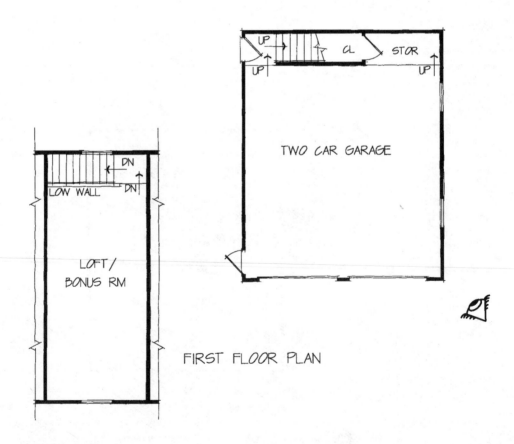

UP

UP

CL   STOR

UP

TWO CAR GARAGE

FIRST FLOOR PLAN

DN

LOW WALL   DN

LOFT/
BONUS RM

SECOND FLOOR PLAN

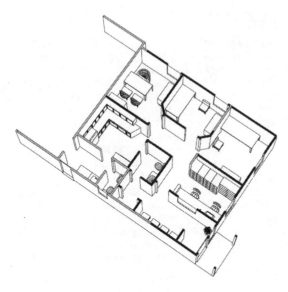

APT06

YOUR GOAL IS TO CREATE A PROFESSIONAL SUITE FROM A TWO-CAR GARAGE, BUT THE REQUIREMENTS OF THE PROGRAM EXCEED THE SPACE AVAILABLE. THE SOLUTION SHOWN HERE ADDS 10'0" TO THE SIDE, CREATING AN OFFICE EQUAL TO THAT OF A THREE-CAR GARAGE.   THE RESULTING SUITE IS SPACIOUS ENOUGH TO ACCOMMODATE TWO EXAMINATION (OR TREATMENT) ROOMS, A PRIVATE OFFICE, A LABORATORY, PLUS RECEPTION AND WAITING SPACE. THE GARAGE DOORS ARE CLOSED, OF COURSE, AND THE WINDOWS IN THE GARAGE, PLUS THE SIDING AND WINDOWS IN THE ADDITION, SHOULD ALL MATCH THE HOUSE.   ENTRANCE TO THE SUITE IS FROM THE SIDE, VIA A NEW COVERED PORCH.   THIS ENTRANCE WOULD LIKELY BE CONVENIENT TO ADDITIONAL PARKING WHICH IS USUALLY REQUIRED BY MOST ZONING ORDINANCES.

EXISTING PLAN

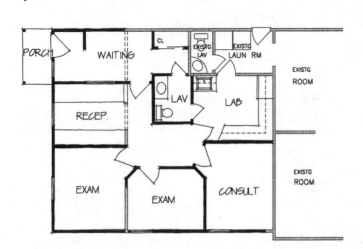

REMODELED FIRST FLOOR PLAN

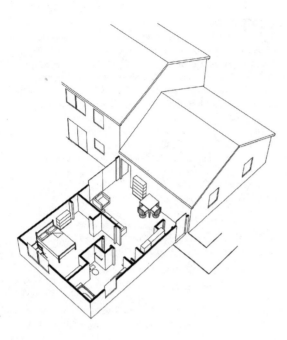

HAPT2

FINDING OR CREATING SPACE TO HOUSE ELDERLY PARENTS IS AN INCREASINGLY REQUESTED NEED EXPRESSED BY MANY HOMEOWNERS. WHERE TO PUT THEM IS OFTEN AN EXTREMELY DIFFICULT DECISION; SINCE STAIRS POSE A PROBLEM, AND ADEQUATE FIRST FLOOR SPACE USUALLY DOES NOT EXIST, AN ADDITION IS A FREQUENT CONSIDERATION, ESPECIALLY IF ITS A FULL APARTMENT YOU ARE SEEKING. THIS 20'4"×28'0" ADDITION IS PROPOSED AT THE REAR OF A DEEP GARAGE; IT PROVIDES DIRECT ACCESS TO THE HOUSE THROUGH THE LAUNDRY ROOM, YET FUNCTIONS VERY INDEPENDENTLY WITH ITS OWN SIDE ENTRANCE AND ACCESS TO THE REAR PATIO. THE BATH, HALLS, DOORS AND BEDROOM HAVE ALL BEEN DESIGNED TO BE BARRIER-FREE, THEREBY ACCOMMODATING THE NEEDS OF AN ADULT CONFINED TO A WHEELCHAIR, SHOULD THAT NEED ARISE.

REMODELED FIRST FLOOR PLAN

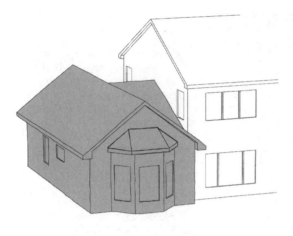

HAPT3

IF THE PROGRAM SEEKS TO HOUSE ELDERLY
PARENTS, OR A HANDICAPPED CHILD, THIS PLAN
PRESENTS ANOTHER OPTION TO CONSIDER. IT IS A
VERY ATTRACTIVE LOOKING ADDITION, 15'8" WIDE,
THAT CAN BE ATTACHED TO THE SIDE OF A ONE- OR
TWO-STORY HOME. THE COMFORTABLE, BARRIER-
FREE, TWO-ROOM APARTMENT DOES NOT INCLUDE
ITS OWN SEPARATE ENTRY OR KITCHEN; IT PRESUMES
THAT THE PARENTS (OR CHILD) WILL BE DINING IN THE
MAIN HOUSE ALL THE TIME, AND THAT THEY WILL
ENTER THROUGH THE MAIN—OR SOME OTHER—
ENTRANCE TO THE HOME, WHICH, IF THEY WERE
CONFINED TO A WHEELCHAIR, WOULD HAVE TO BE
MADE ACCESSIBLE. SEVERAL OTHER BARRIER-FREE
APARTMENTS ARE SHOWN IN CHAPTER 8.

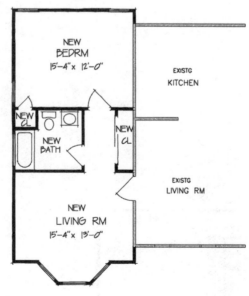

REMODELED FIRST FLOOR PLAN

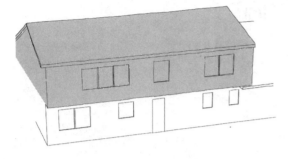

APT0I

PROBLEM: YOU'RE LOOKING TO CREATE A SMALL APARTMENT, BUT YOU DON'T HAVE THE LOT AREA TO GO OUT. LOOK UP. IT MAY BE POSSIBLE TO CREATE AN APARTMENT IN A PARTIAL SECOND FLOOR. SEE WHERE YOUR BASEMENT STAIR IS LOCATED—COULD YOU PUT A STAIR TO THE SECOND FLOOR ABOVE IT? THIS DESIGN SHOWS HOW TO DO IT. THE EXISTING PLAN SHOWN IS THE REAR OF A ONE-STORY HOME THAT IS WELL SUITED TO THIS ADDITION. THE APARTMENT IS 40'0" ACROSS AND CANTILEVERS 2'0" BEYOND THE FIRST FLOOR WALL TO GAIN ADDITIONAL AREA. THE CANTILEVER HAS ANOTHER ADVANTAGE, THAT OF PERMITTING GREATER DESIGN FREEDOM IN THE SIZING AND PLACEMENT OF WINDOWS AT THE SECOND FLOOR, SINCE ALIGNMENT WITH FIRST FLOOR WINDOWS IS NOT A PREREQUISITE.

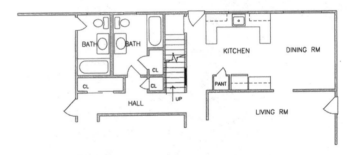

REMODELED FIRST FLOOR PLAN

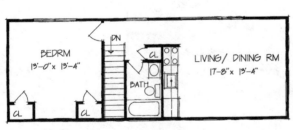

SECOND FLOOR PLAN
ALL NEW

APT07

SECOND FLOOR ADDITIONS ON LONG ONE-STORY HOMES ARE FREQUENTLY A CAUSE FOR CONCERN, AS THE SIZE OF THE ADDITION AND THE RELATIONSHIP OF NEW WINDOWS TO THE FIRST FLOOR ARE POTENTIAL DESIGN PROBLEMS. THIS PLAN SOLVES THE ARCHITECTURAL CONCERNS WELL AND ALSO PROVIDES A SPACIOUS TWO BEDROOM APARTMENT. THE NEW FIRST FLOOR VESTIBULE ALLOWS YOU TO SEPARATE THE APARTMENT, IF NECESSARY, FROM THE HOUSE. THE APARTMENT INCLUDES A LOVELY COUNTRY KITCHEN, ITS OWN OUTDOOR DECK, ONE AND ONE HALF BATHS AND AMPLE CLOSET SPACE. IT UTILIZES THE SPACE OVER AN EXISTING BASEMENT STAIR TO CREATE THE STAIR UP TO THE APARTMENT; IF YOUR STAIR IS NOT IN THIS LOCATION, YOU WOULD HAVE TO TAKE 3 FEET FROM THE BEDROOM OR CLOSETS LOCATED HERE.

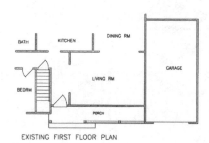

EXISTING FIRST FLOOR PLAN

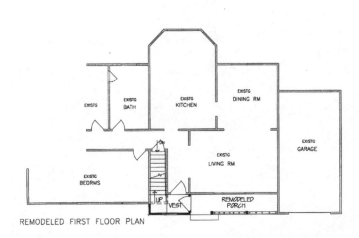

REMODELED FIRST FLOOR PLAN

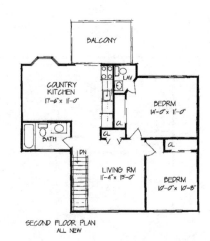

SECOND FLOOR PLAN
ALL NEW

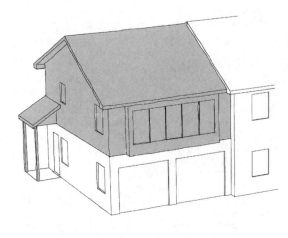

APT02

THE AREA OVER AN ATTACHED GARAGE IS READILY FOUND SPACE; IN THIS PLAN THE 20'0"×26'0" SPACE BECOMES A ONE BEDROOM APARTMENT. THE STAIR TO THE APARTMENT IS TAKEN FROM A STORAGE ALCOVE, A SPACE QUITE COMMON IN MANY DEEP GARAGES. IF YOUR GARAGE DOESN'T HAVE THIS DEPTH, THE STAIR WILL HAVE TO BE ADDED TO THE REAR, WHICH IS A MINOR ADJUSTMENT TO THE PLAN. THE APARTMENT INCLUDES A SMALL KITCHEN AND EATING ALCOVE; TO THE EXTENT THAT YOUR GARAGE IS LARGER THAN THAT PICTURED, THEN THESE CAN BE INCREASED. IF THE APARTMENT IS FOR FAMILY, AND YOU DESIRE AN INTERNAL CONNECTION, IT IS POSSIBLE TO CONNECT TO AN EXISTING SECOND FLOOR BEDROOM, OR EXTEND THE SECOND FLOOR HALL.

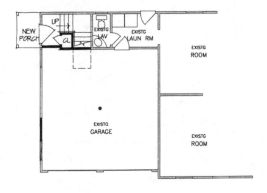

REMODELED FIRST FLOOR PLAN

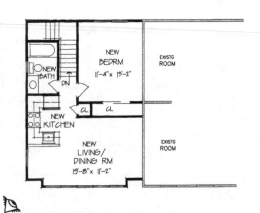

REMODELED SECOND FLOOR PLAN

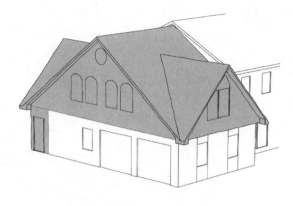

APT03

THE AREA ABOVE THIS 34'6" DEEP GARAGE WING IS FOUND SPACE FOR A SPACIOUS, ELEGANT APARTMENT.   THE ONLY GROUND FLOOR AREA NEEDED IS A 3'6" ADDITION FOR THE STAIR TO THE APARTMENT.   AN INTERESTING BONUS IS THE USE OF THE SPACE BELOW THIS STAIR TO PROVIDE A SECOND STAIR TO THE BASEMENT—AND IT HAS DIRECT ENTRANCE TO THE OUTSIDE.   THE APARTMENT IS HOUSED IN A DISTINCTIVE LOOKING ROOFLINE, FEATURING INTERSECTING REVERSE GABLE FORMS.   HALF-ROUND WINDOWS ADD EXTERIOR INTEREST, AS WELL AS INTERIOR CHARM.   A SPACIOUS LIVING/DINING ROOM AND AN EQUALLY LARGE BEDROOM, WITH PLENTY OF CLOSETS ARE THE NOTEWORTHY ASPECTS OF THIS DELIGHTFUL APARTMENT.

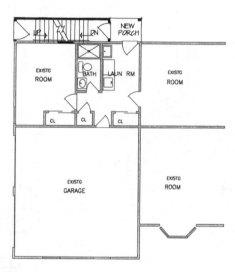

REMODELED FIRST FLOOR PLAN

REMODELED SECOND FLOOR PLAN

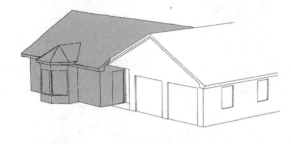

APT04

THE YARD BEHIND A GARAGE IS AN IDEAL LOCATION FOR A NEW GROUND FLOOR APARTMENT; THE REASONS INCLUDE THE FACTS THAT THIS AREA IS FREQUENTLY UNDERUTILIZED, THAT THERE ARE NO ROOMS AFFECTED AT THIS LOCATION, AND ITS PROXIMITY TO THE DRIVEWAY PROVIDES REASONABLY PRIVATE ACCESS. THE COMFORTABLE ONE BEDROOM APARTMENT SHOWN INCLUDES A LARGE LIVING ROOM, A U-SHAPED KITCHEN AND A LOVELY BAYED DINING AREA. AN ENTRANCE FOYER WITH TWO CLOSETS, A DUAL ENTRANCE BATH AND A LARGE WALK-IN CLOSET ARE OTHER FEATURES OF NOTE. THE BLANK WALL FACING THE REAR YARD BEHIND THE HOUSE SHOULD MAINTAIN PRIVACY FOR THE OWNERS.

REMODELED FIRST FLOOR PLAN

APT09

THE NEED TO HOUSE AN AGING PARENT—OR YOUNG
MARRIED COUPLE—IS ONE OF THE INCREASINGLY
POPULAR THEMES WE ARCHITECTS HEAR. MULTI-
GENERATIONAL HOMES ARE BECOMING MORE
POPULAR. THIS PLAN, AS SEVERAL OTHERS, TAKES
ADVANTAGE OF THE SPACE COMMONLY FOUND ON A
LOT BEHIND THE GARAGE. IT CREATES A TWO ROOM
APARTMENT WITH ITS OWN OUTSIDE ENTRANCE
WHILE STILL GIVING ACCESS TO THE REAR YARD FOR
THE MAIN OCCUPANTS. THE PLAN INCLUDES A
GENEROUS LIVING ROOM AND A BEDROOM AND FULL
BATH. DEPENDING ON THE EXISTING HOUSE,
ROOFLINES MIGHT NEED TO BE STUDIED, AS THEY
COULD BE TRICKY.

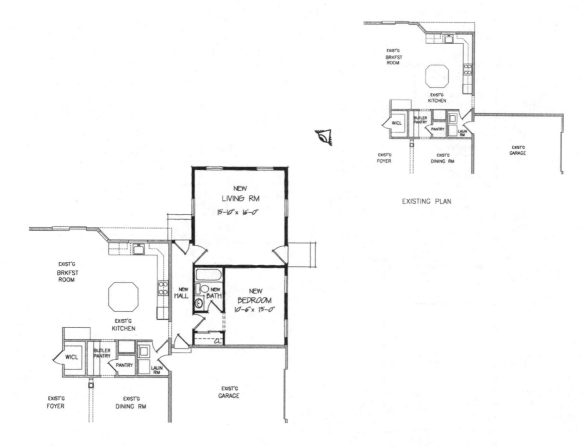

EXISTING PLAN

REMODELED FLOOR PLAN

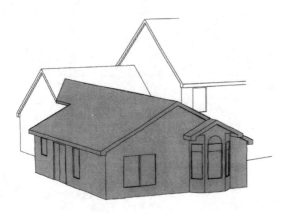

APT IO

THIS PLAN, AS THE PRIOR ONE, DEALS WITH THE ISSUE OF ADDING AN APARTMENT TO THE LOT SPACE LOCATED BEHIND A GARAGE. IT TOO SOLVES THE NEED FOR THE NEW MULTI-GENERATIONAL FAMILY, BUT SINCE IT ALSO PROVIDES FOR A KITCHEN IT COULD BE AN INCOME-PRODUCING APARTMENT AS WELL. YOU NEED TO CHECK YOUR LOCAL ZONING ORDINANCES, THOUGH, TO SEE IF A SECOND KITCHEN IS ALLOWED. THE PLAN PROVIDES A FORMAL ENTRANCE, SPACIOUS LIVING ROOM AND KITCHEN PLUS TWO BEDROOMS AND A FULL BATH. A NEW BASEMENT STAIR IS SHOWN PROVIDING ACCESS TO A FULL BASEMENT WHICH CAN BE LOCATED UNDER THE NEW ADDITION.

EXISTING FLOOR PLAN

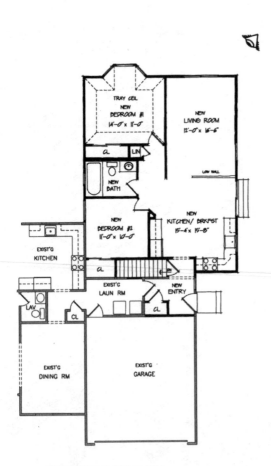

REMODELED FLOOR PLAN

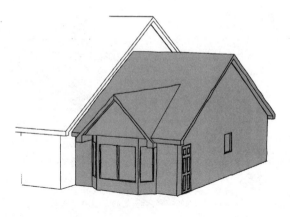

APT II

ANOTHER APARTMENT SOLUTION FOR A PARENT, CHILD—OR FOR RENT—IS THE SUBJECT OF THIS PLAN. THIS PLAN PRESUMES THERE IS AMPLE LOT SPACE LEFT ON THE GARAGE SIDE OF THE HOME. WHAT IT DOES, THOUGH, IS PROVIDE AN ATTRACTIVE WAY TO ADD ALONGSIDE A GARAGE. THE ELEMENT MUST BE SET BACK FROM THE GARAGE WALL SO IT ESTABLISHES ITS OWN FORM AND CHARACTER, AND IS NOT MERELY A CONTINUATION OF THE GARAGE ROOF. THIS PLAN, AS MANY OF THE OTHERS, CREATES ITS CONNECTION TO THE EXISTING HOUSE THROUGH THE LAUNDRY ROOM, WHICH IS FREQUENTLY LOCATED NEAR THE REAR OF A GARAGE. THIS PROVIDES A "NEUTRAL" MEETING SPACE FOR THE TWO FAMILIES.

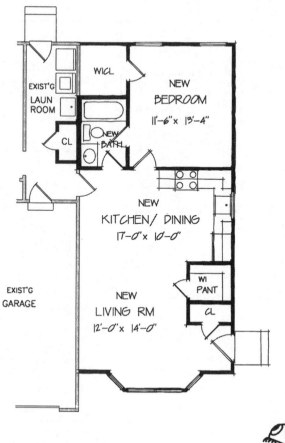

REMODELED FLOOR PLAN

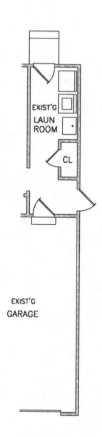

EXISTING FLOOR PLAN

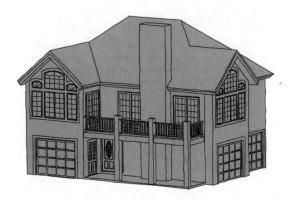

APT08

THIS PLAN IS ANOTHER UNIQUE ONE FOR THIS BOOK; IT IS A FULLY DETACHED STRUCTURE—ALMOST A LITTLE HOUSE—THAT OFFERS THE REMODELOR A VERY DIFFERENT SOLUTION THAT SATISFIES THE NEED FOR AN APARTMENT AND A GARAGE.   THE APARTMENT, SOMETIMES CALLED A "GRANNY FLAT," IS LOCATED ABOVE THE GARAGE.   IT INCLUDES A BEAUTIFUL GREAT ROOM, DINING ROOM, KITCHEN AND A SPACIOUS BEDROOM WITH A FULL BATH; THERE IS A PORCH FOR OUTDOOR ENJOYMENT.   THE FIRST FLOOR IS VERY FLEXIBLE; ALTHOUGH IT IS SHOWN AS A THREE-CAR GARAGE, ONE OR TWO OF THE GARAGE BAYS COULD BE FINISHED AS ADDITIONAL LIVING SPACE, IF SO DESIRED.

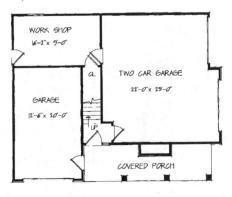

FIRST FLOOR PLAN

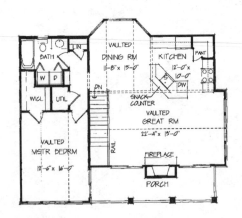

SECOND FLOOR PLAN

Remodel Plans—Bumps, Bays, Extensions and Interior Remodeling

The prior chapter presented an extensive assortment of room additions. This chapter presents an equally varied collection of plans; however, the scope of these projects is usually smaller, and typically—but not necessarily—less costly than room size additions. Again the plans are generally grouped by room type, and all of the plan viewing conventions previously referred to still apply, so if you are reading this section first, please review the introductions to chapters 5 and 8 before trying to view these plans.

There are several types of designs presented here; the most prominent is a design for one specific room, such as a bathroom, or a kitchen. The plan could be a remodeling of interior space only, or it might include a small addition, or a "bump", or a bay. These small space additions can have an affect on the interior space that is significantly greater than their area.

There are also several designs in this section that remodel multiple rooms; however, these are not new room additions, but extensions to existing rooms. They are typically under 8'0". If you are seeking larger additions, that is the subject of chapters 8 and 11. This section is a collection of smaller projects.

Some of the designs pictured here are also not necessarily specific to a given room. For example, there are front porches that can change the appearance of the home, vestibules, or even some plans that show you how to add natural light to the interior of the home, and even some that can light up a basement. A larger number of these plans are pictured with interior perspective views as they do not add much, if any, new exterior space.

It is also possible that some of these designs will be incorporated within, or together with, larger room additions presented in the prior chapter. These designs could also become integral components to a new facelift to the home, as pictured in the next section, or even a part of a whole house renovation as shown in chapter 11. Space additions of this nature do have one common inherent difficulty: they are more difficult to live with during construction than a new room addition, therefore extra planning is necessary to help cope with the project. A discussion on staging, which can be very helpful to mitigate living with construction, is included in chapter 13.

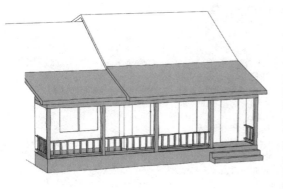

P0007

TODAY'S NEW HOME IS LIKELY TO HAVE A FRONT
PORCH, AS THAT HAS BEEN IN VOGUE, AND IS LIKELY
TO REMAIN POPULAR FOR SOME TIME. THE PORCH
BRINGS NOSTALGIA, CHARM AND A THEME OF
RELAXATION, WHILE IT ALSO HAS THE USEFUL
FUNCTION OF PROVIDING SHELTER TO THE ENTRY;
AND IT IS STILL A PLACE TO SIT AND WATCH THE
WORLD. BUT ONE DOES NOT HAVE TO MOVE TO
FIND A PORCH; IT IS EASY TO ADD ONE TO ANY
CURRENT HOME. YOU WILL HAVE TO CHECK THE
ZONING ORDINANCES, ESPECIALLY IF YOUR HOME IS
CURRENTLY AT THE MINIMUM SETBACK. MANY
ORDINANCES ALLOW A ONE-STORY OPEN PORCH TO
ENCROACH INTO A REQUIRED FRONT YARD. IF NOT, A
VARIANCE MAY BE REQUIRED. THIS INFORMALLY-
STYLED, SHED-ROOFED PORCH WILL ADAPT TO EITHER
A ONE OR TWO-STORY HOME.

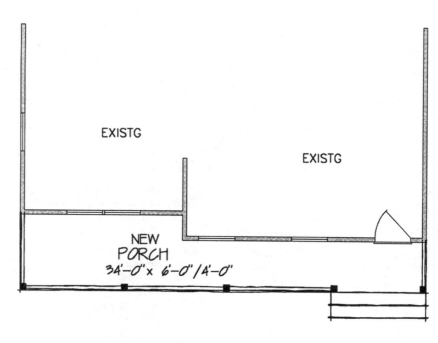

EXISTG

EXISTG

NEW
PORCH
34'-0" x 6'-0" / 4'-0"

REMODELED FIRST FLOOR PLAN

P0013

SIMPLE, FLUSH-FRONT FAÇADES DOMINATED THE STYLING OF MANY TWO-STORY HOMES BUILT FIFTEEN TO THIRTY YEARS AGO, AND IN SOME REGIONS THEY ARE STILL POPULAR.   THERE IS, HOWEVER, A DEFINITE STYLISTIC CHANGE OCCURRING.   IT IS CALLED "COUNTRY" AS IT RELIES ON THE HOMINESS AND WARMTH ASSOCIATED WITH RURAL LIFE.   THE COUNTRY FRONT PORCH IS "IN" — AND, SINCE THE STYLE IS NOT NEW AND FLASHY, BUT OLD AND LAID BACK, IT IS LIKELY TO BE WITH US FOR A LONG TIME. THEREFORE, IF ONE IS DREAMING OF A WRAP-AROUND, COUNTRY-STYLE PORCH, GO AHEAD AND DO IT; ONE WON'T HAVE TO WORRY THAT IT WILL BE OUT OF FASHION WHEN ONE DECIDES TO SELL.   IN FACT, IN SOME REGIONS, ONE MAY BE OUT OF FASHION WITH AN OLD FLUSH FRONT.

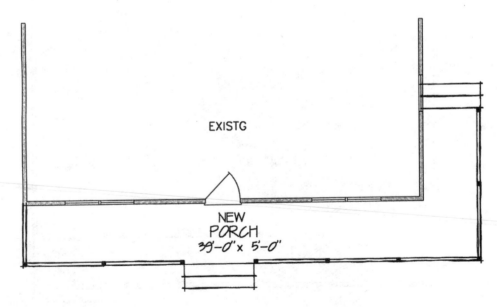

EXISTG

NEW
PORCH
39'-0" x 5'-0"

REMODELED FIRST FLOOR PLAN

P0008

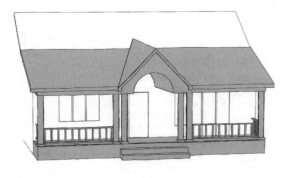

THIS BEAUTIFUL, CONTINUOUS FRONT PORCH
CREATES A MORE FORMAL, STATELY ENTRANCE THAN
THE RAMBLING SHED ROOF IN P0007 OR THE
COUNTRY LOOK IN P0013. HEAVY ROUND COLUMNS
AND THE REVERSE GABLE CENTER SECTION HELP
DELINEATE THIS UNDERSTATED FORMALITY. AS WITH
ANY OF THESE PORCHES, THE MAIN IMPETUS IS A
DESIRE TO CHANGE OR UPDATE THE EXTERIOR OF
YOUR HOME; THEREFORE, THERE IS A VARIETY OF
STYLES TO HELP CREATE THE PARTICULAR MOOD OR
FEELING YOU ARE SEEKING. THE PORCH MAY
BECOME THE FOCUS FOR CHANGE, AND YOU SHOULD
REVIEW THE NEW FAÇADES SHOWN IN CHAPTER II
FOR FURTHER IDEAS. UNLESS INDICATED OTHERWISE
MOST OF THE PORCHES SHOWN IN THIS CHAPTER
ARE ADAPTABLE TO BOTH ONE- OR TWO-STORY
HOMES.

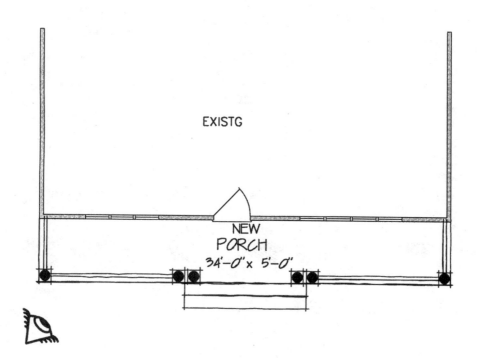

EXISTG

NEW
PORCH
34'-0" x 5'-0"

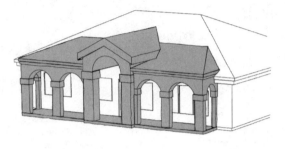

P0010

PORCHES CAN BE DESIGNED IN ALL SIZES, SHAPES AND STYLES TO MATCH ANY HOME—OR THE STYLE YOU WANT TO MAKE THE HOME. THIS SOUTHWESTERN, SPANISH-STYLE PORCH IS AN EXAMPLE. IT COULD BE AFFIXED TO A STUCCO SOUTHWESTERN HOME—OR IT COULD BE THE DOMINANT FEATURE TO RECAST A SIMPLE FLUSH-FRONT HOME FROM ORDINARY TO SPECTACULAR. A RAISED CENTER GABLE PROVIDES A FOCUS TO THE ENTRY, AND THIS CENTER SECTION COULD BE BUILT BY ITSELF. AN IMPORTANT DESIGN TIP IS TO KEEP THE PORCH AT LEAST 3' SHORT OF THE ENDS. THIS ALLOWS YOU TO PROPERLY RAISE THE WALL AND ROOF OF THE PORCH, WHICH IS NECESSARY TO ACHIEVE THE DESIRED EFFECT.

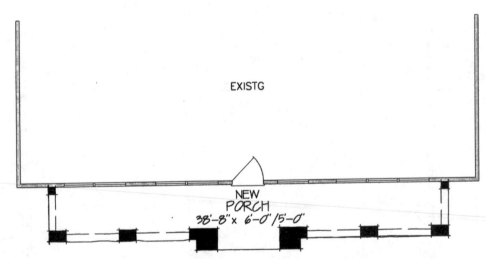

EXISTG

NEW
PORCH
38'-8" x 6'-0"/5'-0"

REMODELED FIRST FLOOR PLAN

P0009

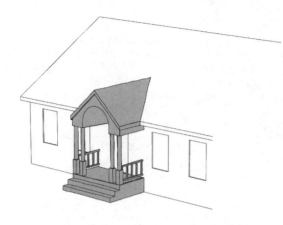

THIS ENGAGING LITTLE FRONT PORCH COULD DO MUCH TO UPDATE THE APPEARANCE OF ANY HOME. IT ALSO WILL SERVE THE PRACTICAL PURPOSE OF PROVIDING COVER TO THE FRONT DOOR. THE ATTRACTIVE REVERSE GABLE, ARCHED ENTRYWAY, CLUSTERED ROUND COLUMNS AND WOOD RAILS HAVE BEEN EXQUISITELY DETAILED AND WILL FOSTER AN INITIAL APPEARANCE OF QUALITY. THE TRIM 9'×5' SIZE WILL BE APPROPRIATE FOR MOST AVERAGE HOMES. IT SHOULD BE DECREASED FOR A HOME UNDER 30' IN WIDTH AND INCREASED FOR A HOME GREATER THAN 45' IN WIDTH. A CONTINUOUS PORCH MIGHT BE PREFERABLE FOR A HOME LESS THAN 30' WIDE.

EXISTG

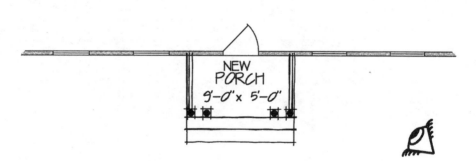

NEW
PORCH
9'-0" x 5'-0"

REMODELED FIRST FLOOR PLAN

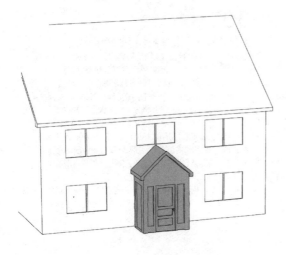

P0011

IS THE OWNER OF THE HOME TIRED OF THAT COLD BLAST OF ARCTIC AIR IN WINTER WHEN SOMEONE OPENS THE FRONT DOOR? WELL, THEN, YOU SHOULD CONSIDER RECOMMENDING A VESTIBULE. A VESTIBULE SERVES AS AN AIR LOCK—OR "DECOMPRESSION CHAMBER"—KEEPING THE COLD AIR OUTSIDE YOUR LIVING SPACES. AS WITH A FRONT PORCH, IT IS NECESSARY TO CHECK YOUR ZONING ORDINANCE, TO SEE IF YOU CAN BUILD ONE "AS-OF-RIGHT" OR IF YOU MIGHT NEED A VARIANCE. THE LOVELY LOOKING 7'8"×4'10" REVERSE GABLE VESTIBULE PICTURED HERE IS ADAPTABLE TO MOST ONE- AND TWO-STORY HOMES. ON A TWO-STORY IT IS IMPORTANT TO VERIFY THE HEIGHT OF THE WINDOWS OVER THE FRONT DOOR TO SEE IF THE VESTIBULE FITS WITHOUT HAVING TO MAKE WINDOW CHANGES.

EXISTG

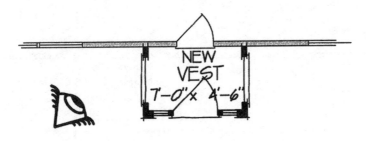

NEW
VEST
7'-0" x 4'-6"

P0012

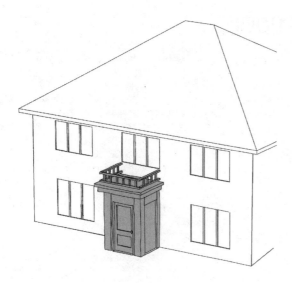

THIS 6'4"×4'10" FLAT-ROOF VESTIBULE IS THE MOST MODEST OF THE VESTIBULES SHOWN IN THE BOOK. IT IS COMPRISED OF THREE DOORS, ONE IN THE FRONT AND TWO FIXED ONES ON THE SIDES. THE GLAZED DOORS PROVIDE AN ABUNDANCE OF LIGHT WHILE ATTRACTIVELY ENCLOSING THIS SPACE. THE FLAT ROOF IS CAPPED BY A LOW DECORATIVE RAILING. ON A TWO-STORY HOME WITH DEEP SECOND FLOOR WINDOWS, THIS WOULD BE THE MORE PRACTICAL SOLUTION. THIS VESTIBULE, AS WITH ANY OF THE VESTIBULES OR PORCHES, ALSO PERFORMS A SECONDARY FUNCTION, THAT OF DRESSING UP THE FAÇADE OF THE HOME IT IS ATTACHED TO. IT BECOMES A COST-EFFECTIVE METHOD TO EFFECT A MODEST FAÇADE CHANGE.

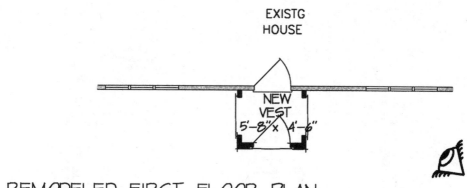

EXISTG
HOUSE

NEW
VEST
5'-8" x 4'-6"

REMODELED FIRST FLOOR PLAN

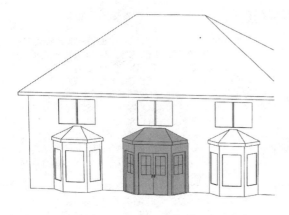

POOI5

THIS TASTEFUL LOOKING, GLASS ENCLOSED, VESTIBULE IS DESIGNED SPECIFICALLY FOR A CENTER HALL TWO-STORY HOME. IT IS EXCEPTIONALLY WELL SUITED TO A HIP-ROOFED HOME, WITH MATCHING BAY WINDOWS AND A RECESS AT THE FRONT DOOR, AS SHOWN. IT WILL, HOWEVER, BE APPROPRIATE TO ANY FLUSH-FRONT TWO-STORY HOME. THE ENCLOSURE UTILIZES FOUR GLAZED DOORS, WITH THE SIDE ONES BEING FIXED IN PLACE. THE SPACE IS COVERED WITH A HIP ROOF DESIGNED TO COMPLEMENT THE BAYS (IF THEY EXIST). A TRULY STUNNING LOOKING OPTION MIGHT BE A GLAZED ROOF IN THE SHAPE SHOWN; IF HOWEVER, YOURS IS A VERY SUNNY LOCATION AND IT GETS HOT IN SUMMER, THAT WOULD NOT BE ADVISABLE.

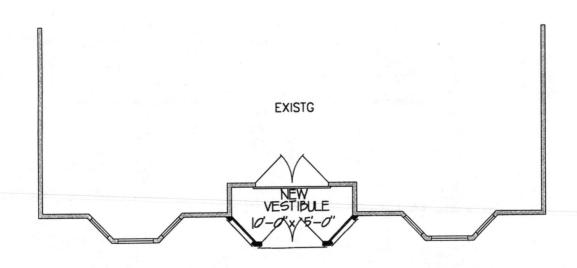

EXISTG

NEW
VESTIBULE
10'-0" x 5'-0"

REMODELED FIRST FLOOR PLAN

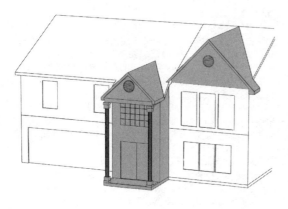

POOI9

ONE OF THE MOST UNFORTUNATE ASPECTS OF THE TYPICAL HI-RANCH (SPLIT-FOYER, BI-LEVEL) PLAN IS THE LACK OF AN ATTRACTIVE ENTRY. THERE IS USUALLY NO SHELTER AT THE DOOR, YOU FREQUENTLY HAVE TO CLIMB A STEEP STOOP TO GET THERE, AND ONCE INSIDE, THERE IS NO TRUE FOYER; THE MID-LEVEL PLATFORM IS NOT A PLACE TO STAY. THIS NEAT LITTLE ADDITION SOLVES ALL THESE PROBLEMS. IT REPLACES THE STOOP WITH A LOVELY COVERED PORCH AND AN ELEGANT LITTLE GRADE LEVEL FOYER THAT SEEMS TO SAY "WELCOME." ALSO INCLUDED IN THIS PLAN IS A SUGGESTED REMODELING OF THE LIVING ROOM WHICH CALLS FOR NEW DRAMATIC WINDOWS AND A RAISING OF THE CEILING AS A CONSEQUENCE OF INSTALLING A REVERSE GABLE ROOF. ALTHOUGH UNRELATED TO THE NEW FOYER, IT DOES HELP CREATE THE STYLISH NEW EXTERIOR DESIGN PICTURED.

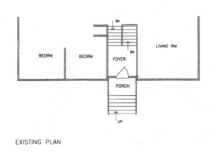

EXISTING PLAN

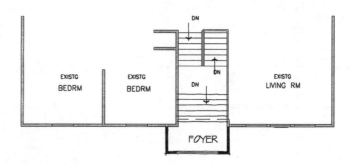

REMODELED SECOND FLOOR PLAN

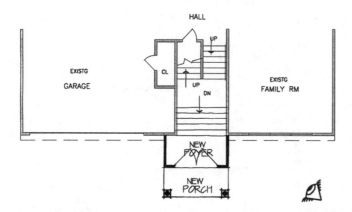

REMODELED FIRST FLOOR PLAN

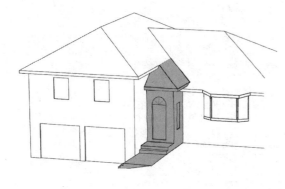

P0016

THERE ARE SOME ADDITIONS THAT LOOK SO NATURAL THAT IT IS A WONDER THEY WERE NOT PART OF THE ORIGINAL HOME. THIS NEW LITTLE VESTIBULE IS AN EXAMPLE. DESIGNED SPECIFICALLY FOR THE L-SHAPED SPLIT-LEVEL, IT CREATES AN ATTRACTIVE SEPARATELY DEFINED ENTRANCE FOYER, POTENTIALLY FREEING YOUR LIVING ROOM FROM SERVING THIS DOUBLE DUTY. IT IS PLACED DOWN TWO STEPS, WHICH WILL REDUCE THE HEIGHT OF THE OUTSIDE STOOP. THIS LOWER FLOOR ALSO ALLOWS THE HEIGHT FOR A HALF-ROUND WINDOW OVER THE NEW DOOR, WHILE CREATING A MORE INVITING ENTRANCE. A WINDOW AT THE SIDE FURTHER ENHANCES THE SPACE. FOR SOME NEW IDEAS ON ENTRANCE STEPS, SEE PLANS SML02/3 ON PAGE 229.

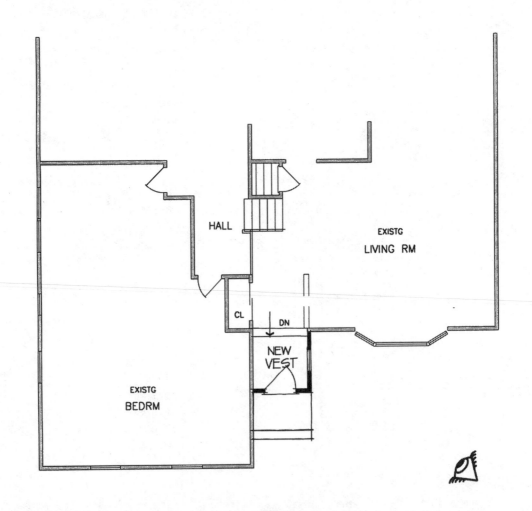

HALL

EXISTG
LIVING RM

CL

DN

NEW
VEST

EXISTG
BEDRM

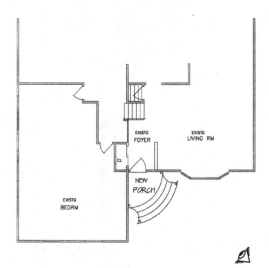

SML02/SML03

THESE TWO PLANS ARE A DEPARTURE; THEY DO NOT DEAL WITH INTERIOR SPACE AT ALL, BUT ARE IDEAS THAT ENHANCE AN ENTRANCE WITHOUT ADDING ON. MANY HOMES, PARTICULARLY SPLIT-LEVEL DESIGNS, HAVE AN OLD CONCRETE PORCH AND STEPS THAT ARE PROBABLY IN NEED OF REPAIR. FREQUENTLY THE STEPS ARE STEEP, AND THE OVERALL EFFECT MAY NOT PRESENT A VERY APPEALING ENTRANCE TO THE HOME. BEFORE YOU PATCH OR COVER THEM, GIVE SOME THOUGHT TO COMPLETELY REPLACING THEM. THESE TWO DESIGNS DO THAT WITH FLAIR. BOTH MOVE THE PATH OF TRAVEL AWAY FROM THE WALL AND ENLARGE THE PLATFORM SO THAT MORE THAN ONE PERSON CAN STAND THERE. THE CURVED SOLUTION IS AN ELEGANT PLAN BEST EXECUTED IN MASONRY; THE ANGULAR PLAN COULD BE BUILT AS A WOOD DECK, OR IN MASONRY. EITHER ONE WILL ENHANCE THE ENTRANCE TO THE HOME.

EXISTG
FOYER

EXISTG
LIVING RM

CL

NEW
PORCH

EXISTG
BEDRM

REMODELED FIRST FLOOR PLAN

EXISTG
LIVING RM

EXISTG
FOYER

CL

EXISTG
BEDRM

NEW
PORCH

REMODELED FIRST FLOOR PLAN

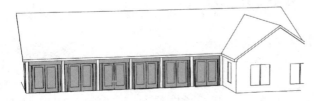

P0021

IS THE FRONT OF THE HOME ADORNED BY A LONG, COVERED PORCH THAT YOU THINK MIGHT BE BETTER UTILIZED? THIS DESIGN SHOWS YOU HOW TO INCORPORATE THE PORCH INTO THE HOME. IT CREATES A CONTINUOUS LOGGIA, PARTS OF WHICH CAN BE ADDED TO THE ACTUAL FLOOR AREA OF THE ADJOINING ROOM. IN FRONT OF OTHER ROOMS, SUCH AS A KITCHEN, COST CONSIDERATIONS MIGHT DICTATE LEAVING THE EXISTING WALL. EVEN IN THAT SITUATION, THOUGH, THE INTERIOR ROOM BENEFITS FROM NATURAL LIGHT THAT THE NEW LOGGIA HAS PROVIDED IN THE FORM OF CONTINUOUS SKYLIGHTS AND GLAZED DOORS. THE NUANCES OF YOUR HOME WOULD DETERMINE THE BEST UTILIZATION OF THE NEW FOUND SPACE.

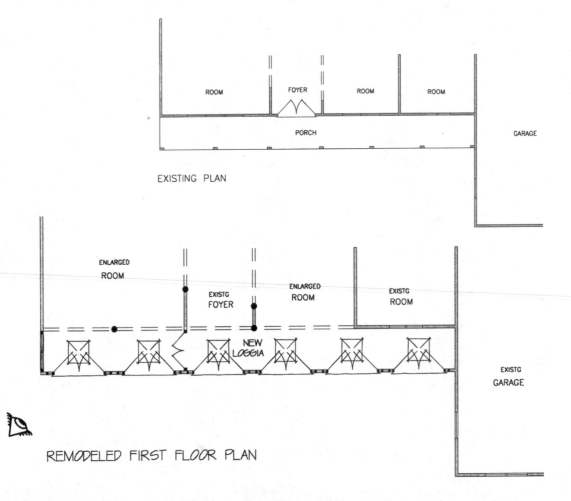

EXISTING PLAN

REMODELED FIRST FLOOR PLAN

PFOOI

PROBLEM: AN UNINSPIRED LOOKING, FLAT-ROOFED, ONE-STORY HOME WITH A RECESSED ENTRANCE THAT SEEMS TO BE SPACE WAITING TO BE PUT TO BETTER USE. SOLUTION: ENCLOSE THE COURT WITH A SMART LOOKING REVERSE GABLE ADDITION THAT SUCCEEDS IN ENHANCING THE APPEARANCE OF THE HOME WHILE BENEFITING THE ROOMS IT ADJOINS. THE GLAZED ENDS OF THIS GABLE, AND AN EXPANSIVE ROOF SKYLIGHT, BATHE THE NEW ENCLOSED FOYER WITH NATURAL LIGHT, WHICH ALSO SERVES TO VISUALLY ENHANCE THE ADJOINING LIVING AND DINING ROOMS. THE DRAMATIC NEW FRONT TO REAR INTERIOR VISTA WILL UNDOUBTEDLY GENERATE MANY POSITIVE COMMENTS.

EXISTING PLAN

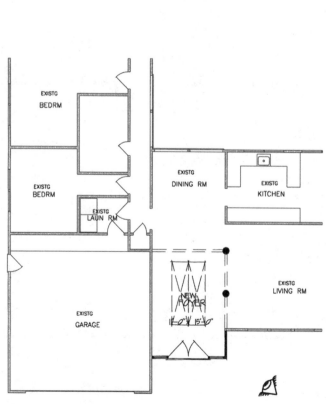

REMODELED FIRST FLOOR PLAN

P0014

THE HOMEOWNER KEEPS DRIVING BY THAT BRAND NEW TWO-STORY AND ENVIES ITS DRAMATIC MAIN ENTRANCE. WELL, IF THEIR HOME IS A SIMPLE, FLUSH FRONT, CENTER HALL TWO-STORY, THEY NEED ENVY NO MORE, AS THIS MODEST CHANGE WILL CREATE THE NEW LOOK THEY ARE SEEKING. A 13'0"×3'6" DEEP, REVERSE GABLE BUMP IS CREATED IN THE PLAN SHOWN. PRACTICAL BENEFITS INCLUDE A RECESSED SHELTERED ENTRY, AND A 3'6" INCREASE TO THE SECOND FLOOR ROOM ABOVE. AN ALTERNATIVE MIGHT BE TO REMOVE THE ROOM OVER THE FOYER AND CREATE A DRAMATIC TWO-STORY FOYER. THIS ADDITION REQUIRES MINIMAL CHANGE TO THE EXISTING HOME, YET COULD ACCOMPLISH MUCH FOR OTHERS TO ENVY.

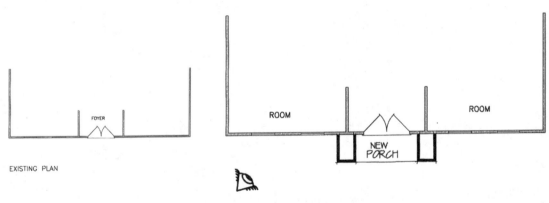

EXISTING PLAN

REMODELED FIRST FLOOR PLAN

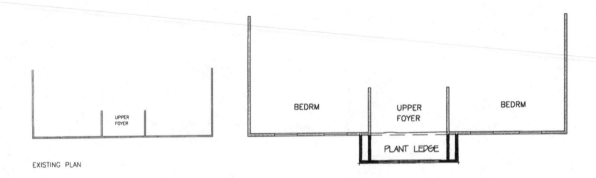

EXISTING PLAN

REMODELED SECOND FLOOR PLAN

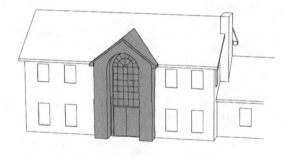

PF002

A DRAMATIC NEW ENTRANCE IS THE MAIN FOCUS OF THIS DESIGN. TWO SMALL 3'0" DEEP CLOSETS ARE BUMPED OUT AT EACH SIDE OF THE FIRST FLOOR FOYER; THEY EXTEND TWO STORIES IN HEIGHT, AND TERMINATE IN A ROUNDED ARCH UNDER A REVERSE GABLE ROOF. A FABULOUS WINDOW OCCUPIES THE ENTIRE SPACE OVER THE NEW DOUBLE DOOR ENTRY. THE FLOOR OVER THE FOYER HAS BEEN REMOVED, AND THIS WINDOW FLOODS THE NEW TWO-STORY HIGH FOYER WITH NATURAL LIGHT. THE OVERALL EFFECT IS STUNNING, AND IT PROVIDES A 30-YEAR-OLD HOME WITH A NEW PRESENCE. THERE IS A ROOM REMOVED AT THE SECOND FLOOR, OF COURSE, WHICH IS THE TRADE OFF.

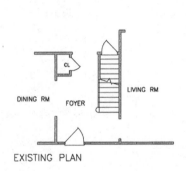

EXISTING PLAN

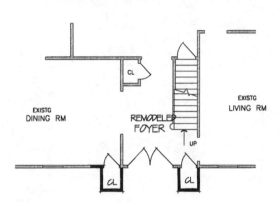

REMODELED FIRST FLOOR PLAN

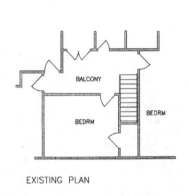

EXISTING PLAN

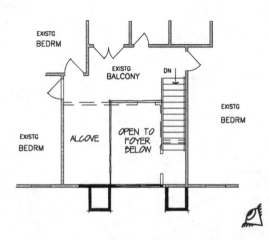

REMODELED SECOND FLOOR PLAN

PFB0I

ENLARGING AND MODERNIZING SECOND FLOOR FRONT BATHROOMS IS A THORNY DESIGN PROBLEM. PLAN PFB02 ON PAGE 235 ACCOMPLISHES IT BY REMOVING A BEDROOM AND RELOCATING THE BATHS TO THE REAR. THIS PLAN ACHIEVES SIMILAR RESULTS, WITHOUT THE LOSS OF THE BEDROOM, BY ADDING A 7'0" DEEP, TWO-STORY EXTENSION TO THE FRONT. IT OBVIOUSLY REQUIRES THE ABILITY TO BUILD IN FRONT, WHICH MIGHT REQUIRE A VARIANCE. THE RESULTS, HOWEVER, ARE WORTH IT; A SPARKLING NEW MASTER BATH AND DRESSING ROOM ARE THE RESULT. A REMODELED FRONT FAÇADE PLUS AN ENHANCED ENTRANCE FOYER, WITH AN APPEALING VISUAL OPENING TO THE SECOND FLOOR, ARE EXTRA BENEFITS. A WORD OF CAUTION DURING CONSTRUCTION: IF YOU WANT A FUNCTIONING SECOND FLOOR BATH, YOU WILL HAVE TO STAGE THEM ONE AT A TIME, DOING THE HALL BATH FIRST.

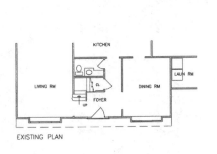

EXISTING PLAN

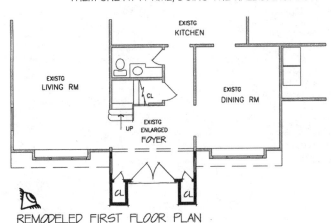

REMODELED FIRST FLOOR PLAN

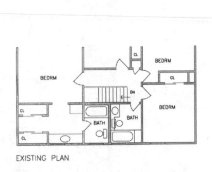

EXISTING PLAN

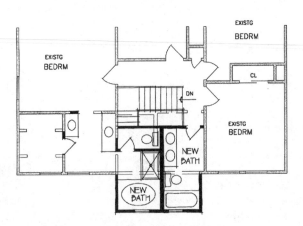

REMODELED SECOND FLOOR PLAN

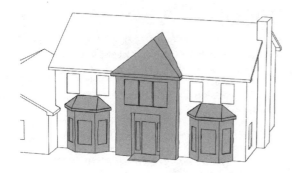

PFB02

SOME WILL SAY, "IT'S CRAZY, YOU LOSE A BEDROOM". BUT, IF ONE CAN LIVE WITH THREE BEDROOMS ON THE SECOND FLOOR (AND IN MANY MATURING FAMILIES THAT IS NOW POSSIBLE), THEN THIS REMODEL MIGHT MAKE SENSE. IT WILL BE MORE SENSIBLE IF A GOAL IS TO UPDATE THE ENTRANCE TO THE HOME PLUS THE DATED SECOND FLOOR BATHROOMS. TWO NEW BATHS, INCLUDING A STYLISH NEW COMPARTMENTED MASTER BATH ARE RECREATED FROM THE REAR MIDDLE BEDROOM. A LARGE NEW WALK-IN CLOSET AND DRESSING ROOM ARE ALSO INCLUDED, AND A CHIC NEW MASTER SUITE RESULTS. THE FIRST FLOOR FOYER NOW OPENS TO THE SECOND FLOOR, THEREBY CREATING A DRAMATIC NEW ENTRY. A SIGNIFICANT BONUS OF THIS PLAN IS THE UP-DATED NEW FAÇADE THAT RESULTS. ALSO SEE PLAN PFB01 ON PAGE 234.

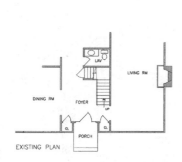

EXISTING PLAN

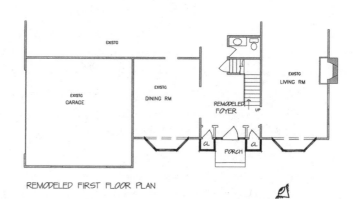

REMODELED FIRST FLOOR PLAN

EXISTING PLAN

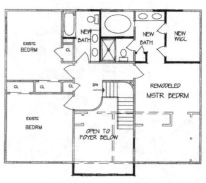

REMODELED SECOND FLOOR PLAN

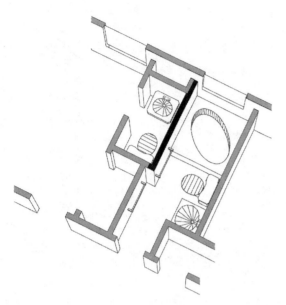

B0001

THE FOLLOWING THREE PLANS DEAL WITH ANOTHER COMMON PROBLEM: HOW DO YOU CREATE TWO BATHS (OR 1½) WHERE THERE'S PRESENTLY ONLY ONE HALL BATH. THE THREE EXISTING PLANS SHOWN ARE EXTREMELY POPULAR LAYOUTS DERIVED FROM TYPCIAL ONE-STORY, SPLIT-LEVEL, OR BI-LEVEL (HI-RANCH) HOMES. IF THIS IS YOUR NEED, ONE OF THESE SHOULD BE FAIRLY CLOSE TO THE LAYOUT OF YOUR HOME. THE PLAN PICTURED ON THIS PAGE SHOWS HOW TO GAIN AN EXTRA HALF BATH, WITHOUT ANY EXTERIOR ADDITIONS, FROM AN EXISTING BATH ONLY 11' DEEP. AS YOU CAN SEE, THE EXTRA HALF BATH IS GAINED FOR THE MASTER BEDROOM, WITH VERY LITTLE CHANGE. WITH A SMALL EXTERIOR BUMP OF 2' YOU COULD GET TWO FULL BATHS; SEE THE PLANS THAT FOLLOW.

EXISTING PLAN

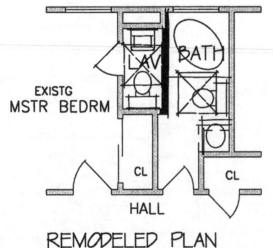

REMODELED PLAN

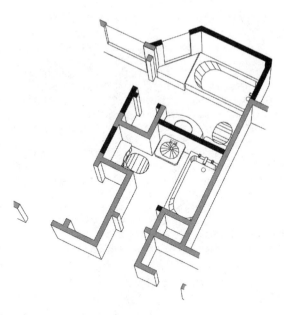

B0002

THIS PLAN CREATES TWO FULL TUB BATHS FROM THE ONE 13'0" DEEP HALL BATH COMMONLY FOUND IN TYPICAL 25- TO 35-YEAR-OLD ONE-STORY, SPLIT-LEVEL OR BI-LEVEL HOMES. IT REQUIRES A SMALL EXTERIOR BAY TO BE POPPED OUT, AND DOES RESULT IN THE LOSS OF SOME CLOSET AREA FOR THE MASTER BEDROOM. HOWEVER, THERE IS A RESPECTABLE GAIN OF WALL SPACE IN THE BEDROOM, WHICH, WITH THE USE OF BUILT-INS OR ADDITIONAL CHESTS, COULD MORE THAN COMPENSATE FOR THE SMALL LOSS OF CLOSET SPACE. COMMON TO MANY HOMES OF THIS VARIETY IS A CHIMNEY OR DUCT CHASE LOCATED IN THIS AREA. IF ONE DOES NOT EXIST IN YOUR HOME, YOU COULD GAIN BACK SOME OF THE CLOSET SPACE LOST IN THIS LAYOUT, OR REDUCE THE SIZE OF THE BAY. THE MASTER BATH CREATED IN THIS DESIGN INCLUDES ITS OWN TUB BATH WITH A RAISED PLANT LEDGE ALONGSIDE.

EXISTING PLAN

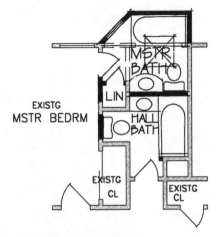

REMODELED PLAN

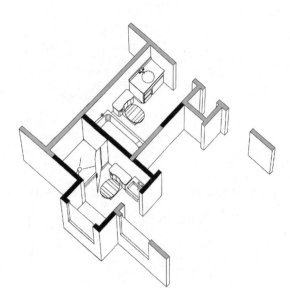

B0003

THE THIRD VERSION CREATES TWO FULL BATHS FROM A 12' HALL BATH. THE NEW MASTER BATH IS A SHOWER BATH WITH A SMALL BOX BAY BUMPED OUT OF THE WALL THAT ADDS VISUAL ENHANCEMENT TO THE SPACE. IN ALL 3 PLANS, THE END RESULT IS TWO (OR 1½) NEW MODERN BATHS; 30"×30' SKYLIGHTS SHOULD BE INSTALLED, IF POSSIBLE, IN EACH. ONE OF THE MAJOR CONCERNS OF ALL OF THESE PLANS IS THE STAGING PROBLEM. BECAUSE OF THE TIGHT AREAS, NONE OF THESE ENJOY THE LUXURY WHERE YOU CAN FINISH ONE BATHROOM WHILE LEAVING AN OLD ONE ALONE FOR DAILY USE. ALL REQUIRE GUTTING AND REMODELING THE ENTIRE SPACE AT ONE TIME, WHICH CALLS FOR A WELL-COORDINATED CONSTRUCTION SCHEDULE TO REDUCE THE LENGTH OF INCONVENIENCE.

EXISTING PLAN

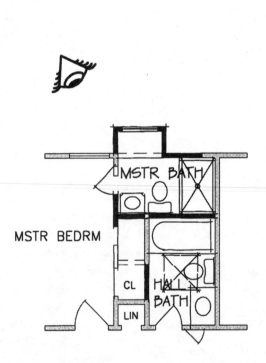

REMODELED FIRST FLOOR PLAN

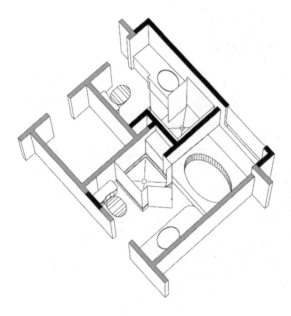

B0004

YOU HAVE TWO FULL BATHS, BUT THE TILE NEEDS REGROUTING AGAIN, THE SHOWER LEAKS AND THE BATHS ARE TIRED AND DATED! DOES THIS SOUND FAMILIAR? THIS PLAN TAKES TWO SUCH BATHS FROM ONE OF THE MORE COMMONLY FOUND LAYOUTS, AND TURNS THEM INTO MODERN, STYLISH PLACES. A 1'6" CANTILEVERED BAY IS ADDED THAT PROVIDES ENOUGH SPACE TO ACCOMMODATE A LUXURIOUS PLATFORM WHIRLPOOL TUB AND A SEPARATE STALL SHOWER IN THE REMODELED HALL BATH. BUT THAT LITTLE EXTRA SPACE DOES WONDERS FOR THE MASTER BATH TOO, WHICH NOW HAS BOTH A LARGE STALL SHOWER AND A LARGE VANITY, PLUS SOME EXTRA FLOOR AREA TO MOVE AROUND IN. THIS PLAN DOES ENJOY THE LUXURY OF STAGING WHEREBY YOU CAN FINISH OFF THE NEW MASTER BATH, WHILE LEAVING THE OLD ONE ALONE UNTIL THE MASTER HAS BEEN FINISHED AND IS READY FOR USE.

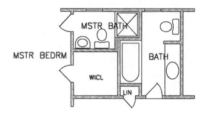

EXISTING PLAN

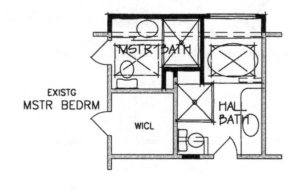

REMODELED FIRST FLOOR PLAN

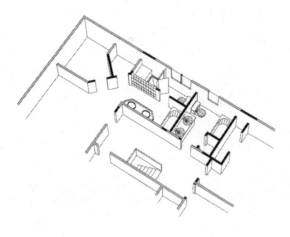

B0006

HOMES OF EACH PERIOD REFLECT CONSUMER PREFERENCES POPULAR AT THE TIME. AS AN EXAMPLE, TWO-STORY HOMES BUILT 15 TO 30 YEARS AGO, SUCH AS THE ONE SHOWN HERE, FREQUENTLY FEATURED A HALL BATH LARGER THAN THE MASTER BATH. TODAY'S STANDARD IS REVERSED, AND THE REMODELED PLAN SHOWS HOW TO ACHIEVE IT IN THE HOME PICTURED. BY REDUCING ONE BEDROOM BY 4'0", ENOUGH SPACE IS GAINED TO CREATE A SPARKLING NEW MASTER BATH WHILE ALSO INCREASING THE SIZE OF THE WALK-IN CLOSETS. THE NEW BATH FEATURES A SEPARATE SHOWER AND WATER CLOSET COMPARTMENT, A LARGE DOUBLE VANITY AND A WHIRLPOOL TUB; EVEN THE ENTRANCE IS CHANGED WITH THE INTRODUCTION OF A DRAMATIC ANGLED CLOSET WALL. THIS RENOVATION, ALTHOUGH IT REMODELS BOTH BATHS, IS EASILY STAGED.

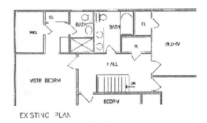

EXISTING PLAN

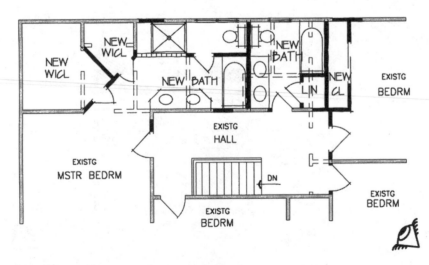

REMODELED FIRST FLOOR PLAN

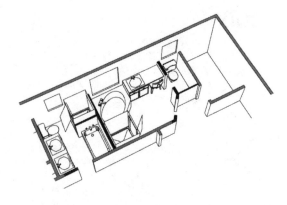

B0011

THE SUBJECT IS A TYPICAL 30 YEAR OR OLDER HOME WITH TWO BATHS WHICH REFLECT THE DESIGN THINKING OF THAT TIME: A LARGER HALL BATH AND MINISCULE MASTER BATH. THE PLAN SHOWN REVERSES THAT THINKING TO TODAY'S STYLE; THE HALL BATH IS TIGHTER, EVEN THOUGH IT INCLUDES A SEPARATE STALL SHOWER FOR THE CHILDREN. THE NEW MASTER BATH ALSO INCLUDES A SEPARATE STALL SHOWER, BUT IT HAS A LARGE WHIRLPOOL TUB AND A SEPARATE COMPARTMENT FOR THE TOILET AS WELL. THIS PLAN COULD BE STAGED INTO 2 PARTS: THE HALL BATH WOULD BE DONE FIRST, AND AFTER IT IS COMPLETE THE MASTER COULD BE GUTTED AND REDONE.

EXIST'G BATHROOM

EXIST'G MSTR BATH

EXIST'G WICL

EXIST'G MSTR BEDRM

EXISTING FLOOR PLAN

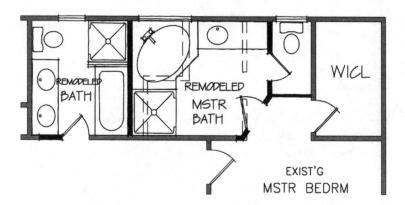

REMODELED BATH

REMODELED MSTR BATH

WICL

EXIST'G MSTR BEDRM

REMODELED FLOOR PLAN

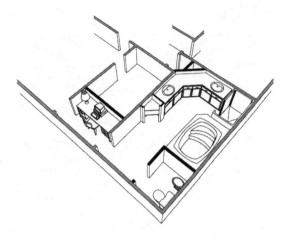

B0012

IF THE PROGRAM CALLS FOR AN EXPANSIVE NEW MASTER BATH AND MORE CLOSET SPACE, AND WE DON'T WANT TO ADD NEW SPACE, THE ONLY SOLUTION IS TO TAKE OVER ANOTHER SPACE. THIS PLAN SHOWS A SPACIOUS, COMPARTMENTED, NEW MASTER BATH IN THE BEDROOM THAT WAS ADJACENT TO THE EXISTING MASTER BEDROOM. THERE IS A COMPARTMENT FOR THE TOILET AND BIDET PLUS AN EXPANSIVE SPACE REMAINING FOR A LARGE WHIRLPOOL TUB, STALL SHOWER AND DRAMATIC CORNER VANITY. AN EXTRA BONUS OF THE PLAN IS THE NEW COMPUTER ALCOVE THAT IS DEVELOPED IN THE ALCOVE LEADING TO THE NEW BATHROOM.

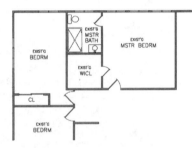

EXISTING FLOOR PLAN

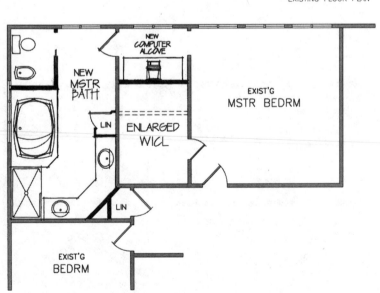

REMODELED FLOOR PLAN

B0007

HOW DO YOU MAKE A TINY FIRST FLOOR HALL BATH LOOK AND FEEL TWICE AS BIG WITHOUT DOUBLING ITS SIZE? BY CREATING THE ILLUSION OF SPACE BY "BLOWING OPEN" THE REAR WITH GLASS, AND ENCLOSING OUTDOOR SPACE WITH THE USE OF GARDEN WALLS. THE NEW USE OF GLASS AT THE TUB END REQUIRES THE CREATION OF A SPECIAL FIXTURE. SUCH USE OF THE "FIXTURE" IS ACTUALLY A SITE BUILT CERAMIC TILE STALL SHOWER, WITH AN 18" HIGH TILED CURB AND SEAT THAT ENABLES IT TO FUNCTION AS A TUB AS WELL. THIS TUB/SHOWER EXTENDS 3' INTO THE REAR, PERMITTING GLASS TO WRAP THE CORNER, ENHANCING THE AMOUNT OF LIGHT AND THE ILLUSION OF SPACE. THE 3'0" BUMP OUT ALSO PERMITS THE INSTALLATION OF A LARGER VANITY. FOR A REALLY OUTRAGEOUS LOOK, YOU COULD CONSIDER A GLASS ROOF OVER THE ADDITION.

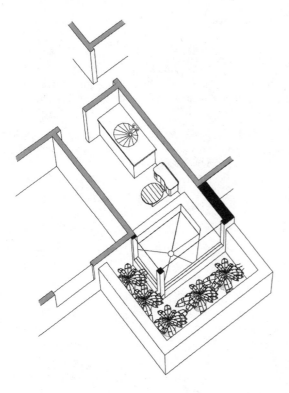

BEDRM   BATH   BEDRM

HALL

EXISTING PLAN

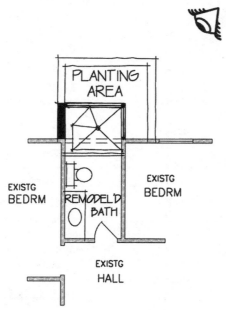

PLANTING AREA

EXISTG BEDRM

REMODEL'D BATH

EXISTG BEDRM

EXISTG HALL

REMODELED FIRST FLOOR PLAN

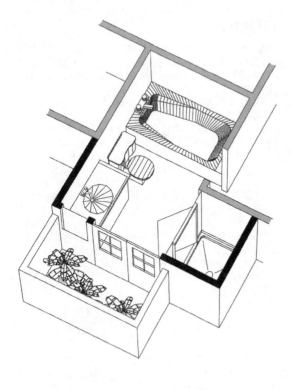

B0009

A TIME WORN MODEST MASTER BATH IS TURNED INTO AN ENGAGINGLY ATTRACTIVE NEW SPACE IN THIS MODEST 4'4" DEEP GARDEN BATH ADDITION. THE NEW ROOM NOW SPORTS A SEPARATE STALL SHOWER PLUS A WHIRLPOOL TUB AND AN EXPANDED VANITY. A FIXED LIGHT, AT THE SIDE OF THE VANITY, PLUS FRENCH DOORS, BRING AN ABUNDANCE OF NATURAL LIGHT TO THE ROOM, AND VISUALLY EXPAND THE SPACE TO THE REAR. GARDEN WALLS ARE PROPOSED TO PROVIDE THE REQUISITE PRIVACY, ELIMINATING THE NEED TO HEAVILY SHADE THE GLASS. YOU COULD ALSO CONSIDER ADDING A SKYLIGHT TO FURTHER ENHANCE THE SPACE.

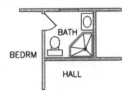

EXISTING PLAN

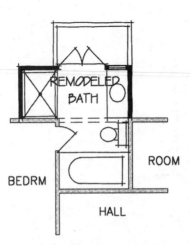

REMODELED FIRST FLOOR PLAN

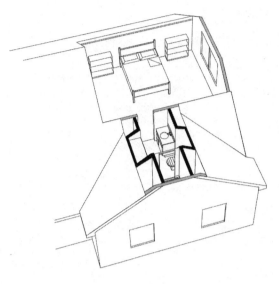

B0010

THIS IS ANOTHER CLEVER EXAMPLE OF THE ART OF FINDING SPACE. IF YOU HAVE A SECOND FLOOR BEDROOM, AND ADJACENT TO IT, IS AN ATTIC AREA THAT IS CREATED BY A ROOFLINE OVER A FIRST FLOOR ROOM (OR GARAGE), IT IS POSSIBLE THAT ENOUGH SPACE EXISTS TO CREATE A BATH. THE NEW BATH NEEDS AN AREA 8' TO 10' LONG AND IT SHOULD ALLOW YOU TO STAND UP COMFORTABLY FOR A MINIMUM WIDTH OF 3' THIS WOULD CREATE THE BATH PICTURED WITH A SHOWER AT THE END. IT WILL HAVE SLOPED CEILINGS AND SOME LOW WALLS, BUT WOULD BE A LOVELY BATH FOR MOST OF US. A WORD OF CAUTION: CHECK THE LOCATION OF THE NEAREST PLUMBING CONNECTIONS ON THE FIRST FLOOR—IT COULD CAUSE A LARGER MESS THAN YOU WOULD OTHERWISE ANTICIPATE.

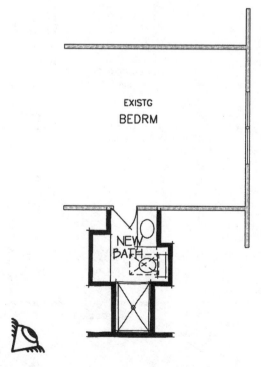

EXISTG
BEDRM

NEW
BATH

EXISTING SECOND FLOOR PLAN

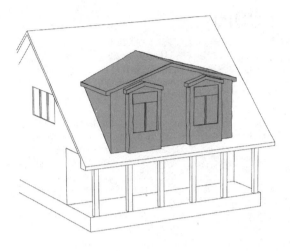

BR002

THIS ATTRACTIVE LOOKING SECOND FLOOR "BUMP" IS CERTAIN TO PLEASE, IF YOU NEED A LITTLE EXTRA ELBOW ROOM FOR TWO SMALL SECOND FLOOR BEDROOMS.   THE ADDITION IS LOCATED OVER AN EXISTING FIRST FLOOR PORCH COMMON TO MANY OLDER TWO-STORY HOMES, AND REPLACES A TINY DORMER WITH A 19'8"×8'0" DORMERED ADDITION. EACH BEDROOM GAINS AN ALCOVE APPROXIMATELY 7'6"×7'6", AND A NICE SIZED CLOSET.   THE ALCOVES ARE IDEALLY FURNISHABLE AS PLAY OR STUDY SPACES TO COMPLEMENT THE SLEEPING AREAS. THE REVERSE GABLE ROOFLINES SHOULD BLEND WELL WITH THE EXISTING ROOF.

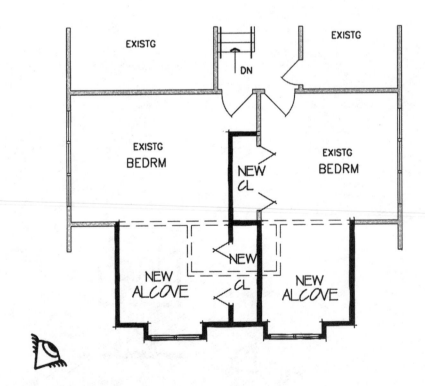

SECOND FLOOR PLAN

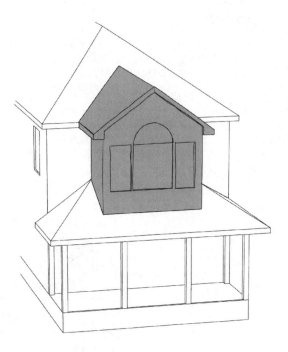

BR001

FOUND SPACE OVER A FRONT PORCH (OR A SIDE OR REAR ONE FOR THAT MATTER) IS OFTEN OVERLOOKED. THIS LITTLE 10'0"×5'6" ADDITION OVER A FIRST FLOOR PORCH PROVIDES AN ATTRACTIVE ALCOVE ENLARGEMENT FOR A SECOND FLOOR BEDROOM. THE ALCOVE IS PERFECT FOR STUDY OR PLAY, AND IS AESTHETICALLY PLEASING AS WELL. THE DESIGN CALLS FOR AN ATTRACTIVELY CONCEIVED WINDOW IN A WELL-DESIGNED GABLE WALL THAT IS VERY APPEALING. IT SHOWS THAT GABLES CAN BE MIXED AND CONTRASTED AGAINST HIPS TO ACHIEVE A MORE UP-TO-DATE LOOK. IF YOUR GOAL IS ALSO TO ENHANCE THE HOME, THEN THIS ADDITION HAS ACCOMPLISHED THAT FOR YOU TOO.

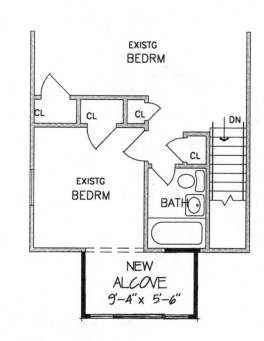

SECOND FLOOR PLAN

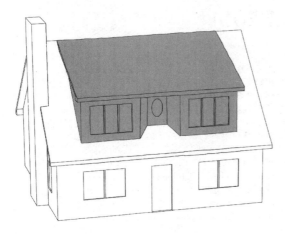

BR003

THIS PLAN MODIFIES AN EXISTING 1½-STORY ROOFLINE (COTTAGE, CAPE, ETC.) THAT HAS TWO TINY SHED-ROOF DORMERS; THE GOAL IS TO PROVIDE A NEW LOOK, MORE LIGHT AND POSSIBLY MORE SPACE TO THE BEDROOMS. THE PLAN LINKS THE TWO DORMERS TOGETHER. THERE IS A SIGNIFICANT GAIN IN LIVING SPACE TO THE TWO BEDROOMS AND AN AESTHETIC IMPROVEMENT TO THE HOME. AN ELLIPTICAL WINDOW PROVIDES LIGHT TO THE STAIR HALL.

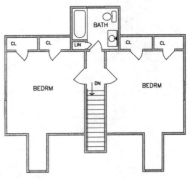

EXISTING PLAN

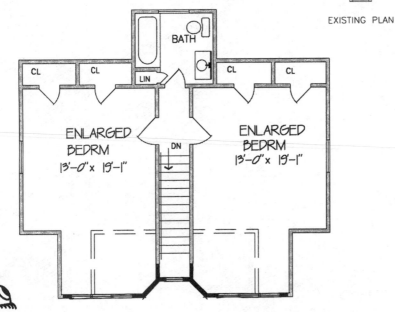

REMODELED SECOND FLOOR PLAN

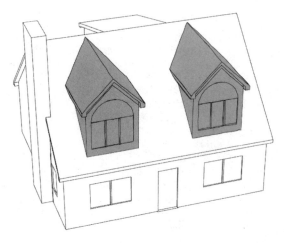

BR004

THIS, THE SECOND ALTERNATIVE ROOFLINE CHANGE, REPLACES THE EXISTING NARROW SHED DORMERS WITH TWO NEW EXTRA WIDE REVERSE GABLE DORMERS. EACH DORMER FEATURES A TRIPLE WINDOW WITH A STYLISH HALF-ROUND LIGHT OVER; THE OVERALL EFFECT IS ONE OF UPDATING, WHERE, BY SIMPLY CHANGING THESE DORMERS, THE HOME TAKES ON A NEW CHARACTER. ALTHOUGH THE BEDROOMS HAVE BENEFITED BY INCREASED LIGHT AND SIZE, THE ACTUAL INCREASE IN AREA IS A LITTLE LESS THAN IN THE PRIOR PLAN. WITH THE ADDITION OF A NEW PORCH YOU HAVE A CONTEMPORARY, UPDATED HOME.

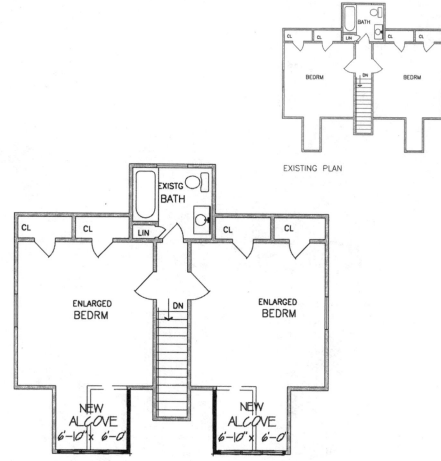

EXISTING PLAN

REMODELED SECOND FLOOR PLAN

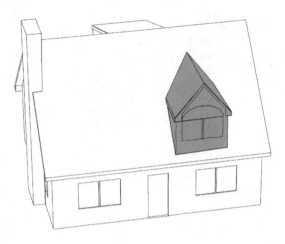

BR005

THE THIRD PLAN EFFECTS A SIGNIFICANT
TRANSFORMATION OF SEVERAL AREAS. IT ACTUALLY
DOES NOT PROVIDE ANY GAIN IN LIVING AREA—THERE
IS, IN FACT, A SLIGHT LOSS—BUT IT RESULTS IN AN
IMPORTANT CHANGE TO THE EXTERIOR FORM AND
THE INTERIOR SPACES AS WELL. BOTH DORMERS ARE
REMOVED, AND THE BEDROOM ON JUST ONE SIDE IS
INCREASED BY THE ADDITION OF A LARGE REVERSE
GABLE, WHICH HAS BEEN DESIGNED AS A GABLE
WALL RATHER THAN A DORMER. THIS IS NOT
MIRRORED ON THE OPPOSITE SIDE, WHERE THE
BEDROOM HAS BEEN REPLACED WITH A DRAMATIC
OPEN LOFT. PART OF THE CEILING OF THE LIVING
ROOM BELOW IS REMOVED AND AN EXPANSIVE
VAULTED CEILING RESULTS.

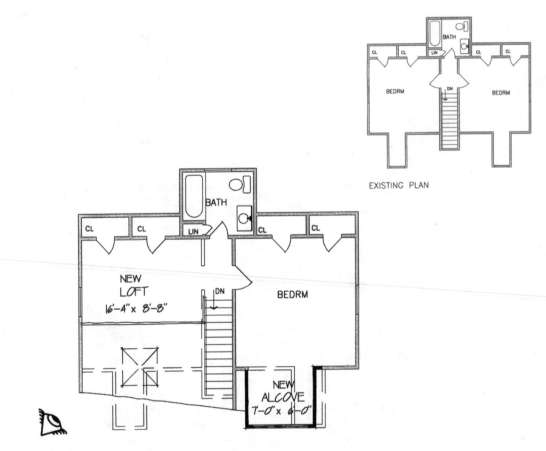

EXISTING PLAN

REMODELED SECOND FLOOR PLAN

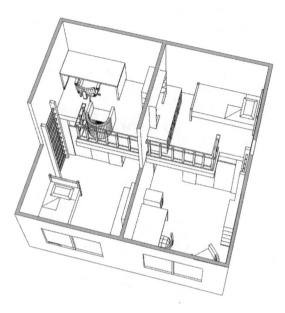

BR006

THE ART OF FINDING SPACE REQUIRES THAT YOU
CONSIDER THE ATTIC. IF THE HOME IS A ONE-STORY
DESIGN WITH A FAIRLY STEEP ROOFLINE, THE ATTIC
OVER THE CHILDREN'S BEDROOMS COULD BECOME A
FIND INDEED. THE DESIGN ILLUSTRATED ON THIS
PAGE SHOWS YOU HOW TO TAKE TWO SMALL
BEDROOMS, AND VIRTUALLY DOUBLE THEM IN SIZE, BY
CREATING A LOFT AREA ACCESSIBLE BY LADDER.
THIS IS NOT FOR EVERYONE, BUT IF YOU ARE NOT
INHIBITED, OR RESTRICTED BY CODE, THE SOLUTION
PICTURED COULD BE A LOT OF FUN. THE LOFTS
EXTEND OUT OVER THE HALL BELOW, AND COULD
EXTEND EVEN FURTHER OVER THE ROOMS ON THE
OPPOSITE SIDE; THE LOFT COULD PROVIDE STUDY,
PLAY OR SLEEPING SPACE. WHATEVER USES YOU
ASCRIBE TO THE LOFT, THIS PLAN LEAVES THE
BEDROOM TO SATISFY THE OTHERS. THE VIEW
SHOWS ALTERNATE LAYOUTS FOR EACH BEDROOM.

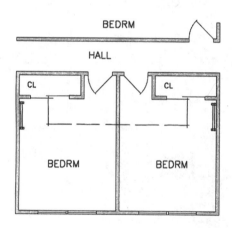

FIRST FLOOR PLAN

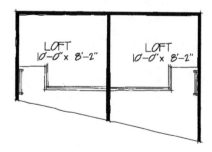

LOFT PLAN

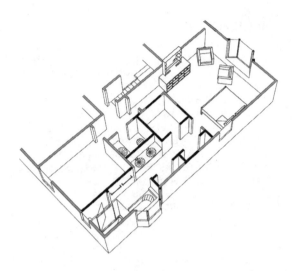

B0005

WHETHER THEY CALL IT A FARM-RANCH, EXPANDED CAPE, ONE AND ONE-HALF-STORY, OR WHATEVER, IT IS YOUR BELIEF THAT THE SECOND FLOOR BEDROOMS ARE AMPLE FOR THE FAMILY'S CHILDREN, BUT THE EXTRA BEDROOM ACROSS FROM THE FIRST FLOOR MASTER BEDROOM COULD BE BETTER UTILIZED. WHAT BETTER PURPOSE THAN REDISTRIBUTING THE EXISTING SPACE TO CREATE A FABULOUS NEW MASTER SUITE, THAT INCLUDES A SMART, NEW, COMPARTMENTED BATH AND SPACIOUS DRESSING AREA? AND WE DO IT WITHOUT ADDING ON (OTHER THAN THE LOVELY NEW BAY WINDOW AT THE TUB), AND WITHOUT LOSING THE EXTRA BEDROOM. THE BEDROOM BECOMES A USEFUL HOME OFFICE, AND THE OLD HALL BATH IS SCALED DOWN TO A TIDY POWDER ROOM. A GREAT PLAN IF IT FITS YOUR NEEDS.

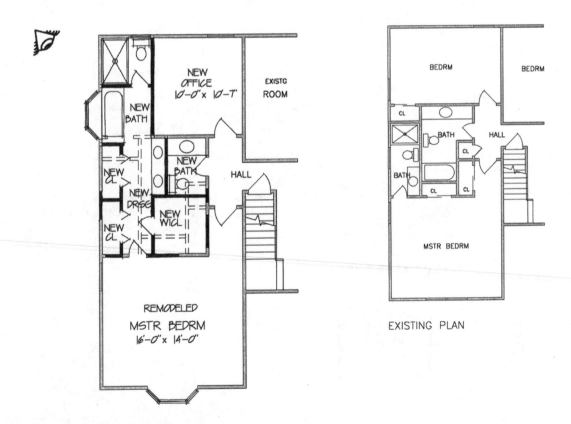

REMODELED FIRST FLOOR PLAN

EXISTING PLAN

BRB22

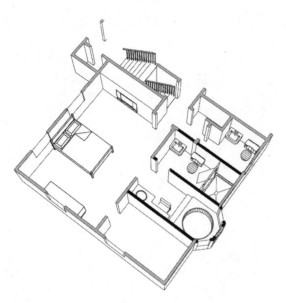

THAT EXTRA FIRST FLOOR BEDROOM, NEXT TO THE MASTER, IS SELDOM USED ANYMORE, AND ITS SPACE IS VERY APPEALING.   THAT IS PARTICULARLY SO, SINCE THE GOAL IS TO HAVE A NEW PRIVATE BATH AND DRESSING AREA WITH ALL THE MODERN ACCOUTREMENTS.   THIS PLAN SHOWS YOU HOW TO DO IT.   SINCE THE OLD HALL BATH IS NO LONGER NEEDED, IT IS CONVERTED TO A POWDER ROOM FOR GUESTS; THE SPACE LEFT OVER IS ADDED TO HELP CREATE A FABULOUS NEW MASTER BATH.   A SEPARATE STALL SHOWER IS LOCATED IN ONE SECTION OF THE TWO COMPARTMENT BATH.   A NEW ANGLE BAY WINDOW ENCLOSES THE REAR OF A LUXURIOUS WHIRLPOOL TUB WHICH SHARES SPACE WITH A DRESSING TOP VANITY IN THE NEW DRESSING ROOM.   THE OLD CLOSET IS REPLACED BY A SPACIOUS NEW WALK-IN CLOSET, AND ITS FORMER SPACE IS NOW IDEAL FOR BUILT-INS.

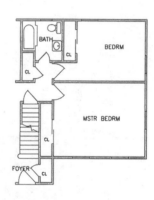

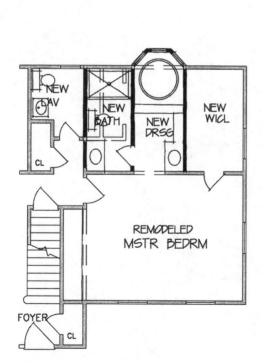

EXISTING PLAN

REMODELED FIRST FLOOR PLAN

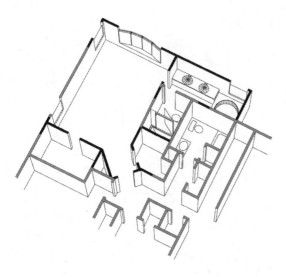

BRB13

THIS MINIMAL 5'4" DEEP ONE-STORY ADDITION IS EXPRESSLY DESIGNED TO ATTACH TO THE REAR OF A TYPICAL MASTER BEDROOM AND TWO STANDARD BATHS; THOUGH MODEST IN AREA, IT PROVIDES ALL THE ROOM NECESSARY TO CREATE AN UP-TO-DATE, SPLASHY, NEW MASTER SUITE. THE HALL BATH REMAINS, BUT THE OLD MASTER BATH IS REMODELED TO CREATE A TWO COMPARTMENT ROOM—ONE FOR A STALL SHOWER AND TOILET—AND THE NEW ADDITION PART FOR A LARGE ROUND WHIRLPOOL TUB AND A LONG DUAL BASIN VANITY. THE OLD BATH AND CLOSET AREAS ARE ALSO REMODELED TO CREATE TWO NEW WALK-IN CLOSETS, AND THE ENTRANCE TO THE SUITE IS CHANGED TO A DRAMATIC NEW ANGLE. CONSTRUCTION BLUEPRINTS PROVIDE THE ADDITION AS A SIMPLE SHED ROOF, BUT YOU COULD HAVE IT CHANGED TO A GABLE OR HIP, AS MAY BE NECESSARY, TO SUIT YOUR HOME.

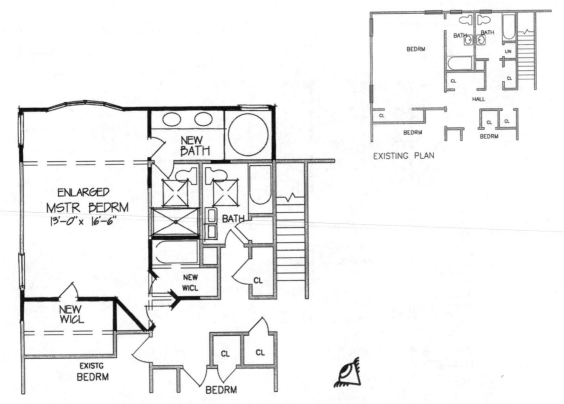

EXISTING PLAN

REMODELED FIRST FLOOR PLAN

BRB30

THE EXISTING FLOOR PLAN PICTURED IS A COMMON
BEDROOM LAYOUT FROM A HOME 30 YEARS OLD OR
MORE.   WHETHER IT IS A ONE- OR TWO-STORY PLAN,
THE PROBLEM IS THE SAME—DATED BATHROOMS IN
NEED OF REMODELING. IF THE HOMEOWNER IS
WILLING TO GIVE UP ONE BEDROOM TO ENLARGE THE
MASTER BATH, THE RESULT CAN BE A FABULOUS
NEW MASTER SUITE AS PICTURED. WE REARRANGE
THE FIXTURES IN THE HALL BATH AND BUILD A NEW
MASTER BATH WITH A CORNER TUB, SEPARATE STALL
SHOWER AND SEPARATE TOILET COMPARTMENT.
THE NEW WALK-IN CLOSET COULD BE ACCESSED
DIRECTLY FROM THE BEDROOM, IF YOU PREFER.

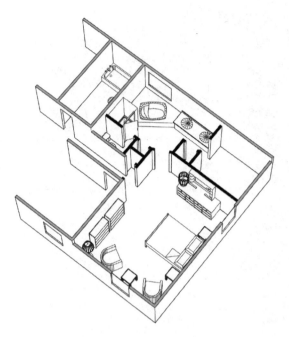

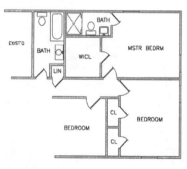

EXISTING FLOOR PLAN

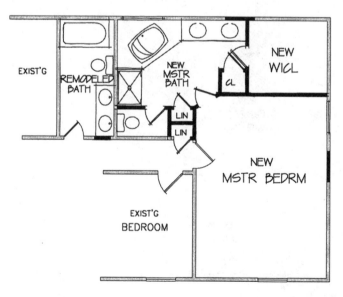

REMODELED FLOOR PLAN

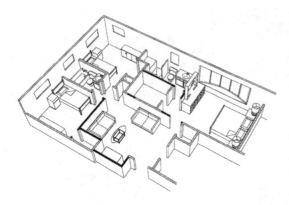

BRB31

GIVEN A TINY ONE BATH, THREE BEDROOM RANCH; THERE'S A NICE LIVING ROOM, BUT THERE IS ALSO A FAMILY ROOM BEYOND THE KITCHEN, AND THERE IS A SPACIOUS ENTRY. THE LARGE LIVING ROOM AND FOYER ARE SUPERFLUOUS FOR TODAY'S LIFESTYLES. NICER BEDROOMS ARE MORE IMPORTANT. THE SOLUTION IS TO SHRINK THE FORMER MASTER BEDROOM (BEDROOM #3) AND CREATE A FUNCTIONAL, IF TINY, LIVING ROOM AND FORMAL ENTRY. THE EXISTING LIVING ROOM AND SMALL ADJACENT BEDROOM ARE COMBINED TO CREATE A LOVELY NEW MASTER SUITE COMPLETE WITH A NEW PRIVATE FULL BATH AND A LARGE WALK-IN CLOSET.

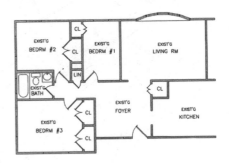

EXISTING FLOOR PLAN

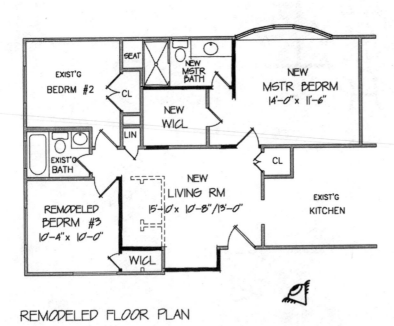

REMODELED FLOOR PLAN

BRB21

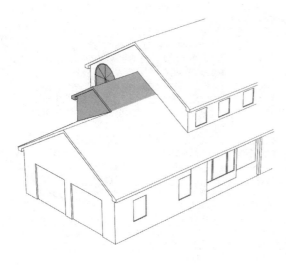

THE FABULOUS NEW MASTER BATH, SHOWN HERE, IS A MARVELOUS EXAMPLE OF HOW THE ART OF FINDING SPACE, AS DISCUSSED IN CHAPTER 3, CAN PRODUCE A REMODELING PROJECT THAT FAR EXCEEDS EXPECTATIONS. YOUR HOUSE IS A WIDE TWO-STORY WITH AN ATTACHED GARAGE; THE MASTER BEDROOM IS SITUATED ON THE GARAGE SIDE OF THE SECOND FLOOR AND ITS DATED BATHROOM AND DRESSING AREA IS CRAMPED AND RIPE FOR REMODELING. BY UTILIZING THE FOUND SPACE OVER THE REAR CORNER OF THE GARAGE FOR AN EXPANSIVE NEW WALK-IN CLOSET, THE FORMER CLOSET AND DRESSING AREA BECOME AVAILABLE TO CREATE THE SMART NEW TUB AND VANITY SECTION OF THE NEW COMPARTMENTED BATH. THE OLD SHOWER AREA AND WATER CLOSET REMAIN, ALTHOUGH THEY'LL LIKELY BE REPLACED.

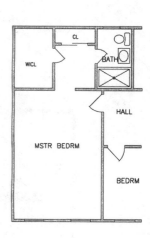

EXISTING PLAN

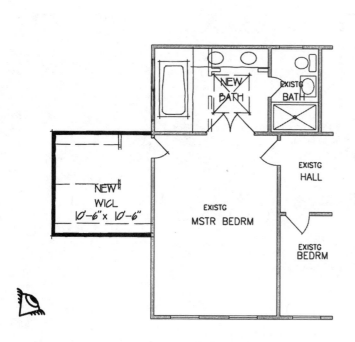

REMODELED SECOND FLOOR PLAN

BRB26

MANY OF THE PLANS FOR NEW MASTER SUITES INVOLVE EXPANSIVE NEW ROOMS AND SPACIOUS NEW BATHS, BUT THERE ARE ALSO MANY PLANS, SUCH AS THIS ONE, THAT SIMPLY ADD A MODEST AMOUNT OF SPACE TO EXPAND AN EXISTING BEDROOM. THIS BUMP-OUT DOES JUST THAT. IT IS PICTURED AS A SHED ROOF ADDITION TO A TWO-STORY HOME, BUT IT COULD ALSO BE ROOFED AS A REVERSE GABLE ADDITION, WHICH WOULD FIT EITHER A ONE- OR TWO-STORY HOME. THERE IS A NEW WALK-IN CLOSET PROVIDED, AS WELL AS A NEW DOOR ALLOW DIRECT ACCESS TO THE EXISTING HALL BATH. ONE OF THE CRITICAL THINGS WE MUST DEAL WITH IN A SHED ROOF ADDITION TO A TWO-STORY HOME IS THE FACT THAT WE MUST USE A FLATTER ROOF PITCH TO KEEP THE ROOF BELOW SECOND FLOOR WINDOWS.

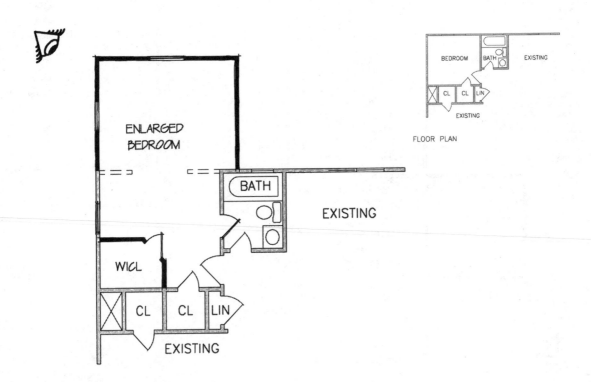

FLOOR PLAN

REMODELED FLOOR PLAN

FBR05

THERE ARE ESSENTIALLY THREE APPROACHES TO PROVIDE AN EXTRA BATH TO THE TYPICAL SPLIT LEVEL WHERE THREE BEDROOMS SHARE ONE BATH: AN INTERNAL REMODEL; AN ADDITION THAT ADDS A WHOLE NEW MASTER SUITE; OR THE PLAN PICTURED HERE. THIS PLAN IS A MIDDLE ROAD; IT ADDS A COMPARTMENTED NEW BATH, DRESSING ALCOVE AND WALK-IN CLOSET TO THE EXISTING MASTER BEDROOM—AND DOES SO WITH A LITTLE STYLE. A COVERED PRIVATE DECK IS PART OF THE PLAN AS IS AN EXPANDED LOWER LEVEL FAMILY ROOM. THE ADDITION MEASURES 22'4"×8'4".

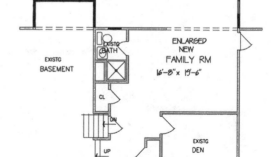

LOWER LEVEL PLAN

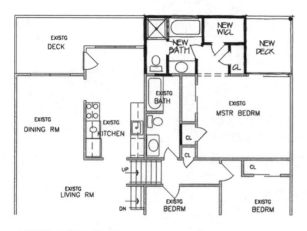

UPPER LEVEL PLAN

KB001

WHAT IS THE BEST WAY TO CREATE A MASTER BATH AND EXPAND THE KITCHEN IN A SPLIT-FOYER (HI-RANCH, BI-LEVEL) PLAN? THE BEST WAY PROBABLY INVOLVES PUSHING OUT THE LOWER LEVEL, AS SHOWN IN PLAN KBR02 ON PAGE 262, BUT IF BUDGETING IS A REAL CONCERN, THE PLAN PICTURED ACCOMPLISHES THE TASK AS ECONOMICALLY AS POSSIBLE. THE 5'4" DEEP ADDITION PROVIDES A NEW MASTER BATH, WITH ITS OWN TUB (A STALL SHOWER COULD BE SUBSTITUTED IF DESIRED), AND ADDS ENOUGH SPACE TO CREATE A LOVELY ISLAND KITCHEN. THIS REMODELED KITCHEN PROVIDES TWO PLACES FOR INFORMAL MEALS; THE FIRST IS THE SNACK COUNTER AT ONE SIDE OF THE ISLAND, THE OTHER IS A SPACIOUS SKYLIT BREAKFAST AREA UNDER A NEW TRIPLE WINDOW.

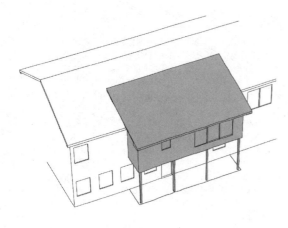

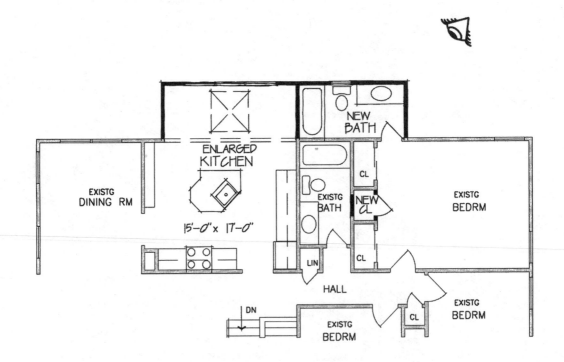

NEW BATH

ENLARGED KITCHEN

EXISTG DINING RM

15'-0" x 17'-0"

EXISTG BATH

NEW CL

CL

EXISTG BEDRM

LIN

CL

HALL

DN

EXISTG BEDRM

CL

EXISTG BEDRM

REMODELED SECOND FLOOR PLAN

KB002

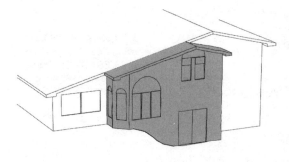

A DESIRE FOR BOTH AN EXPANDED KITCHEN AND A SECOND BATH CERTAINLY RANKS HIGH ON MANY HOMEOWNER'S WISH LISTS. THE SOLUTIONS ARE INFINITE, PARTICULARLY IN ONE-STORY HOMES. AS YOU STUDY MULTI-LEVEL PLANS, AND PARTICULARLY A SHED-ROOFED SPLIT-LEVEL, AS THE ONE SHOWN, THE DESIGN BECOMES MUCH MORE DIFFICULT AND LIMITING. THE DESIGN SOLUTION FOR THE CREATION OF A SMALL 5' "BUMP" ON SUCH A HOME REQUIRES MESHING WITH THE EXISTING ROOFLINE; THE RESULTS CAN BE DRAMATIC AND EXCITING, AS SHOWN. SPECIAL WINDOWS IN THE NEW MASTER BATH AND NEW BREAKFAST AREA PROVIDE THE HOME WITH A REFRESHING APPEARANCE. THE EXTRA 5' ALSO ENHANCES THE LOWER-LEVEL FAMILY ROOM.

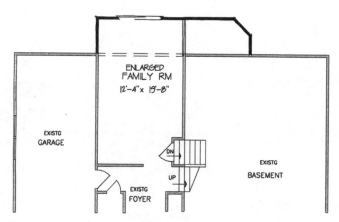

REMODELED FIRST FLOOR PLAN

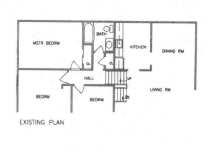

EXISTING PLAN

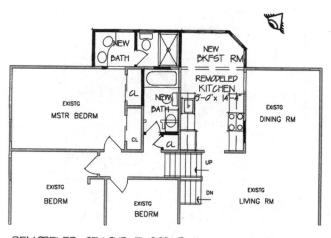

REMODELED SECOND FLOOR PLAN

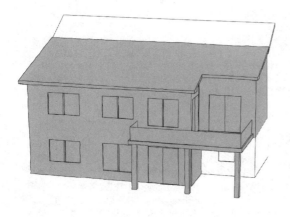

KBR02

ADDING TO A HI-RANCH (ALSO KNOWN AS A RAISED RANCH, BI-LEVEL OR SPLIT-FOYER—DEPENDING ON WHERE YOU RESIDE) ADDS THE QUESTION OF WHAT TO DO WITH THE LOWER FLOOR. MANY TIMES WE DESIGN TO CANTILEVER OUT OR BUILD ON POSTS WHEN DOING A RENOVATION TO SUCH A HOME. THIS PLAN, HOWEVER, ADDS 8'0" TO BOTH FLOORS AND ACCOMPLISHES BENEFITS FOR BOTH. THE PRIME BENEFICIARIES ARE A NEW, PRIVATE, MASTER BATH AND AN EXPANDED KITCHEN WITH A LOVELY OUTSIDE BREAKFAST CORNER. THE DINING ROOM HAS BEEN BUMPED OUT A FEW FEET AND A NEW LARGE DECK IS PROPOSED. THE LOWER LEVEL IS ENHANCED WITH A NEW WORKSHOP OFF THE GARAGE AND AN EXTENSION TO THE FAMILY ROOM, WHICH MAKES FOR A GREAT EXERCISE OR PLAY AREA.

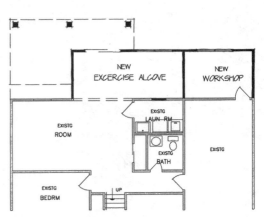

REMODELED FIRST FLOOR PLAN

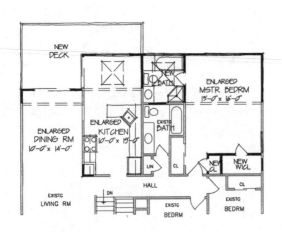

REMODELED SECOND FLOOR PLAN

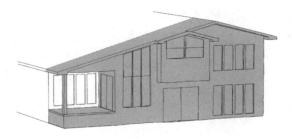

KFBR4

ADDING TO A SPLIT LEVEL APPEARS EASY—BUT MANY HOMEOWNERS HAVE FOUND, AFTER THE FACT, THAT THE AESTHETICS OF THEIR ADDITION ELUDED THEM. THE SPLIT-LEVEL DEMANDS UNYIELDING ATTENTION TO ROOF FORMS, AND THE SHED-ROOFED VERSION, SHOWN HERE, EVEN MORE; BUT THE RESULTS CAN BE MOST PLEASUREABLE—AND EVEN DRAMATIC, AS WITNESSED BY THE LARGE EXPANSES OF HIGH GLASS. EIGHT FEET HAS BEEN ADDED ACROSS THE ENTIRE REAR OF THIS HOME AND IT IS SEAMLESSLY MARRIED TO THE EXISTING ROOFLINE. A WONDERFUL NEW MASTER SUITE WITH A LUXURIOUS PRIVATE BATH IS ONE OF THE MAIN IMPROVEMENTS. A NEW BREAKFAST ROOM ENABLES THE ADDITION OF MORE CABINETS IN THE REMODELED KITCHEN. "EXTRAS" INCLUDE THE COVERED PORCH, ENLARGED FAMILY ROOM AND SUNROOM OR EXERCISE ALCOVE.

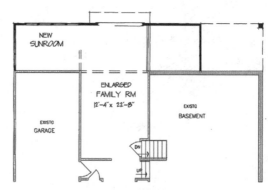

LOWER LEVEL PLAN

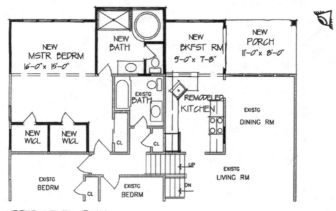

UPPER LEVEL PLAN

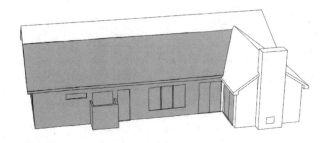

KBR03

THE REAR OF THIS 30-YEAR-OLD ONE-STORY
LOOKS LIKE IT HAS HAD ITS SHARE OF
ADDITIONS, BUT THEY DO NOT FLOW
TOGETHER. THIS LATEST 5'10" ADDITION
ACROSS THE REAR TIES THE KITCHEN TO THE
FAMILY ROOM, AND ADDS A NEW REAR ENTRY,
LAUNDRY, MASTER BATH AND DRESSING AREA,
TO CREATE A THOROUGHLY UP-DATED PLAN.
THE CONNECTION FROM THE ENLARGED, AND
NEWLY REMODELED KITCHEN, TO THE
REMODELED FAMILY ROOM IS THROUGH A NEW
REAR FOYER LOCATED BEHIND THE EXISTING
DINING ROOM. THERE ARE MANY EXTRA
BONUSES IN THE PLAN, INCLUDING THE VISUAL
ENLARGEMENT OF THE DINING ROOM, THE
ENLARGED MASTER BEDROOM AND THE WET
BAR IN THE FAMILY ROOM, WHICH REPLACES A
MISPLACED LAVATORY THAT MAY NO LONGER
BE NEEDED, SINCE THERE ARE NOW TWO FULL
BATHS.

EXISTING PLAN

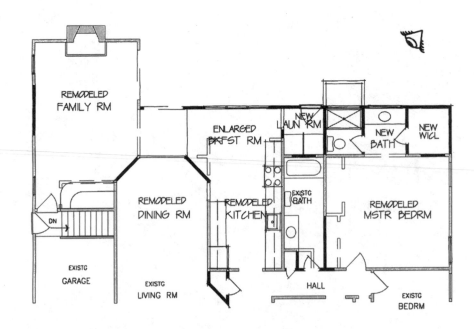

REMODELED FIRST FLOOR PLAN

F0005

DO YOU HAVE A CHARMING OLDER HOME WITHOUT A
FAMILY ROOM, BUT WITH AN UNDER-UTILIZED REAR
PORCH? IS THERE 8'6" OR SO OF SPACE TO EXPAND
TO THE REAR? THEN TAKE A HARD LOOK HERE. THE
OLD PORCH AND THE NEW AREA ARE COMBINED TO
PROVIDE A BEAUTIFUL, REVERSE GABLED, FAMILY
ROOM MATCHING THE WIDTH OF THE OLD PORCH.
REMEMBER, IF THE DIMENSIONS SHOWN AREN'T AN
EXACT MATCH TO YOUR HOME, THIS PLAN, AS ANY
OTHER OF OUR DESIGNS CAN BE ADAPTED TO FIT
YOUR SPECIFIC DIMENSIONS OR REQUIREMENTS. THE
REAR BAY WINDOW AND SIDE FRENCH DOORS ADD
BOUNTIFUL LIGHT TO THE ROOM. THE MARRYING OF
ROOFLINES IS CRITICAL TO ANY SUCCESSFUL
ADDITION, AND THIS ONE DOES IT ADMIRABLY.

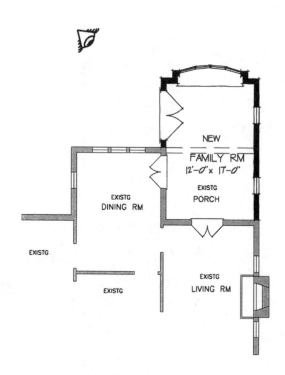

REMODELED FIRST FLOOR PLAN

F0007

JUST A FEW FEET CAN MAKE A WORLD OF DIFFERENCE IN THE USE AND FURNISHABILITY OF A ROOM. TAKE THE REAR-FACING FAMILY ROOM SHOWN; ITS CURRENT 16'2"×12'4" SIZE WAS ALWAYS TIGHT, PARTICULARLY BECAUSE IT SERVES AS THE ACCESS TO THE KITCHEN. WHEN PART OF A ROOM HAS TO PROVIDE A CIRCULATION PATH TO AN ADJOINING ROOM, IT DECREASES THE FURNISHING OPTIONS. THE ADDITION SHOWN ADDS 6' TO THIS FAMILY ROOM; A WOOD STOVE IS SUGGESTED AS A FOCAL POINT, BUT YOU COULD SUBSTITUTE A FIREPLACE. SLIDING DOORS, WITH TRANSOM LIGHTS ABOVE, FLANK EACH SIDE. THE ADDED SPACE NOW PROVIDES ENOUGH DEPTH TO CREATE A COMFORTABLE SEATING ARRANGEMENT, INCLUDING LOVE SEATS AND WRAP-AROUND COUCHES. THE KITCHEN COULD ALSO BE MODERNIZED, AS SHOWN, IF DESIRED.

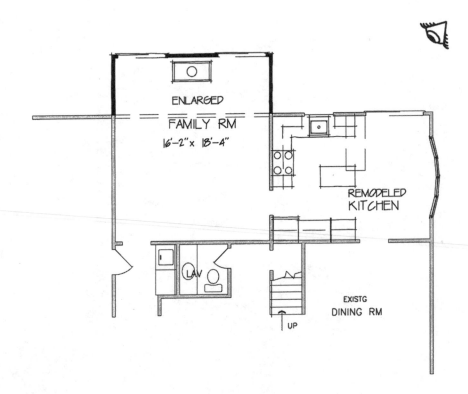

ENLARGED
FAMILY RM
16'-2" x 18'-4"

REMODELED
KITCHEN

LAV

EXISTG
DINING RM

UP

REMODELED FIRST FLOOR PLAN

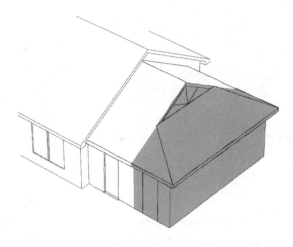

F0009

THERE'S A FAMILY ROOM IN THE PROGRAM—BUT THE BUDGET IS TIGHT AND THE FAMILY ROOM IS MORE IMPORTANT THAN THAT ONE-CAR GARAGE. BEWARE! MANY ONE-CAR GARAGES ARE TOO NARROW TO CREATE A WORKABLE FAMILY ROOM; 12' IS THE MINIMUM, ESPECIALLY FOR THE LENGTH; 14' IS BETTER. IF YOURS IS A NARROW GARAGE, BUT YOU HAVE THE SIDE YARD SPACE (ALBEIT IT NEEDING A VARIANCE), GIVE SOME THOUGHT TO ADDING 4' AS IN THE PLAN SHOWN. IT WILL COST MORE, BUT THE HOMEOWNER WON'T BE SORRY; WITH THE EXTRA SPACE YOU COULD TAKE SOME AREA FOR A LAUNDRY ROOM, BUILT-IN MEDIA CENTER AND EVEN RECOUP SOME SPACE FOR STORAGE OF AUTO OR GARDEN SUPPLIES. AN EXTRA BENEFIT IS THE INTERESTING ROOFLINE AND A HIGH CLEAR-STORY WINDOW THAT THE ADDITION PERMITS.

EXISTING PLAN

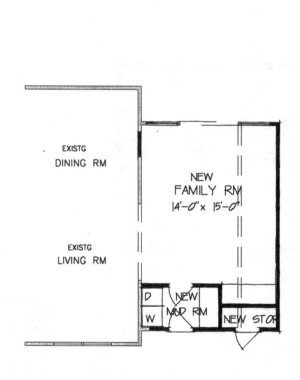

REMODELED FIRST FLOOR PLAN

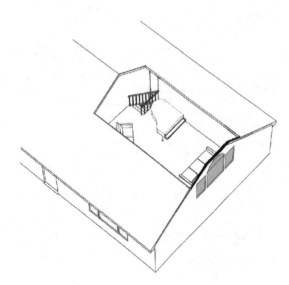

F0013

IF YOU CAN STAND UP STRAIGHT IN AN ATTIC FOR
SOME SIZEABLE DISTANCE, IT SHOULD BE ABLE TO BE
CONVERTED TO LIVING SPACE.   THIS DESIGN SHOWS
YOU HOW.   IT CREATES A ROOM 11' WIDE, BY
WHATEVER LENGTH YOU HAVE AVAILABLE (19'6"
SHOWN ON THE PLAN).   NO STRUCTURAL WORK IS
REQUIRED OTHER THAN THE PLACEMENT OF LARGE
ATTRACTIVE GABLE-END WINDOWS FOR LIGHT, AND
THE INSTALLATION OF A STAIR.   THE LATTER IS NO
SMALL TASK, AS YOU DO HAVE TO FIND AN AREA
APPROXIMATELY 3' × 10' FOR A STAIR, THE TOP END
OF WHICH SHOULD BE FAIRLY CLOSE TO THE MIDDLE
OF YOUR HOME, UNDER THE RIDGE, WHERE YOU HAVE
MAXIMUM HEADROOM.   NOTE THAT IF YOUR ATTIC
BECOMES A THIRD FLOOR ABOVE GRADE, SOME
CODES MAY NOT PERMIT IT.

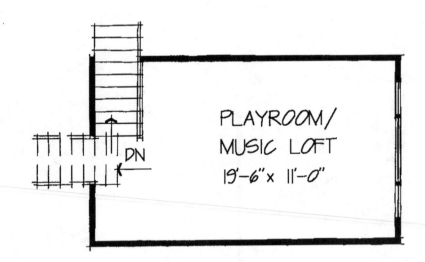

DN

PLAYROOM/
MUSIC LOFT
19'-6" x 11'-0"

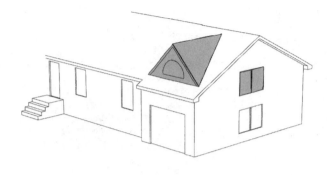

FBR08

THE ART OF FINDING SPACE FREQUENTLY REQUIRES THAT YOU LOOK UP OVERHEAD FOR WASTED VOLUME. A COMMON EXAMPLE OF SUCH WASTE IS FOUND IN THE EXCESS HEIGHT ABOVE A GARAGE, WHICH OFTEN OCCURS IN HOMES WITH BASEMENTS. IT IS USUALLY AN UNPLANNED BY-PRODUCT THAT RESULTED FROM THE BUILDER TRYING TO KEEP THE BASEMENT WINDOWS ABOVE GROUND. THIS PLAN SHOWS YOU HOW TO GAIN A ROOM OVER THE GARAGE; IT IS AN IDEAL PLAYROOM, OR IT COULD SERVE AS ANOTHER BEDROOM. A STAIR IS REQUIRED TO GET TO THIS LEVEL WHICH IS LIKELY TO BE 4' TO 6' ABOVE THE FIRST FLOOR. THE DESIGN PICTURED ALSO SHOWS A NEW REVERSE GABLED DORMER WITH A SPECIAL SHAPED WINDOW THAT SHEDS EXTRA LIGHT TO THIS NEW FOUND SPACE.

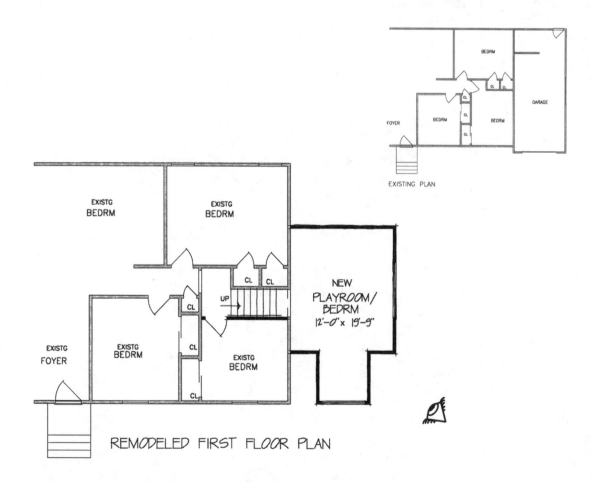

EXISTING PLAN

REMODELED FIRST FLOOR PLAN

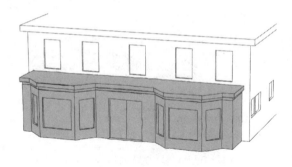

KFOOI

A COMMON PROBLEM: A STATELY OLDER TWO-STORY HOME, BUT LITTLE ROOM TO EXPAND OUT, THE KITCHEN IS DATED AND HAS NO EATING SPACE—AND YOU WOULD LOVE TO HAVE A LARGE FAMILY ROOM. SOLUTION: REMOVE THE TYPICAL OLD REAR PORCH (5'6" DEEP IN THIS PLAN AS DRAWN) AND PUSH OUT TO THAT LINE WITH A BEAUTIFULLY BALANCED EXTENSION THAT RESULTS IN A SENSATIONAL KITCHEN AND AN EXPANDED FAMILY ROOM.   EACH ROOM INCLUDES A WIDE BAY WINDOW FLANKING THE DOUBLE CENTER DOORS, WHICH PROVIDE DIRECT ACCESS TO THE PATIO.   THE KITCHEN FEATURES A LARGE CENTER ISLAND WITH A BAR SINK.   THE DRAMATIC SURROUNDING CABINET LAYOUT SHOWS YOU HOW TO WORK EXISTING CONSTRAINTS, SUCH AS A CHIMNEY BUMP, TO YOUR ADVANTAGE.   REVIEW THE PLAN FOR SEVERAL INTERNAL CHANGES SUGGESTED TO IMPROVE CIRCULATION.

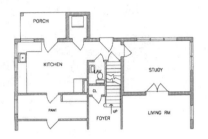

EXISTING PLAN

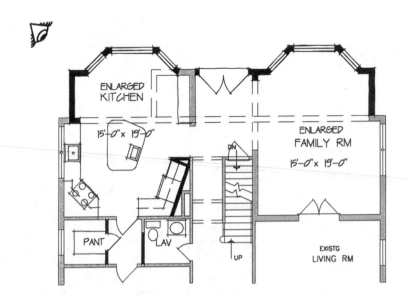

REMODELED FIRST FLOOR PLAN

KF005

THE REAR-FACING FAMILY ROOM AND THE ADJOINING KITCHEN OF THIS HOME ARE OF ADEQUATE LENGTH, BUT THEIR 11' WIDTH IS TIGHT. THE 4'4" ADDITION, PROPOSED FOR BOTH, PROVIDES ENOUGH SPACE TO CREATE A NEW KITCHEN AND A COMFORTABLE FAMILY ROOM. YOU COULD ADD MORE IF YOU WANT, THE ONLY LIMITATION BEING A CONCERN WITH THE ROOF PITCH OF THE EXTENSION SO AS TO CLEAR THE BOTTOM OF SECOND FLOOR WINDOWS IF YOURS IS A TWO-STORY HOME. THE KITCHEN, WHICH HAD A PENINSULA RETURN BEFORE, IS NOW LARGE ENOUGH TO HOUSE A CENTER ISLAND. SKYLIGHTS ARE SUGGESTED IN THE NEW AREAS OF BOTH ROOMS.

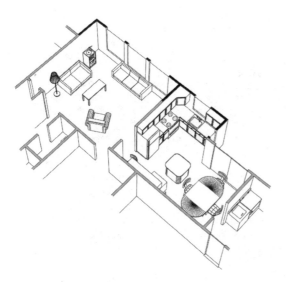

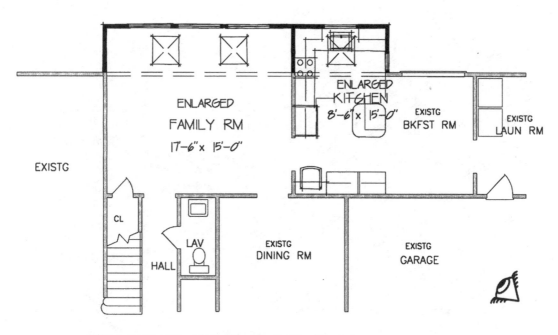

ENLARGED
FAMILY RM
17-6" x 15'-0"

ENLARGED
KITCHEN
8'-6" x 15'-0"

EXISTG
BKFST RM

EXISTG
LAUN RM

EXISTG

CL

LAV

HALL

EXISTG
DINING RM

EXISTG
GARAGE

REMODELED FIRST FLOOR PLAN

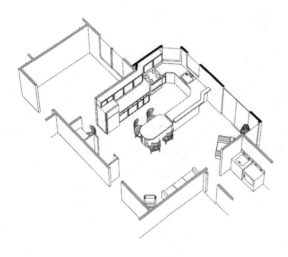

KF006

DOES THIS HOME INCLUDE A NARROW U-SHAPED KITCHEN, WITH A PENINSULA EATING BAR RETURN, THAT IS FOREVER CROWDED—ESPECIALLY SO AT MEALTIME? THIS 8'8" ADDITION TO THE KITCHEN (3'8" AT THE FAMILY ROOM SIDE) PROVIDES ALL THE SPACE NEEDED TO CREATE A WONDERFUL COUNTRY KITCHEN. THE EXTRA AREA PERMITS THE CREATION OF A STYLISH WORKING KITCHEN, AND A LOVELY EATING AREA THAT BRIDGES THE SPACE BETWEEN THE KITCHEN AND THE FAMILY ROOM. ANGLED CORNERS SERVE TO EXPAND AND ENHANCE THE KITCHEN. A DESK AND PANTRY ARE LOCATED AT THE INSIDE WALL, AND A HIGH COUNTER SERVES TO DEFINE THE KITCHEN FROM THE FAMILY ROOM WITHOUT ACTUALLY SEPARATING THEM.

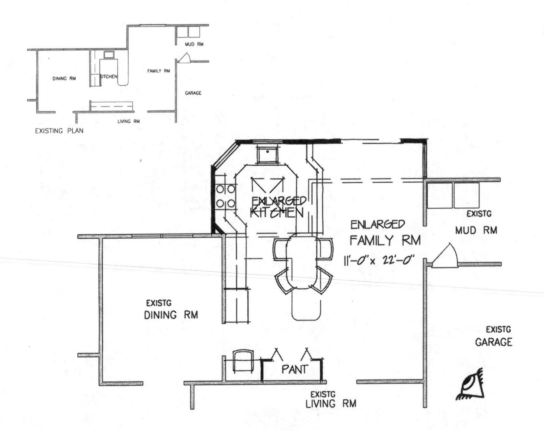

EXISTING PLAN

REMODELED FIRST FLOOR PLAN

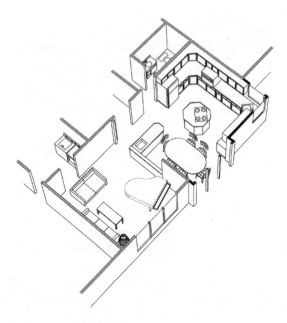

KF007

THE SUBJECT IS A COMFORTABLE, SPACIOUS HOME, BUT THE CRAMPED U-SHAPED KITCHEN AND TABLE SPACE IS WEAR-DATED. THE SOLUTION IS A 5'0" ADDITION (6'0" AT THE BREAKFAST AREA) ACROSS THE WIDTH OF THE ROOM. THE RESULT: A FABULOUS NEW KITCHEN, WITH SMART, UP-DATED STYLING. FEATURES INCLUDE A DOUBLE CORNER SINK WITH CORNER WINDOWS ABOVE, AND AN ABUNDANCE OF CABINETS IN A SPACIOUS U-SHAPE SURROUNDING AN OCTAGONALLY-SHAPED COOKING ISLAND. A NEW SERVING COUNTER, WITH ITS OWN SINK, IS IDEALLY LOCATED TO AID SERVING THE DINING ROOM AND FAMILY ROOM. THE NEW BREAKFAST TABLE SPACE IS NO LONGER CROWDED, AND TRIPLE FRENCH DOORS AND A SKYLIGHT PROVIDE IT WITH AN ABUNDANCE OF NATURAL LIGHT.

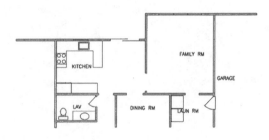

EXISTING PLAN

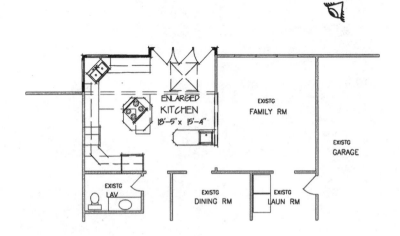

REMODELED FIRST FLOOR PLAN

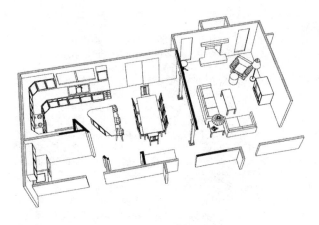

KF016

THERE'S NOTHING NECESSARILY WRONG WITH THE EXISTING KITCHEN THAT NEW CABINETS AND FLOORING COULDN'T RESOLVE—EXCEPT IF THE GOAL IS TO ACHIEVE MORE OF AN OPEN RELATIONSHIP TO THE FAMILY ROOM. THIS IS ONE OF TODAY'S STRONGEST DESIGN TRENDS; IT REFLECTS A MORE INFORMAL WAY OF LIVING THAT CREATES POTENTIAL CONFLICTS WITH MOST OLDER HOMES. HOWEVER, IT IS READILY CURED BY SIMPLY FLIPPING THE KITCHEN AND BREAKFAST ROOM. THE DEAD END KITCHEN LOCATION PERMITS A BETTER CABINET LAYOUT AND THE VISUAL OPENNESS WE SEEK IS CREATED BY REMOVING THE WALL ADJOINING THE EXISTING FAMILY ROOM AND REPLACING IT WITH DECORATIVE (OR STRUCTURAL) COLUMNS.

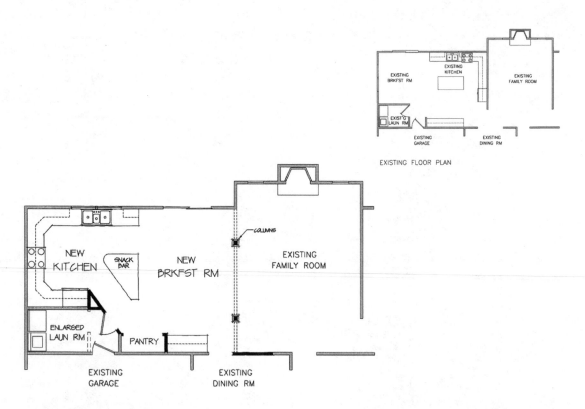

EXISTING FLOOR PLAN

REMODELED FLOOR PLAN

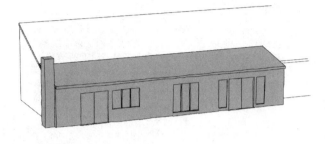

KFD01

THE KITCHEN, DINING ROOM AND OLD DEN ARE ALL JUST A LITTLE TOO TIGHT FOR CURRENT NEEDS? THIS SIMPLE, EASY TO CONSTRUCT, 5'4" WIDE, SHED ROOF ADDITION ACROSS THE REAR OF ALL THREE ROOMS AFFORDS ALL THE SPACE NECESSARY TO SOLVE THE PROBLEM. OF COURSE, THE SAME COULD BE ACCOMPLISHED ON ANY ONE OF THE ROOMS, IF THAT'S ALL THAT WAS NEEDED. THE KITCHEN IS NOW LARGE ENOUGH TO INCLUDE A CENTER ISLAND AND THE SKYLIT BREAKFAST AREA IS JUST DELIGHTFUL. THE FAMILY ROOM IS NOW SPACIOUS ENOUGH FOR ENTERTAINING. A NEW CORNER FIREPLACE, SLIDING DOORS AND SKYLIGHTS ADD TO THE ROOM'S NEW-FOUND ATTRACTION.

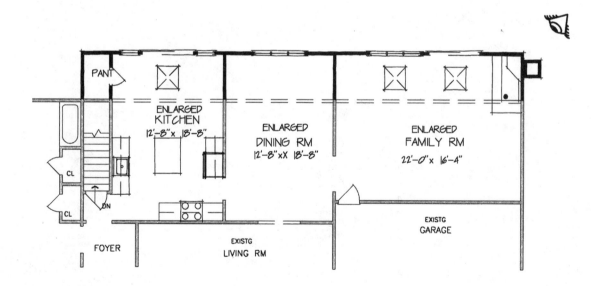

REMODELED FIRST FLOOR PLAN

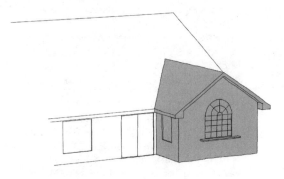

KFD02

A SMART, NEW, BRIGHT AND CHEERFUL KITCHEN, WITH A MUCH MORE CONNECTED RELATIONSHIP TO THE ADJOINING FAMILY ROOM, IS THE RESULT OF THIS TRIM 14'8"×7'4" REAR ADDITION. EVEN THE DINING ROOM GAINS A FEW FEET IN LENGTH, BUT THE MAIN BENEFICIARY IS THE KITCHEN, WHICH NOW INCLUDES SOME BULK STORAGE, IN THE FORM OF A PANTRY, AND A SERVING BUFFET TO THE DINING ROOM. A STYLISH, ANGLED, SNACK COUNTER NOW SEPARATES THE KITCHEN AND FAMILY ROOM, AND AN EQUALLY STYLISH HALF-ROUND WINDOW IS THE FOCAL POINT OF THE NEW REAR WALL. SKYLIGHTS COULD BE ADDED TO THE KITCHEN ADDITION IF DESIRED.

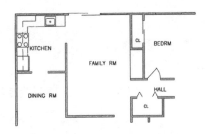

EXISTING PLAN

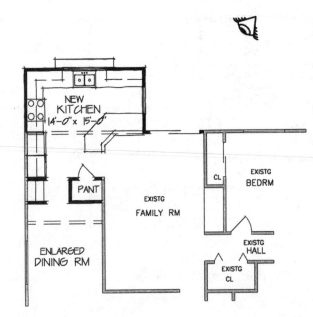

REMODELED FIRST FLOOR PLAN

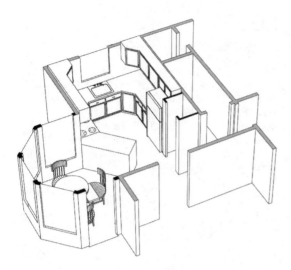

K0001

THE FIRST OF THREE VARIATIONS ON REMODELING A
NARROW KITCHEN WITH INADEQUATE EATING AREA.
THIS VERSION ADDS THE MOST SPACE IN THE FORM
OF A 9'2"×6'6" ADDITION, IN THE SHAPE OF A HALF
OCTAGON. THIS DELIGHTFULLY SUNNY SPACE IS
LARGE ENOUGH TO ACCOMMODATE A BREAKFAST
TABLE, ENABLING THE INTRODUCTION OF A DRAMATIC
ANGLED COUNTERTOP TO THE WORKING PART OF
THE KITCHEN. THE ANGLES ARE MIRRORED IN THE
CORNER CABINETS AT THE FAR END OF THE KITCHEN,
THUS CREATING AN OVERALL STYLE AND ARTISTRY TO
THE REMODELED KITCHEN. THE KITCHEN WINDOW
AND DOORWAY TO THE DINING ROOM CAN REMAIN
WITHOUT CHANGE.

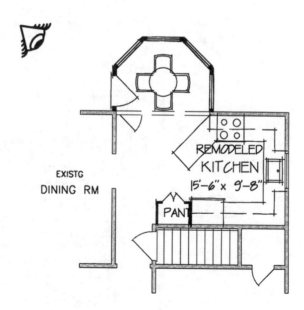

EXISTG
DINING RM

REMODELED
KITCHEN
15'-6" x 9'-8"

PANT

REMODELED FIRST FLOOR PLAN

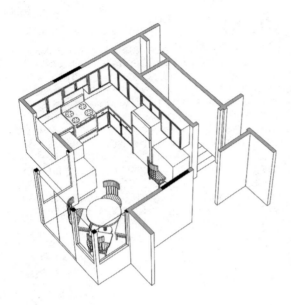

K0002

THE SECOND VARIATION, REMODELING THE SAME
KITCHEN, ADDS AN 8'6"×3'6" "GREENHOUSE." THIS
TYPE OF ADDITION, AVAILABLE FROM SEVERAL
MANUFACTURERS, IS PROVIDED IN A PRE-FABRICATED
KIT THAT IS SITE ERECTED; A FOUNDATION, FLOOR
AND THE NECESSARY MECHANICALS (ELECTRICAL,
HEATING, ETC.) ARE PROVIDED ON-SITE. AS AN ALL
GLASS SPACE, IT PROVIDES AN ABUNDANCE OF
LIGHT- AND SUN-OPENING UP THE SMALLISH KITCHEN,
WHILE AT THE SAME TIME PROVIDING JUST ENOUGH
SPACE TO LOCATE A SMALL TABLE. A DEEPER
GREENHOUSE WOULD, OF COURSE, AFFORD EVEN
MORE TABLE SPACE. THIS PLAN SHOWS THE
KITCHEN WINDOW MOVED, ALONG WITH THE SINK, TO
THE REAR WALL.

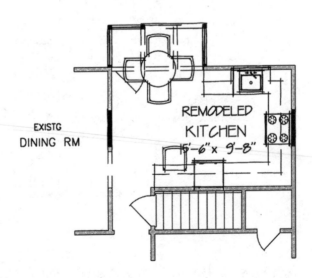

EXISTG
DINING RM

REMODELED
KITCHEN
5'-6" x 9'-8"

REMODELED FIRST FLOOR PLAN

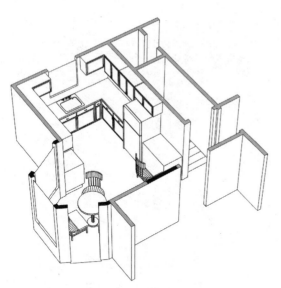

K0003

THE THIRD VARIATION, REMODELING THE SAME NARROW, LONG KITCHEN, INCORPORATES A BUMP IN THE FORM OF AN 8'4"×4'0" ANGLED BAY. THIS IS LIKELY TO BE THE LEAST COSTLY OF THE THREE ADDITIONS, YET IT ACCOMPLISHES ALMOST THE SAME AS THE OTHERS. THE BAY PROVIDES PLENTY OF LIGHT, SPACE FOR A SMALL BREAKFAST TABLE, AND ACCESS TO THE YARD, AS DO ALL THREE PLANS. THE TABLE SPACE IS A LITTLE TIGHTER, BUT BY MOVING THE DOORWAY TO THE DINING ROOM DOWN, YOU CAN ALMOST ACHIEVE THE SAME TABLE SPACE AS IN THE LARGEST ADDITION. THE PLAN PROVIDES FOR A CONVENIENT DESK, AND LEAVES THE KITCHEN WINDOW ON THE SIDE WALL.

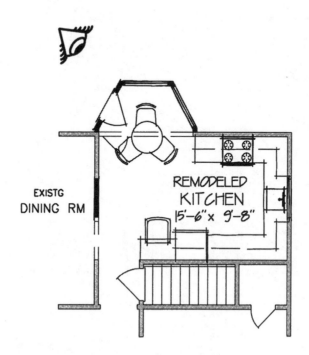

EXISTG DINING RM

REMODELED KITCHEN 15'-6" x 9'-8"

REMODELED FIRST FLOOR PLAN

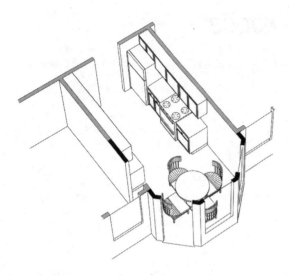

K0007

THIS PLAN DEMONSTRATES HOW LITTLE BUMP-OUTS CAN ACCOMPLISH BIG THINGS. THE 3'8" ANGLED BAY ADDITION TO THE OUTSIDE WALLS OF A NARROW 9'0"×13'4" KITCHEN PROVIDES ALL THE SPACE NECESSARY TO THOROUGHLY MODERNIZE THIS ROOM. THE BIGGEST DEFICIENCY IN THE EXISTING KITCHEN IS THE TIGHT, DARK, INSIDE CORNER FOR THE BREAKFAST TABLE; BY ADDING 3'8", THE ROOM IS NOW LONG ENOUGH TO PROVIDE A LOVELY BREAKFAST AREA WITHIN THE NEW BAY AT THE END. ALTHOUGH THE WORKING PART OF THE KITCHEN MOVES TO THE INSIDE, IT NOT ONLY GAINS CABINETS AND COUNTER SPACE, BUT IT ALSO BENEFITS FROM ALL THE LIGHT THAT IS PROVIDED BY THE BAY WINDOW.

KITCHEN   DINING RM

EXISTING PLAN

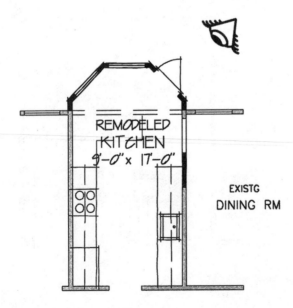

REMODELED KITCHEN 9'-0" x 17'-0"

EXISTG DINING RM

REMODELED FIRST FLOOR PLAN

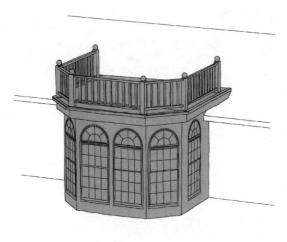

KD008

TODAY'S LIFESTYLE PREFERENCES DIFFER IN MANY RESPECTS FROM THOSE THAT GOVERNED THE DESIGN OF HOMES YEARS AGO. TAKE THE EXISTING KITCHEN PICTURED; EATING WAS RELEGATED TO A DARK INSIDE CORNER, BARELY BIG ENOUGH FOR A TABLE OF FOUR. THE KITCHEN WORKSPACE WAS A SIMPLE "L" SHAPE. TODAY WE DEMAND MORE KITCHEN WORK AREA AND WE PREFER A BRIGHT SUNNY PLACE TO SET OUR BREAKFAST TABLE; THE 13'×9' BUMP-OUT PICTURED ALLOWS US TO DO ALL OF THAT HANDSOMELY. THE KITCHEN NOW ENJOYS USE OF ALL THE FOUR WALLS, AND IT INCLUDES A RAISED COUNTER FACING THE NEW BREAKFAST ROOM. THE ADDITION IS SHOWN WITH A FLAT ROOF AND RAIL, BUT IT COULD HAVE A PITCHED ROOF, IF DESIRED.

EXISTING FLOOR PLAN

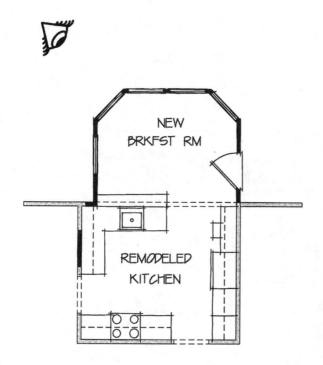

REMODELED FLOOR PLAN

K0006

MODERNIZING THE FRONT-FACING KITCHEN IS POTENTIALLY MUCH MORE LIMITING THAN ANY OTHER LOCATION, SINCE IT AFFECTS THE FRONT FAÇADE. ANYTHING OTHER THAN MERE CABINET REPLACEMENT SHOULD BE UNDERTAKEN WITH CARE. IF YOUR DESIRE IS ALSO TO EXPAND THE KITCHEN, THE STUDIED DESIGN OF ROOFLINES AND WINDOWS BECOME CRITICAL. SETBACK LIMITATIONS WILL LIKELY GOVERN, AS IN THE HOME SHOWN; THE ADDITION TO THE KITCHEN IS DESIGNED TO ALIGN WITH THE FORWARD BEDROOM WING. ALTHOUGH ONLY 4'4", IT ACCOMPLISHES BOTH A SPARKLING NEW U-SHAPED KITCHEN AND A SMART NEW FRONT FAÇADE. THE DRAMATIC WINDOW REFLECTS THE NEW VAULTED CEILING INSIDE.

EXISTING PLAN

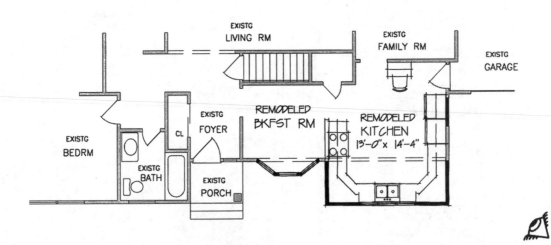

REMODELED FIRST FLOOR PLAN

K0005

EXPANDING A FRONT-FACING KITCHEN CAN BE HAZARDOUS. TECHNICAL CONSIDERATIONS ASIDE (LANDSCAPING, BURIED UTILITIES, SEWERS, WALKS, ETC.) THE NEW EXTENSION CAN REDEFINE THE CHARACTER OF YOUR WHOLE HOUSE. THIS HOME, AS SHOWN, TAKES ON A NEW PRESENCE, BY INFILLING THE RECESS BETWEEN THE EXISTING BEDROOM WING AND GARAGE, WITH A FASHIONABLE NEW REVERSE GABLED WING. A STYLISH NEW COVERED PORCH AND EXPANDED FOYER ARE THE "EXTRAS" TO THE MAIN SUBJECT, THE OUTRAGEOUS NEW KITCHEN. FEATURES INCLUDE A DRAMATIC ANGULAR LAYOUT WITH A CORNER RANGE, AN UNUSUAL ISLAND THAT DEFINES THE NEW BREAKFAST TABLE AREA AND A FABULOUS WALL OF BUILT-INS.

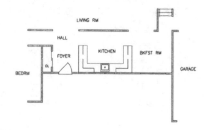

EXISTING FIRST FLOOR PLAN

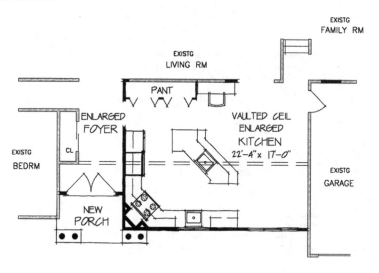

REMODELED FIRST FLOOR PLAN

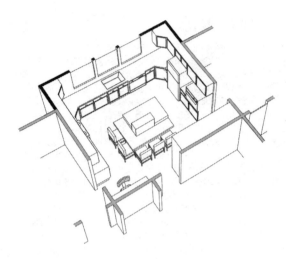

K0009

YOU MAY HAVE NOTICED THAT THERE ARE TIMES WHEN A REMODELING PROJECT COMBINES ROOMS IN WHAT MAY APPEAR TO BE A LOSS OF A ROOM. WELL THIS NEW KITCHEN IS SUCH A PLAN. THE EXISTING 17'0" WIDTH IS SOMEWHAT CRAMPED FOR BOTH A KITCHEN AND BREAKFAST SPACE; ASSUMING THE GOAL IS A DAZZLING EXPANDED KITCHEN—AND YOUR ONLY WAY TO EXPAND IS OUT—ELIMINATING THE SEPARATE BREAKFAST AREA IS AN IDEA TO CONSIDER. THE 4'0" ADDITION PROVIDES ALL THE SPACE NEEDED TO CREATE A WINNING KITCHEN. THE NEW PLAN IS AN EXPANSIVE U-SHAPE WITH AN ABUNDANCE OF NATURAL LIGHT. A LARGE MULTI-LEVEL CENTER ISLAND PROVIDES A COMFORTABLE TABLE HEIGHT EATING AREA ON TWO SIDES, WHILE LEAVING A LARGE WORK SURFACE FOR KITCHEN PREPARATION ON THE OPPOSITE SIDES.

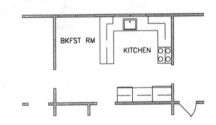

EXISTING PLAN

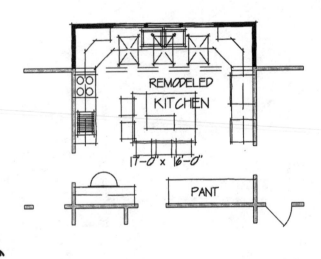

REMODELED FIRST FLOOR PLAN

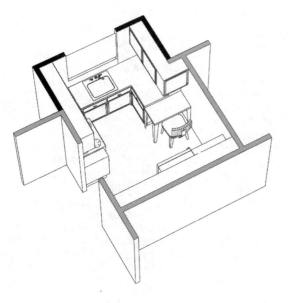

K0010

REMODELING A GALLEY KITCHEN WITH NEW LIGHTING, APPLIANCES, CABINETS AND FLOORING CAN HELP IMPROVE ITS APPEARANCE, BUT IT CAN'T HELP REMOVE THE PHYSICAL TIGHTNESS OF THE SPACE. THAT PROBLEM CAN ONLY BE RESOLVED BY ADDING SOME SPACE TO THE KITCHEN. THE 8'0"X4'0" BUMP-OUT SHOWN DOES WONDERS TO THE GALLEY KITCHEN. IT REMOVES THE DULL, SINGLE, WORK AISLE AND REPLACES IT WITH A BEAUTIFULLY FUNCTIONAL, AND ATTRACTIVE, U-SHAPED KITCHEN. A NEW WRAP-AROUND COUNTER IS PLACED IN THE ADDITION WITH THE SINK CENTERED UNDER A NEW LARGE WINDOW WITH A SKYLIGHT ABOVE. A BUILT-IN DESK IS PLACED IN A TRAFFIC-FREE INSIDE CORNER.

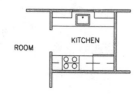

ROOM   KITCHEN

EXISTING PLAN

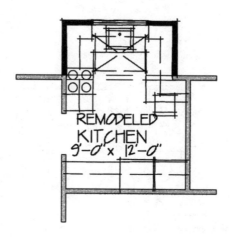

REMODELED KITCHEN 9'-0" x 12'-0"

REMODELED FIRST FLOOR PLAN

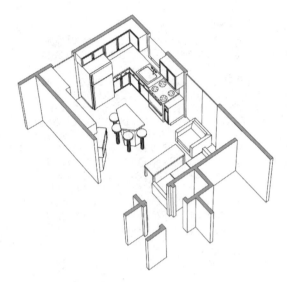

K0008

GIVEN: A VERY TIGHT KITCHEN THAT IS REALLY TOO SMALL TO ALLOW THE OWNERS TO SET UP A TABLE, SO THEY EAT IN THE ADJOINING DINING ROOM ALL THE TIME, BUT EVEN THAT IS AN UNATTRACTIVE, CRAMPED ROOM.   A SOLUTION: IF FORMAL DINING IS NOT THEIR STYLE ANYWAY, CONSIDER CREATING A STUNNING NEW COUNTRY KITCHEN FROM THE TWO SPACES.   THE RESULT IS AN INVITING ROOM WITH A KITCHEN WORK AREA EQUAL TO WHAT EXISTED, BUT WITH A SIGNIFICANT NEW STORAGE COMPONENT IN THE WAY OF A PANTRY, A BUILT-IN DESK, A CORNER FOR A BUILT-IN TV, AND A CENTER ISLAND EATING COUNTER.   BUT BEYOND THIS, THERE IS NOW SPACE FOR A COMFORTABLE, INFORMAL, FAMILY AREA.   TO SATISFY THE OCCASIONAL NEED FOR LARGE DINING, THEY WOULD MOVE THE COUCH AND CHAIR AND SET UP A TABLE, BUT SINCE THE SPACE IS NOW OPEN, IT WILL NO LONGER FEEL CRAMPED.

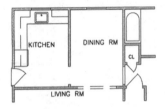

EXISTING PLAN

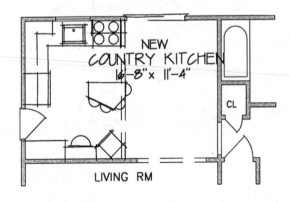

REMODELED FIRST FLOOR PLAN

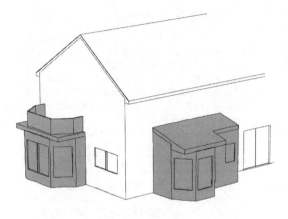

KD003

THIS PLAN IS ACTUALLY TWO SEPARATE ADDITIONS THAT COMPLEMENT EACH OTHER, BUT WHICH COULD BE UNDERTAKEN INDEPENDENTLY. THE HOME FEATURED IS TYPICALLY AN OLDER COLONIAL STYLED TWO-STORY WITH A NICE DINING ROOM AND KITCHEN, BUT MISSING IS A HALL THAT WOULD ALLOW DIRECT ACCESS TO THE KITCHEN. WHILE THE KITCHEN IS AMPLE, IT'S A LITTLE TOO TIGHT TO PROVIDE ATTRACTIVE TABLE SPACE. THE TWO ADDITIONS, SHOWN WITH TWO DIFFERENT ROOFLINES, PROVIDE NOT ONLY THE SPACE NECESSARY TO ACCOMPLISH THE GOALS, BUT DO SO TASTEFULLY AND IN HARMONY WITH THE HOME. TWO COLUMNS AND A DROPPED HEADER DEFINE THE NEW HALL SPACE WITHOUT THE CONFINING USE OF WALLS. THE DINING ROOM BUMP IS 5'4", AND THE REAR EXTENSION IS 14'4"×7'10", INCLUDING THE LAVATORY AS SHOWN.

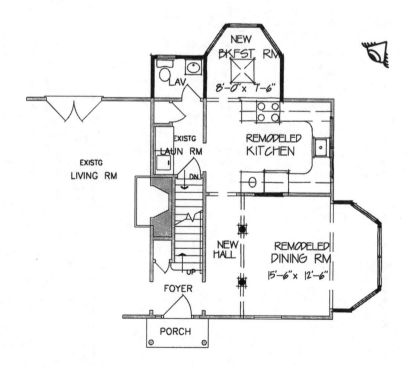

REMODELED FIRST FLOOR PLAN

KD005

A NARROW, SIDE-FACING, KITCHEN IS COMMON
TO MANY ONE-STORY HOMES.   ENLARGING ONE
TO CREATE A FABULOUS, UP-TO-DATE SPACE
IS THE SUBJECT OF THIS PLAN; IT REQUIRES 6'
OF YOUR SIDE YARD, ALTHOUGH WITHOUT A
NEW LAUNDRY ROOM IT COULD BE BUILT IN 4'.
THE KITCHEN IS A SENSATIONAL U,
SURROUNDING A DRAMATIC CENTER ISLAND;
BUILT-INS, INCLUDING A DESK AND PANTRY,
LINE THE INSIDE WALL.   IT IS STRONGLY
SUGGESTED THAT THE FAMILY ROOM BE
REMODELED AND OPENED TO THE NEW
KITCHEN, THEREBY CREATING A UNIFIED
INFORMAL FAMILY LIVING AREA.   THE DINING
ROOM EXPANSION, NEW LAUNDRY AND
COVERED PORCH ARE THE "BONUSES" THAT
GO ALONG WITH THIS PLAN.

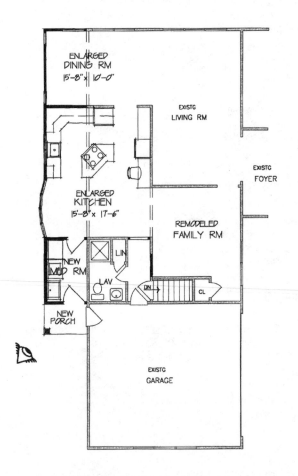

REMODELED FIRST FLOOR PLAN

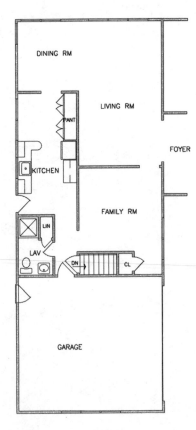

EXISTING PLAN

KD007

HOMES BUILT 25 TO 35 YEARS AGO, WHEN FAMILY ROOMS WERE FIRST BECOMING POPULAR, OFTEN PLACED A "DEN," OR SMALL FAMILY ROOM, BEHIND THE GARAGE AND SEPARATED, BY THE DINING ROOM FROM THE KITCHEN. THE CONNECTION BETWEEN THE KITCHEN AND INFORMAL DEN WAS THUS THROUGH THE FORMAL DINING ROOM, AFFECTING THE FURNISHABILITY OF THE DINING ROOM. THE SOLUTION PICTURED PUSHES OUT AN ADDITION TO ENLARGE THE DINING ROOM SUFFICIENTLY TO CREATE A "GALLERY" OR DESIGNATED CIRCULATION SPACE TO THE DEN. THE KITCHEN IS ALSO COMPLETELY REMODELED IN THIS PLAN WITH THE ADDITION OF A NEW BREAKFAST ROOM FACING THE REAR.

EXISTING FLOOR PLAN

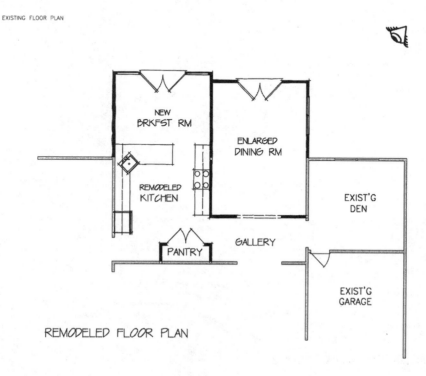

REMODELED FLOOR PLAN

KDBEI

IT'S AMAZING WHAT 5' CAN ACCOMPLISH; ADDED ACROSS THE REAR OF THIS TWO-STORY, IT HELPS CREATE A GREAT NEW KITCHEN, AN EXPANDED DINING ROOM, A LARGE NEW LAUNDRY/EXERCISE ROOM, AND A SPACIOUS NEW MASTER BATH AT THE SECOND FLOOR. IT ALSO ENABLES A COMPLETE MODERNIZATION OF THE REAR FAÇADE PERMITTING LOTS OF GLASS TO BRIGHT LIGHT INSIDE. THE REMODELED KITCHEN IS A VISUAL DELIGHT; A CORNER SINK, AN INTERESTINGLY-SHAPED CENTER ISLAND AND SKYLIGHTS IN THE NEW ADDITION, CREATE A DRAMATIC NEW SPACE. THE EXPANDED LAUNDRY PROVIDES AN IDEAL SPACE FOR EXERCISE EQUIPMENT, OR FOR SEWING OR A HOME OFFICE—MAYBE EVEN ALL THREE. THE NEW MASTER BATH AND SECOND WALK-IN CLOSET ARE THE NOTABLE CHANGES TO THE SECOND FLOOR.

EXISTING PLAN

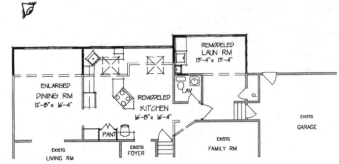

REMODELED FIRST FLOOR PLAN

EXISTING PLAN

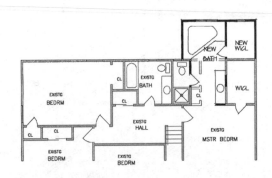

REMODELED SECOND FLOOR PLAN

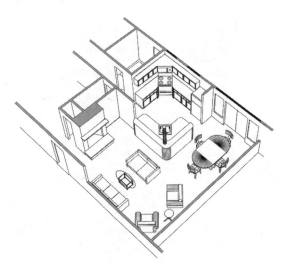

KDLOI

WHEN THERE IS NO ROOM TO EXPAND OUT, AND YOUR GOAL IS TO MODERNIZE A TIGHT KITCHEN, CONSIDER THE CHOICE OF OPENING THE SPACE TO CREATE A GREAT ROOM. THIS OPTION, WHILE NOT FOR EVERYONE, IS A TECHNIQUE FREQUENTLY USED TO MAXIMIZE LIMITED SPACE. THE KITCHEN, WHILE NOT INCREASED IN SIZE, BENEFITS FROM A VISUAL INTEGRATION WITH THE ADJOINING LIVING AND DINING ROOMS. INTERIOR WALLS ARE ELIMINATED TO THE MAXIMUM EXTENT POSSIBLE, AND A COLUMN IS USED AS NECESSARY. THE OLD KITCHEN DOOR AND WINDOW ARE REMOVED, SINCE EXTERIOR ACCESS AND AN ABUNDANCE OF LIGHT ARE NOW PROVIDED FROM THE REAR OF THE GREAT ROOM. THE KITCHEN LAYOUT IS SIGNIFICANTLY ENHANCED, AND THE ENTIRE SPACE TAKES ON A SHINING NEW CHARACTER.

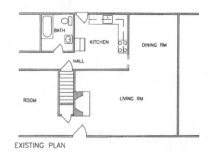

EXISTING PLAN

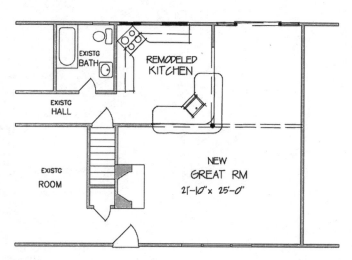

REMODELED FIRST FLOOR PLAN

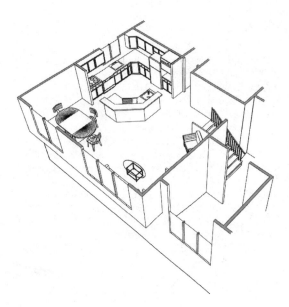

KDL02

HOW DO YOU MODERNIZE THE L-SHAPED LIVING/
DINING ROOM AND THE CLOSED-IN, SIDE-FACING,
KITCHEN IN AN OLD BI-LEVEL (HI-RANCH) HOME?
CONSIDER REMOVING THE WALLS AND MAKING A
FABULOUS NEW GREAT ROOM. THE LIKELIHOOD IS
THAT THE LOWER LEVEL HAS ALL THE NECESSARY
LIVING SPACE FOR THE KIDS (IF THEY'RE STILL THERE)
SO WHY NOT CREATE A STYLISH ENTERTAINMENT
AREA FOR THE ADULTS THAT INCORPORATES THE
KITCHEN. THE REMODELED KITCHEN IS A
DESIGNER'S—AND GOURMET'S—DELIGHT; THE
SMART-LOOKING, ANGULAR ISLAND INCLUDES A
BARBECUE AND SECOND SINK. A WIDE, BAR STOOL
HEIGHT COUNTER PROVIDES THE NECESSARY VISUAL
SCREENING, WHILE CREATING AN INVITING PLACE FOR
GUESTS TO CONGREGATE.

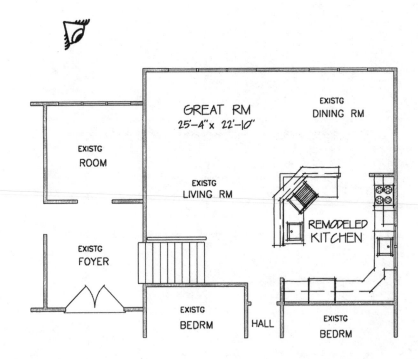

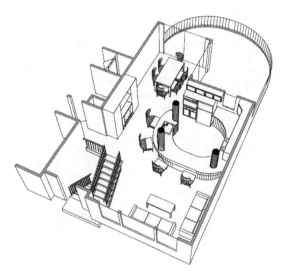

KDL03

IT'S NOT A NEED FOR MORE SPACE THAT HAS THE OWNERS CONSIDERING THE REMODELING OF THE ENTIRE LIVING AREA OF THIS BI-LEVEL (HI-RANCH)—IT'S THE DESIRE FOR A CHANGE IN LIFESTYLE. THEY ARE TIRED OF CHASING UP AND DOWN THE STAIRS TO THE LOWER LEVEL FAMILY ROOM, AND, WHAT'S MORE, THEY ARE EXCITED BY THOSE SPLASHY NEW GREAT ROOMS. THIS PLAN CAN HELP TURN DREAMS INTO REALITY; WALLS ARE ELIMINATED, REPLACED BY DECORATIVE COLUMNS, AND THE ENTIRE AREA BECOMES A SENSATIONAL LIVING AND ENTERTAINING SPACE, THAT HAS A DRAMATIC NEW KITCHEN AS ITS FOCAL POINT. THE ONLY EXPANSION IS THE REAR DECK WHICH HAS BEEN ENLARGED, IN THE FORM OF A HALF CIRCLE, TO ENHANCE THE ABILITY TO ENTERTAIN OUTDOORS AT THIS LEVEL.

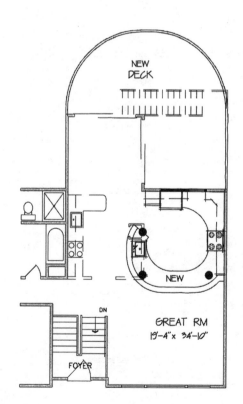

NEW DECK

NEW

GREAT RM
19'-4" x 34'-10"

DN

FOYER

REMODELED SECOND FLOOR PLAN

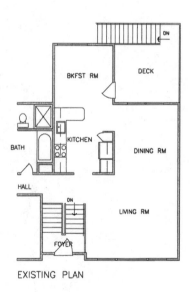

DN

BKFST RM

DECK

BATH

KITCHEN

DINING RM

HALL

DN

LIVING RM

FOYER

EXISTING PLAN

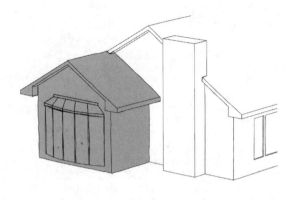

D0001

DINING ROOM MUCH TOO SMALL FOR THOSE FEW OCCASIONS WHEN IT IS NEEDED? WELL, THAT'S NOT AN UNUSUAL COMPLAINT. THERE ARE NUMEROUS PLANS THAT TACKLE THAT PROBLEM IN CONJUNCTION WITH THE REMODELING OF OTHER ROOMS. THIS PLAN DEALS WITH THE SIMPLE SIDE EXTENSION OF ONLY A DINING ROOM. IF YOURS IS AN L-SHAPED LIVING / DINING ROOM, THIS PLAN WILL WORK, REGARDLESS OF THE HOUSE STYLE OR TYPE. THE ADDITION ADDS 7'0" TIMES THE DEPTH OF YOUR ROOM, AND CALLS FOR A LARGE BOW WINDOW AT THE END, TO SERVE AS A FOCAL POINT OF THE REMODELED ROOM. THE OLD WALL ADJOINING THE KITCHEN MAKES A GOOD WALL FOR A BREAKFRONT.

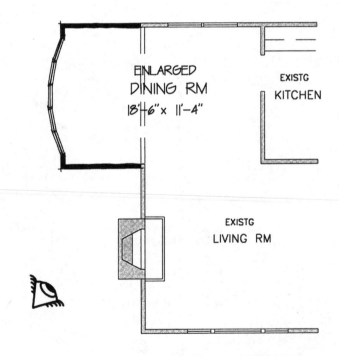

ENLARGED
DINING RM
18'-6" x 11'-4"

EXISTG
KITCHEN

EXISTG
LIVING RM

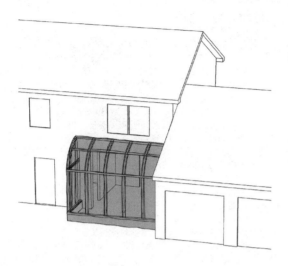

D0002

EXPANDING A FRONT-FACING DINING ROOM IN A CENTER HALL TWO-STORY DESIGN CAN BE RISKY BUSINESS. MOST FLOOR PLANS WILL ONLY ALLOW YOU TO EXTEND FORWARD, WHICH BECOMES A MINOR STRUCTURAL CONCERN AND A MAJOR AESTHETIC ONE. TRYING TO EMULATE AND DESIGN AN ADDITION WITHIN THE STYLE OF THE EXISTING HOME FREQUENTLY PRESENTS AN UNWORKABLE SOLUTION, PARTICULARLY BECAUSE THE NEW ELEMENT IS TOO SMALL. ALTHOUGH MAYBE NOT FOR EVERYONE, THIS GLASS-ENCLOSED GREENHOUSE-STYLE ADDITION COULD BE THE ANSWER. ALTHOUGH IT CREATES A MAJOR DEPARTURE FROM THE STYLE OF THE FRONT, IT DOES SO DRAMATICALLY AND TASTEFULLY. THE COLOR OF THE STRUCTURE SHOULD BLEND WITH YOUR WINDOWS, AND THE USE OF TRADITIONAL DRAPERIES COULD TIE IT IN BEAUTIFULLY.

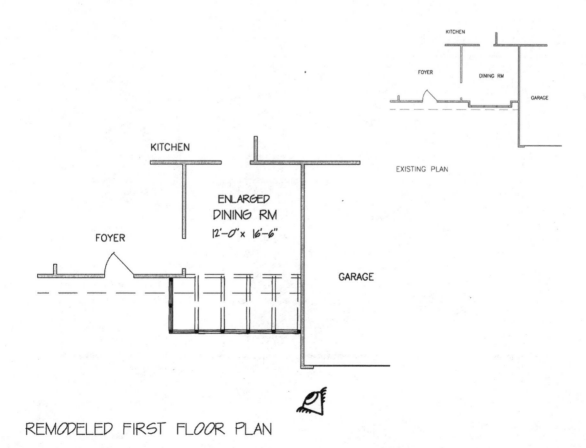

EXISTING PLAN

ENLARGED
DINING RM
12'-0" x 16'-6"

FOYER

KITCHEN

GARAGE

REMODELED FIRST FLOOR PLAN

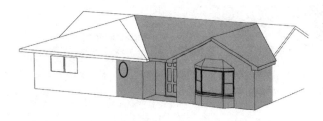

D0003

ADDING TO THE FRONT OF ANY HOME CAN BE TREACHEROUS; UNLESS WE ARE PREPARED TO REDO THE ENTIRE FRONT, THE ADDITION HAS TO BE CAREFULLY CONCEIVED SO IT WILL MESH AND NOT LOOK LIKE A TACK-ON. ALSO, MANY HOMES ARE FREQUENTLY SET AT THE MINIMUM SET BACK, THEREFORE THE ZONING ORDINANCE WOULD PREVENT YOU FROM ADDING TO THE FRONT. THE HOME PICTURED, A ONE-STORY L-SHAPED HOME AVOIDS THE SECOND PROBLEM, BY ALLOWING US TO INFILL THE BALANCE OF THE YARD UP TO THE FRONT LINE OF THE "L." THE ROOM WE ARE ADDING TO IS THE DINING ROOM, BUT WE ALSO ARE ABLE TO IMPROVE THE ENTRANCE FOYER AND ADD A LARGE CLOSET TO THE EXISTING BEDROOM. WHATEVER ROOMS ARE INVOLVED IN YOUR HOME, THE GUIDING PRINCIPLE IS TO MAKE IT LOOK GOOD, AND MAKE SURE IT MESHES WITH THE EXISTING.

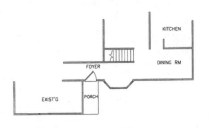

EXISTING FLOOR PLAN

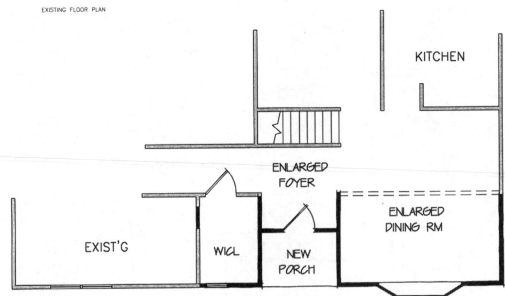

REMODELED FLOOR PLAN

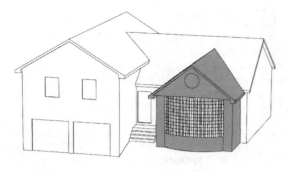

L0003

THE INHERENT FLEXIBILITY FOR CHANGE THAT MOST SPLIT-LEVEL HOMES ENJOY IS DEMONSTRATED IN THIS LIVING ROOM ADDITION. THE SPLIT-LEVEL ALSO LENDS ITSELF TO CONTEMPORARY ADAPTATIONS, AND IF YOU WILL BE ADDING TO THE FRONT, AS IN THIS DESIGN, IT IS A MARVELOUS OPPORTUNITY TO CREATE A STRIKING CHANGE. THIS REVERSE GABLED ADDITION FEATURES A DRAMATIC CURVED GLASS BLOCK WALL THAT EMITS LIGHT, PROVIDES PRIVACY, AND IS HANDSOME TO LOOK AT. THE SPACE THAT IS ADDED IS IDEAL AS A LIBRARY OR MUSIC ALCOVE, AND IS A PERFECT ENHANCEMENT FOR THE ENTERTAINING CAPABILITIES OF THE LIVING AND DINING ROOMS.

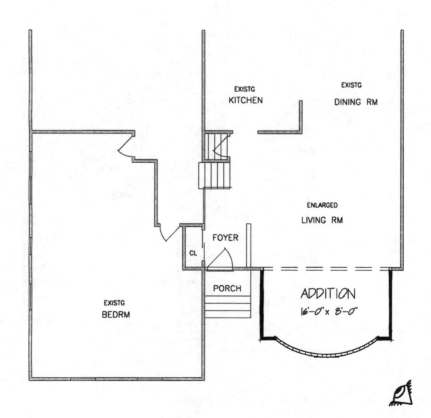

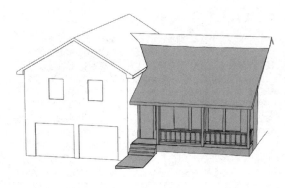

LP00I

JUST AS THE OPEN SITE AREA FORMED BY THE WINGS OF AN L-SHAPED ONE-STORY OFFERS POTENTIAL FOR NEW SPACE, THE AREA IN FRONT OF THE LIVING ROOM ON AN L-SHAPED SPLIT-LEVEL IS ALSO SPACE WAITING TO BE FOUND. IN THE DESIGN SHOWN, THE LIVING ROOM HAS BEEN GRACIOUSLY INCREASED BY 5', AND A NEW FRONT PORCH IS ALSO ADDED. BONUSES OF THIS ADDITION INCLUDE A NEW ENTRANCE FOYER AND A NEW FOUND EXTERIOR APPEAL. WHEN PLANNING ANY FRONT ADDITION, REMEMBER TO INVESTIGATE THE LOCATION OF ALL UNDERGROUND UTILITY CONNECTIONS.

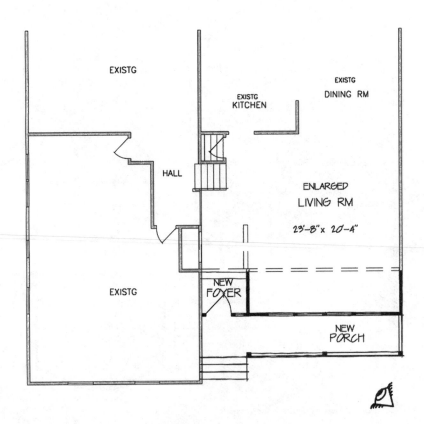

REMODELED FIRST FLOOR PLAN

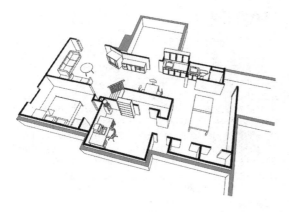

BSMT1

THIS IS THE ONLY PLAN INCLUDED THAT DEALS WITH THE FINISHING OF A BASEMENT. BASEMENTS VARY SO MUCH, AS DO INDIVIDUAL PROGRAMS, BUT THE BASICS SHOULD BE THE SAME. I TRY TO AVOID DARK HALLS AND TRY TO LOSE THE COLUMNS AND GIRDERS IN PARTITIONS. I ALSO OPEN THE STAIRCASE UP AS MUCH AS POSSIBLE, LEAVE AMPLE UTILITY AND STORAGE SPACE AND ADD NATURAL LIGHT WITH LARGER WINDOWS AND SLIDING DOORS, ESPECIALLY IF IT IS A WALK-OUT CONDITION. EVEN IF IT IS NOT AND YOU INTEND TO PLACE A BEDROOM IN THE BASEMENT, VIRTUALLY ALL BUILDING CODES REQUIRE A LARGE EGRESS WINDOW, THE SILL OF WHICH IS NO HIGHER THAN 42 INCHES ABOVE THE FLOOR. THIS WINDOW NEEDS TO LEAD INTO A LARGE WELL THAT ENABLES ONE TO CLIMB TO GRADE. THERE ARE PRE-FABRICATED PRODUCTS THAT ACCOMPLISH THAT FOR YOU.

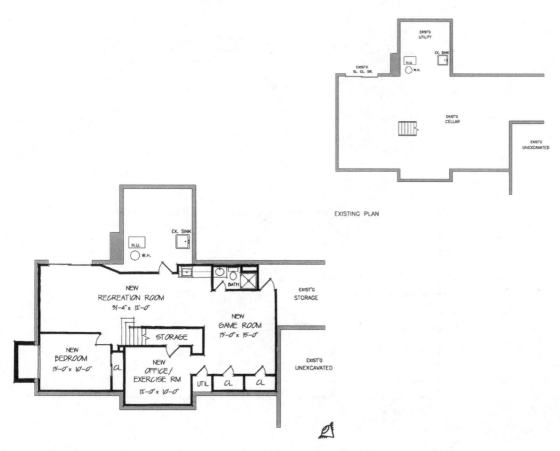

EXISTING PLAN

REMODELED PLAN

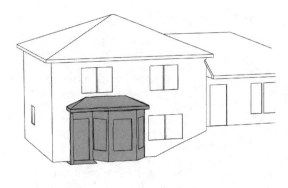

HAPT4

THIS IS ONE OF SEVERAL PLANS IN THE BOOK THAT IS DESIGNED TO CREATE AN ATTRACTIVE BARRIER-FREE APARTMENT. THE LOCATION IS PERFECT: IT IS THE GROUND FLOOR OF A SPLIT-LEVEL, WHERE DIRECT ACCESS TO THE OUTSIDE IS EASILY ACHIEVED. THE PLAN TAKES UP THE AREA OF THE GARAGE AND RECREATION ROOM, AN AREA APPROXIMATELY 27'×26' IT INCLUDES A SEPARATE EAT-IN KITCHEN, A LARGE LIVING ROOM WITH A NEW BAY WINDOW, AND A WHEELCHAIR-ACCESSIBLE BATHROOM THAT IS LOCATED ALONG THE MAIN PLUMBING WALL OF THE HOME. THE CONVERSION EVEN LOOKS ATTRACTIVE, SOMETHING THAT IS OFTEN OVERLOOKED, DESPITE THE NEW WINDOWS AND DOORS WHICH ARE NECESSARY. PLANS THAT ADD BACK A FAMILY ROOM AND GARAGE ARE SHOWN IN THE PRECEDING CHAPTER.

EXISTING PLAN

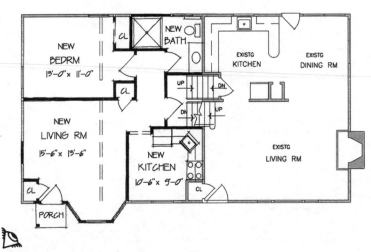

REMODELED FIRST FLOOR PLAN

HAPTI

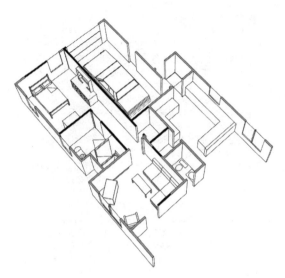

THIS BARRIER-FREE CONVERSION CREATES AN ATTRACTIVE ONE BEDROOM, FULLY HANDICAPPED ACCESSIBLE APARTMENT FROM AN EXISTING GARAGE AND ADJACENT ROOM—MOST LIKELY A DINING ROOM AS SHOWN. THE PLAN ASSUMES A TWO-CAR SIDE ENTRY GARAGE, AND STILL LEAVES A ONE-CAR GARAGE WITH DIRECT INTERIOR ACCESS. THE HALF GARAGE UTILIZED IS CONVERTED INTO A BEDROOM AND A FULLY WHEELCHAIR-ACCESSIBLE BATHROOM WITH A ROLL-IN SHOWER. THE DINING ROOM MAKES A FINE LIVING ROOM, BUT NEED NOT BE CONVERTED IF ONLY A BEDROOM IS NECESSARY. OTHER THAN THE CLOSURE OF ONE GARAGE DOOR, THERE ARE NO OTHER CHANGES REQUIRED TO THE EXTERIOR OF THE HOME.

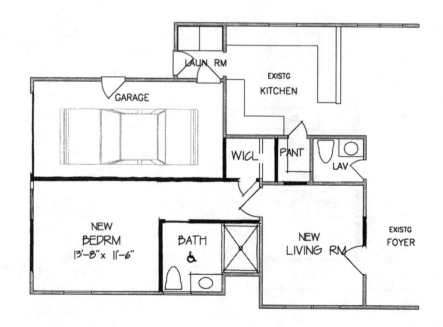

REMODELED FIRST FLOOR PLAN

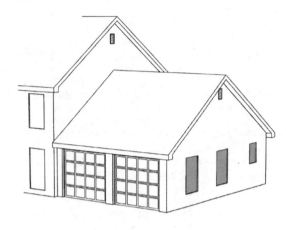

HAPT5

WHAT IF ONE NEEDS TO CREATE A HANDICAPPED-ACCESSIBLE BEDROOM FOR A PARENT, BUT THERE IS NO SPACE—OR BUDGET—TO ADD ON. THIS PLAN SHOWS YOU HOW TO ATTRACTIVELY CONVERT ONE BAY OF AN EXISTING TWO CAR GARAGE. THE HALLS, BATH AND DOORS ARE EXTRA WIDE TO ACCOMMODATE A WHEELCHAIR. THE REASON TO KEEP THE BEDROOM SHORT OF THE FRONT GARAGE WALL IS NOT TO HIDE THE CONVERSION FROM THE AUTHORITIES; IT IS DONE FOR AESTHETIC CONCERNS. PUTTING A WINDOW IN THE SAME FRONT WALL AS THE REMAINING EXISTING GARAGE DOOR LOOKS AWFUL. IT IS USUALLY AT A DIFFERENT HEAD HEIGHT AND IT FORESHORTENS THE HOME'S APPEARANCE. ALTHOUGH IT WOULDN'T HURT IF WE COULD CREATE A BEDROOM WIDER THAN 10'0", THAT'S IMPOSSIBLE IF THE GARAGE IS ONLY 20'0" WIDE, BUT THE 13 FOOT DEPTH IS AMPLE.

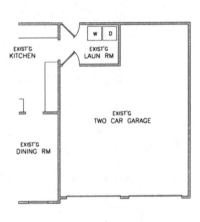

EXIST'G KITCHEN

EXIST'G LAUN RM

W   D

EXIST'G DINING RM

EXIST'G TWO CAR GARAGE

EXISTING FLOOR PLAN

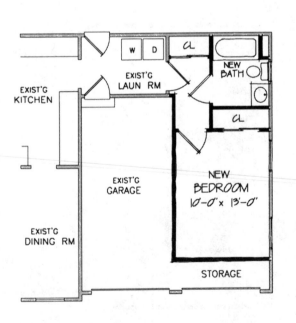

EXIST'G KITCHEN

W   D

EXIST'G LAUN RM

NEW BATH

EXIST'G GARAGE

NEW BEDROOM 10'-0" x 13'-0"

EXIST'G DINING RM

STORAGE

REMODELED FLOOR PLAN

APT05

IF YOU ARE CONSIDERING CONVERTING AN ATTACHED TWO-CAR GARAGE TO A PROFESSIONAL APARTMENT, GIVE SOME THOUGHT TO MAKING IT OTHER THAN TWO WINDOWS AND A DOOR "STUCK IN THE HOLES" OF THE GARAGE DOORS. THE LITTLE REVERSE GABLE ROOF, COVERING THE BAY AND ENTRANCE DOOR, SHOWN IN THIS DESIGN, DO MUCH TO GIVE THE NEW OFFICE AN APPEAL OF ITS OWN. THE PLAN, ALBEIT A LITTLE TIGHT, DOES PROVIDE FOR TWO EXAM ROOMS, A PRIVATE OFFICE AND AN OPEN RECEPTION—WAITING AREA. HALLS ARE WIDE ENOUGH FOR HANDICAP ACCESS, AS IS THE LAVATORY. CONNECTION TO THE HOUSE CAN REMAIN THROUGH THE PRIVATE OFFICE.

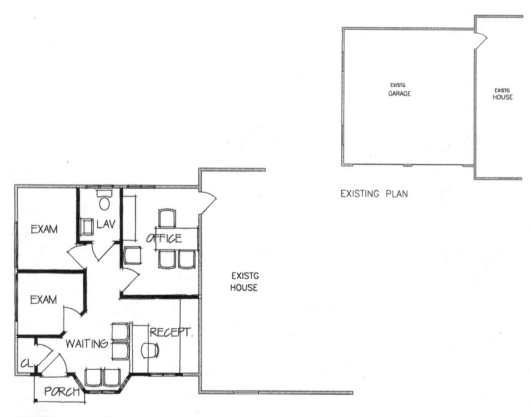

EXISTING PLAN

REMODELED FIRST FLOOR PLAN

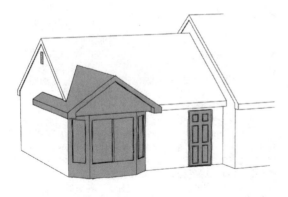

APT12

THIS IS ANOTHER, AMONGST THE MANY, APARTMENT
SOLUTIONS IN THIS BOOK, ALL OF WHICH ARE ON CAD
AND AVAILABLE FOR MODIFICATION AND CONVERSION.
THIS PLAN IS ONE OF THE LEAST COSTLY, AS IT
UTILIZES ONLY EXISTING SPACE, BUT YOU DO GIVE UP
THE GARAGE IN ITS ENTIRETY. IMPORTANT TO NOTE
IS, THAT, IF YOU WANT TWO ROOMS AND THE
GARAGE IS THE TYPICAL 20'×20', YOU DO NEED TO
PUSH OUT A LITTLE. THE REAR BAY BUMP-OUT
PROVIDES THAT LITTLE EXTRA BIT OF SPACE NEEDED
TO MAKE THIS TWO ROOM APARTMENT WORK. IF
YOU DO NEED TO ADD BACK A GARAGE, THERE ARE
MANY GARAGE PLANS, INCLUDING A FEW FULLY-
DETACHED GARAGES, IN THE BOOK.

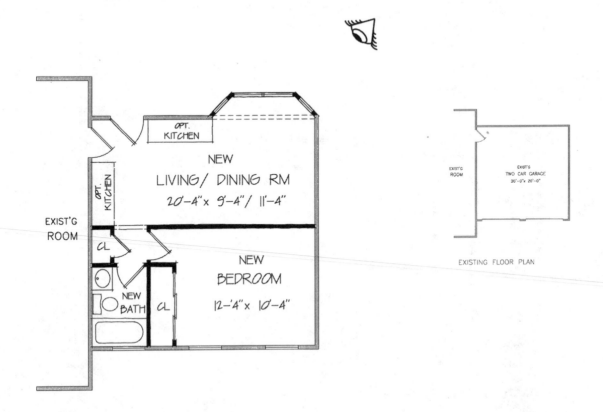

OPT.
KITCHEN

NEW
LIVING/ DINING RM
20'-4"x 9'-4"/ 11'-4"

OPT. KITCHEN

EXIST'G
ROOM

CL

NEW
BEDROOM
12-'4"x 10'-4"

NEW
BATH

CL

EXIST'G
ROOM

EXIST'G
TWO CAR GARAGE
20'-0"x 20'-0"

EXISTING FLOOR PLAN

REMODELED FLOOR PLAN

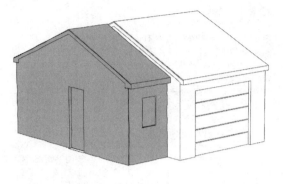

STR01

IF THE PROGRAM IS ASKING FOR SOME STORAGE OR WORKSHOP SPACE, AND THE LOT GIVES YOU 5 OR 6' TO EXPAND ALONGSIDE THE GARAGE, YOU COULD CONSIDER THE ADDITION SHOWN HERE. THERE ARE SOME PITFALLS TO BE AWARE OF; EVEN THOUGH YOU COULD USE ALL THE SPACE, THE SMALL SET-BACK AT THE FRONT IS ADVISABLE. IT CREATES AN ATTRACTIVE FORM AND ROOFLINE BREAK, AND WITH SOME ACCENTS, LIKE A SPECIALTY WINDOW, OR SOME STONE VENEER, IT COULD BECOME AN ATTRACTIVE ADDITION. IF YOU HAVE 7 OR 8' THAT CAN BE ADDED, CONSIDER MAKING THE ADDITION FLUSH WITH THE GARAGE AND RECONSTRUCTING THE GARAGE FRONT WITH ONE OR TWO OVERHEAD DOORS. BEAR IN MIND, HOWEVER, THAT A TWO-CAR GARAGE SHOULD HAVE A MINIMUM OF 17 OR 18' IN WIDTH.

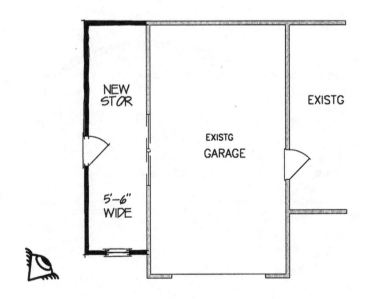

REMODELED FIRST FLOOR PLAN

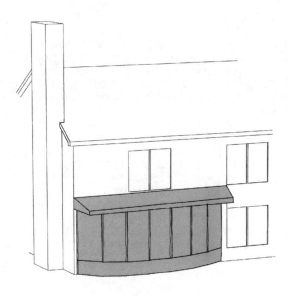

SML01

IS THERE A GREAT VIEW THAT YOU WANT TO TAKE ADVANTAGE OF? OR A SUNNY SIDE OF THE HOME THAT YOU WANT TO CAPTURE INSIDE? OR YOU JUST WANT TO MAKE A STATEMENT IN GLASS AND ADD A FEW FEET OF SPACE IN THE PROCESS? WELL ANY ONE OF THESE GOALS IS ACHIEVED IN THIS PLAN. IT IS A ROOM-WIDE BOW WINDOW THAT PROTRUDES OUT A FEW FEET AND BRINGS GLASS FROM CORNER TO CORNER OF THE ROOM. WHATEVER TYPE OF ROOM IT IS, AND WHETHER THE ROOM IS 10' WIDE OR 20' WIDE (AS SHOWN), THE SAME CONCEPT APPLIES. THE BIGGEST CONSTRUCTION CONCERN IS CALCULATING THE GIRDER NECESSARY TO SUPPORT THE ROOF (AND FLOORS) ABOVE, AND THE DETAILS NECESSARY TO INSTALL THIS GIRDER; SEE PAGES 369 THROUGH 380 IN CHAPTER 12 ON HOW TO ACCOMPLISH THIS.

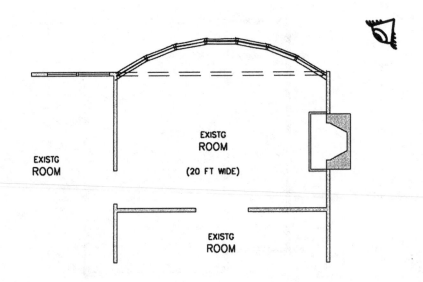

EXISTG
ROOM

EXISTG
ROOM
(20 FT WIDE)

EXISTG
ROOM

REMODELED FIRST FLOOR PLAN

SML04/05

THE TWO-ROOF CLEARSTORY PLANS PICTURED HERE
ARE AMONGST THE MANY PLANS IN THIS BOOK THAT
HAVE AS THEIR FOCUS THE ADDITION OF LIGHT.   THIS
PROPENSITY FOR LIGHT IS A DRIVING FORCE IN
CONTEMPORARY DESIGN.   IT HAS ALSO BECOME A
YEARNING OF MANY HOMEOWNERS WHEN
UNDERTAKING A REMODELING PROJECT.   WE REMOVE
WALLS, OPEN OUTSIDE WALLS AND INSTALL NEW
LARGER WINDOWS AND WE ALSO INSTALL SKYLIGHTS.
TO MANY PEOPLE, THOUGH, THE SKYLIGHT PROVIDES
TOO DIRECT A SOURCE OF LIGHT; SKYLIGHTS ARE
ALSO DIFFICULT TO SHADE.   THE CLEARSTORY (OR
ROOF MONITOR, AS SOME CALL IT) BRINGS IN LIGHT
THROUGH ITS WALLS.   SHOWN ON THIS PAGE IS A
SHED-ROOF CLEARSTORY AND A REVERSE GABLE
CLEARSTORY.   TWO OTHER DESIGNS FOLLOW.

RIDGE LINE — HIGH CEIL

FIRST FLOOR WALLS —

CLERESTORY PLAN

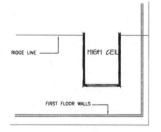

RIDGE LINE — HIGH CEIL

FIRST FLOOR WALLS —

CLERESTORY PLAN

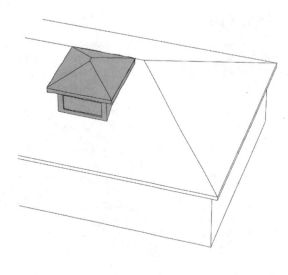

SML06/07

THIS PAGE PRESENTS A HIP-ROOFED CLEARSTORY AND A MULTI-SIDED CONICAL STYLE CLEARSTORY OR MONITOR. WITH ROOF OVERHANGS, ANY OF THESE CLEARSTORIES CAN BE DESIGNED TO ELIMINATE DIRECT SUN, IF THAT IS DESIRED. THE CLEARSTORY ALSO PROVIDES LIGHT MORE DIRECTLY TO WALLS BELOW IT, AND CAN BE USED AS AN EFFECTIVE DESIGN TOOL TO LIGHT SPECIFIC AREAS OF THE FLOOR BELOW. THE INSTALLATION OF A CLEARSTORY REQUIRES THE REMOVAL OF SOME CEILING BELOW, AND MAYBE EVEN THE ENTIRE CEILING OF A ROOM. AS SUCH, A CLEARSTORY ALSO HAS THE EFFECT OF ELEVATING THE VOLUME OF A ROOM, AND CAN VISUALLY ENHANCE THE APPEARANCE OF THE SPACE. THEY ARE ALSO EXTERIOR FORMS THAT ADD INTEREST AND APPEAL TO THE ROOFLINE OF YOUR HOME.

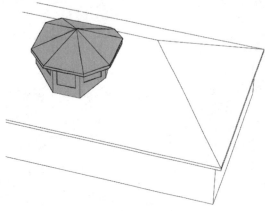

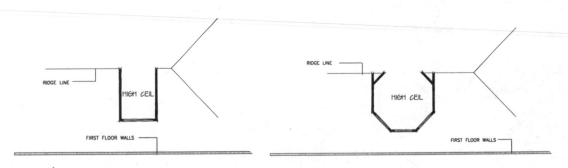

RIDGE LINE

HIGH CEIL

FIRST FLOOR WALLS

CLERESTORY PLAN

RIDGE LINE

HIGH CEIL

FIRST FLOOR WALLS

CLERESTORY PLAN

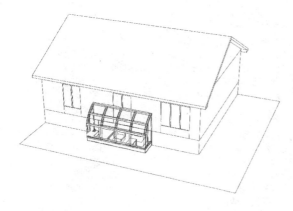

SML08

HERE IS A FABULOUS WAY TO GET SOME NATURAL DAYLIGHT INTO A BASEMENT ROOM. THE SEARCH FOR NATURAL LIGHT IS CERTAINLY ONE OF TODAY'S PREVALENT DESIGN THEMES. REMOVING CEILINGS AND INSTALLING SKYLIGHTS IS A GIVEN TO MOST REMODELING PROJECTS, AS IS THE INSTALLATION OF LARGER EXPANSES OF NEW WINDOWS. BUT HOW DO YOU ACHIEVE THAT IN A BASEMENT? THIS PLAN SHOWS HOW. PICK AN AREA WHERE THE GROUND IS BELOW THE BASEMENT WINDOWS. A WIDE NEW AREAWAY WALL IS BUILT, AND ABOVE THAT IS A GLASS ENCLOSED GREENHOUSE STRUCTURE IS INSTALLED. THE TOUGHEST PART IS REMOVING THE OLD BASEMENT WALL, BUT WHEN IT'S DONE YOUR BASEMENT ROOM WILL FEEL AS THOUGH IT HAS BEEN MOVED OUT OF THE GROUND.

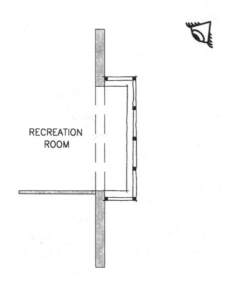

BASEMENT LEVEL

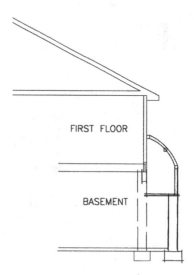

SECTION

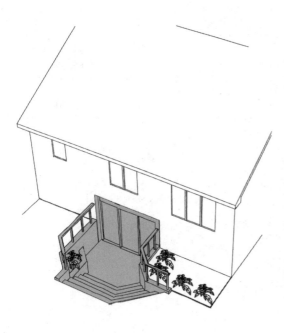

SML09

THE DESIGN PRESENTED HERE IS ANOTHER IDEA FOR YOU TO CONSIDER THAT BRINGS LIGHT INTO A BASEMENT RECREATION ROOM (OR ANY OTHER ROOM IN THE BASEMENT).   THIS DESIGN GOES ONE STEP FURTHER THAN PLAN SML08, ON PAGE 309, BY ALSO PROVIDING EXTERIOR ACCESS TO THE BASEMENT.   A BROAD, STYLISH, ANGULAR SET OF STEPS BUILT FROM EITHER WOOD TIES OR CONCRETE GOES DOWN FROM THE EXTERIOR GRADE TO A WIDE, COMFORTABLE, SUNKEN ENTRY.   TRIPLE FRENCH DOORS PROVIDE LIGHT AND ACCESS.   THE KEY IS THE LARGE SIZE OF THE SUNKEN ENTRY AND THE BROAD STEPS, WHICH ELIMINATES THE NEGATIVE IMPRESSION OF THE TYPICAL NARROW OUTSIDE BASEMENT STAIR.   THIS SOLUTION IS BEST IF THE DISTANCE FROM GRADE TO THE BASEMENT FLOOR IS 4'6" OR LESS.

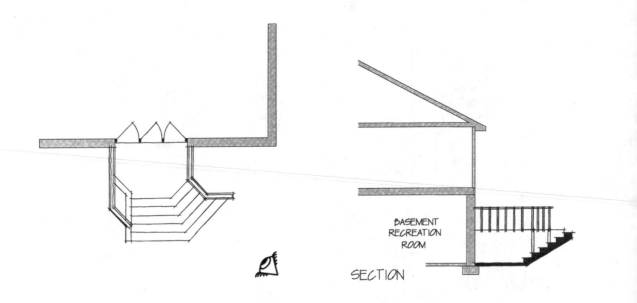

BASEMENT
RECREATION
ROOM

SECTION

Remodel Plans — New Faces

As you have likely noted by now, the exterior designs pictured thus far have been devoid of materials and details. This should not at all suggest that this is the way to design. On the contrary, when preparing a custom design, I am always studying façade details simultaneously as the plan develops. However, for the purpose of preparing this sketchbook of prototype plans, it is helpful to deal with the subject of façades as a separate topic. There are three different scenarios in which the following drawings will prove helpful.

New Faces as a Planned Product of the Remodeling

Almost every remodeling project simultaneously produces some exterior redesign. Even if you are just remodeling a bathroom or a kitchen, you are likely to change a window. What impact does this have on the outside of the home? One window change could be major, particularly if it's a front wall.

Changing a window might require some fixing of siding or brickwork. What if that siding is no longer available, or what if the brick can't be matched? Will you repaint the whole house? Well, if you do, you might as well change some other windows too!

These same types of questions multiply significantly, the more complex the remodeling. You've likely read my comments on certain plans where I cautioned that making an addition flush with existing walls requires the perfect match of siding and roofing.

Yet this is the opportune time to consider a new face. Additions, especially those that affect the forms and massing of the home, may even trigger the question of changing style. As you undertake a major addition, if yours is one of those homes built over the last fifty years that lacked any real discernible character, I strongly recommend that you now give it some character — budget permitting, of course.

Virtually all of the additions shown in the prior chapters have already been designed from the point of view of forms and mass; all they need are materials and trim to complete the picture. That you can do on you own—or you could pick from the drawings in this chapter. To the extent that you may prefer one style over another, and that suggests changing window designs, that is perfectly acceptable. A custom sketch could be prepared if you are unsure.

New Faces as an Unplanned Product of the Remodeling

This can be a most unfortunate experience. It usually happens when there has been a lack of proper design. Just as I sketched some "don'ts" in chapter 4 on forms, I could do the same here; but that would take a great deal of space, and I would rather show what to do. The best advice for the do-it-yourselfer is to hire a professional or to try to mimic the ready-made designs in this book. Remember, for professional and laymen alike, make sure you study all sides of the project, or even build a scale model to study all four sides.

New Faces Per se

Many remodeling projects are only skin deep; the project that only replaces windows, siding and trim is quite common. The motivation is generally a practical consideration, stemming from the fact that the windows are rotted or the siding is broken and the trim is peeling. Yet all too often the homeowner fails to seize upon this as a golden opportunity to give their home some character.

If one is considering window replacement, give some thought to also changing their location, size and style. As many have learned, the mere changing of the windows can have a profound affect on the home's appearance. The enormous variety of window shapes, sizes and styles that are readily available today provide today's remodeler a wonderful opportunity to help create a new look, whatever its style. Years ago an arched head window with intricate lacy divided lights was a custom order that could blow the budget—today you can pick it up at the local lumberyard.

If you are planning to redo the exterior, there are 26 prototypes for you to look at that follow. Hopefully they will give you some direction that can be developed and embellished further as warranted.

New Faces as the Motivation for the Remodeling

As a society, we have become more involved with our homes; we care how they look, how they appear to ourselves and to others. Forty years ago the obsession was pure shelter; today it is style. As a consequence, some remodeling projects start with the exterior. Typically such a renovation starts out where the owners have a strong feeling for the way they would like their home to appear; all other aspects of the program, then, take a back seat to that direction. It is not wrong. In fact it can lead to a very successful renovation because there is a strong cohesive direction to the project.

Frequently this type of program leads to a veritable gutting of the existing home, although this need not be the rule. Several of the new façades shown on the following pages are of this nature, whereas any of the façades presented could serve as the prototype for an exterior directed remodeling project.

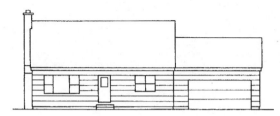

FAC01

THIS SIMPLE ONE AND ONE-HALF STORY (A.K.A. A CAPE COD, FARM RANCH, COTTAGE, ETC.) CAN BE TRANSFORMED INTO A SEDUCTIVE COUNTRY-STYLE HOME WITH THE MERE ADDITION OF A FRONT PORCH. TWO PLANS SHOWING SUCH PORCHES ARE PRESENTED IN THE PRIOR CHAPTER, AS PLAN P0008 ON PAGE 221 AND PLAN P0013 ON PAGE 220. SIDING AND WINDOWS MUST BE REPLACED OF COURSE, AS WELL AS TRIM, BUT CHANCES ARE THEY WERE DUE ANYWAY.

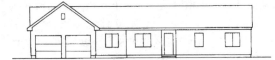

FAC08

TODAY'S NEW FAÇADES ARE TRENDING AWAY FROM
THE UNADORNED TRACT LOOK TO A RICHLY DETAILED,
TRADITIONAL OR COUNTRY LOOK.   THIS PLAIN, LONG,
ONE-STORY HOME IS RECAST WITH ITS NEW APPEAL
BY ADDING A PORCH FROM THE GARAGE TO THE
FRONT DOOR, WITH AN APPROPRIATE ROOF BREAK,
AND ALSO ADDING SOME DORMER FORMS OVER THE
BEDROOM WINDOWS.   NEW WINDOWS, SIDING AND
TRIM COMPLETE THE PICTURE.   PLAN P0007 ON PAGE
219 PROVIDES A PLAN FOR SUCH A PORCH.

FACIO

THE PROBLEM WITH THE FAÇADES OF SO MANY POST-WORLD WAR II HOMES WAS THAT THEY WERE BUILT WITHOUT ANY ATTENTION TO EXTERIOR DETAIL. THIS SPLIT-LEVEL WAS NO EXCEPTION. FORTUNATELY, THERE ARE SEVERAL WAYS TO GIVE IT SOME STYLE AND SOME FLAIR. BY INSTALLING A REVERSE GABLE ROOF, AND RAISING THE CEILING IN THE LIVING ROOM, IT IS NOW POSSIBLE TO INSTALL TWO OF THOSE GREAT LOOKING NEW WINDOWS WITH ROUNDED TOPS. NEW FRONT STEPS, A NEW FRONT DOOR, AND NEW WINDOWS COMPLETE THE REFURBISHING. THE HIGHER ROOF IS A FUNCTION OF ADDING SPACE OVER THE LIVING ROOM, BUT IT DOESN'T HAVE TO BE DONE TO CREATE A SIGNIFICANT IMPROVEMENT.

FAC34

TODAY'S PREDOMINANT THEME IS COUNTRY STYLING.
IT CAN BE ACCOMPLISHED VERY READILY ON MANY
SIMPLE ONE-STORY HOMES.   A PORCH ADDITION IS A
MUST, BUT IT DOESN'T HAVE TO BE HUGE.   ADDING
REVERSE GABLE ELEMENTS TO FURTHER DELINEATE
THE FAÇADE IS ANOTHER IMPORTANT ELEMENT;
THESE ARE EASY TO DO.   THE CHANGE OF WINDOWS
IS ANOTHER REQUIREMENT, BUT THEY WERE
PROBABLY DUE TO BE REPLACED ANYWAY.

FAC03

THIS CHANGE FROM A PLAIN TWO-STORY TO A
STYLISH POST-MODERN FAÇADE GOES HAND-IN-HAND
WITH PLAN UPDATING.   TO CREATE A TWO-STORY
ENTRANCE FOYER, WE NEED TO RELOCATE THE
SECOND FLOOR BEDROOMS AND USE THE SPACE
OVER THE GARAGE; A NUMBER OF PLANS LIKE PFB02,
BRB05 AND BRB20 DO JUST THAT.   THE ONE-STORY
ADDITION TO THE FRONT OF THE LIVING ROOM, LIKE
L0002, HELPS CREATE FAÇADE INTEREST.

FAC07

THE HI-RANCH (A.K.A. BI-LEVEL OR SPLIT-FOYER) IS A COMMON TARGET FOR FAÇADE REMAKES. BECAUSE OF ITS DIFFERENT DOOR AND WINDOW HEIGHTS, AND THE ABSENCE OF SYMMETRY, IT IS FREQUENTLY REFACED IN A CONTEMPORARY MODE. IN THE PLAN SHOWN, NOT ONLY ARE WINDOWS AND DOORS CHANGED AND THE HOUSE RE-SIDED, BUT A REVERSE GABLE IS PROPOSED FOR THE LIVING ROOM. THIS WOULD ALLOW YOU TO RAISE THE CEILING AND INSTALL A DRAMATIC NEW FLOOR-TO-CEILING WINDOW WALL.

FAC20

OH, THAT UGLY BIG STOOP! OWNERS OF HI-RANCHES (A.K.A. BI-LEVEL, SPLIT-ENTRY OR SPLIT-FOYER) HAVE COVERED THEM IN WOOD, MARBLE, BRICK, YOU NAME IT. IF YOU HAVE WISHED THERE WAS A WAY TO GET RID OF IT, THIS REMODEL SHOWS HOW. IT DOES REQUIRE REMOVING THE STOOP, BUT IF YOU'RE UP TO THAT, YOU CAN RECAST YOUR HOME AS A TWO-STORY, AS SHOWN. A NEW PORCH AND FOYER ARE CREATED, AND THE DESIGN FOR THESE IS PLAN P0019 ON PAGE 227. YOU CAN ALSO REVERSE GABLE THE LIVING ROOM, AS PICTURED, AND RAISE THE VOLUME TO CREATE A HIGH-VAULTED CEILING.

FAC04

THIS IS A FORTY-YEAR-OLD ONE AND ONE-HALF STORY HOME WITH A BREEZEWAY CONNECTING TO A DETACHED TWO-CAR GARAGE.   IN THE REMODEL PICTURED, THE BREEZEWAY IS ENCLOSED, AND A SHALLOW REVERSE GABLE "BUMP" IS ATTACHED TO THE LIVING ROOM.   THE CEILING OF THE LIVING ROOM IS OPENED UP AS FAR AS YOU CAN GO, AND A DRAMATIC WINDOW WALL IS INSTALLED.   A PORCH NOW ADORNS THE ENTRY, AND ENLARGED WINDOWS AND NEW SIDING COMPLETELY REMAKE THE EXTERIOR.   ROOM ADDITIONS TO INFILL A BREEZEWAY ARE SHOWN IN CHAPTER 8 AND "BUMPS" ARE PICTURED IN CHAPTER 9.

FAC05

DRESSING UP A VERY PLAIN SPLIT-LEVEL REQUIRES A
LITTLE WORK.   THE FAÇADE SHOWN BUMPS OUT THE
FRONT TO PROVIDE A COVERED PORCH; IT ALSO
ENLARGES THE TWO BEDROOMS UPSTAIRS IN THE
FRONT.   THE OTHER MAJOR CHANGE, WHICH IS THE
CREATION OF A LARGE ROOFLINE, IS A FUNCTION OF
ADDING SPACE OVER THE LIVING ROOM LEVEL.
SEVERAL OTHER VARIATIONS OF THIS CAN BE SEEN IN
PLANS BR007 AND BRB18.

FAC14

NO BIG ADDITION IS NEEDED TO TURN THIS FLUSH-
FRONT CENTER HALL TWO-STORY INTO THE COUNTRY
VICTORIAN PICTURED BELOW. A TWO FOOT REVERSE
GABLED ADDITION IS ALL THAT IS NEEDED AT THE
LEFT SIDE OF THE ENTRANCE. THEN ADD A WRAP-
AROUND COUNTRY PORCH LIKE THE ONE SHOWN IN
PLAN P0013 ON PAGE 220 AND YOU HAVE ACHIEVED
THE NEW LOOK. THE DORMER ON THE GARAGE ROOF
IS NICE—BUT NOT NECESSARY—AND IT DOESN'T
HAVE TO BE REAL SPACE ANYWAY.

FAC24

IF YOUR TASTE LEANS TOWARD A SPANISH OR
SOUTHWESTERN STYLE, YOU COULD READILY CHANGE
THIS SIMPLE ONE-STORY TO THAT PICTURED BELOW.
THE MAIN ELEMENT IS THE PORCH ADDITION, WHICH
IS SHOWN WITH AN ENTIRE NEW, HIGHER ROOF.
HOWEVER, YOU COULD ALSO ADD THE PORCH TO
YOUR EXISTING ROOF AS SHOWN IN PLAN P0010
ON PAGE 222, AND ACHIEVE A SATISFACTORY
APPEARANCE.   REMEMBER, IT IS IMPORTANT,
REGARDLESS OF STYLE, TO FINISH WITH APPROPRIATE
TRIM; IN THIS INSTANCE IT SHOULD BE ROUGH SAWN,
DARK-STAINED WOOD.

FAC25

THERE IS ABSOLUTELY NOTHING WRONG WITH THIS EXISTING FAÇADE; THAT IS, UNLESS YOU WANT TO CHANGE IT. WHILE THERE ARE COUNTLESS AESTHETIC RULES THAT I WAS TAUGHT, THAT PRACTICE CONFIRMED OR DENIED, AND WHICH I HAVE TAUGHT TO OTHERS, THERE IS ONE RULE THAT ONLY PRACTICE TAUGHT; IT IS THAT THE HOME IS EACH OWNER'S PERSONAL STATEMENT AND I SHOULD ONLY ADVISE AND SUGGEST—NOT DICTATE—TASTE. I NEVER HAVE AND NEVER WILL. IN THAT REGARD, IF YOU WANT TO TURN THIS LOVELY CENTER HALL INTO A COUNTRY STYLE HOME WITH A WRAP-AROUND PORCH—AND YOU DO IT TASTEFULLY, AS PICTURED— GO AHEAD.

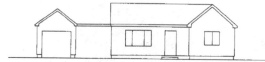

FAC06

THIS TINY, UNAPPEALING RANCH CAN BECOME A
SOPHISTICATED LOOKING COUNTRY-STYLED CHARMER
WITH SOME SPACE ADDITIONS. THE GARAGE AND
BREEZEWAY ARE UNSIGHTLY, SO WE ENCLOSE THE
BREEZEWAY AND TIE THE TWO TOGETHER TO
CREATE A NEW TWO CAR GARAGE—OR MAYBE IT'S
EVEN A MASTER BEDROOM. WE ALSO ADD A FRONT
PORCH, CHANGE WINDOWS, AND WRAP IT ALL IN A
NEW STEEP ROOFLINE WITH A STAND-UP SECOND
FLOOR ATTIC.

FAC36

HOW DO YOU UPDATE THE APPEARANCE OF A DATED U-SHAPED HIP ROOFED RANCH?   THE EXAMPLE SHOWN IS ONE WAY.   OTHER THAN INSTALLING A BAY UNDER THE PORCH AND CHANGING THE WINDOWS AND SIDING, THE BIG CHANGE IS TO ELIMINATE THE TWO FRONT HIPS AND TO CHANGE THEM TO DRAMATIC REVERSE GABLE ELEMENTS, USING LARGE HALF-ROUND, OR OTHER SPECIAL SHAPED, WINDOWS, AND TO PUT A DIFFERENT MATERIAL IN THE TWO GABLES.

FAC37

THIS IS ANOTHER EXAMPLE OF A LONG, LOW, WIDE-LINE, ONE-STORY RANCH HOME WITH LITTLE APPEAL. OTHER THAN PROPOSING NEW WINDOWS AND SIDING, THE ONLY CHANGE HERE IS THE ADDITION OF A NEW FRONT PORCH WITH A HIGHER CEILING HEIGHT. THIS EXTRA HEIGHT COULD BE CARRIED INTO THE ROOMS BEHIND (MOST LIKELY THE ENTRY AND LIVING ROOM) AND PROVIDE A HUGE INTERIOR ENHANCEMENT AS WELL. ALTHOUGH THE CHANGE IS SHOWN IN A CONTEMPORARY MODE, IT COULD BE IN ANY STYLE YOU WANT; JUST CHANGE THE WINDOWS, SIDING AND TRIM DETAILS.

FACII

THIS L-SHAPED TWO-STORY IS A GOOD CHOICE FOR REMODELING IN A CONTEMPORARY POST-MODERN APPROACH. BY CREATING TWO-STORY VOLUME OVER THE LIVING ROOM AND ENTRY, WE EXPAND THE APPEARANCE OF THE SECOND FLOOR—EVEN WITHOUT NECESSARILY ADDING FLOOR SPACE. THIS ENABLES US TO CREATE A LARGE EXPANSIVE ROOF OVER THE SECOND FLOOR WHICH MAKES THE HOME APPEAR MUCH LARGER. NEW SIDING AND WINDOWS COMPLETE THE JOB.

FAC12

THE EXISTING ONE-STORY FAÇADE IS A REFLECTION
OF THE ERA WHEN COST EFFICIENCY DICTATED
SIMPLE, UNADORNED LINES. THE REMODEL PICTURED
DOES MORE THAN JUST CHANGE WINDOWS, SIDING
AND TRIM; IT ALSO ADDS A SMALL SECOND FLOOR
REVERSE GABLE WING, PLUS A COVERED PORCH AT
THE ENTRY. A PLAN SHOWING SUCH A CHANGE IS
PLAN BRB23 ON PAGE 127. OF COURSE, IF YOU HAVE
THE ROOM TO CHANGE YOUR GARAGE TO A SIDE
ENTRY, YOU WILL FURTHER ENHANCE THE
APPEARANCE OF YOUR HOME.

FAC17

THIS ONE AND ONE-HALF STORY IS 40 YEARS OLD, AND IT LOOKS IT. IT'S TIME FOR A CHANGE AND YOUR TASTE LEANS TOWARD COUNTRY. NEW WINDOWS ARE CERTAIN, ESPECIALLY THE LARGE ONES IN THE REMODELED GABLE WALL. A NEW COUNTRY PORCH, SIMILAR TO PLAN P0017 ON PAGE 93, IS PART OF THE PICTURE, AS ARE TWO MORE ROOF DORMERS. THE BREEZEWAY COULD BE ENCLOSED, SEE PLAN F0002 ON PAGE 154, AND YOU COULD CONSIDER RAISING THE ROOF OF THE GARAGE, BUT THAT IS LEAST NECESSARY TO ACHIEVE THE LOOK.

FAC39

IN SOME PARTS OF THE COUNTRY, PSEUDO-EUROPEAN STYLING IS IN VOGUE. SOMETIMES THEY ALSO CALL IT "FRENCH COUNTRY," BUT THE COMMON ELEMENT THAT MAKES THEM STAND OUT IS THE FACT THAT THEY ARE FINISHED IN STUCCO AND INCLUDE STUCCO QUOINS AND SOME CURVED OR ROUND-TOP WINDOWS. IF THE SUBJECT HOME NEEDS NEW SIDING AND NEW WINDOWS, TURNING IT INTO A EUROPEAN-STYLED HOME COULD BE EASY. SOME ROOFLINE MODIFICATION MIGHT BE CALLED FOR, BUT LITTLE ELSE NEED BE DONE.

FAC19

I WOULD BE REMISS IF I DIDN'T PRESENT AT LEAST ONE TUDOR FAÇADE OPTION. ALTHOUGH THERE APPEARS TO BE VERY LITTLE CALL FOR NEW TUDOR HOMES THESE DAYS, IT IS NOT ABSENT. MORE IMPORTANTLY, THOUGH, IF YOU ARE LOOKING TO MAKE A CHANGE FROM "BUILDER'S BASIC," TUDOR IS A READILY ACHIEVABLE STYLE THAT CAN BE COST-EFFECTIVE. THE REMODEL PICTURED IS ACCOMPLISHED BY WINDOW REPLACEMENT, MINIMAL FRAMING FOR THE REVERSE GABLE AND ROOF DORMERS, REFACING WITH THIN BRICK VENEER AND STUCCO, AND THE ADDITION OF A SMALL FRONT PORCH.

FAC27

THE EXISTING FAÇADE OF THIS LONG ONE-STORY
HOME HAS ONE DISTINGUISHING FEATURE—IT IS
LONG. IT IS DEVOID OF ANY CHARACTER, BECAUSE
THAT WAS NOT THE CONCERN OF ITS BUILDER.
YOUR CONCERNS ARE PERSONAL; WHEREAS YOU CAN
DEVELOP ALMOST ANY STYLISTIC LEANING ON SUCH
A HOME, I HAVE SHOWN IT WITH A COUNTRY STYLE
THEME. A PORCH, SIMILAR TO THOSE SHOWN IN
CHAPTER 9, PLUS NEW, LARGER WINDOWS, PANELED
SHUTTERS, FRIEZES AND CORNER BOARDS ARE THE
ELEMENTS THAT CREATE THIS NEW FAÇADE.
BREAKING THE ROOFLINE BEFORE THE GARAGE HELPS,
BUT IS NOT ESSENTIAL TO THE OVERALL THEME.

FAC28

THERE IS TRULY NOTHING WRONG WITH THIS HIPPED-ROOF TWO-STORY THAT SOME COSMETICS COULDN'T REPAIR.   HOWEVER, IF YOU PINE FOR A FRESH LOOK, THE REMODEL PICTURED DOES MAKE FOR A STRIKING NEW APPEARANCE.   A BUMP TO CREATE A NEW SHELTERED ENTRANCE CAN BE FOUND IN PLANS PF002, PFB01 & PFB02 WITHIN CHAPTER 9, AND THE NEW REVERSE GABLE OVER THE GARAGE REPRESENTS AN APARTMENT (OR IT COULD BE A SECOND FLOOR PLAYROOM) WHICH CAN BE SEEN IN PLAN APT03 ON PAGE 211.   A NEW BRICK FRONT COULD BE ACHIEVED WITH THE USE OF THIN BRICK THAT DOES NOT REQUIRE A FOUNDATION.

FAC30

IF YOU'RE TIRED OF THE FORMAL BALANCE OF YOUR CENTER HALL TWO-STORY, IT IS POSSIBLE TO UNBALANCE IT, IF YOU LEAN TOWARD A WHIMSICAL STYLE, SUCH AS THE VICTORIAN PICTURED. BAYED ADDITIONS TO THE LIVING ROOM AND THE BEDROOM ABOVE, PLUS THE ADDITION OF A HUGE WRAP-AROUND PORCH, ARE THE MAJOR STRUCTURAL CHANGES. THE BALANCE OF THE NEW FAÇADE IS A FUNCTION OF SECOND FLOOR BUMP-OUTS, A BRAND NEW STEEP ROOF, SIGNIFICANT WINDOW CHANGES AND TRIM DETAIL.

FAC32

OTHER THAN BEING DATED, THE EXISTING TWO-STORY FAÇADE IS NOTHING TO BE ASHAMED OF. HOWEVER, FOR THE RESTLESS, WE CAN ALWAYS IMPROVE AND UPDATE. THIS FAÇADE REMAKE DOES INVOLVE SEVERAL ADDITIONS, AS WELL, INCLUDING AN ENTIRE ROOM OVER THE GARAGE AND AN EXTENSION TO THE FRONT ROOMS. THE NEW FAÇADE IS AN ELEGANT POST-MODERN DESIGN THAT IS CERTAIN TO PLEASE. ONE OF THE MAIN DESIGN ELEMENTS NEEDED TO EFFECTIVELY CREATE SUCH A NEW FAÇADE IS THE NEW, STEEPER, ROOFLINE, AN ITEM OF SIGNIFICANT EXPENSE, BUT WITHOUT WHICH THE NEW FAÇADE WOULD NOT WORK.

FAC38

IN SOME URBAN AND SUBURBAN AREAS, THERE ARE
OCCASIONAL EXAMPLES OF ONE-OF-A-KIND "FUNKY"
POST-MODERN CONVERSIONS. SUCCESSFULLY
CREATING ONE OF THESE REQUIRES THE DESIGN
SKILL OF A PROFESSIONAL. THE EXAMPLE PICTURED
IS THE CONVERSION OF AN ORDINARY CENTER HALL
TWO-STORY; THE CRITICAL ELEMENTS ARE
ROOFLINES, WINDOWS, SIDING AND TRIM DETAILS.
WINDOWS TRANSCEND THEIR FUNCTION OF
PROVIDING LIGHT, AND BECOME EXCITING
SCULPTURAL ELEMENTS IN A HOME REDONE IN THIS
FASHION.

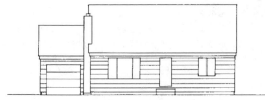

FAC33

THIS IS NOT A MISTAKE. THE NEW FAÇADE WAS
BUILT ON THE SAME HOME AS SHOWN TO THE LEFT.
WELL, DON'T FEEL BAD IF YOU CAN'T FIGURE IT OUT.
THE SMALL ONE AND ONE-HALF STORY WAS
COMPLETELY REDESIGNED, ADDED TO, RIPPED APART,
YOU NAME IT, AND THE RESULT IS WHAT IS PICTURED.
THE POINT TO BE MADE IS THAT, WHEREAS MOST OF
THIS SECTION HAS DEALT WITH FAÇADE CHANGES
PER SE, ONE OF THE OTHER MORE COMMON WAYS
WE CHANGE A HOME'S FAÇADE IS THE PRODUCT OF
A CUSTOM DESIGN UNDERTAKEN BY A QUALIFIED
DESIGN PROFESSIONAL.

Remodel Plans–Whole House Remakes

There are times when a remodeling project involves such a large addition, or additions, or so many bumps, bays and remodeling of interior space, that it takes on the scope of a virtual remodeling of the entire home. There is no precise definition of when that threshold occurs, but I like to think that it occurs when your project begins to involve 40% or more of the home. Remodeling projects of this nature are expensive—and frightening to many; but they are also very exciting. A renovation of this nature can completely transform an inadequate home into a palace.

These kinds of projects are frequently featured in the home journals because they can be beautiful; but they also can be more realistic for a homeowner to consider if they realize that an undertaking of this nature need not be done all at once. I will deal in greater detail on the subject of staging in the next chapter, but briefly stated, staging involves some pre-planning on how you will accomplish the project while living there. In a whole house renovation, proper staging can frequently make the project palatable.

The plans that follow are like all the prior plans, readily duplicated on the subject home, presuming of course that there's a match. Let's talk about that a bit. There are two types of whole house remakes presented. The first type involves the complete renovation of a small home that is likely to be at least fifty years old or more. These are typically old bungalows, cottages, split-levels, or one and one-half stories (cape codes, expansion attic homes, etc.) that are so poorly suited to contemporary living needs that the only solution to many of their deficiencies frequently involves a complete remodeling. You will find a number of these to peruse. Although your home may not precisely match the existing floor plan, it could be similar enough for these plans to work, or it is very possible that you can modify the plans to suit your home. The end result of all these is to create an exciting new beautiful home from one that is somewhat sour.

Whereas this first type of plan involves a remodeling project that is frequently motivated by the need to correct a home with grossly inadequate features, there are other motivations that lead to a whole house renovation. These are usually not as corrective or mandatory in nature, but more selective, representing individual desires or needs. Whole house projects of this nature frequently add more space of special needs, and may significantly renovate the exterior design of the home by choice. Projects of this nature usually do not have to correct circulation problems, or reutilize poorly functioning space, and are inherently more flexible. This second group of whole-house remakes is further divided into two types. The first are plans that are unique custom designs, which derive from projects created in my office; the second type are plans created by combining designs shown in the prior chapters.

The potential number of variations on such plans is, as such, limitless; but they have some very common ground that we have already explored in the plans of the prior chapters. Whether the subject home is a one- or two-story, or a split-level, and one wants to add a new family room, country kitchen, master suite, guest apartment, or whatever, these have already been shown. So, if the program presents a large wish list, it is possible to combine many of the plans previously shown, and create a personal whole house renovation.

I have presented a number of examples of such potential whole house renovations. These, which show one-story, two-story and split-level styles, take various plans from the prior chapters and combine them to create several wonderful new homes that are each worth studying in detail. The numbers of the plans utilized are referenced on each page, so you can see the small modifications that may have been required to incorporate them into the grand scheme. It is my hope that with these examples you may be able to see your way through the process of creating many other unique remodeling projects from the plans shown.

CAP04

ALMOST ALL THE SPACE NEEDED TO DESIGN THIS WHOLE HOUSE RENOVATION IS FOUND ON THE SECOND FLOOR. BY CAREFULLY PUSHING OUT THE SECOND FLOOR WALLS, A VERY APPEALING TWO-STORY HOME IS CREATED FROM THIS 34'0"×26'0", VERY ORDINARY, ONE AND ONE-HALF STORY PLAN. A VERY SMALL SIDE BAY IS ALL THAT IS ADDED TO THE FIRST FLOOR; IT EXPANDS THE FABULOUS NEW GREAT ROOM JUST ENOUGH TO PROVIDE EXTRA LIGHT AND A BUILT-IN MEDIA CENTER. THIS OPEN CONCEPT KITCHEN AND GREAT ROOM IS A TRENDY WAY TO DEAL WITH LIMITED SPACE, WHICH IS ALSO VERY MUCH IN KEEPING WITH TODAY'S LESS FORMAL LIFESTYLE. DO NOTE THE NEW CENTER HALL, CREATED FROM PART OF THE FORMER FRONT BEDROOM; IT'S A MODEST, BUT IMPORTANT, CONTRIBUTION TO THE FUNCTIONALITY OF THE GREAT ROOM.

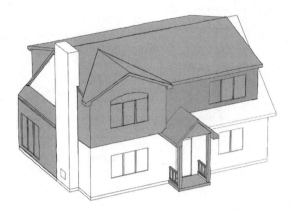

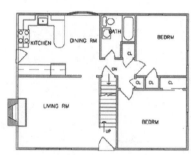

EXISTING FIRST FLOOR PLAN

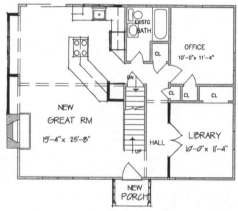

REMODELED FIRST FLOOR PLAN

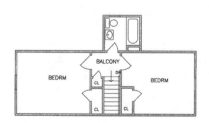

EXISTING SECOND FLOOR PLAN

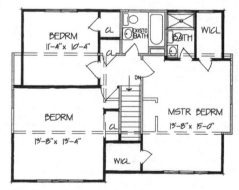

REMODELED SECOND FLOOR PLAN

RANOI

THE L-SHAPED RANCH OFFERS MULTIPLE SOLUTIONS FOR IMPROVEMENT FROM GOING UP TO ADDING ON.   THIS WHOLE HOUSE RENOVATION IS ONE THAT ADDS ON BY FILLING IN THE SITE AREA OF THE L, WHILE REMODELING THE EXISTING PLAN, TO CREATE AN IMPRESSIVE, UP-TO-DATE, ONE-STORY HOME.   THE AREA OF THE HANDSOME LOOKING FRONT ADDITION PROVIDES FOR A NEW LIVING ROOM, ENTRANCE FOYER, PART OF THE NEW DINING ROOM AND A NEW MASTER BATH AND DRESSING ROOM.   THE CHANGES TO THE EXISTING PART ARE DESIGNED TO CREATE MINIMAL DISTURBANCE, ALLOWING ONE TO STAGE THIS REMODELING WHILE LIVING HERE. IF THE FRONT OF THE HOME IS TURNED 90 DEGREES (BEDROOM WING AT FRONT), A SIMILAR PLAN IS POSSIBLE BY SIMPLY ROTATING THE NEW LIVING ROOM TO THE GARAGE WALL.

REMODELED FIRST FLOOR PLAN

EXISTING PLAN

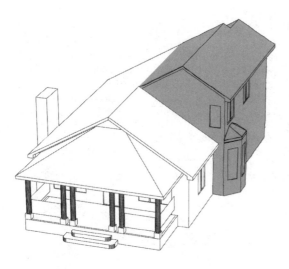

CTG01

IT'S A LOVELY OLD THREE-BEDROOM BUNGALOW OR NARROW ONE AND ONE-HALF STORY HOME, BUT MORE SPACE IS NEEDED, AND THERE'S ONLY A FEW FEET TO EXPAND IN EACH DIRECTION. NOW TAKE A HARD LOOK HERE! A MAJOR RENOVATION OF THIS 28'0"×39'6" PLAN ADDS JUST A FEW FEET, BUT GOES UP TOO, AND MAKES A STUNNING OVERALL IMPROVEMENT. THE RESULTING RENOVATION TO THE ORIGINAL FIRST FLOOR PROVIDES A REMODELED EAT-IN KITCHEN, A LARGE FAMILY ROOM, AND A GENEROUS SIZED MASTER SUITE. THE SPACE FOR ALL THIS IS ACHIEVED BY LOCATING TWO CHILDREN'S BEDROOMS (AND A FULL BATH) ON A NEW PARTIAL SECOND FLOOR. THE FRONT END OF THE HOME REMAINS TOTALLY UNAFFECTED IN THIS REMODEL, ALLOWING ONE TO STAGE THE RENOVATION WHILE LIVING HERE.

EXISTING PLAN

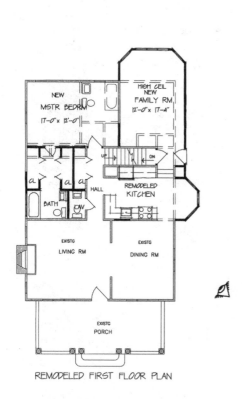

REMODELED FIRST FLOOR PLAN

SECOND FLOOR PLAN
ALL NEW

TWS03

THE LOT IS LOVELY, THE EXISTING ONE AND ONE-HALF STORY COTTAGE IS CHARMING, BUT IT IS OUT-OF-DATE AND CRAMPED. FURTHERMORE, THERE IS NO ROOM TO EXPAND OUT, SO YOUR ONLY SOLUTION IS TO GO UP; BUT TO DO IT WITH STYLE, BUILDING UPON AND REINFORCING THE CHARM OF THE EXISTING HOME IS A CHALLENGE. THIS WHOLE HOUSE RENOVATION MEETS THAT TASK WITH FLAIR. THE RESULTING HOME IS A WONDERFUL THREE BEDROOM TWO-STORY THAT RETAINS—AND ENHANCES—THE APPEAL OF THE OLD COTTAGE, WHILE PROVIDING A STYLISH, CONTEMPORARY LIVING ENVIRONMENT. THE FORMER FIRST FLOOR BEDROOMS ARE REMODELED TO CREATE A CENTER HALL CIRCULATION PATTERN AND SPACE FOR A BREAKFAST ROOM AND FAMILY/MEDIA ROOM. THE KITCHEN IS ENLARGED AND REMODELED, AND THE SECOND FLOOR IS COMPLETELY REBUILT.

REMODELED SECOND FLOOR PLAN

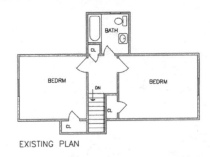

EXISTING PLAN

EXISTING PLAN

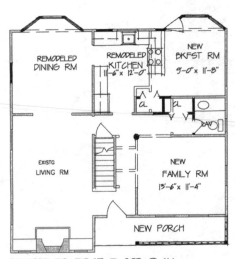

REMODELED FIRST FLOOR PLAN

TWS08

THE EXISTING HOME IS A BASIC THREE-BEDROOM RANCH; MORE SPACE IS NEEDED, BUT THE ONLY PLACE TO GO IS UP. THE SOLUTION ADDS TWO NEW BEDROOMS UPSTAIRS, INCLUDING A LAVISH NEW MASTER SUITE AND TOTALLY UPDATES THE HOME THROUGHOUT, INCLUDING THE CREATION OF A SPARKLING NEW EXTERIOR LOOK. A SPACIOUS NEW FOYER WITH TWO-STORY VOLUME FLOWS INTO THE ADJACENT LIVING ROOM WHICH ALSO SHARES THE NEW HIGH VOLUME. THERE IS A NEW ENLARGED KITCHEN AND A NEW BAYED BREAKFAST ROOM, PLUS A NEW DINING ROOM CARVED FROM THE OLD GARAGE. YOU COULD ADD A DETACHED GARAGE IF THERE IS SPACE ON YOUR LOT, AS LESS RESTRICTIVE SIDE AND REAR YARDS USUALLY APPLY.

NEW SECOND FLOOR PLAN

EXISTING FLOOR PLAN

REMODELED FLOOR PLAN

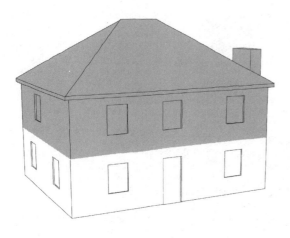

CAP0I

A GREAT NEIGHBORHOOD, A NICE LOT AND THE EXISTING 32'×26' COTTAGE IS MUCH TOO SMALL, BUT THERE IS NO ROOM TO EXPAND OUT. BUT, YOU CAN GO UP! THIS WHOLE HOUSE RENOVATION DOUBLES THE SQUARE FOOTAGE BY TURNING THE MODEST COTTAGE INTO A FULL THREE- OR FOUR-BEDROOM CENTER HALL-STYLE TWO-STORY. THE OLD BASEMENT STAIR IS RELOCATED TO THE FRONT CENTER WHERE IT BECOMES PART OF A DRAMATIC TWO-STORY HIGH ENTRANCE FOYER. THE EXPANDED KITCHEN IS NOW A DELIGHT, WITH ITS LARGE CENTER ISLAND AND CONVENIENT LAUNDRY. THE NEW SECOND FLOOR MASTER SUITE IS SPACIOUS AND UP-TO-DATE, AND IT INCLUDES A LARGE WALK-IN CLOSET AND A FIVE-FIXTURE PRIVATE BATH.

EXISTING PLAN

REMODELED FIRST FLOOR PLAN

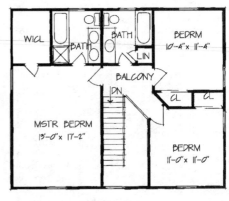

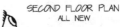

SECOND FLOOR PLAN
ALL NEW

RAN02

BY COMBINING FOUR OF THE PLANS SHOWN IN PRIOR CHAPTERS, THIS ORDINARY, L-SHAPED, ONE-STORY HAS BEEN REFASHIONED AS A SENSATIONAL SPANISH COURTYARD RESIDENCE OF IMPRESSIVE PROPORTIONS. THE DESIGN EXPANDS INTO THE OPEN SITE AREA CREATED BY THE L AND ALSO UTILIZES A REAR YARD ADDITION. THE CHILDREN'S BEDROOMS MOVE TO THEIR OWN SECOND-FLOOR WING WITH THE MASTER BEDROOM NOW ENCOMPASSING THE AREA VACATED BY THEM. THERE IS A DRAMATIC NEW FOYER AND A FABULOUS NEW KITCHEN IN AN OPEN ARRANGEMENT WITH THE NEW FAMILY ROOM. THE FORMER GARAGE IS UTILIZED TO CREATE A LOVELY APARTMENT, WITH ITS OWN SIDE ENTRANCE, AND A SPACIOUS OFFICE IS CREATED ALONGSIDE THE NEW GARAGE.

NOTE: THIS PLAN IS A COMPOSITE OF PLAN NUMBERS GAR03, BRB02, FD001 AND APT04

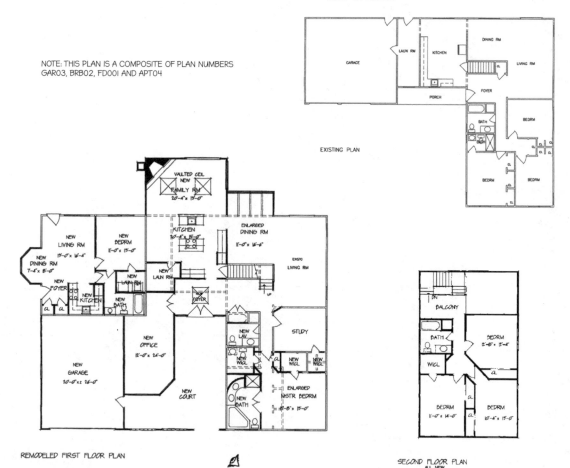

REMODELED FIRST FLOOR PLAN

SECOND FLOOR PLAN
ALL NEW

EXISTING PLAN

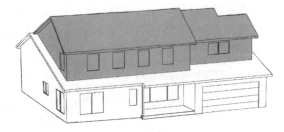

SPL01

THE FRONT TO REAR SPLIT-LEVEL IS ONE OF THOSE FEW HOMES THAT I FIND GREAT DIFFICULTY IN PROVIDING PARTIAL HELP FOR. MOST ARE CONSTRUCTED ON SMALL LOTS THAT LEAVE LITTLE ROOM TO SOLVE THE MANY DEFICIENCIES THAT OWNERS COMPLAIN OF. THE TIDY SOLUTION PRESENTED HERE IS A WHOLE HOUSE RENOVATION THAT GOES UP. IT ADDS A FULL FLOOR OVER THE FIRST FLOOR AND RELOCATES ROOMS FROM TOP TO BOTTOM. THE NEW SECOND FLOOR IS NOW A SELF-CONTAINED CHILDREN'S WING, COMPLETE WITH ITS OWN STUDY AREA AND RECREATION ROOM. THE FORMER BEDROOMS ARE NOW OCCUPIED BY A STUNNING LIVING ROOM AND AN EQUALLY BEAUTIFUL MASTER SUITE. THE GROUND FLOOR NOW HAS AMPLE SPACE FOR A LARGE KITCHEN AND BREAKFAST ROOM, WIDER STAIRCASES AND A NEW DINING ROOM. IT ISN'T AN EASY PROJECT, BUT, IT IS READILY CONSTRUCTED IN 3 OR 4 STAGES.

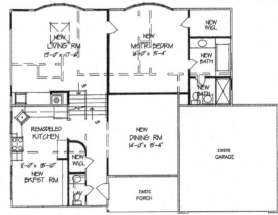

 REMODELED FIRST FLOOR PLAN

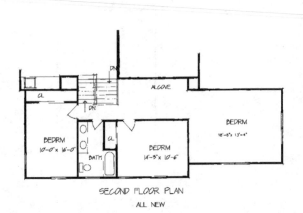

SECOND FLOOR PLAN

ALL NEW

EXISTING PLAN

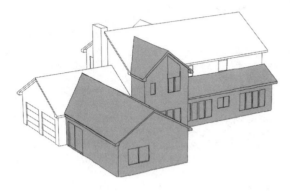

TWS05

THIS IS ANOTHER WHOLE HOUSE PROJECT DRAWN FROM THE HUNDREDS OF PLANS PRESENTED. IT IS A REMAKE OF A 25–35-YEAR-OLD TWO-STORY THAT PROVIDES A NEW FACELIFT AMONGST ITS IMPROVEMENTS. THIS NEW FAÇADE CAN BE SEEN IN PLAN PF002 ON PAGE 233. THE REAR VIEW PICTURED HERE SHOWS AN ENLARGED FIRST FLOOR REAR, COMPRISING A FABULOUS NEW KITCHEN AND EXPANDED DINING ROOM, A NEW MASTER BATH AND DRESSING AREA, AND AN APARTMENT ON THE FIRST FLOOR, WHICH IS LOCATED BEHIND THE GARAGE. THE APARTMENT IS DESIGNED TO HOUSE ELDERLY PARENTS, AND IS A BARRIER-FREE DESIGN. THE CONNECTION TO THE APARTMENT IS THROUGH AN ENLARGED LAUNDRY / EXERCISE ROOM.

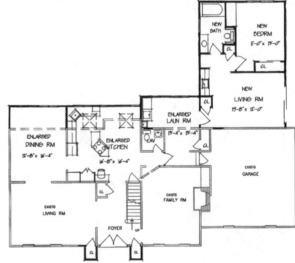

REMODELED FIRST FLOOR PLAN

EXISTING PLAN

NOTE: THIS PLAN IS A COMPOSITE OF PLAN NUMBERS KDEBI, PF002 AND HAPT2

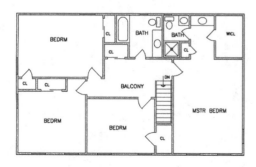

EXISTING PLAN

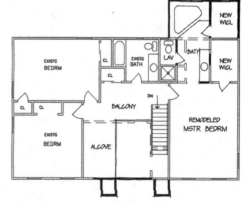

REMODELED SECOND FLOOR PLAN

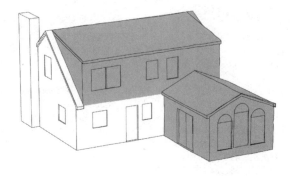

CAP02

A COMFORTABLE, DELIGHTFUL, THREE BEDROOM, ONE AND ONE-HALF STORY HOME IS THE RESULT OF THE WHOLE HOUSE RENOVATION OF THE SAME BASIC 32'×26' TWO-BEDROOM COTTAGE. THE PLAN FEATURES A ONE-STORY REAR ADDITION THAT PROVIDES THE SPACE FOR A LOVELY NEW MASTER SUITE, WITH ITS OWN PRIVATE, COMPARTMENTED BATH, THAT IS CARVED FROM AN EXISTING SMALL BEDROOM. THE BASEMENT STAIR IS RELOCATED TO THE FRONT, THEREBY ENLARGING THE EXISTING REAR KITCHEN, WHILE ALSO PROVIDING A LOGICAL LOCATION FOR A SECOND FLOOR STAIR. THE FORMER MASTER BEDROOM IS ENLARGED TO CREATE A LIVING ROOM, AND A NEW DINING ROOM RESULTS FROM THE DECREASED FORMER LIVING ROOM. UNLESS THE ORIGINAL ROOFLINE WAS A MINIMUM OF AN 8:12 PITCH, IT IS LIKELY THAT A NEW, STEEPER ROOF WILL HAVE TO BE FRAMED TO ENCLOSE THE TWO BEDROOMS AND BATH AT THE NEW SECOND FLOOR.

NOTE: THIS PLAN IS A COMPOSITE OF PLAN NUMBERS BRB11 AND BRB12

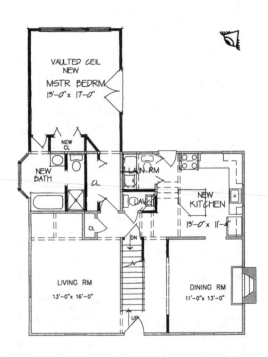

REMODELED FIRST FLOOR PLAN

EXISTING PLAN

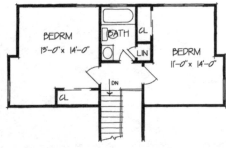

SECOND FLOOR PLAN
ALL NEW

TWS12

THIS CLEVER ADDITION TURNS A TINY TWO-BEDROOM COTTAGE INTO A FOUR-BEDROOM TWO-STORY. IT IS AN EASILY STAGED ADDITION THAT ENABLES ONE TO LIVE THERE WHILE IT IS ACCOMPLISHED. THE ADDITION ADDS A NEW KITCHEN, DINING ROOM AND FOYER ON THE FIRST FLOOR AND TWO BEDROOMS ON THE SECOND FLOOR. THE EXISTING COTTAGE IS REMODELED TO CREATE A LARGE MASTER BEDROOM AND A SECOND BEDROOM. MANY VARIATIONS OF THIS PLAN CAN BE CREATED, INCLUDING ADDING ADDITIONAL BATHS ON EACH FLOOR. A SMALL BUMP-OUT BEHIND THE KITCHEN WOULD ADD A BREAKFAST ALCOVE. MOST IMPORTANTLY, THE COMPLETED REMODELING WILL LOOK LIKE IT WAS MEANT TO BE.

EXISTING FLOOR PLAN

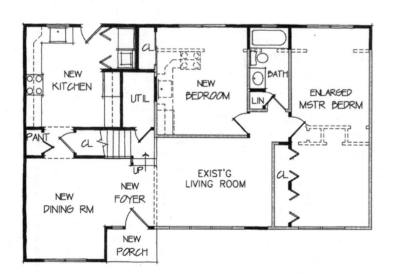

REMODELED FLOOR PLAN

REMODELED FLOOR PLAN

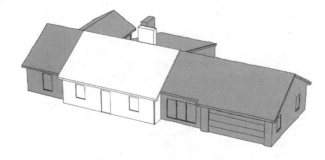

RAN03

A TINY FOUR-ROOM STARTER HOME IS CONVERTED INTO A SPRAWLING AND COMFORTABLE SEVEN-ROOM RESIDENCE IN THIS WHOLE HOUSE RENOVATION. THE FRONT TWO ROOMS REMAIN, BUT THE REAR IS COMPLETELY REMODELED, AND ADDITIONS ARE ADDED ON BOTH SIDES PLUS THE REAR. THE RESULTING HOME PROVIDES A LOVELY NEW MASTER SUITE, A STYLISH NEW FAMILY ROOM, A SEPARATE DINING ROOM, A LAUNDRY ROOM AND TWO CAR GARAGE, PLUS A BRAND NEW KITCHEN AND MODERNIZED BATHS. THE PLAN IS AN ADAPTATION OF THREE DESIGNS PRESENTED IN CHAPTER 8, AND IS ANOTHER EXAMPLE OF HOW YOU CAN SUCCESSFULLY USE THE PLANS PRESENTED TO CREATE YOUR OWN HOME. THIS IS A PROJECT THAT CAN BE READILY STAGED OVER A LONG TERM.

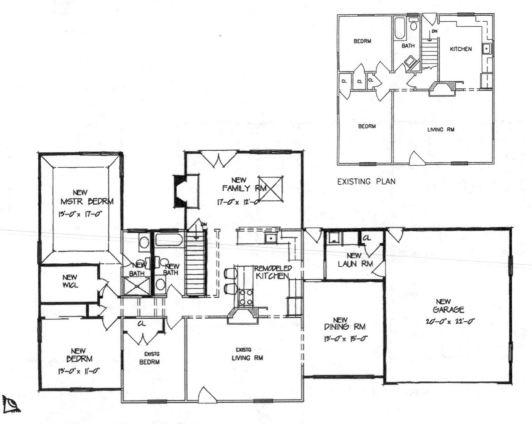

EXISTING PLAN

REMODELED FIRST FLOOR PLAN

CTG02

THIS 23'0"×40'6" TWO-BEDROOM COTTAGE HAS BEEN GIVEN A REFRESHINGLY NEW INSIDE, WHILE RETAINING MOST OF ITS CHARMING EXTERIOR CHARACTER. OTHER THAN THE AREA OF THE REAR BEDROOM AND BATH, THE BALANCE OF THE FIRST FLOOR HAS BEEN "BLOWN WIDE-OPEN," WHICH ESTABLISHES A SMART, CREATIVE INTERIOR WITH LOTS OF NOOKS, CORNERS AND NEW WINDOWS AND SKYLIGHTS FOR LIGHT. A GREAT NEW KITCHEN RESULTS, AS DOES A BEAUTIFULLY FLOWING LIVING AND DINING ROOM, AND THERE'S A LITTLE CORNER FOR AN OFFICE. A DRAMATIC CIRCULAR STAIR PROVIDES ACCESS TO A NEW SECOND FLOOR WING THAT HOUSES A VERY CHIC NEW MASTER SUITE. BALCONIES AND MUCH OPEN VOLUME HELP ENHANCE THE UPDATED NEW CHARACTER OF THIS OLD CHARMER.

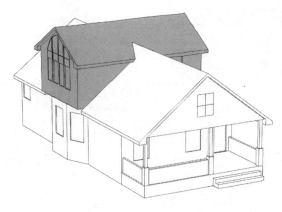

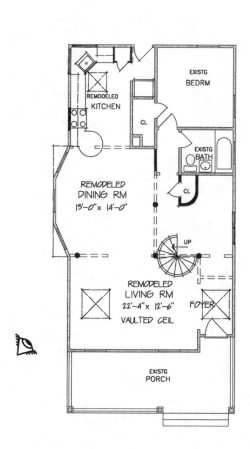

REMODELED FIRST FLOOR PLAN

SECOND FLOOR PLAN
ALL NEW

EXISTING PLAN

TWS06

LOOKING TO DOUBLE THE AREA OF THIS THREE-
BEDROOM, 40-YEAR-OLD ONE-STORY, BUT THE LOT
PREVENTS IT? YOUR ANSWER THEN IS TO GO UP AS
SHOWN IN THIS WHOLE HOUSE RENOVATION. AFTER
IT HAS BEEN COMPLETED, CHANCES ARE THAT NO
ONE WOULD REALIZE THAT THIS WAS ONCE A ONE-
STORY HOME. THE BUILDING FORMS, ROOFLINES AND
WINDOW DESIGNS HAVE BEEN SKILLFULLY DESIGNED,
SO THAT THE SECOND FLOOR DOESN'T LOOK
LIKE A HAT—A COMMON RESULT OF MANY SUCH
RENOVATIONS. BEARING WALLS HAVE BEEN
RETAINED, BUT THE REMAINING FLOOR PLAN
FUNCTIONS AS BEAUTIFULLY AS ANY NEW FOUR-
BEDROOM, TWO AND ONE-HALF BATH, CENTER HALL
TWO-STORY. THIS IS A RENOVATION THAT CAN BE
STAGED WHILE LIVING THERE.

EXISTING PLAN

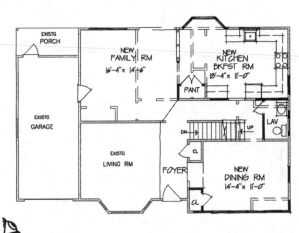

REMODELED FIRST FLOOR PLAN

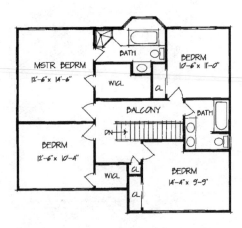

SECOND FLOOR PLAN
ALL NEW

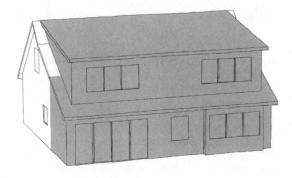

CAP03

AN 8'0" DEEP, TWO-STORY HIGH ADDITION ACROSS THE REAR, PROVIDES ALL THE SPACE NEEDED TO TRANSFORM THIS 36'0" WIDE, MODEST SIZED, ONE AND ONE-HALF STORY HOME INTO A SPACIOUS AND COMFORTABLE TWO-STORY. AS VIEWED FROM THE REAR, THE FORMS OF THE OLD STEEPER ROOFLINES ARE RETAINED AT EACH SIDE: AN IMPORTANT DESIGN CONSIDERATION TO KEEP IN MIND. THE REMODELED FIRST FLOOR NOW INCLUDES A TIDY NEW MASTER SUITE, WITH ITS OWN TUB BATH, AND A CHARMING NEW COUNTRY KITCHEN. SINCE THE SECOND FLOOR NOW PROVIDES THREE BEDROOMS AND A PLAY LOFT, YOU COULD CONSIDER MULTIPLE OTHER USES FOR THE OLD FRONT BEDROOM ON THE FIRST FLOOR, SUCH AS A MEDIA ROOM, OFFICE, OR EVEN A DINING ROOM.

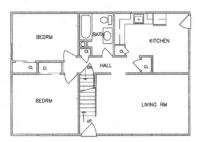

EXISTING FIRST FLOOR PLAN

EXISTING SECOND FLOOR PLAN

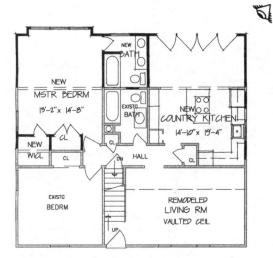

REMODELED FIRST FLOOR PLAN

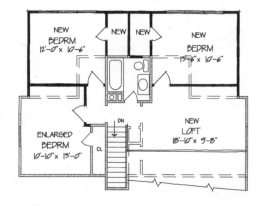

REMODELED SECOND FLOOR PLAN

SPL02

EVERYTHING ONE MIGHT NEED TO ADD, OR REMODEL, HAS BEEN INCORPORATED INTO THE REMAKE OF THIS SPLIT-LEVEL. THE ARCHITECTURAL DESIGN TAKES FOUR PLANS PICTURED IN THE PREVIOUS SECTIONS AND MODIFIES THEM, AS NECESSARY, TO ACHIEVE THIS WINNING NEW HOME. A BEAUTIFUL MAIN LEVEL FAMILY ROOM, LOCATED OFF THE REMODELED KITCHEN, IS ONE OF THE STRIKING HIGHLIGHTS. A FABULOUS NEW MASTER SUITE OVER THE LIVING ROOM IS ANOTHER. THE FORMER RECREATION ROOM IS NOW THE LOCATION FOR A GROUND LEVEL APARTMENT THAT IS PLANNED FOR HANDICAP ACCESSIBILITY. A ONE-CAR GARAGE IS ALSO ADDED TO COMPENSATE FOR THE GARAGE AREA THAT WAS INCLUDED IN THE APARTMENT.

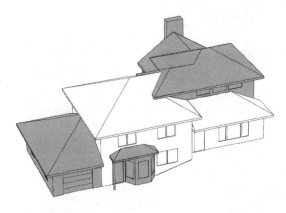

NOTE: THIS PLAN IS A COMPOSITE OF PLAN NUMBERS BRB18, F0006, HAPT4, AND GAR05

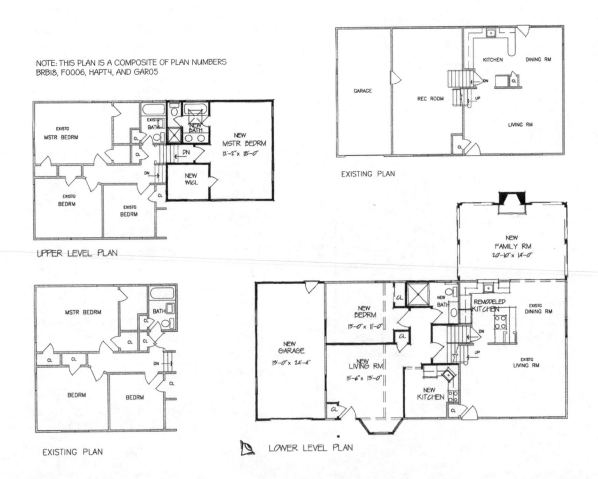

UPPER LEVEL PLAN

EXISTING PLAN

EXISTING PLAN

LOWER LEVEL PLAN

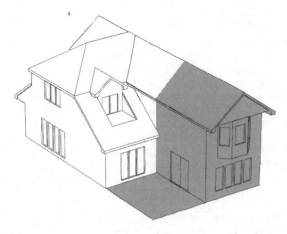

TWSOI

MANY HOMES 60 OR MORE YEARS OLD SUFFER BADLY IN TERMS OF TODAY'S AMENITIES, PARTICULARLY AS CONCERNS THEIR BATHS AND KITCHENS; THEY ALSO ARE LIKELY TO BE DEVOID OF GOOD CIRCULATION PATTERNS AND ARE SURELY MISSING A FAMILY ROOM. BUT DESPITE THESE DEFICIENCIES, MANY ENJOY SUCH A WONDERFUL CHARACTER THAT THEY ARE WORTH THE INVESTMENT TO MODERNIZE. THIS TWO-STORY IS SUCH A HOME; THE RENOVATION SHOWN ADDS A FAMILY ROOM AND A NEW MASTER SUITE. IT CONVERTS A COVERED REAR PORCH TO A DINING ROOM. THE OLD DINING ROOM NOW BECOMES A SENSATIONAL NEW KITCHEN, IDEALLY SITUATED IN RESPECT TO THE NEW FAMILY ROOM. FINALLY, THE OLD KITCHEN NOW HOUSES A LARGE LAUNDRY ROOM, POWDER ROOM, AND CENTER HALL.

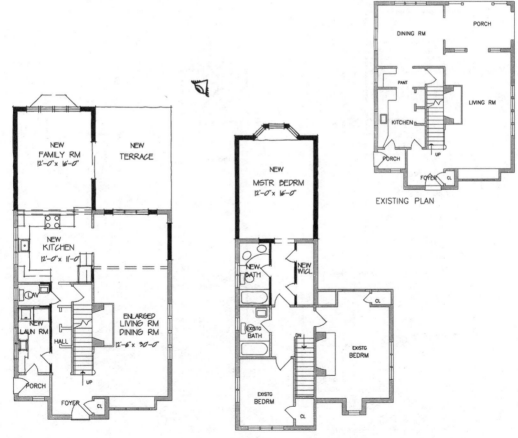

EXISTING PLAN

REMODELED FIRST FLOOR PLAN   REMODELED SECOND FLOOR PLAN

CAP05

WHEN DOES A SMALL ONE AND ONE-HALF STORY CAPE COD STYLE COTTAGE BECOME AN EXPANSIVE, FABULOUS HOME? WHEN YOU ADD A 49'8" DEEP ADDITION TO ITS REAR, AS SHOWN. THE SCALE OF THIS ADDITION IS LARGE AND SUGGESTS A LOT WITH EXTRA DEPTH THAT MIGHT ALSO BE LACKING IN WIDTH. THE IMPROVEMENTS TO THE HOME ARE ALL THE ELEMENTS THAT ARE IN DEMAND TODAY. A NEW KITCHEN AND BREAKFAST ROOM PLUS A NEW FAMILY ROOM ARE THE CENTERPIECES OF THE ADDITION, AND BEYOND IS A TWO-CAR GARAGE. ABOVE IT ALL IS AN EXTENSIVE NEW MASTER SUITE, BUILT WITHIN ROOFLINES THAT ECHO THE ORIGINAL HOUSE. THE MASTER BEDROOM IS REACHED FROM A NEW STAIRCASE IN THE ADDITION, BUT IT ALSO RETAINS A CONNECTION TO THE OLD BEDROOM HALL. EXTENSIVE REMODELING OF THE EXISTING FIRST FLOOR WOULD FOLLOW THE ADDITIONS.

EXISTING FIRST FLOOR PLAN

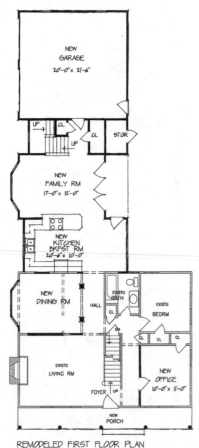

REMODELED FIRST FLOOR PLAN

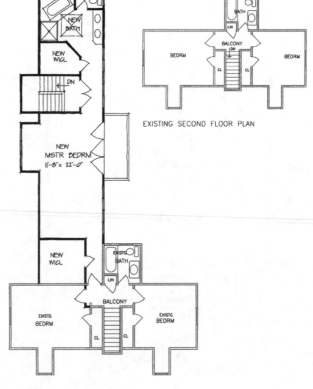

EXISTING SECOND FLOOR PLAN

REMODELED SECOND FLOOR PLAN

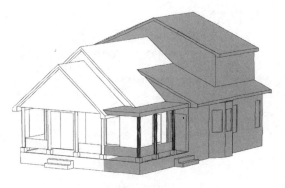

CTG03

A CHARMING 24'0"×32'8" COTTAGE BECOMES A STYLISH NEW THREE- OR FOUR-BEDROOM WINNER IN THIS WHOLE HOUSE REMAKE. BY ADDING 5'4" TO ONE SIDE AND GOING UP IN THE REAR, AMPLE SPACE IS GAINED TO ENABLE A COMPLETE TRANSFORMATION, WHILE STILL RETAINING THE INTEGRITY AND CHARM OF THE ORIGINAL HOME. THE FRONT PORCH IS WRAPPED AROUND ONE SIDE, THEREBY MOVING THE ENTRANCE AND CREATING A FOYER AND CENTER HALL. A PRIVATE FIRST FLOOR MASTER SUITE IS PROVIDED WITH ITS OWN BATH AND WALK-IN CLOSET, AND TWO CHILDREN'S BEDROOMS ARE PLACED IN THE NEW SECOND FLOOR ALONG WITH THEIR OWN BATH. THE KITCHEN IS REMODELED IN-PLACE, AND A SMALL GREENHOUSE "BUMP" IS SUGGESTED AS A BREAKFAST NOOK. PROPER STAGING ALLOWS ONE TO UNDERTAKE THIS WHILE RESIDING IN HOUSE.

EXISTING PLAN

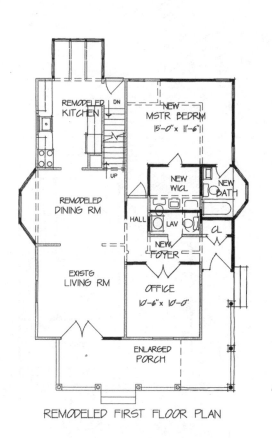

REMODELED FIRST FLOOR PLAN

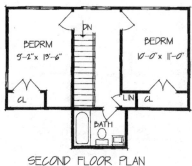

SECOND FLOOR PLAN

ALL NEW

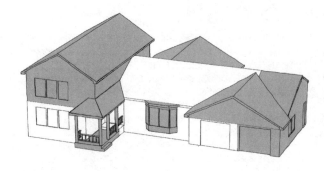

RAN04

THE WHOLE HOUSE RENOVATION OF THIS DATED U-SHAPED ONE-STORY EXPANDS OUT IN ALMOST EVERY DIRECTION TO CREATE A LOVELY NEW HOME THAT IS STYLISH AND UP-TO-DATE THROUGHOUT. MAJOR REMODELING INCLUDES A BRAND NEW CHILDREN'S WING ON THE SECOND FLOOR, A BEAUTIFUL NEW FIRST FLOOR MASTER SUITE, AN EXPANDED KITCHEN WITH A LOVELY NEW BREAKFAST ROOM, AN ENLARGED DINING ROOM, AND A NEW GARAGE ADDITION. OTHER BENEFITS OF THE REMODELING INCLUDE AN IMPROVED ACCESS TO THE DEN, AND A CHARMING NEW FRONT PORCH. THIS DESIGN IS ONE OF THOSE CULLED FROM OTHER PLANS IN THE BOOK, AND IT DEMONSTRATES HOW EASILY YOU CAN CREATE A WHOLE HOUSE SCHEME FOR YOURSELF.

NOTE: THIS PLAN IS A COMPOSITE OF PLAN NUMBERS BRB04, KD002 AND GAR01

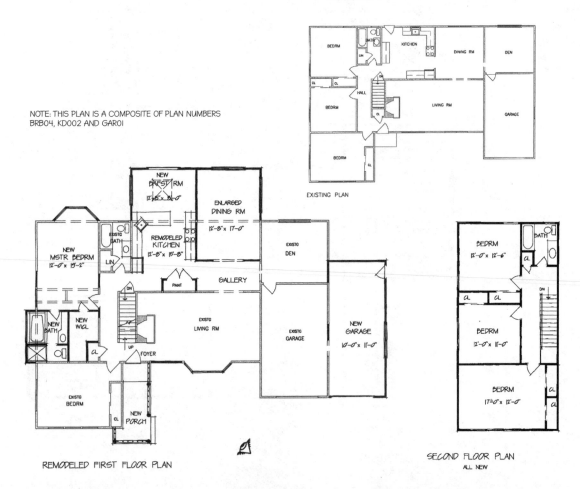

EXISTING PLAN

REMODELED FIRST FLOOR PLAN

SECOND FLOOR PLAN
ALL NEW

TWS02

WHEN DOES A 24'0"×40'0" ONE-STORY BUNGALOW OR CAPE TRANSFORM INTO A 24'0"×40'0" THOROUGHLY UPDATED TWO-STORY? THIS IS LIKELY TO OCCUR WHEN ONE LOVES THE LOCATION OF THE OLD CHARMER AND THERE'S NO ROOM TO EXPAND OUT, YET THE PROGRAM DEMANDS NO LESS THAN WE WOULD ACHIEVE IN A BRAND NEW HOME. THAT'S THE SUBJECT OF THIS WHOLE HOUSE REMAKE. THE REMODELED FIRST FLOOR INCLUDES A DRAMATIC NEW TWO-STORY HIGH RECEPTOR FOYER, A TRUE CENTER HALL LAYOUT, A LAUNDRY ADJACENT TO A NEW SIDE DOOR ENTRY, A GREAT NEW EAT-IN KITCHEN, AND AN ADJOINING NEW FAMILY ROOM. THE ALL NEW SECOND FLOOR HAS A DRAMATIC BALCONY AND THREE BEDROOMS. THE MASTER SUITE FEATURES A COMPARTMENTED PRIVATE BATH, TWO WALK-IN CLOSETS, AND A LOVELY LITTLE LOUNGE OR OFFICE ALCOVE.

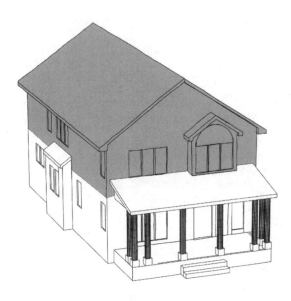

EXISTING PLAN

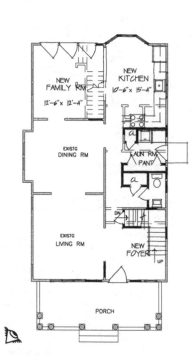

REMODELED FIRST FLOOR PLAN

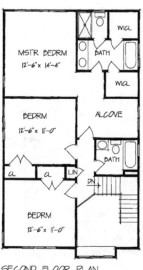

SECOND FLOOR PLAN
ALL NEW

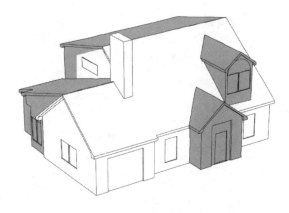

CAP06

THE MOST UNFORTUNATE ASPECTS OF THIS EXISTING ONE AND ONE-HALF STORY HOME ARE ITS LACK OF RELATIONSHIP TO THE REAR YARD AND ITS POOR CIRCULATION. THE WHOLE HOUSE REDESIGN PICTURED ELIMINATES THESE DEFICIENCIES, WHILE ESTABLISHING AN EXCITING NEW ENVIRONMENT FOR LIVING. A LOVELY NEW FIRST FLOOR MASTER SUITE IS CREATED BY UTILIZING ONE REAR BEDROOM AND ADDING THE UNUSED SPACE BEHIND THE GARAGE. THE OTHER REAR BEDROOM IS NOW INCORPORATED INTO A CHARMING COUNTRY KITCHEN. A SMALL FRONT VESTIBULE IS ADDED TO EXPAND THE CIRCULATION SPACE, AS WELL AS TO HELP DEFINE A FRESH NEW LOOK FOR THE HOUSE. THE NEW SECOND FLOOR NOW HOUSES THREE BEDROOMS AND A SMALL LOFT. REMOVAL OF THE OLD DORMERS HELPS COMPLETE THE NEW LOOK.

EXISTING FIRST FLOOR PLAN

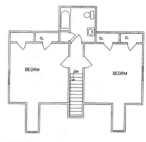

EXISTING SECOND FLOOR PLAN

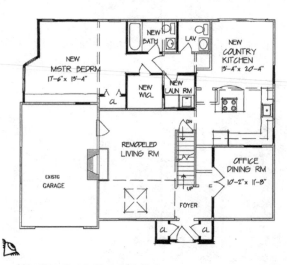

REMODELED FIRST FLOOR PLAN

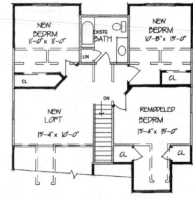

REMODELED SECOND FLOOR PLAN

RAN05

A WHOLESALE CHANGE IS NECESSARY IF YOUR GOAL IS TO PROPERLY BRING THE EXISTING HIP-ROOFED ONE-STORY HOME PICTURED TO TODAY'S STANDARDS. ONE SERIOUS PROBLEM WITH THE HOME IS ITS LACK OF RELATIONSHIP TO THE REAR YARD, AND THE SOLUTION REQUIRES A RELOCATION OF THE KITCHEN. TWO NEW WINGS ARE ADDED, ONE FOR A NEW FAMILY ROOM, THE OTHER FOR A NEW MASTER BEDROOM SUITE; BOTH FEATURE VAULTED CEILINGS AND LOTS OF GLASS FOCUSING ABOUT THE BEAUTIFUL NEW CENTER COURT THAT THEY CREATE. AS COMPLEX AS THESE CHANGES MAY APPEAR, THEY CAN BE STAGED OVER A PERIOD OF TIME ALLOWING THE OWNER TO LIVE THERE WHILE THE TRANSFORMATION IS BEING MADE.

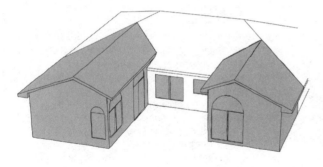

EXISTING PLAN

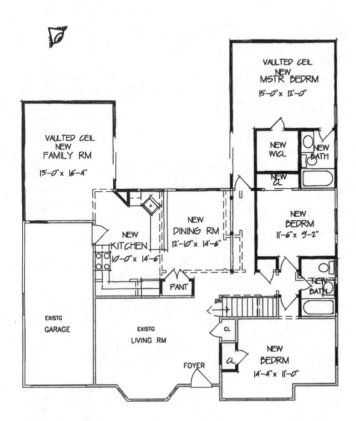

REMODELED FIRST FLOOR PLAN

TWS09

THIS IS ANOTHER EXAMPLE OF HOW AN ORDINARY ONE-STORY RANCH CAN BE TRANSFORMED INTO A SPARKLING, NEW, DRAMATIC TWO-STORY HOME WITH A BRAND NEW CHARACTER AND APPEAL. SMALL CHILDREN'S BEDROOMS IN THE OLD RANCH HOME ARE NOW SPACIOUS SECOND FLOOR ROOMS ACCESSED FROM A DRAMATIC TWO-STORY ENTRANCE FOYER. THE MASTER SUITE IS RATHER NOVEL IN THAT IT IS A TWO-STORY SUITE WITH ITS OWN INTERNAL STAIR. THE PLAN SHOWS THE FIRST FLOOR PROVIDING AN EXERCISE ROOM, DRESSING AREA AND BATH, WHILE THE SECOND FLOOR PROVIDES FOR A BED LOFT. YOU COULD REVERSE THAT OR CREATE YOUR OWN TWO-STORY SUITE.

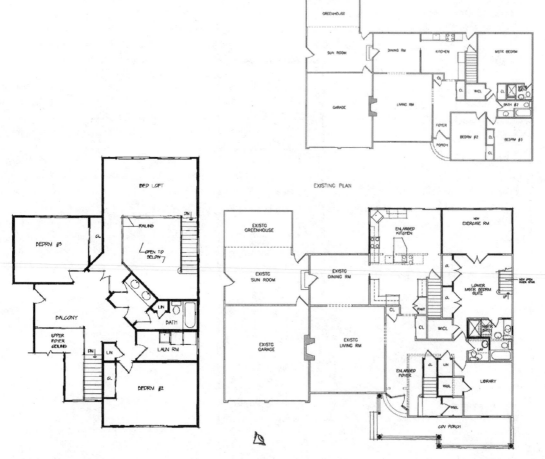

EXISTING PLAN

REMODELED FLOOR PLAN

REMODELED FLOOR PLAN

TWS04

MOST OBSERVERS WOULD LOOK AT THIS
EXISTING TWO-STORY HOME AND SAY IT LOOKS
JUST FINE; BUT IF ONE HAS LIVED IN IT FOR 15
YEARS OR MORE, THEY MIGHT HAVE A WISH
LIST THAT ENCOMPASSES THE ADDITIONS AND
RENOVATIONS PICTURED. INCLUDED ARE A
REMODELED KITCHEN, A FABULOUS NEW
GREAT ROOM, A LUXURIOUS NEW FIRST FLOOR
MASTER SUITE, A NEW APARTMENT OVER THE
GARAGE, A NEW TWO-STORY HIGH ENTRANCE
FOYER, A REMODELED SECOND FLOOR, AND A
RESTYLED FRONT FAÇADE. IT IS, WITHOUT
DOUBT, AN EXTENSIVE, VERY LAVISH
UNDERTAKING, BUT IT TOO COULD BE STAGED
IN PARTS. THE PLAN IS DRAWN FROM FOUR
PARTIAL PLAN PROJECTS PRESENTED IN THE
PRIOR CHAPTERS, AND IS ANOTHER EXAMPLE
THAT SHOWS YOU HOW TO ADAPT THE IDEAS
IN THIS BOOK TO YOUR HOME.

NOTE: THIS PLAN IS A COMPOSITE OF PLAN NUMBERS
PFB02, BRB24, APT03, AND KF009

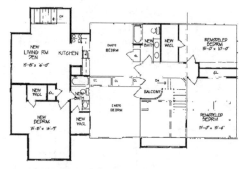

REMODELED SECOND FLOOR PLAN

EXISTING PLAN

REMODELED FIRST FLOOR PLAN

EXISTING PLAN

TWS10

THERE'S NOT MUCH LEFT UNTOUCHED IN THIS WHOLE HOUSE REMAKE OF A THREE BEDROOM RANCH. THE NEW PLAN BASICALLY GUTS THE ENTIRE EXISTING HOUSE AND PUSHES OUT THE FRONT AND REAR TO CREATE AN EXCITING, NEW AND VERY DRAMATIC NEW HOME THAT IS AS UP-TO-DATE AS ANY BRAND NEW HOME. THIS IS A ONE-OF-A-KIND CUSTOM PLAN THAT REQUIRES CREATIVE, THOROUGH ARCHITECTURAL SKILL TO PULL OFF PROPERLY. IT ALSO IS NOT CHEAP TO EXECUTE AND IT CERTAINLY REQUIRES THAT THE HOME BE VACANT FOR AN EXTENDED PERIOD OF TIME TO ACCOMPLISH, BUT THE END RESULT WILL BE THE ENVY OF THE NEIGHBORHOOD.

EXISTING FLOOR PLAN

REMODELED FLOOR PLAN

NEW SECOND FLOOR PLAN

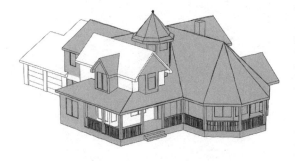

TWSII

AS WITH THE PREVIOUS PLAN, THIS IS A UNIQUE ONE-OF-A-KIND CUSTOM PLAN THAT REQUIRES CREATIVE ARCHITECTURAL SKILL TO ACCOMPLISH. ALTHOUGH THE PLAN IS ON THE CAD DISK, AS ARE ALL OUR PLANS, IT IS NOT LIKELY THIS WILL BE USEFUL TO COPY BECAUSE OF ITS SCOPE AND SPECIFICITY. IT IS PRESENTED HERE, HOWEVER, TO SHOW THAT EVEN A MINUSCULE OLD VICTORIAN COTTAGE CAN BE ADDED TO AND THOROUGHLY UPDATED, WHILE RETAINING ITS OLD VICTORIAN CHARM AND APPEAL. THERE ARE MANY SUCH OLD HOMES SITUATED ON BEAUTIFUL, MATURE PROPERTY, BUT THEY MAY BE SO DEVOID OF CURRENT APPEAL THAT MOST PEOPLE CAN'T SEE THE POTENTIAL; BUT THE PERSON WHO DOES, CAN CREATE A VERY SPECIAL NEW HOME LIKE THE ONE CREATED HERE.

EXISTING FLOOR PLAN

EXISTING FLOOR PLAN

REMODELED FLOOR PLAN

NEW SECOND FLOOR PLAN

Building and Finishing the Project

Construction Details

I have stated that this is not a how-to book, but a what-to book, so why is there a chapter on construction details? Because the construction subjects dealt with here are generally design related, and may be missing from the how-to books most do-it-yourselfers will consult. The professional should find these very useful as well. I may have also referred to a number of these in the text matter associated with individual designs. Furthermore, there are a few details shown that are frequently misunderstood or overlooked by the do-it-yourselfer and professional alike, and which could cause severe problems, as well as some favorite details of mine that lead to successful remodelings. As necessary, there is a brief discussion on each page, but let's talk about two of the subjects here.

An inordinate amount of time has gone into our preparation of the girder charts. Since I emphasize the opening up of walls to visually enhance or combine space, I believe you will find this to be extremely valuable in your pursuit of the open plan. It also will prove helpful during construction when you suddenly realize a wall is bearing, or should you decide to open a wall more than originally planned. A discussion on how to use the charts is included therein. These are obviously generalized conditions, but hopefully you will find that a condition of yours falls somewhere within those tabulated. Local codes could require some modifications of the spans.

The details on staging in the following chapter present proposed staging plans for two plans shown in prior chapters. These clearly show how each remodeling can proceed in several pre-defined steps that will enable one to cope with the construction. There is also informative text that delves further into this important subject.

FOUNDATION DETAILS

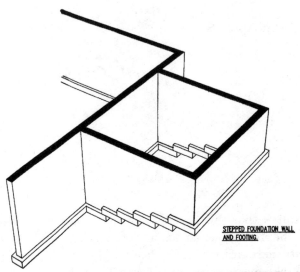

STEPPED FOUNDATION WALL
AND FOOTING.

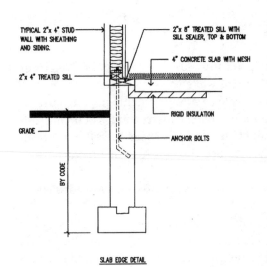

TYPICAL 2"x 4" STUD WALL WITH SHEATHING AND SIDING.

2"x 4" TREATED SILL

GRADE

BY CODE

2"x 8" TREATED SILL WITH SILL SEALER, TOP & BOTTOM

4" CONCRETE SLAB WITH MESH

RIGID INSULATION

ANCHOR BOLTS

SLAB EDGE DETAIL

A COMMON ERROR FREQUENTLY OVERLOOKED IN BUILDING AN ADDITION IS THE NEED TO STEP THE FOOTING AND FOUNDATION WALL TO THE DEPTH OF THE EXISTING FOOTING AND FOUNDATION. WHY? TO PREVENT THE ADDITION FROM SETTLING INDEPENDENTLY OF THE EXISTING HOUSE. THE PROCESS IS ALWAYS NECESSARY WHEN ADDING AN ADDITION ON A CRAWL SPACE ADJACENT TO A BASEMENT, ALTHOUGH IT COULD ALSO OCCUR IN SOME OTHER CIRCUMSTANCES. THE PROCESS REQUIRES THAT EXCAVATING TO THE TOP OF THE EXISTING FOOTING AND THEN REDUCING THE EXCAVATION TO THE MINIMUM REQUIRED BY YOUR CODE, OR THAT REQUIRED FOR THE CRAWL SPACE. THE FOOTING IS HAND DUG TO THE BOTTOM OF THE EXISTING FOOTING AND "STEPPED" UP TO THE PERIMETER GRADE IN SEVERAL STEPS.

IF YOU INTEND TO BUILD WITH SLAB CONSTRUCTION, I HAVE DEVELOPED A WALL EDGE DETAIL THAT I WOULD RECOMMEND YOU CONSIDER. THE MAIN PURPOSE OF THE DETAIL IS TO PROVIDE A POSITIVE METHOD FOR INSULATING THE EDGE OF THE SLAB FROM THE EXTERIOR. IT MAY NOT BE NECESSARY IN SOUTHERN CLIMATES, BUT IS IMPORTANT IN COLDER AREAS. THE DETAIL REQUIRES A 2×8 TREATED TOP SILL MEMBER, WHICH COVERS THE TOP OF THE FOUNDATION WALL AND THE EDGE OF THE INSULATION. SOME POSSIBLE CONCERNS: IT ADDS 2 INCHES EXTRA IN HEIGHT TO THE EXTERIOR WOOD WALL AND DOES LEAVE A STRIP AROUND THE PERIMETER IN WOOD, RATHER THAN CONCRETE. HOWEVER, THIS STRIP IS PERFECT FOR NAILING CARPET INTO, AND WILL NOT BE NOTICED UNDER CERAMIC TILE. IT COULD BE A CONCERN WITH A THIN VINYL TILE OR LINOLEUM.

DOUBLE FLOOR CONSTRUCTION

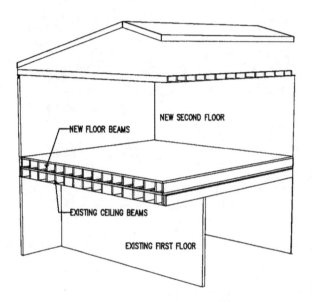

NEW SECOND FLOOR

NEW FLOOR BEAMS

EXISTING CEILING BEAMS

EXISTING FIRST FLOOR

<u>CUT-AWAY VIEW</u>

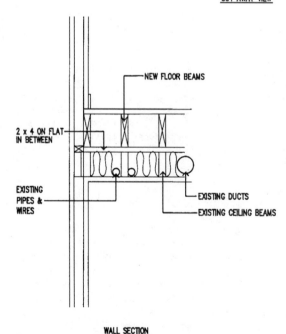

NEW FLOOR BEAMS

2 x 4 ON FLAT
IN BETWEEN

EXISTING
PIPES &
WIRES

EXISTING DUCTS

EXISTING CEILING BEAMS

<u>WALL SECTION</u>

WHEN ADDING A NEW ADDITION UP AND OVER EXISTING ROOMS IT COULD BE VERY ADVANTAGEOUS TO CONSIDER USING A DOUBLE FLOOR. WHY? IT IS LIKELY THAT THE EXISTING CEILING BEAMS ARE INADEQUATE TO SUPPORT A FLOOR, SO NEW BEAMS WILL BE NEEDED. IF THAT IS SO, THESE NEW BEAMS COULD BE SET WITH THEIR BOTTOM FLUSH WITH THE EXISTING CEILING BEAMS, AND EXTEND HIGHER AS REQUIRED. HOWEVER, THIS FREQUENTLY REQUIRES THE CUTTING OF WIRES AND THE RELOCATION OF PIPES AND DUCTS; IT IS ALSO VERY MESSY AND DOES POSE A GREATER DISRUPTION FACTOR TO THE ROOMS BELOW.

BY SETTING THE NEW BEAMS STARTING 2 INCHES ABOVE THE EXISTING CEILING BEAMS THERE IS NO NEED TO RELOCATE ANY WIRING, LIGHT FIXTURES, PIPES, ETC. IT ALSO CREATES AN EXCELLENT SOUND-INSULATING FLOOR. THERE ARE TWO POTENTIAL PROBLEMS, THOUGH, YOU MUST CONSIDER. THE STAIR TO THIS NEW FLOOR WILL BE LONGER; IT WILL REQUIRE AT LEAST ONE EXTRA STEP, MAYBE TWO, AND YOU WILL NEED THE FLOOR SPACE TO ACCOMMODATE THIS STAIR. THE SECOND FACTOR TO CONSIDER IS THE EXTRA HEIGHT ADDED TO THE HOUSE, WHICH COULD CREATE AN AESTHETIC CONCERN, ESPECIALLY IF THE ADDITION IS A SMALL ELEMENT ON A VERY LARGE ROOF, SOMETHING I CAUTIONED ABOUT BACK IN CHAPTER 3.

GIRDER DETAILS FOR NEW OPENINGS

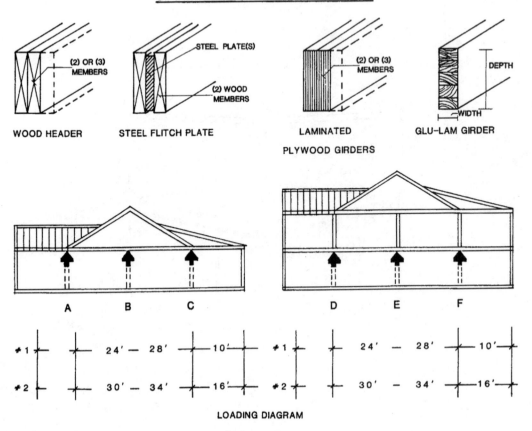

WOOD HEADER   **STEEL FLITCH PLATE**   **LAMINATED**   **GLU-LAM GIRDER**

PLYWOOD GIRDERS

LOADING DIAGRAM

THE GIRDER DETAILS PICTURED ABOVE ILLUSTRATE THE MOST COMMON TYPES OF WOOD GIRDERS. THE CHARTS ON THE NEXT PAGE ARE BASED ON THESE TYPES.

VARIOUS LOADING CONDITIONS FOUND IN A TYPICAL HOME ARE SHOWN JUST BELOW THE GIRDER DETAILS. IT IS NECESSARY FOR YOU TO PICK THE CORRECT LOCATION. POINTS A, B, C REPRESENT CEILING AND ROOF LOADS ONLY, AND ARE FOR A ONE-STORY HOME WITHOUT ANY SECOND FLOOR, AND FOR THE SECOND FLOOR OF A TWO-STORY HOME. POINTS D, E, F REFLECT CONDITIONS THAT ALSO CARRY A SECOND FLOOR LOAD. THE CHARTS DO NOT COVER BASEMENT GIRDERS. POINTS A & D REFLECT AN OUTSIDE WALL WITH NO LOADS FROM ANY NEW ADDITION (THESE WOULD ALSO BE USED FOR NEW WINDOWS IN AN EXISTING OUTSIDE WALL). POINTS B & E REPRESENT A CENTER BEARING PARTITION. POINTS C & F REFLECT AN EXISTING OUTSIDE WALL THAT WILL ALSO CARRY LOADS FROM A NEW ADDITION.

CONDITION #1 REFLECTS A HOME 24 TO 26 FEET WIDE AND AN ADDITION NO DEEPER THAN 10 FEET. CONDITION #2 REFLECTS A HOME 30 TO 34 FEET WIDE AND AN ADDITION UP TO 16 FEET DEEP. THE THREE CHARTS ON THE FOLLOWING PAGE PROVIDE GIRDER SIZE INFORMATION BASED ON THE LOADING DIAGRAMS AND THE SPAN OF THE GIRDER. THE SNOW LOAD 0-30-60 IS THE ONLY VARIABLE WHICH MUST BE OBTAINED FROM YOUR LOCAL BUILDING CODE. ENTER THE APPROPRIATE SNOW LOAD CHART, ONCE YOU HAVE SELECTED THE LOADING CONDITION THAT CORRESPONDS TO YOUR SPECIFIC LOCATION. CROSS REFERENCE YOUR LOADING CONDITION A, B, C ETC., WITH THE WIDTH OF YOUR HOUSE CONDITION INDICATED AT POSITIONS #1 OR #2 IN THE DIAGRAMS. THEN SELECT A GIRDER FROM THE SNOWLOAD CHART BASED ON THE APPROXIMATE OPENING (8 FT., 12 FT., OR 16 FT.) THAT YOUR GIRDER WILL SPAN. THESE GIRDER OPENINGS REFLECT TYPICAL CONDITIONS AND MAY VARY SLIGHTLY. IF ANY OF YOUR ACTUAL CONDITIONS FALL IN THE MIDDLE, OPT FOR SAFETY AND GO TO THE HIGHER REQUIREMENT.

0 SNOW LOAD

	8 FT. OPENING				12 FT. OPENING				16 FT. OPENING			
	WOOD HEADER	STEEL FLITCH PL.	LAM-PLYWOOD	GLU-LAM	WOOD HEADER	STEEL FLITCH PL.	LAM-PLYWOOD	GLU-LAM	WOOD HEADER	STEEL FLITCH PL.	LAM-PLYWOOD	GLU-LAM
A-1	(2) 2x 8		(2) 1 3/4"x 9 1/2"	5 1/8"x 6"	(3) 2x10	1/4"x 11"	(2) 1 3/4"x 9 1/2"	5 1/8"x 9"	(3) 2x12	1/4"x 11"	(2) 1 3/4"x 11 7/8"	3 1/8"x 12"
B-1	(3) 2x10	1/4"x 9"	(3) 1 3/4"x 7 1/4"	5 1/8"x 6"	(3) 2x12	1/4"x 11"	(3) 1 3/4"x 9 1/2"	3 1/8"x 10 1/2"		3/8"x 11"	(3) 1 3/4"x 11 7/8"	3 1/8"x 13 1/2"
C-1	(3) 2x10		(2) 1 3/4"x 9"	3 1/8"x 6"		1/4"x 9"	(2) 1 3/4"x 11 7/8"	3 1/8"x 9"		3/8"x 9"	(3) 1 3/4"x 11 7/8"	3 1/8"x 12"
D-1	(3) 2x10	1/4"x 9"	(3) 1 3/4"x 7 1/4"	3 1/8"x 7 1/2"		1/2"x 9"	(3) 1 3/4"x 9 1/2"	5 1/8"x 9"		1/2"x 9"	(3) 1 3/4"x 11 7/8"	6 3/4"x 12"
E-1	(3) 2x12	1/4"x 11"	(2) 1 3/4"x 9 1/2"	5 1/8"x 7 1/2"		(2)1/2"x 9"	(2) 1 3/4"x 11 7/8"	6 3/4"x 10 1/2"	(2) 1/2"x 9"		(3) 1 3/4"x 16"	5 1/8"x 15"
F-1	(3) 2x12	1/4"x 11"	(3) 1 3/4"x 9 1/2"	5 1/8"x 7 1/2"		1/2"x 11"	(3) 1 3/4"x 11 7/8"	6 3/4"x 13 1/2"		1/2"x 11"	(3) 1 3/4"x 16"	5 1/8"x 13 1/2"
A-2	(2) 2x 8		(3) 1 3/4"x 7 1/4"	3 1/8"x 6"	(3) 2x10	1/4"x 9"	(3) 1 3/4"x 9 1/2"	3 1/8"x 9"	(3) 2x12	1/4"x 9"	(3) 1 3/4"x 11 7/8"	5 1/8"x 10 1/2"
B-2	(3) 2x10	1/4"x 7"	(3) 1 3/4"x 7 1/4"	3 1/8"x 7 1/2"	(3) 2x12	1/4"x 11"	(3) 1 3/4"x 9 1/2"	3 1/8"x 9"	(3) 2x12	1/2"x 9"	(3) 1 3/4"x 14"	5 1/8"x 12"
C-2	(2) 2x10	1/4"x 7"	(3) 1 3/4"x 7 1/4"	3 1/8"x 6"	(3) 2x12	3/4"x 11"	(3) 1 3/4"x 11"	5 1/8"x 9"		3/4"x 9"	(3) 1 3/4"x 14"	5 1/8"x 12"
D-2	(3) 2x12	1/2"x 9"	(3) 1 3/4"x 9 1/2"	5 1/8"x 9"		1/2"x 11"	(3) 1 3/4"x 11"	5 1/8"x 10 1/2"		3/4"x 9"	(3) 1 3/4"x 14"	5 1/8"x 13 1/2"
E-2		1/2"x 9"	(2) 1 3/4"x 11 7/8"	5 1/8"x 9"		3/4"x 11"	(3) 1 3/4"x 14"	5 1/8"x 13 1/2"				5 1/8"x 16"
F-2		1/2"x 11"	(3) 1 3/4"x 11 7/8"	5 1/8"x 9"		3/4"x 11"	(3) 1 3/4"x 14"	5 1/8"x 13"				5 1/8"x 19 1/2"

† Indicates use of a steel "T" beam

30 SNOW LOAD

	8 FT. OPENING				12 FT. OPENING				16 FT. OPENING			
	WOOD HEADER	STEEL FLITCH PL.	LAM-PLYWOOD	GLU-LAM	WOOD HEADER	STEEL FLITCH PL.	LAM-PLYWOOD	GLU-LAM	WOOD HEADER	STEEL FLITCH PL.	LAM-PLYWOOD	GLU-LAM
A-1	(3) 2x12	1/4"x 11"	(2) 1 3/4"x 9 1/2"	3 1/8"x 9"	(3) 2x12	1/4"x 9"	(3) 1 3/4"x 9 1/2"	5 1/8"x 10 1/2"	(3) 2x14	(2) 1/2"x 9"	(2) 1 3/4"x 13"	5 1/8"x 13 1/2"
B-1	(3) 2x10		(2) 1 3/4"x 7 1/4"	5 1/8"x 6"		1/4"x 11"	(3) 1 3/4"x 11 7/8"	3 1/8"x 10 1/2"		1/2"x 11"	(2) 1 3/4"x 14"	3 1/8"x 13 1/2"
C-1		1/4"x 9"	(2) 1 3/4"x 11 7/8"	5 1/8"x 7 1/2"		1/2"x 11"	(3) 1 3/4"x 14"	6 3/4"x 10 1/2"		1/2"x 11"	(3) 1 3/4"x 14"	5 1/8"x 15"
D-1		3/4"x 11"	(2) 1 3/4"x 9 1/2"	5 1/8"x 7 1/2"	(2) 1/2"x 11"		(3) 1 3/4"x 14"	6 3/4"x 10 1/2"		1/2"x 11"	(3) 1 3/4"x 16"	5 1/8"x 15"
E-1		1/4"x 11"	(3) 1 3/4"x 9 1/2"	5 1/8"x 9"		1/2"x 11"	(3) 1 3/4"x 14"	6 3/4"x 10 1/2"		1/2"x 11"	(3) 1 3/4"x 16"	5 1/8"x 15"
F-1		1/2"x 11"	(3) 1 3/4"x 11 7/8"	5 1/8"x 7 1/2"		1/2"x 11"	(3) 1 3/4"x 14"	6 3/4"x 13"			(3) 1 3/4"x 16"	6 3/4"x 15"
A-2	(3) 2x12	1/4"x 11"	(3) 1 3/4"x 7 1/4"	6 3/4"x 9"	(3) 2x14	1/4"x 11"	(3) 1 3/4"x 11 7/8"	3 1/8"x 10 1/2"	(3) 2x14	1/2"x 11"	(3) 1 3/4"x 14"	3 1/8"x 13 1/2"
B-2	(3) 2x12	1/4"x 7"	(3) 1 3/4"x 9 1/2"	5 1/8"x 9"		3/4"x 11"	(3) 1 3/4"x 14"	5 1/8"x 10 1/2"		3/4"x 9"	(3) 1 3/4"x 14"	5 1/8"x 16"
C-2	(3) 2x10	1/2"x 9"	(3) 1 3/4"x 9 1/2"	5 1/8"x 11"		3/4"x 11"	(3) 1 3/4"x 14"	5 1/8"x 12"			(3) 1 3/4"x 14"	5 1/8"x 16"
D-2		1/2"x 9"	(3) 1 3/4"x 11 7/8"	5 1/8"x 11"		3/4"x 11"	(3) 1 3/4"x 14"	5 1/8"x 12"				5 1/8"x 16"
E-2		1/2"x 11"	(3) 1 3/4"x 11 7/8"	6 3/4"x 11"		1/2"x 14"	(3) 1 3/4"x 16"	5 1/8"x 12"			(3) 1 3/4"x 18"	
F-2		3/4"x 11"	(3) 1 3/4"x 11 7/8"	5 1/8"x 12"		1/2"x 16"	(3) 1 3/4"x 16"	5 1/8"x 15"				

† Indicates use of higher grade lumber

60 SNOW LOAD

	8 FT. OPENING				12 FT. OPENING				16 FT. OPENING			
	WOOD HEADER	STEEL FLITCH PL.	LAM-PLYWOOD	GLU-LAM	WOOD HEADER	STEEL FLITCH PL.	LAM-PLYWOOD	GLU-LAM	WOOD HEADER	STEEL FLITCH PL.	LAM-PLYWOOD	GLU-LAM
A-1	(3) 2x12	1/4"x 11"	(2) 1 3/4"x 9 1/2"	5 1/8"x 10 1/2"	(3) 2x14	1/2"x 9"	(3) 1 3/4"x 14"	6 3/4"x 10 1/2"	(3) 2x14	1/2"x 11"	(3) 1 3/4"x 14"	6 3/4"x 15"
B-1		1/2"x 11"	(2) 1 3/4"x 11"	3 1/8"x 12"	(3) 2x14	1/4"x 11"	(3) 1 3/4"x 14"	3 1/8"x 12"		1/2"x 11"	(3) 1 3/4"x 16"	3 1/8"x 16 1/2"
C-1		1/2"x 9"	(3) 1 3/4"x 9 1/2"	6 3/4"x 9"	(2) 1/2"x 11"		(3) 1 3/4"x 16"	6 3/4"x 12"			(3) 1 3/4"x 16"	6 3/4"x 16 1/2"
D-1		3/4"x 11"	(3) 1 3/4"x 11 7/8"	5 1/8"x 9"	(2) 1/2"x 11"		(3) 1 3/4"x 16"	6 3/4"x 13"		1/2"x 11"	(3) 1 3/4"x 16"	6 3/4"x 15"
E-1		1/4"x 11"	(3) 1 3/4"x 11 7/8"	5 1/8"x 11"		1/2"x 11"	(3) 1 3/4"x 16"	6 3/4"x 15"			(3) 1 3/4"x 16"	5 1/8"x 15"
F-1		1/2"x 11"	(3) 1 3/4"x 11 7/8"	6 3/4"x 11"		1/2"x 11"	(3) 1 3/4"x 16"	3 1/8"x 13 1/2"				5 1/8"x 16 1/2"
A-2	(3) 2x12	1/4"x 11"	(3) 1 3/4"x 9 1/2"	4 3/4"x 11"	1 (2) 2x14	3/4"x 11"	(3) 1 3/4"x 14"	3 1/8"x 13 1/2"	1 (3)2x14	3/4"x 9"	(3) 1 3/4"x 16"	3 1/8"x 16 1/2"
B-2	(3) 2x12	1/4"x 7"	(3) 1 3/4"x 11 7/8"	4 3/4"x 11"		1/2"x 11"	(3) 1 3/4"x 16"	5 1/8"x 15"			(3) 1 3/4"x 16"	5 1/8"x 16 1/2"
C-2	(3) 2x12	1/2"x 9"	(3) 1 3/4"x 11 7/8"	4 3/4"x 11"		1/2"x 11"	(3) 1 3/4"x 16"	5 1/8"x 15"	1 (3)2x14		(3) 1 3/4"x 16"	3 1/8"x 16 1/2"
D-2		1/2"x 9"	(3) 1 3/4"x 11 7/8"	5 1/8"x 12"		1/2"x 14"	(3) 1 3/4"x 18"	3 1/8"x 13 1/2"			(4) 1/2"x 14"	6 3/4"x 16 1/2"
E-2		1/2"x 11"	(3) 1 3/4"x 11 7/8"	6 3/4"x 11"		3/4"x 14"	(3) 1 3/4"x 18"	5 1/8"x 13 1/2"			(3) 1 3/4"x 18"	6 3/4"x 16 1/2"
F-2		3/4"x 11"	(3) 1 3/4"x 11 7/8"	6 3/4"x 13"		1/2"x 16"	(3) 1 3/4"x 18"	5 1/8"x 13"				5 1/8"x 15"

1 Indicates use of higher grade lumber

1 Uniform loading condition assumed for all girders. Deflection limit = L/360.

2 Lumber species - Hem Fir, #2 or better, f=1400 psi for #1, 1150 psi for #2. Higher stress lumber such as D.Fir, S.Y. Pine may be substituted. (National Forest Products Association.)

3 Steel - ASTM A36, Fy (min, yield stress) = 36 ksi, allowable stress = .60 Fy = 22 ksi. (American Institute of Steel Construction, Inc.) Steel Flitch Plates to be assembled with min. 3/8" bolts staggered at 2'0" o.c., top and bottom.

4 Laminated Plywood - Fb=2800 psi, Fv=285 psi, E=2.0 psi. Nailing pattern for assembly of multiple units to be min. (2) rows of 16d nails @ 12" o.c. (3) rows of 16d nails @ 12" o.c. for 14", 16", 18" beams (American National Standards Institute, Inc.).

5 Glu-Lam Timber - Western Species - 1 1/2" thick laminations, Fb=2400 psi, Fv=165 psi, E=1.8 psi (American Institute of Timber Construction).

6 Floor loads: 40 psf live, 10 psf dead—Ceiling loads: 20 psf live, 10 psf dead

ROOF BREAK DETAILS

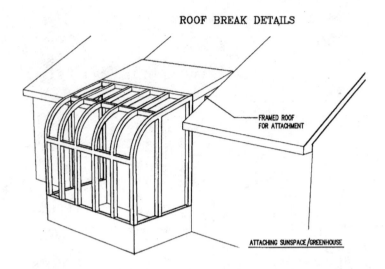

FRAMED ROOF
FOR ATTACHMENT

ATTACHING SUNSPACE/GREENHOUSE

ADDITIONS FREQUENTLY CAUSE A BREAK TO OCCUR IN A ROOFLINE; THIS IS OFTEN A DESIRED EFFECT THAT IS INHERENT TO THE DESIGN. AT OTHER TIMES, PARTICULARLY WHEN THE ADDITION HAS NOT HAD PROPER ARCHITECTURAL PRE-PLANNING, IT COULD BE AN UNFORTUNATE OCCURRENCE. THE UPPER FIGURE SHOWS A ROOF BREAK THAT IS REQUIRED TO ATTACH A GREENHOUSE STRUCTURE TO A ONE OR ONE AND ONE-HALF STORY HOME. THIS LITTLE DETAIL IS OFTEN NOT PLANNED FOR BY THE UNTRAINED PERSON. IF PROPERLY TREATED WITH MATCHING MATERIALS, IT CAN LOOK JUST FINE, BUT DO BE AWARE OF ITS NECESSITY.

WHEN A JOG IN A PLAN OCCURS, A ROOF BREAK IS LIKELY. THE SIZE OF THIS BREAK IS DIRECTLY RELATED TO THE SIZE OF THE JOG IN PLAN, AND THE PITCH OF THE ROOF. A ONE FOOT SETBACK ON AN ADDITION WITH A 6-IN-12 ROOF PITCH WILL PRODUCE A 6 INCH ROOF BREAK; THAT'S FINE, BUT A 4 INCH SETBACK ON THE SAME ADDITION WILL PRODUCE A 2 INCH ROOF BREAK, WHICH, IN MOST INSTANCES, IS UNACCEPTABLE. THE ONLY EXCEPTION WOULD BE A HIP ROOF OFFSET. A 2 INCH BREAK AGAINST A WALL IS DIFFICULT TO FLASH WELL AND WILL BE TOO INSIGNIFICANT—IT MIGHT EVEN LOOK LIKE AN ERROR. SO BE CAREFUL WHEN ADDING ADDITIONS; EITHER MATCH THE ROOFLINES, OR MAKE CERTAIN THAT THERE IS AMPLE OFFSET.

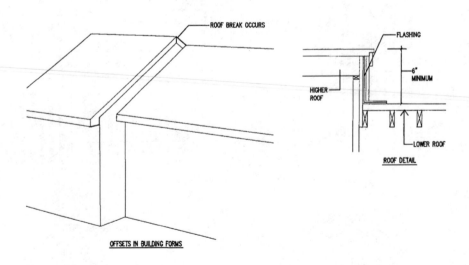

ROOF BREAK OCCURS

FLASHING

6"
MINIMUM

HIGHER
ROOF

LOWER ROOF

ROOF DETAIL

OFFSETS IN BUILDING FORMS

DOUBLE ROOF CONSTRUCTION

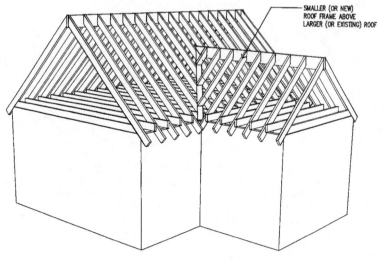

SMALLER (OR NEW)
ROOF FRAME ABOVE
LARGER (OR EXISTING) ROOF

<u>FRAMING PERSPECTIVE</u>

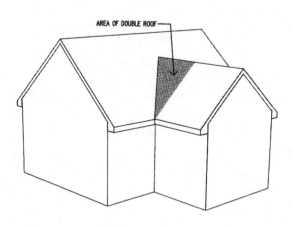

AREA OF DOUBLE ROOF

<u>VIEW WITH SHEATHING</u>

WHENEVER POSSIBLE, MOST CONTRACTORS AND CARPENTERS WILL USE DOUBLE ROOF CONSTRUCTION TODAY WHEN FRAMING INTERSECTING ROOFLINES. MANY DO-IT-YOURSELF CONTRACTORS DO NOT UNDERSTAND IT. THEY HAVE READ ABOUT STRUCTURAL VALLEYS AND HEADERS AND ARE READY TO CUT APART AN OLD ROOF, OR EVEN FRAME TWO NEW ONES THAT WAY. IT IS NOT NECESSARY. THE PRACTICE PICTURED BUILDS ONE ROOF, USUALLY THE SMALLER, ABOVE THE OTHER ROOF; THE RAFTERS OF THE UPPER ROOF ARE ATTACHED TO NAILING STRIPS THAT RUN ALONG THE LOWER ROOF. THESE NAILING STRIPS REPLACE THE STRUCTURAL VALLEYS OF THE OLD PRACTICE.

THIS METHOD IS EASIER AND QUICKER. IT DOES REQUIRE EXTRA LUMBER FOR RAFTERS, BUT ELIMINATES THE NEED FOR STRUCTURAL VALLEYS. IT ALSO IS EASIER TO FRAME A ROOM WITH A VAULTED CEILING THAT RUNS PAST AN INTERSECTING ROOFLINE. IN SUCH A CASE ONE MIGHT FRAME THE SMALLER (VAULTED CEILING) ROOFLINE FIRST AND FRAME THE MAIN ROOF OVER, BUT MAKE SURE YOU INSURE AGAINST THE OUTWARD SPREADING OF THE LOWER ROOF.

CRICKETS

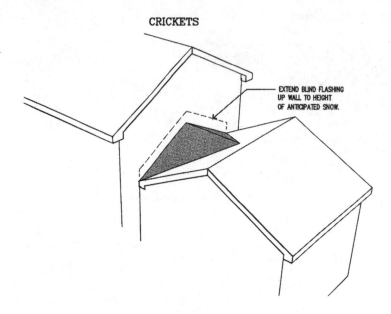

EXTEND BLIND FLASHING UP WALL TO HEIGHT OF ANTICIPATED SNOW.

GABLE ROOF TO WALL

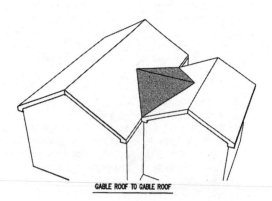

GABLE ROOF TO GABLE ROOF

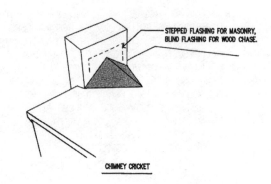

STEPPED FLASHING FOR MASONRY, BLIND FLASHING FOR WOOD CHASE.

CHIMNEY CRICKET

NEW ADDITIONS COULD RESULT IN THE NEED FOR A CRICKET. A CRICKET IS A ROOF STRUCTURE BUILT AT A PITCH OPPOSITE TO THE ROOF IT IS CONSTRUCTED ON, AND IS DESIGNED TO HELP A ROOF SHED SNOW OR RAIN. CRICKETS ARE ESSENTIAL IN AREAS WHERE SNOW IS A CONCERN, BUT MAY ALSO BE USED IN OTHER LOCATIONS. THERE ARE THREE CONDITIONS WHERE CRICKETS COULD BE REQUIRED AND THEY ARE PICTURED HERE. THE CONDITIONS ARE ALL DIFFERENT, BUT THE GOAL IS THE SAME, WHICH IS TO FLASH THESE INTERSECTIONS SO THAT THEY DO NOT LEAK.

THE CRICKET ADDS INSURANCE TO THE FLASHING BY CONSTRUCTING A ROOF THAT CREATES A POSITIVE FLOW FOR RAIN OR MELTING SNOW. THE CRICKET IS USUALLY BUILT AFTER THE MAIN ROOF IS SHEATHED AND IT IS FRAMED WITH RAFTERS AND SHEATHING AS ANY ROOF. IT IS KEPT LOW, AS IT MAY NOT BE THE MOST ATTRACTIVE ELEMENT—ITS PURPOSE IS SIMPLY TO CREATE A POSITIVE PITCH. THERE ARE TIMES WHEN ONE MIGHT PREFER TO RAISE THE HEIGHT OF A CRICKET TO THE HEIGHT OF THE MAIN ROOF, AND THUS CREATE, IN EFFECT, ANOTHER MAIN ROOFLINE AT THE OPPOSITE PITCH.

VAULTING A CEILING/SOUND WALLS

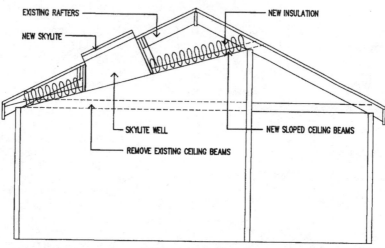

EXISTING RAFTERS

NEW SKYLITE

NEW INSULATION

SKYLITE WELL

REMOVE EXISTING CEILING BEAMS

NEW SLOPED CEILING BEAMS

VAULTING AN EXISTING CEILING

I HAVE OFTEN WRITTEN ABOUT THE DESIRABILITY OF ADDING VOLUME TO SPATIALLY ENHANCE A ROOM. THIS DETAIL SHOWS YOU HOW TO DO IT OVER AN EXISTING ROOM COVERED BY CONVENTIONAL CEILING BEAMS AND RAFTERS. A TRUSSED ROOF REQUIRES REBUILDING THE TRUSSES, BUT A SKYLIGHT COULD BE INSTALLED AS SHOWN HERE. NEW CEILING BEAMS AT A LOWER SLOPE, AS PICTURED, WILL PROVIDE THE DEPTH FOR GOOD ROOF INSULATION, AND ALSO WILL PREVENT AGAINST THE POSSIBLE BOWING OF THE OUTSIDE WALL. THE SKYLIGHT WELL SHOULD BE SPLAYED AS SHOWN TO SPREAD THE LIGHT. THE NEW CEILING BEAMS SHOULD ONLY BE ELIMINATED IF THE EXISTING ROOF IS SUPPORTED AGAINST SPREADING OUT, AND IF THE RAFTERS CAN PROVIDE AMPLE SPACE FOR INSULATION.

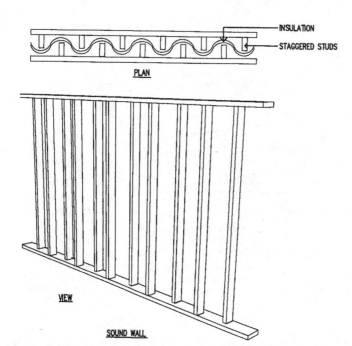

INSULATION

STAGGERED STUDS

PLAN

VIEW

SOUND WALL

SOMETIMES THE REMODELING OF A HOME MAY PLACE A BEDROOM NEAR AN ACTIVITY ROOM AND SOUND INSULATION WOULD BE A NICE LUXURY. FORGET ABOUT JUST INSULATING THE WALL—IT HELPS, BUT IT IS NOT ENOUGH. THE BEST SOLUTION IS TWO SEPARATE, FULLY INDEPENDENT WALLS WITH AN AIR SPACE BETWEEN; BUT THIS COULD TAKE UP TOO MUCH AREA. THE NEXT BEST IS THE STAGGERED STUD WALL ILLUSTRATED HERE. OTHER THAN AT THE TOP AND BOTTOM, THERE ARE NO SURFACES THAT WILL CARRY SOUND FROM ONE SIDE TO THE OTHER. THE INSULATION HELPS BY WEAVING IT THROUGH THE CAVITY. ALSO REMEMBER TO KEEP ANY DUCTS OR PIPES OUT OF THIS WALL, AND DON'T PLACE ELECTRICAL OUTLETS BACK TO BACK.

STAIR WALLS/PLATFORM TUBS

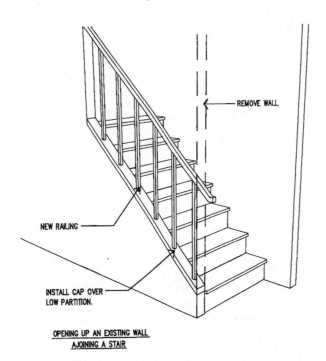

REMOVE WALL

NEW RAILING

INSTALL CAP OVER
LOW PARTITION.

OPENING UP AN EXISTING WALL
ADJOINING A STAIR

I HAVE ALSO WRITTEN ABOUT THE DESIRABILITY OF OPENING EXISTING ROOMS AND SPACES TO ONE ANOTHER TO HELP INCREASE THEIR IMPRESSION OF SIZE, AND TO CREATE A MORE OPEN FLOWING INTERIOR. MANY OLD STAIRHALLS ARE HEMMED BY WALLS ON BOTH SIDES; IT MAKES THEM UNATTRACTIVE AND CLAUSTROPHOBIC. THE DETAIL AT THE LEFT SHOWS YOU HOW TO OPEN THE SIDE OF A STAIR TO AN ADJOINING ROOM BY REMOVING PART OF THE WALL. THE WALL COULD BE REMOVED FOR ITS ENTIRE LENGTH, BUT A LENGTH OF SIX TO SEVEN STEPS WILL ALLOW THE RAIL TO END AT THE WALL BEFORE ONE LOSES THEIR FINGERS. IF YOU DO EXTEND FURTHER, KEEP THIS LATTER ITEM IN MIND.

THE WALL IS NOT REMOVED TO THE FLOOR, BUT WILL STOP AT THE TOP OF THE STRINGER ALONGSIDE THE STEPS AND WILL BE CAPPED THERE WITH AN OAK PIECE. THIS WILL ALLOW THE STAIR TO REMAIN UNTOUCHED. IF THE WALL EXTENDS LOWER, THE SIDE OF THE STAIR MAY HAVE TO BE REFINISHED. YOU COULD OPEN BOTH SIDES OF A STAIR THE SAME WAY.

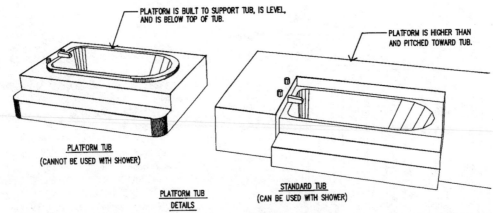

PLATFORM IS BUILT TO SUPPORT TUB, IS LEVEL, AND IS BELOW TOP OF TUB.

PLATFORM IS HIGHER THAN AND PITCHED TOWARD TUB.

PLATFORM TUB
(CANNOT BE USED WITH SHOWER)

PLATFORM TUB
DETAILS

STANDARD TUB
(CAN BE USED WITH SHOWER)

IF YOU PLAN ON HAVING A PLATFORM TUB, THE CARPENTER WILL HAVE TO KNOW HOW TO FRAME THE PLATFORM FOR IT. THERE IS CONFUSION ON THE SUBJECT, AS THERE ARE TWO DISTINCT TYPES OF PLATFORMS, WHICH DEPEND ON THE TYPE OF TUB YOU CHOOSE. THE PLATFORM AT THE LEFT IS FOR A TUB THAT DOES NOT HAVE A SKIRT AND WHICH IS INTENDED TO SIT ON TOP OF A PLATFORM. SUCH A TUB IS NOT TO BE USED WITH AN OVERHEAD SHOWER, UNLESS IT CAN BE SQUARE TO ITS SURROUNDING WALLS, AND COMES WITH OPTIONAL TILING BEADS FOR THE WALL. THE CONVENTIONAL TUB AT THE RIGHT REQUIRES THAT THE PLATFORM BE HIGHER, TO PERMIT TILE TO COVER THE RAISED FLASHING IT COMES WITH ON THREE SIDES. AN OVERHEAD SHOWER IS JUST FINE.

Staging of Construction

I have referred to staging many times. What is it? Staging refers to the construction of a remodeling project in stages—or parts. The natural course of construction events produces staging; it results in every project, as a consequence of the fact that certain tasks can not begin until others are complete. For example, insulation can not be installed until the sheathing is in place and interior floors can not be installed until the roof is made watertight. However, staging can also result from a distinct pre-planning effort that focuses on completing various parts, or various tasks, separately and in a predetermined order. It is this latter aspect of staging that I am focusing on, as this could become a significant design related issue. It may even require some design changes to satisfactorily accommodate the demands for staging.

There are two reasons to plan for staging. The first is to enable the homeowner to maintain sanity while living through an extensive interior remodeling project. The goal here is to plan the construction in such a fashion that one can live as comfortably as possible while the seemingly endless mess is all around. To do this properly requires that this subject be part of the design program, and that as a design is being developed, staging becomes one of the issues that is factored into the design equation.

The plan is usually to start with the exterior shell of the new additions while not opening up to the current rooms. The homeowner may have to stay out of an existing room (or two) during the day, as a safety precaution, but its evening functionality is retained. Frequently, the next step involves the finishing of the addition, so that it can be made livable. The doors, or connections, can wait, or be installed now depending on the project. One then moves into the newly finished rooms and vacates some parts of the old house so that the interior can be changed. You screen off the parts being worked on as best as possible. The number of moves and steps that are required will be dependent on the complexity of the interior renovation, the speed of the construction crews and one's pocketbook, as this will be more costly than if the project were done all at once.

Kitchens and bathrooms present unique problems if they are to be renovated. The easiest solution is to create new rooms at first so they may be utilized while the project continues; that is OK if you are building a new kitchen. If it will be remodeled in place, it has to be carefully coordinated so that "down time" of the kitchen is minimized. The same required coordination is absolutely necessary when remodeling existing bathrooms, and there are no other baths to utilize. It is often possible to do one bathroom at a time, but this is likely to add cost.

There is a second reason to plan for staging, and I have already alluded to it. It is the cost factor. It may be that the wish list far exceeds the capacity to pay, but the homeowner is unwilling—or unable—to pare it down. Staging could present a viable solution so that one ultimately achieves all the items their needs demand, or the home requires. The major difference between this type of staging and the prior is that long gaps of time, even years, may enter the planning process, and you have to consider the potential living condition of the home at each step. But to the homeowner with an extensive wish list and limited means, it may be worth the mess and the wait.

The plans on the next two pages present some graphic examples of the subject.

IDEAS FOR STAGING

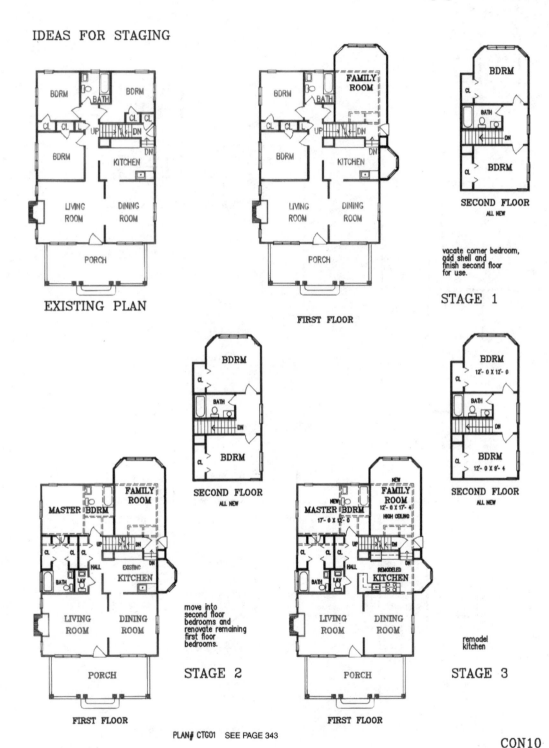

EXISTING PLAN

FIRST FLOOR

vacate corner bedroom,
add shell and
finish second floor
for use.

STAGE 1

SECOND FLOOR
ALL NEW

move into
second floor
bedrooms and
renovate remaining
first floor
bedrooms.

STAGE 2

FIRST FLOOR

remodel
kitchen

STAGE 3

FIRST FLOOR

SECOND FLOOR
ALL NEW

SECOND FLOOR
ALL NEW

PLAN# CTG01   SEE PAGE 343

CON10

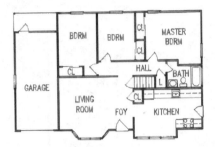

EXISTING PLAN

IDEAS FOR STAGING

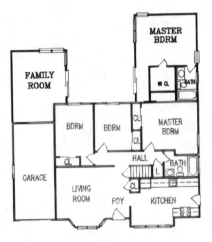

add shell for additions
and finish master suite

STAGE 1

move into new master bedroom,
vacate center and old master bedrooms.
finish new middle bedroom and bath.

STAGE 2

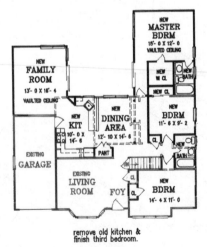

remove old kitchen &
finish third bedroom.

STAGE 4

finish family room, new
kitchen and dining area.

STAGE 3

PLAN# RAN05   SEE PAGE 363

CON11

Finishing the Project

One of the guaranteed, natural occurrences, of every remodeling project is the "finishing squeeze." There are the pressures to finally get it done because, without doubt, it will take longer than anyone estimated. There is another "squeeze," though, that has more crucial bearing on the outcome of the project; it too mounts in tension as the project draws to conclusion. It is the scarcity of funds that can develop as a consequence of under-estimating.

Everyone advises leaving a contingency; the bare minimum should be 5%, but I believe 10% — or more — is a safer bet. Beyond the issue of contingency, however, lies an equally significant concern, that of properly pre-planning all the finish elements to avoid having the project end in an unfinished state. A frequent cause of an unfinished project is the failure to realize that finishing costs could be as much as 50% of the project, particularly if one's tastes are expensive, and that finishing includes planning for carpeting, furnishings, landscaping, walks, patios, lighting, etc. If a detailed specification will be provided before construction, many of these decisions will be made then; however, more often than not, most of these decisions are left to the end, to be decided when budgets are running low. As a planning and design book, space does not allow a detailed analysis of the subject, but I will go through some broad concepts that will help plan to get it done.

Exterior Finishing

In planning an addition you are certainly aware of the need to make choices about windows and siding materials, and the cost ramifications of these choices. I am an advocate of suggesting that if budget constraints are very tight — and they frequently are — that the homeowner is encouraged to postpone those finish elements, which can reasonably be accomplished later.

However, I do not place siding or windows in that category. There are times when someone will want stone veneer, but can only afford vinyl siding, and requests that a stone ledge be prepared in the foundation to accommodate future stone. Do it if you are compelled to, but the likelihood is that the stone will never be added, as the siding of choice will grow on everyone.

So choose the siding carefully; give thought to its texture and its color. Make sure that the color harmonizes with the color of the windows and roof. Obtain samples of all three—plus the exterior fascia or trim—and put them side by side, just as one would match a shirt, tie and jacket. This is at times a difficult decision for many people; photographs in magazines can help enormously, as can a trip around the neighborhood—or to that new subdivision.

Window choices can be equally perplexing, especially because of the proliferation of styles, types and finishes readily available today. Again, this is not the place for a window choice dissertation, but for some design concepts. If one's tastes are very traditional, double hung windows are a likely choice, and they are comparatively inexpensive. That should not rule out casements, awning or sliding windows, though, particularly if they are installed with divided lights. Sliding windows tend to be the least expensive, and casements the most expensive because of the hardware. Give thought to using fixed windows, which can be less costly.

White is the preferred traditional window color. Use darker trimmed windows for a contemporary exterior or for a rustic, woodsy look. But large areas of white framed glass can also be appropriate to a very modern look when used with white stained siding.

Do give thought to the use of those special shapes; they are expensive, but just one can become the focal point of a room. They can be used in any style of home. In a more contemporary home, use them without divided lights. For an eclectic look, mix them with divided lights over large, undivided windows.

Roof choices are somewhat easier; with the exception of those areas where wood shingles or clay tile are the preferred choices, fiberglass roof shingles are the norm. There is a wide choice of textures and colors with these. Pick the texture first, as it could be a significant cost factor. The heavy, layered look, which imitates wood shingles, comes in several styles, each with its own price and selection of colors.

There are a number of other final decisions that are necessary to make to totally pre-plan—and budget for—the exterior finish. An addition will require some new landscaping. It might call for a new patio, or the replacement of walks and entrances, and maybe even a driveway. These must be considered and budgeted for. One might be able to defer a deck, or some landscaping for a year or so, but it could be disheartening if it wasn't planned for at all. Finally, don't forget about exterior lighting; one could defer some fixtures for a while, if necessary, but remember to do the wiring with your project.

Interior Finishing

The same philosophy about postponing certain elements, if necessary, applies to finishing the interior of the remodeling project. But, as with exterior finishes, there are certain areas where we should not plan to use temporary finishes. Items that will be built-in should be permanent; study your choices well, compromise as necessary, but be confident with your compromise. We do not want to replace kitchen cabinets, plumbing fixtures or other built-ins again.

Carefully examine the cost of appliances for the proposed new kitchen; top of the line appliances can cause sticker shock, yet one can not postpone that choice. What is the point of a new kitchen with old, dated, appliances? So budget carefully for these. Your choice of cabinets is a significant cost factor; an imported mica cabinet could be ten times the cost of a simple domestic factory line.

There are similar cost variances in bathroom fixtures and fittings. Every manufacturer produces top of the line fixtures and basic fixtures — plus there's a whole range between. If you are doing it yourself, your local plumbing supply company can provide you cost comparisons. And don't forget about bathroom fittings. There is such an exciting variety of choices available today, and they're all not necessarily budget shattering.

Plan for built-in lighting with your project. It is another item that can not be readily postponed. These are all items that have a significant affect on the budget, and that need to be reconciled before starting. Other items like floor finishes, wall paneling, wallpaper and hanging light fixtures could be deferred, if necessary. The only exception might be certain floorings like ceramic tile or wood, particularly if it's in a kitchen or bathroom; those are tough to defer. However, a ceramic tile family room or an oak living room, could be done later, if necessary. If carpeting initially, one could pick a less expensive carpet, with the intention of replacing it in a few years.

Finally let's talk about furnishings. A completely finished project would include all the elements necessary for the homeowner to enjoy the new or remodeled space, and that includes the furnishings. I strongly suggest budgeting for furnishing, even if it is only for a temporary purchase. If planned for in advance, whatever choices are made will help avoid that "finishing squeeze."

Personal Nuances

The following conclusion is intended primarily for the do-it-yourselfer reading this book. The professional will find that encouraging individuality will result in a more satisfied client or customer. Whether or not you will be adding on, or remodeling from a design in this book, you will be embarking upon a project that will enable you to establish a stronger personal identity with your home. In earlier chapters, I spoke about exerting personal preferences and establishing a program that satisfies personal needs. I also spoke about the likelihood of making changes from these plans, and the special circumstances of your lot, which you should take advantage of. All of these deal with the same issue, that of creating a personally satisfying remodeling project.

The same holds true for this discussion on finishing; exert your tastes and your personality in your choice of finishes. If you do so, you will likely enjoy a completed remodeling that will satisfy your fondest wishes, and be a rewarding achievement for you and your family.

Utilizing the Accompanying
Computer Disk

General

If you have purchased this book with its accompanying computer disk, you will find an enormous wealth of information available for use. In addition to 1,000 plus drawings in plan and 3D views, there are several fully rendered views complete with roof and siding hatches, a sample of a professionally styled presentation plan, and six full sets of construction drawings and a sample outline specification. Most are developed on an extensively developed layering system in 8 colors that provide distinctive color representations for new versus existing construction, and almost everything is readily modified by you. Before I discuss these in greater detail and what you can do with them, let's just review the basic requirements to implement their use.

First, what is on the disk is not a program; they are simply drawings that you must import into your program. We have created all of our work in Auto Cad releases 12 and 14, and as such they will work best in those programs. If you are working with a higher release that should be no problem, but you might have some significant difficulties with lower releases. See the note under "Problem Solving." All the Auto Cad drawings are identified with an Auto Cad .DWG file suffix.

.DWG, .DXF and .TIFF Files

If you are utilizing other CAD programs, what you may be able to do with the drawings is totally dependent on your program. If your program can import a .DWG file, you will have the best results with full 3D capability; you might have some minor text, layer and hatch inconsistencies, but you should be able to resolve these. If your program cannot import .DWG files, we have also provided all of our drawings in a .DXF file format, which is the standard for most CAD programs. Depending on your CAD program, you still may have some 3D capability to work in 3D and rotate and view models as you do with Auto Cad, but that may not be successful with less expensive CAD programs. Depending on your program, the layering system will likely change; most probably all the information will be imported into your program on one layer and in one color. Depending on your program, you may be unable to open hatched drawings, and text could be changed in style and size.

Despite these difficulties, you still should have full capability of use of all the floor plans and you should be able to stretch, modify and change all floor plans at will in any CAD program. You should also be able to download all the drawings as .TIFF or other images onto Corel Draw 7 and other similar newer version desktop publishing, graphic or paint programs. Only minor graphic changes could be made in these programs, but text, color and hatch could be applied, and all the drawings could be printed. This could be useful in creating a brochure or presentation drawing. Hatch, siding and color that are available in some programs might even be applied to the 3D views to create a presentation drawing. As it is impossible for me to know, individual experimentation will be required to determine what your program can, and cannot do, with the drawings on disk.

Working with the Drawings on the Disk

The continuing discussion as to the uses and capabilities of the drawings on the disk is directed to Auto Cad release 12 or higher users. For starters, let's discuss the layering and colors utilized. Most, but not all, drawings will have some 30 to 40 layers utilizing a total of 8 colors. There are separate layers for each new or modified floor level as well as separate layers for existing levels of the house, so you can readily isolate any of the floors and the new from the existing to make modifications. The standard Auto Cad colors utilized in all drawings are as follows:

1. *Red*: used to represent new doors/stairs or dashed lines.
2. *Yellow*: used to represent new walls.
3. *Green*: used for text.
5. *Blue*: used for new windows/headers/sills.
6. *Magenta*: used for fixtures, roofs, cabinets, appliances and porches.
7. *White or black*: used for text or grade lines.
13. *Light brown*: used for existing walls.
15. *Dark brown*: used for existing elements other than walls.

You have the option of working in 2D floor plans or 3D views, or both if you prefer. Every plan in the book is available on the disk in both formats and can be downloaded separately. All drawings have been created in $\frac{1}{4}'' = 1'-0''$, but can be inserted into a new drawing at any scale. Text will be available only on the 2D floor plans, so if you are making changes, you may find it easier to modify the 3D view only which will create a new 3D view, and you could then just plot a new plan view from the 3D model and add new text. If you are not interested in the 3D view, you could work only with the imported 2D view. You should be able to use stretch, cut and paste, move, scale, rotate, mirror or any other Auto Cad command you need, as well as draw new walls, doors, windows, or fixtures, or erase any existing elements. If you retain the existing text styles, text changes should be a snap. Modifying existing hatch should be equally simple. The 2D floor plans do not include shaded walls as shown in the book; however, you can readily shade or hatch the walls within Auto Cad. Also the façades in Chapter 10 are not provided on the disk.

All of the drawings were created also using Softdesk. If you are a Softdesk user, all of the Softdesk capabilities will be available to you. If you are using only Auto Cad or another architectural software, in addition to Auto Cad, your methods of inserting new walls, windows or doors might appear different than the existing elements; however, you could probably convert all to match your program.

3D Views

When you open a typical plan in its 3D format, you will be bringing in a significant amount of 3D information. The plan will come in, in plan view, with each level separate; existing plans will be to one side, and if multi-story, the lower plan will be below the upper floor. The same holds for the new, remodeled, plans. The roof is usually drawn on the topmost floor.

As drawn, each level can be studied separately and revisions made individually to each level. If you look at an elevation view of the overall drawing, you will see that a second floor is drawn so that when brought over the first floor, it will be at the correct height; this enables you to create a new 3D model after you have modified each level. Note that in moving a second floor, do not use a snap command, but simply visually align corners over each other. If you "snap" the matching corners, the levels will merge. Once moved over you can create a new 3D model with the "D-view" command in Auto Cad and then move it to any rendering program; you can then add textures, lighting, shade, etc. and create slides or walk-throughs—or whatever you choose to do for the new model.

The two drawings that follow show a typical 3D drawing in plan view as it will come in. It will of course be in 8 colors to distinguish the elements. Note the separation of each existing and remodeled level. If you look at this very same drawing in the perspective or isometric view, it will appear as shown — in full color of course. It may be hard to see, but each level is properly stacked so when pulled together they produce a full 3D model.

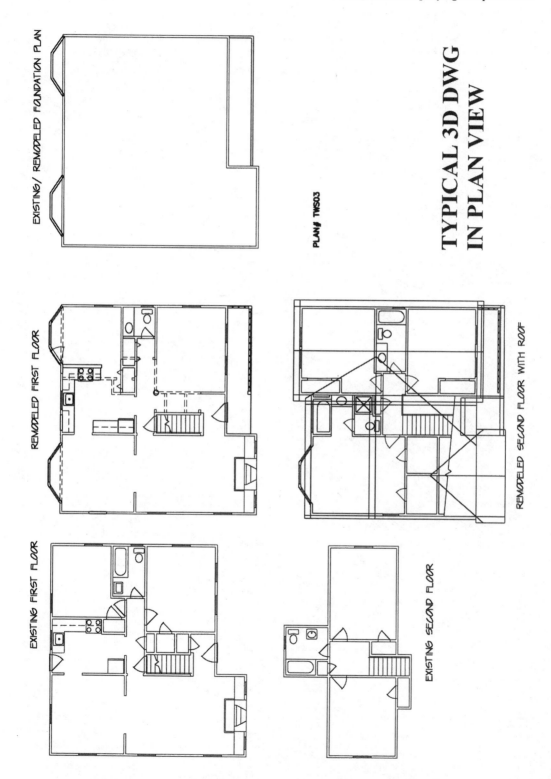

EXISTING/ REMODELED FOUNDATION PLAN

PLAN# TWS03

TYPICAL 3D DWG IN PLAN VIEW

REMODELED FIRST FLOOR

REMODELED SECOND FLOOR WITH ROOF

EXISTING FIRST FLOOR

EXISTING SECOND FLOOR

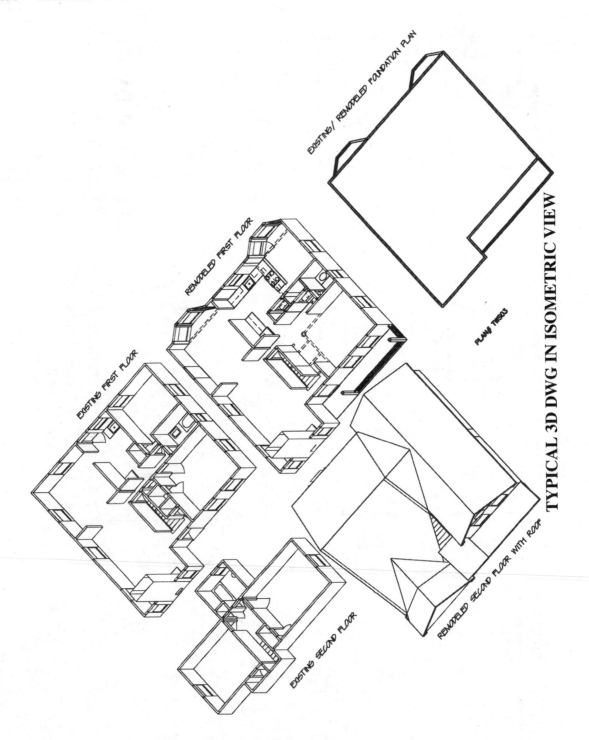

EXISTING/ REMODELED FOUNDATION PLAN

REMODELED FIRST FLOOR

EXISTING FIRST FLOOR

PLAN/ TRIGOS

EXISTING SECOND FLOOR

REMODELED SECOND FLOOR WITH ROOF

TYPICAL 3D DWG IN ISOMETRIC VIEW

2D Files

If you intend to create construction drawings, you will likely use the separate 2D files from the disk, as they are smaller. However nothing would preclude you using plan views of a 3D file to create construction drawings, should you need to. The 2D files for each plan, as indicated before, will come in drawn at 1/4″ = 1′-0″ and include the text as you see it in the book. Once you have modified these plans to suit your specific project, preparing presentation drawings or construction drawings should be a snap. All the auto dimension commands should work; you can add text to match the existing, or change the text to suit your own preferences.

Presentation and Construction Drawings

Preparing your own presentation and construction drawings directly from either the 3D or 2D files should be relatively easy. A sample presentation drawing follows; this drawing used an elevation as the cover page, but you could readily use a 3D presentation view, such as these shown on the following page. You could copy our hatches or create your own.

Creating your own construction drawings should be made easier with the files provided on the disk. However, even if you don't start with a plan file from the disk, much valuable information can be obtained from the sample construction drawings included on the CD. If appropriate, you could cut and paste sections, details, general notes, etc. and add them to your drawings.

I have included six full sets of construction drawings on the disk in both .DWG and .DXF formats. They vary from whole house renovations to a small renovation to a room addition. They are located on the disk with the prefix WKG. You will also find a sample outline specification in text format for your use. Samples of these drawings follow.

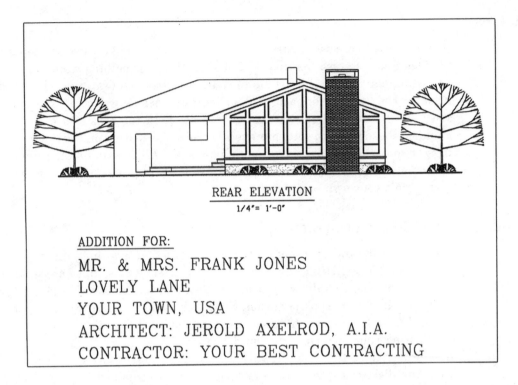

REAR ELEVATION
1/4"= 1'-0"

ADDITION FOR:

MR. & MRS. FRANK JONES
LOVELY LANE
YOUR TOWN, USA
ARCHITECT: JEROLD AXELROD, A.I.A.
CONTRACTOR: YOUR BEST CONTRACTING

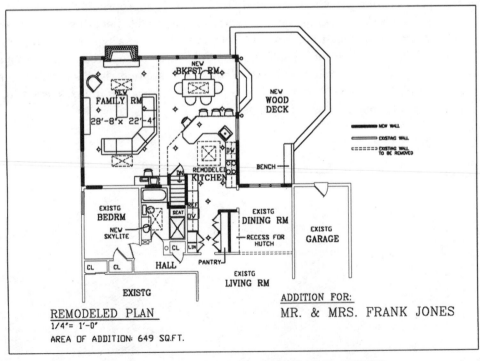

REMODELED PLAN
1/4"= 1'-0"
AREA OF ADDITION: 649 SQ.FT.

CUSTOM PRESENTATION DRAWING

3D: KF013.DWG/DXF

3D: BRG02.DWG/DXF

PRESENTATION VIEWS

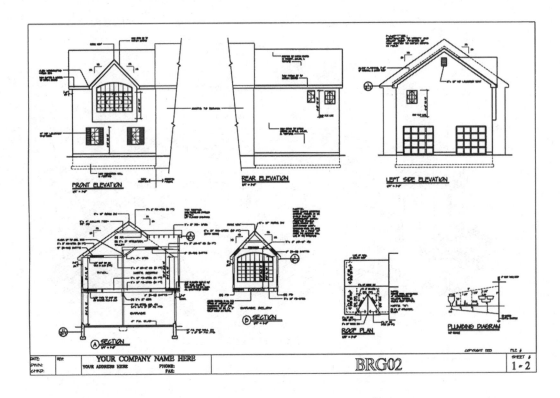

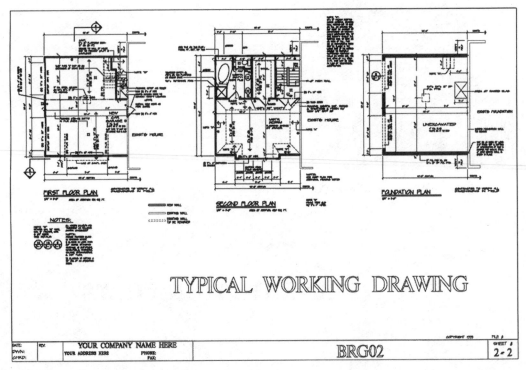

TYPICAL WORKING DRAWING

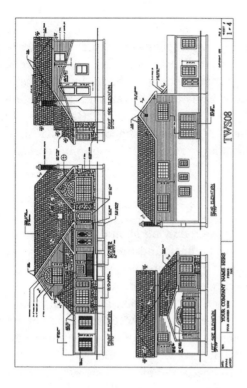

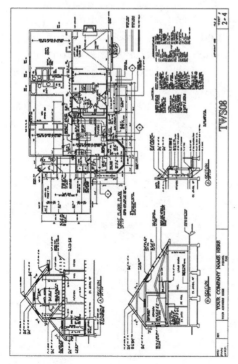

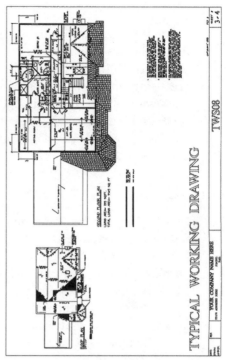

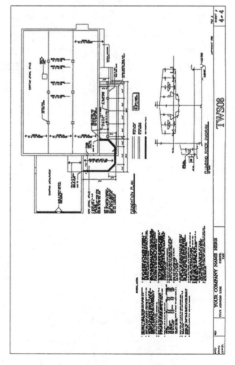

Problem Solving

Because of the multitude of CAD software packages and the hardware platforms they are running on, it is impossible to predict or solve your specific problems. However, there is one generic issue you should be aware of. If you are using an older release of Auto Cad (prior to release 12), the following message will likely appear upon opening the drawings: "Can't open file; incompatible version." You may then only be able to open the .DXF files, or it may be necessary for you to upgrade to release 12 or purchase some other more recent CAD software.

Plan Numbering

In searching for plans on the disk, the following should be helpful. The plan numbering system used throughout the book and the disk tries to be suggestive of the nature of the plan. A five-digit alphanumeric number is used for all plans. The following are the abbreviations used: K = Kitchen, B = Bath, BR = Bedroom, F = Family Room, L = Living Room, D = Dining Room, P = Porch, APT = Apartment, HAPT = Handicapped Accessible Apartment, GAR = Garage. Plans that remodel several spaces would use combined abbreviations, such as KBR = Kitchen and Bedroom, BRB = Bedroom and Bath. Although this will help you focus into specific plans, you should be aware that many plans deal with more than the name suggests; for example, there could be an office alcove in a bedroom plan or some other modification in a garage or apartment plan. Storage is provided in many plans, but is not indicated in the number. Whole-house remakes use the following conventions: Ran = Ranch, TWS = Two-story, SPL = Split level, CTG = Cottage/(Bungalow), CAP = Cape Cod.

Glossary

accessible A term used to describe rooms or facilities designed for persons confined to a wheelchair.

angle bay An extension from a wall, usually containing three sections of windows, the end two of which are at an acute angle to the wall.

as-of-right As used in zoning discussions, a property owner's rights as permitted by the local zoning ordinance.

barrier-free Rooms or facilities that are free of impediments to handicapped persons; *see* accessible.

borrowed light Natural light entering one room which was originated in another adjacent room.

box bay An extension from a wall comprised primarily of windows, the ends of which are perpendicular to the wall.

cantilever A part of a floor that extends out over the wall below; also used as a verb (*to cantilever*).

cape A type of house originating on Cape Cod; it is a one and one-half story design containing steep rooflines with a smaller second floor footprint; also known as a *farm ranch, cottage* or *chalet*.

circulation The paths of travel used for travel from room to room within a home.

colonial A colloquial name used in certain parts of the country for a two-story type of home; is often confused with "colonial" styling.

compartmented bath A bathroom which contains at least two separate spaces, where certain fixtures (usually a water closet) is separated from others.

conical Pertaining to a multi-sided hip roof shaped in the form of a cone.

contemporary style A difficult term to define because of varying regional interpretations; contemporary in the midwest and east usually refers to a modern design that does not follow any classical or traditional styles; in the south and west it can frequently refer to the prevalent "in" style which might be an eclectic style that does borrow from traditional styles.

country kitchen A large multi-function space, usually containing a kitchen, a defined eating area and a sitting area used for informal entertaining and family activities.

country style An informal exterior design and interior decorating style that provides a simple, comfortable, unpretentious quality with frequent references to the past; can be eclectic and very individual.

cricket A small roofed structure set above a main roof to aid the flow of snow and rain from the roof.

dormer A small roofed extension protruding through a roof from a second floor room, with window(s) at the end.

easement As used in property rights, an area of a lot that may be reserved for utilities, or some other third party's use, on which the lot owner's rights of use may be restricted.

eave The low end of a gable or hip roof.

eclectic style A design styling that draws from various sources; a blending of styles.

elevation (front, rear, etc.) The architectural term for the individual views of each side of a house drawn straight-on without perspective; also used for interior walls, cabinets, fixtures.

elevation (height) The height of individual elements of your home or property above some established datum.

elliptical Shaped in the form of an ellipse; a curved shape that is shallower than a circular form; used in windows.

farm ranch *See* cape.

fenestration An architectural term referring to the placement of windows in a building or wall.

frieze An element of exterior wall trim; usually a horizontal band directly below a roof or above an entrance; also known as a *cornice*.

gable end The vertical wall at the end of a gable roof, usually in the shape of a triangle.

gable roof A roof that slopes down in two directions from its top (or ridge) in two planes.

galley kitchen A narrow kitchen usually no more than 9′ wide with cabinets on two opposite sides.

grade The ground surrounding your house; also the slope of the ground.

great room A large room that combines several functions such as living/dining, kitchen/family, living/family or living/dining/kitchen, etc.

header A horizontal structural member carrying loads from other members; in a wall, it is the member over windows, doors and other openings; the word is sometimes interchanged with "girder," the difference being that a girder carries larger loads and is frequently exposed.

high ranch A type of house that has a one-story layout raised out of the ground above an exposed basement (also known as a *hi-ranch, split-foyer* or *bi-level*).

hip roof A roof that slopes down from its peak in all directions, usually having four planes.

knee wall A low wall under a roof that forms the sides of second floor rooms with partially sloping ceilings.

modern style Interchanged with and like "contemporary," it is not always a clearly agreed upon term; more often than not it is a design that is devoid of any references to anything old, but that definition is changing.

peninsula kitchen A kitchen with cabinets that return from a wall into the center of a room.

pitch roof The pitch of a roof is the slope of a roof usually expressed in inches of height per 12″ of width (i.e., 5 in 12).

post-modern style A current architectural style that mixes modern designs with older, classical, elements; an eclectic style.

quoins A decorative treatment of the exterior corners of a house utilizing alternating raised blocks, usually done in masonry (brick, stone) or stucco.

ranch A colloquial name used in many parts of the country for a one-story type of home; also known as a "rambler."

reverse gable A gable roof turned perpendicular to another gable roof, forming intersecting valleys with the main roof and resembling a T in plan.

ridge line The high point of a gable or hip roof; the top member is referred to as a ridge beam.

shed roof A roof that slopes in one direction only from its top to bottom, in one plane.

split-foyer *See* high ranch.

style The "style" refers to exterior design and its related components (i.e., Country, Contemporary, Tudor).

sun porch A term used for an enclosed porch with an abundance of glass in its walls and roof; also sometimes a *greenhouse*.

swale A low point or depression in the grade adjoining a home to carry water away from the structure.

transom A glazed light above a standard height window or door, usually square topped; curves and half-rounds are not usually referred to as transoms, although elliptical units are; it's another area where terminology is not uniform.

trombe wall A masonry wall usually located with a sun porch or greenhouse, its purpose being to store heat obtained by passive solar gain.

type   The "type" refers to the nature of the floor plan (i.e., one-story, two-story, split-level, etc.).

valley roof   The line formed by two intersecting downward sloping rooflines.

variance   In zoning, a waiver of the zoning ordinance which is obtained to permit construction not allowed by the ordinance.

water closet   Technical jargon for a toilet.

Plans Index

General Index

Note to readers: Page numbers appearing in italics refer to illustrations in the book.

About the Author

Jerold L. Axelrod is a practicing architect and president of the architectural firm of Axelrod & Cherveny, A.I.A., Architects, located in Commack, New York. He is also the author of the first edition of this book.